# CHARACTER INTRODUCTIONS

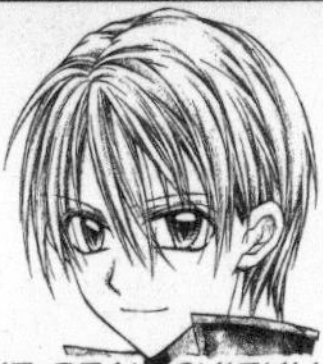

(Younger Twin)

**THE REAL SHIZUMASA**

An illness prevents him from attending school. He helped Haine mend her yanki ways.

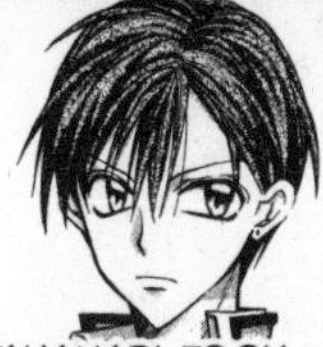

(Elder Twin)

**TAKANARI TOGU**

Student Council President

The double. Referred to as "the Emperor" and is the highest authority in school. Wrote Haine's favorite picture book.

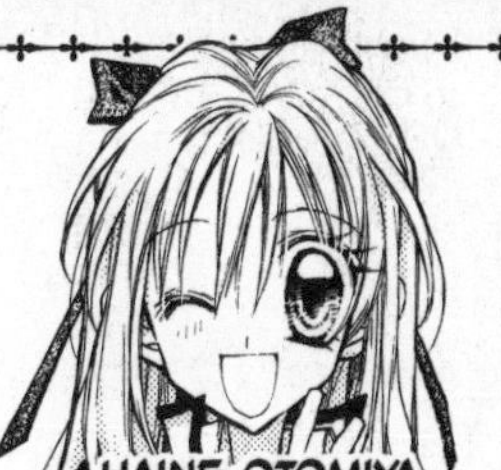

**HAINE OTOMIYA**

Bodyguard & General Affairs

A cheerful girl who is in love with Shizumasa-sama. Former juvenile delinquent. Adopted into the Otomiya family in fourth grade.

**MAGURI TSUJIMIYA**

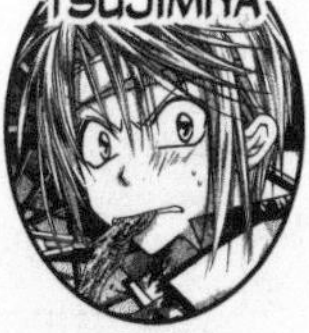

Vice President

Childhood friends with Maora, and now they've become lovers.♥

**MAORA**

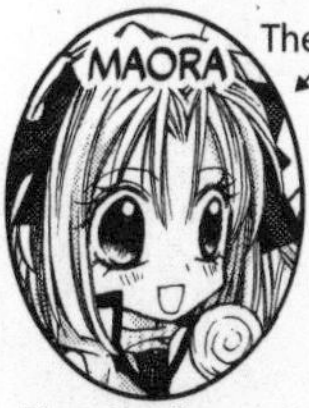

Planning Events & Accounting

Childhood friend of Maguri.

The Same Person!!

**POSTMAN**

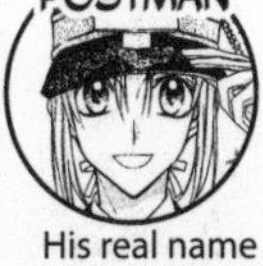

His real name is Ichinomiya Yoshitaka. A very cute boy!!

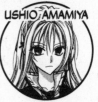

**USHIO AMAMIYA**

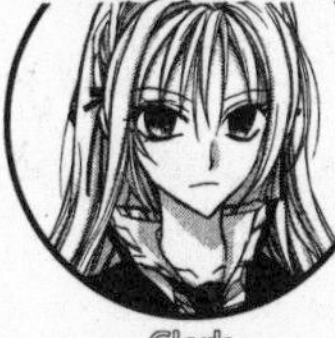

Clerk

Haine's friend. She has gradually started to open up to other people.

## THE GENTLEMEN'S ALLIANCE CROSS

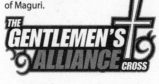

Haine Otomiya is a former juvenile delinquent who attends Imperial Academy. She is in love with Shizumasa Togu, the Emperor, who has the greatest power in the academy. But the current Emperor is Takanari, who is secretly standing in for Shizumasa while Shizumasa is too ill to come to school.

Haine has feelings for both Shizumasa and Takanari, but she finds out that the author of *The Unforgettable Song of the Witch* is Takanari. Haine realizes she is in love with Takanari, but he is taken away, and her engagement to Shizumasa is announced.

Haine visits the old Togu House where Takanari has been locked up, and with the help of the twins' mother Kyoka, she succeeds in finding Takanari. But Takanari, having found out that Shizumasa has leukemia and is in desperate need of a bone marrow transplant, turns his back on Haine.

Shizumasa is ready to face death for the sake of Takanari and Haine's happiness. But Takanari has decided to help Shizumasa by agreeing to the bone marrow transplant. How will this love triangle turn out?

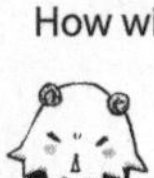

## STORY THUS FAR

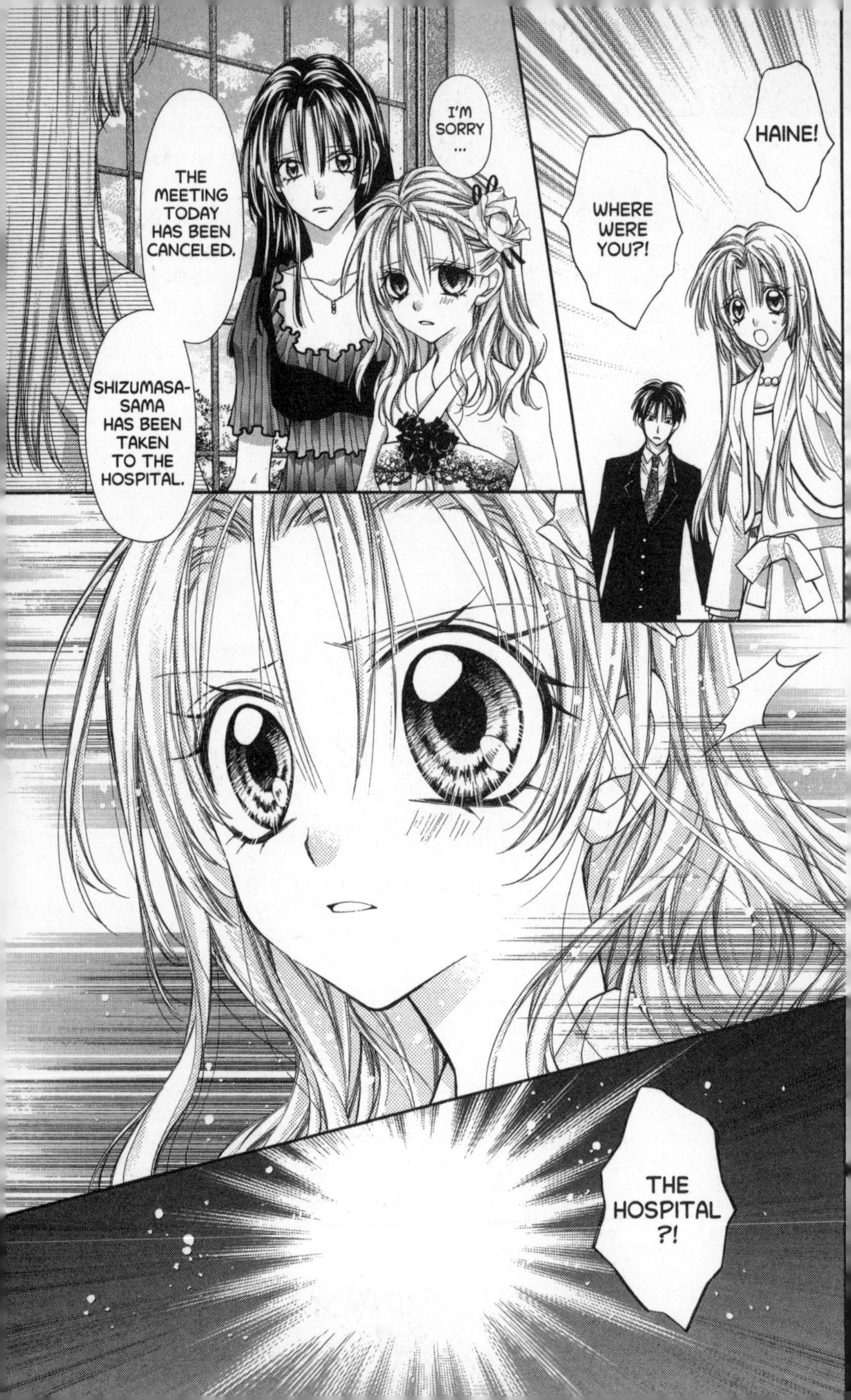
HAINE!
WHERE WERE YOU?!
I'M SORRY ...
THE MEETING TODAY HAS BEEN CANCELED.
SHIZUMASA-SAMA HAS BEEN TAKEN TO THE HOSPITAL.
THE HOSPITAL ?!

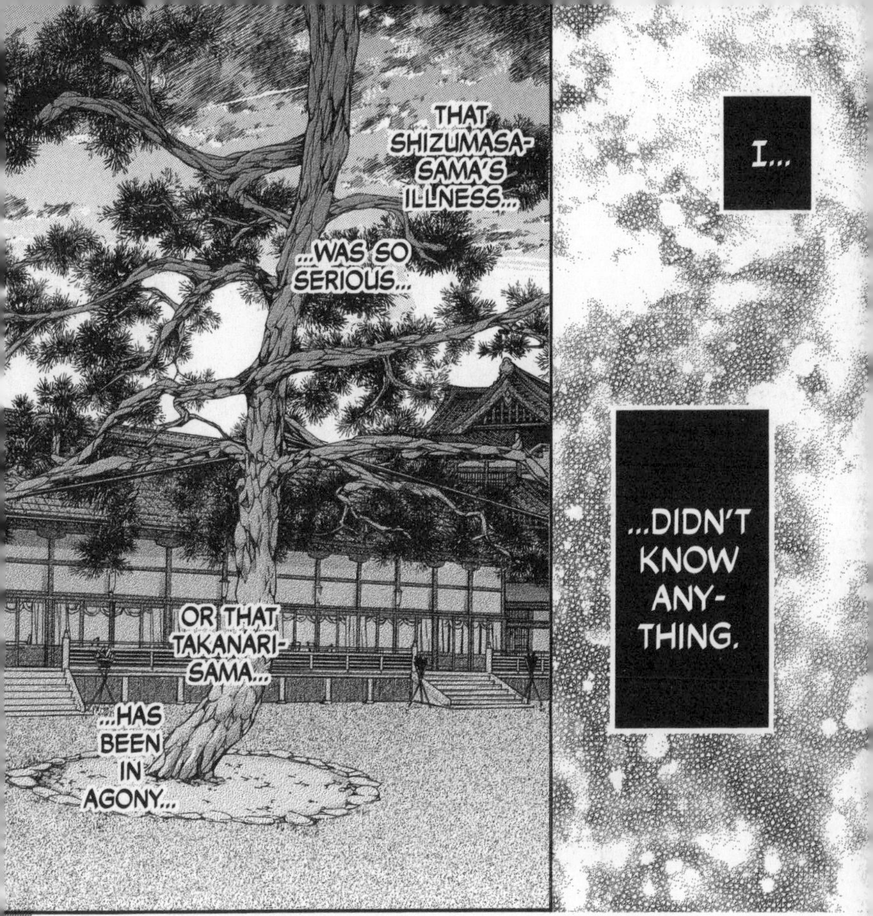
I...
...DIDN'T KNOW ANYTHING.
THAT SHIZUMASA-SAMA'S ILLNESS...
...WAS SO SERIOUS...
OR THAT TAKANARI-SAMA...
...HAS BEEN IN AGONY...

Chapter 45: Leaving One's Grief in the Night

Lead-in Shizumasa's heart. Takanari's feelings. I won't let anyone get in their way anymore...!

Ah... This chapter... This is rather personal, but this was during a time when I was "fighting" against a lot of things, so I drew an image of a brave-looking Haine for the chapter title page.

These characters seem to change their clothes whenever they get the chance... Maora is the one who makes them. I decided to make their uniforms white for the climax since I like the color.

The five members of the student council are completely uncoordinated without Haine-chan. Maora and Maguri may be lovers, but you know what they're like... And I think Maora and Ushio would never get along with each other under normal circumstances.
Maguri and Ushio are like a pet and its owner... ᵕ (I was glad to see them talking to each other at the end of chapter 33 [in volume 8], which is very rare for them.)

I'm sure the other four council members...are glad that Haine is the main character.

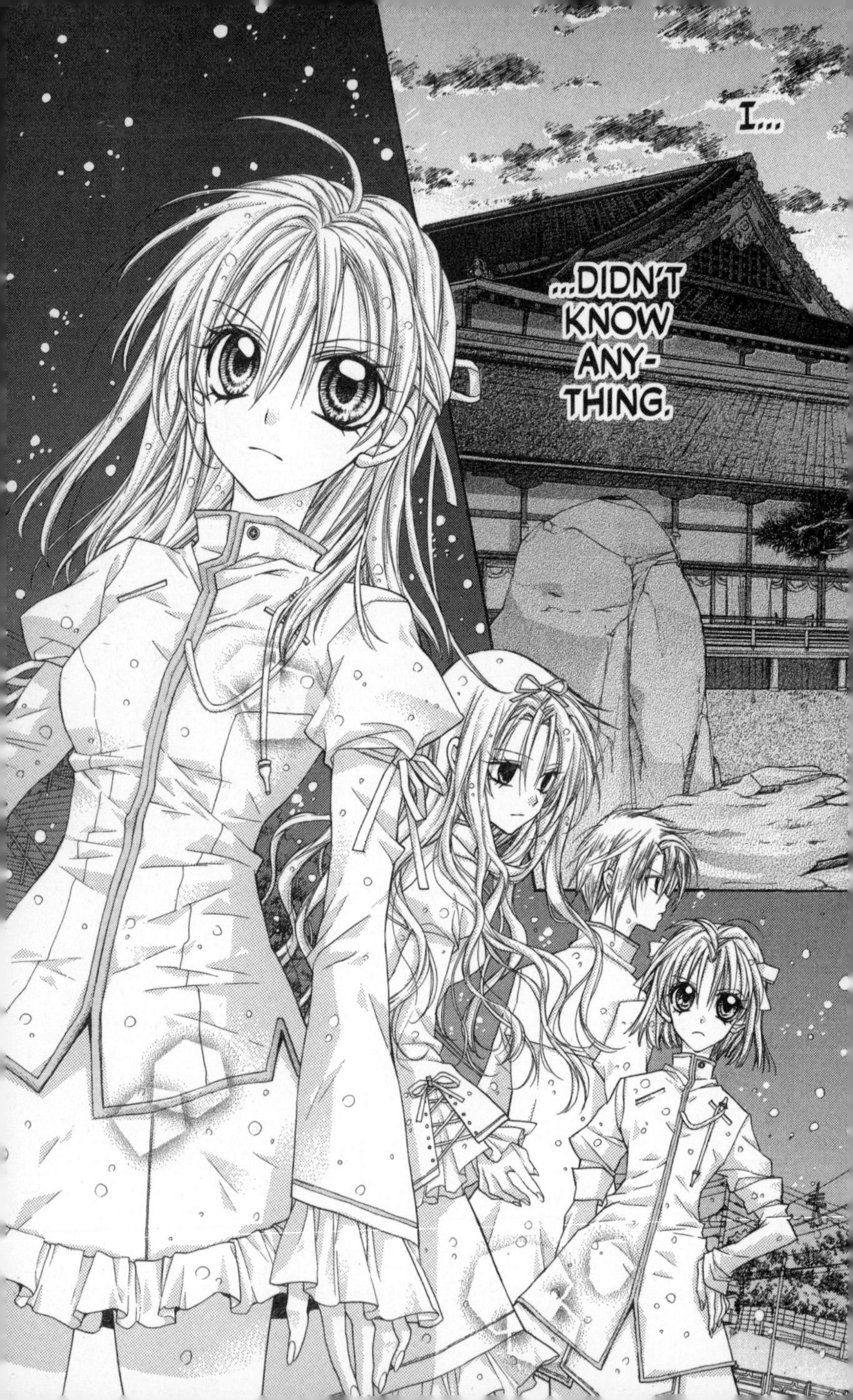
I...
...DIDN'T KNOW ANY-THING.

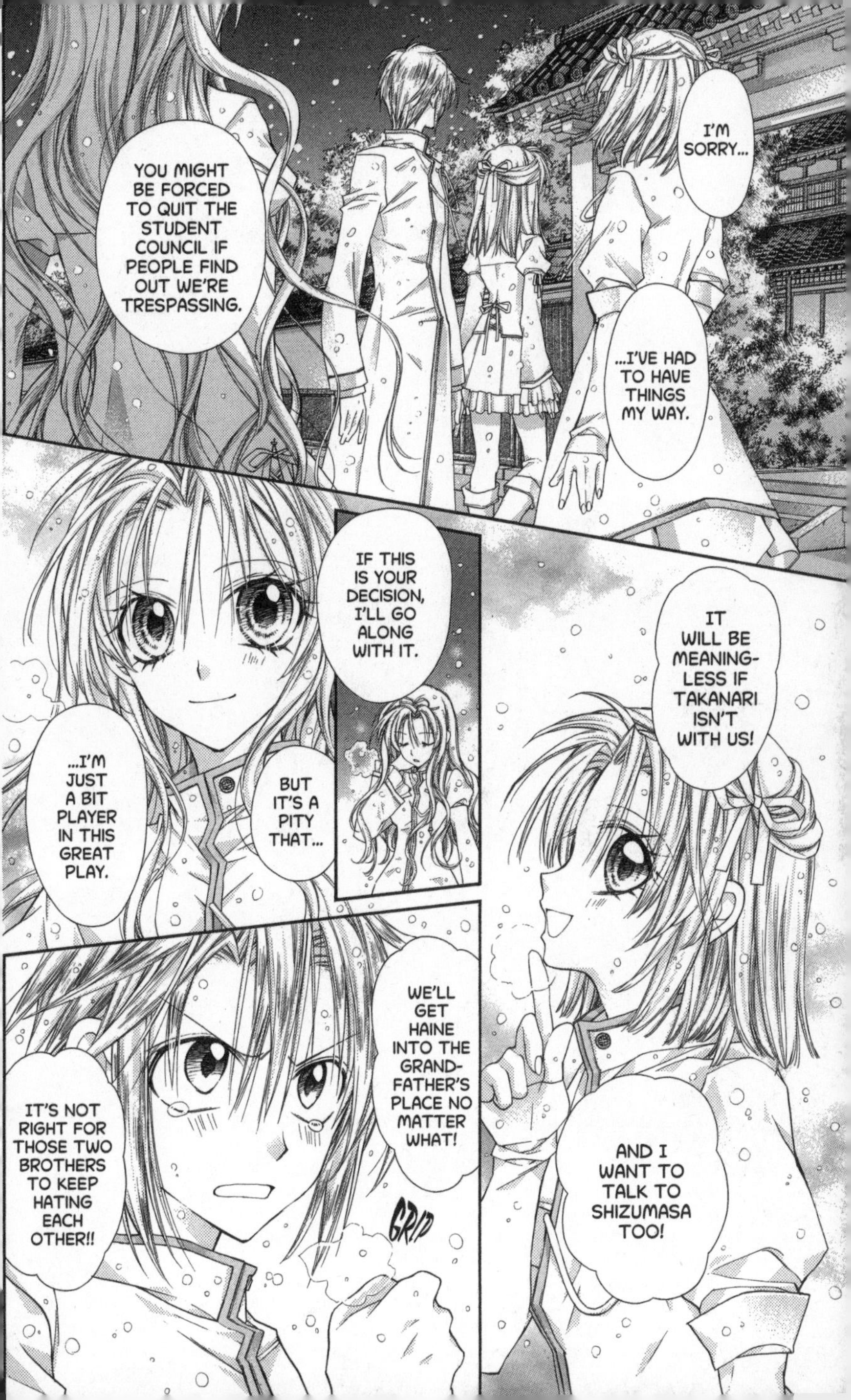
I'M SORRY...
...I'VE HAD TO HAVE THINGS MY WAY.
YOU MIGHT BE FORCED TO QUIT THE STUDENT COUNCIL IF PEOPLE FIND OUT WE'RE TRESPASSING.
IT WILL BE MEANING-LESS IF TAKANARI ISN'T WITH US!
AND I WANT TO TALK TO SHIZUMASA TOO!
IF THIS IS YOUR DECISION, I'LL GO ALONG WITH IT.
BUT IT'S A PITY THAT...
...I'M JUST A BIT PLAYER IN THIS GREAT PLAY.
WE'LL GET HAINE INTO THE GRAND-FATHER'S PLACE NO MATTER WHAT!
GRIP
IT'S NOT RIGHT FOR THOSE TWO BROTHERS TO KEEP HATING EACH OTHER!!

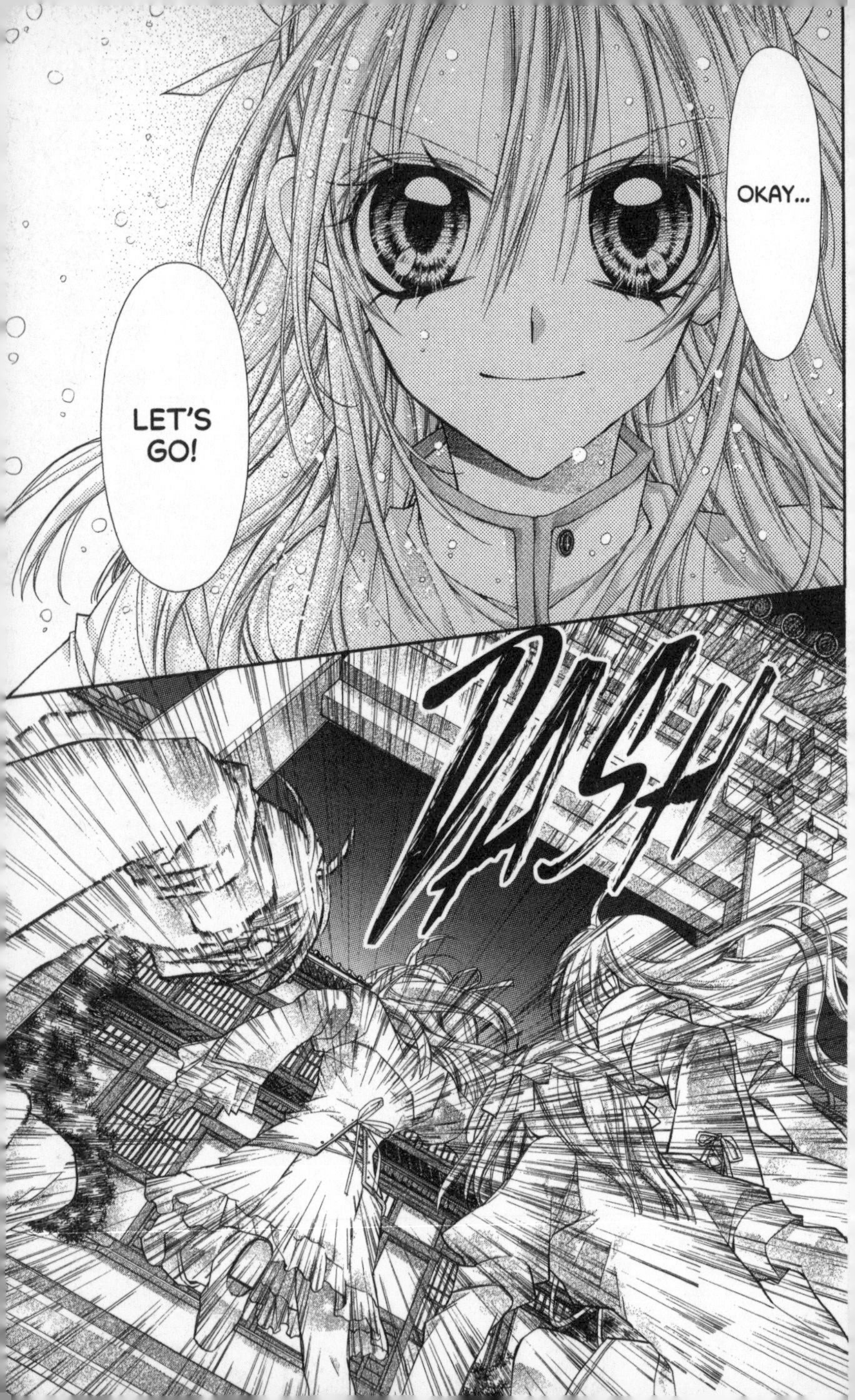
OKAY...
LET'S GO!
DASH

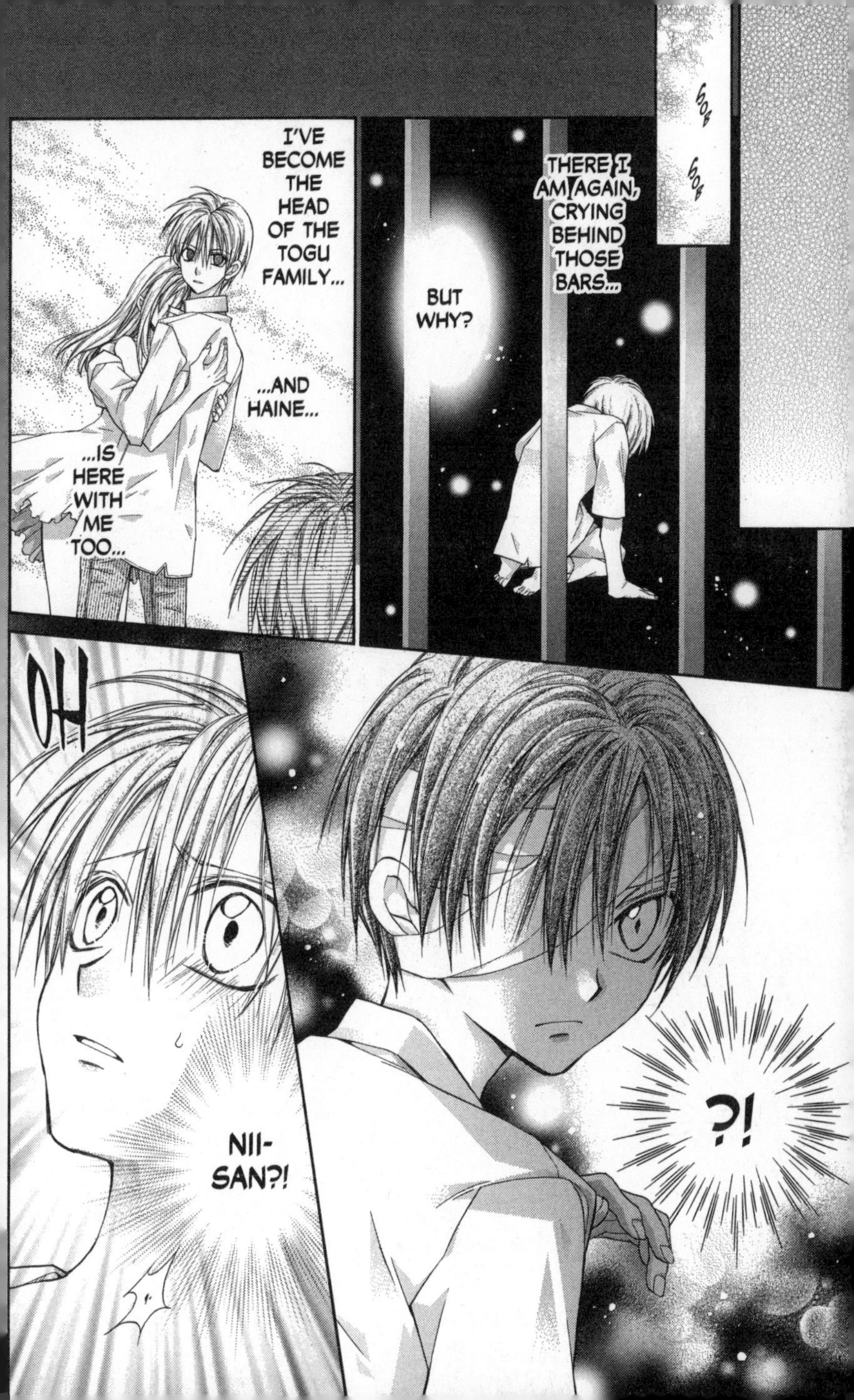
sob
sob
THERE I AM AGAIN, CRYING BEHIND THOSE BARS...
BUT WHY?
I'VE BECOME THE HEAD OF THE TOGU FAMILY...
...AND HAINE...
...IS HERE WITH ME TOO...
?!
OH
NII-SAN?!

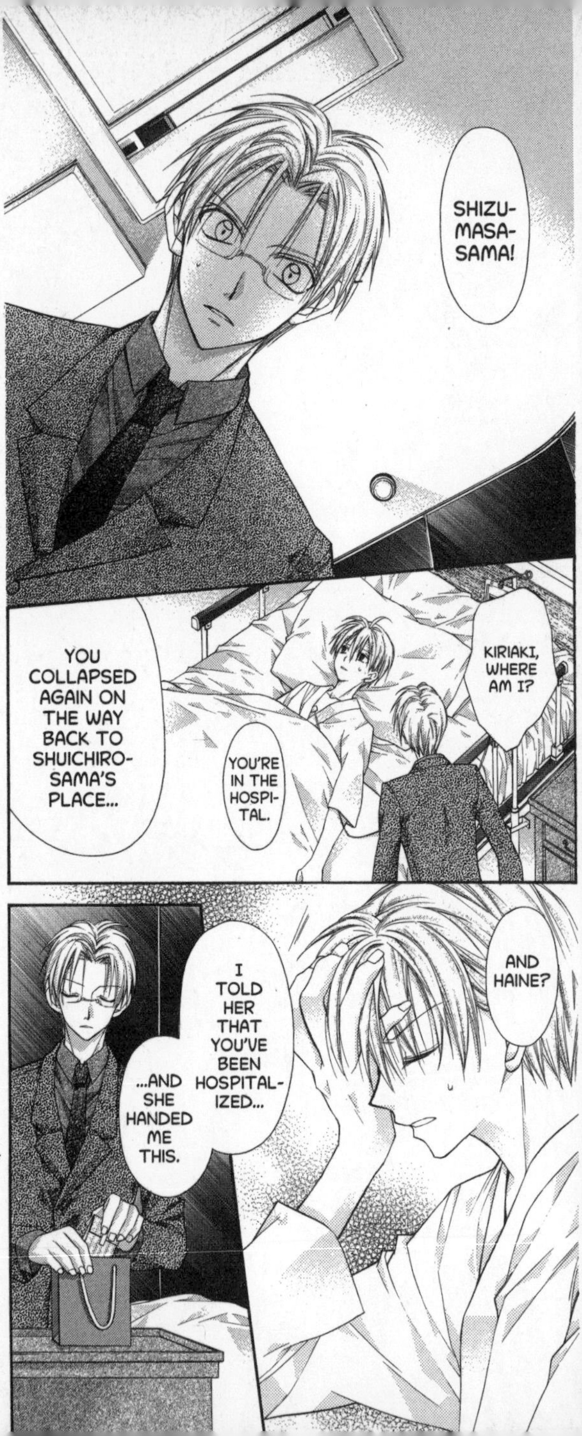
SHIZU-MASA-SAMA!
KIRIAKI, WHERE AM I?
YOU'RE IN THE HOSPI-TAL.
YOU COLLAPSED AGAIN ON THE WAY BACK TO SHUICHIRO-SAMA'S PLACE...
AND HAINE?
I TOLD HER THAT YOU'VE BEEN HOSPITAL-IZED...
...AND SHE HANDED ME THIS.

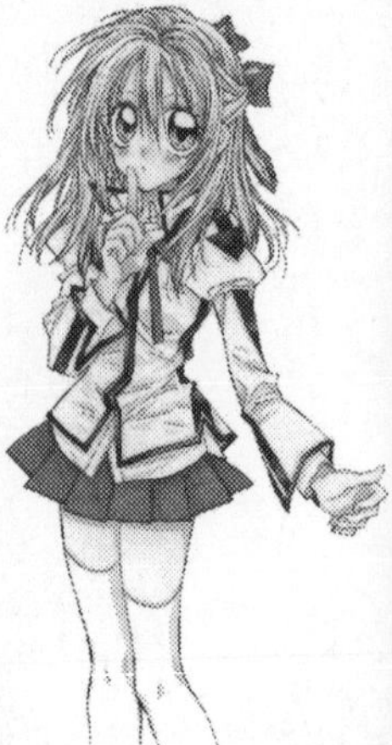

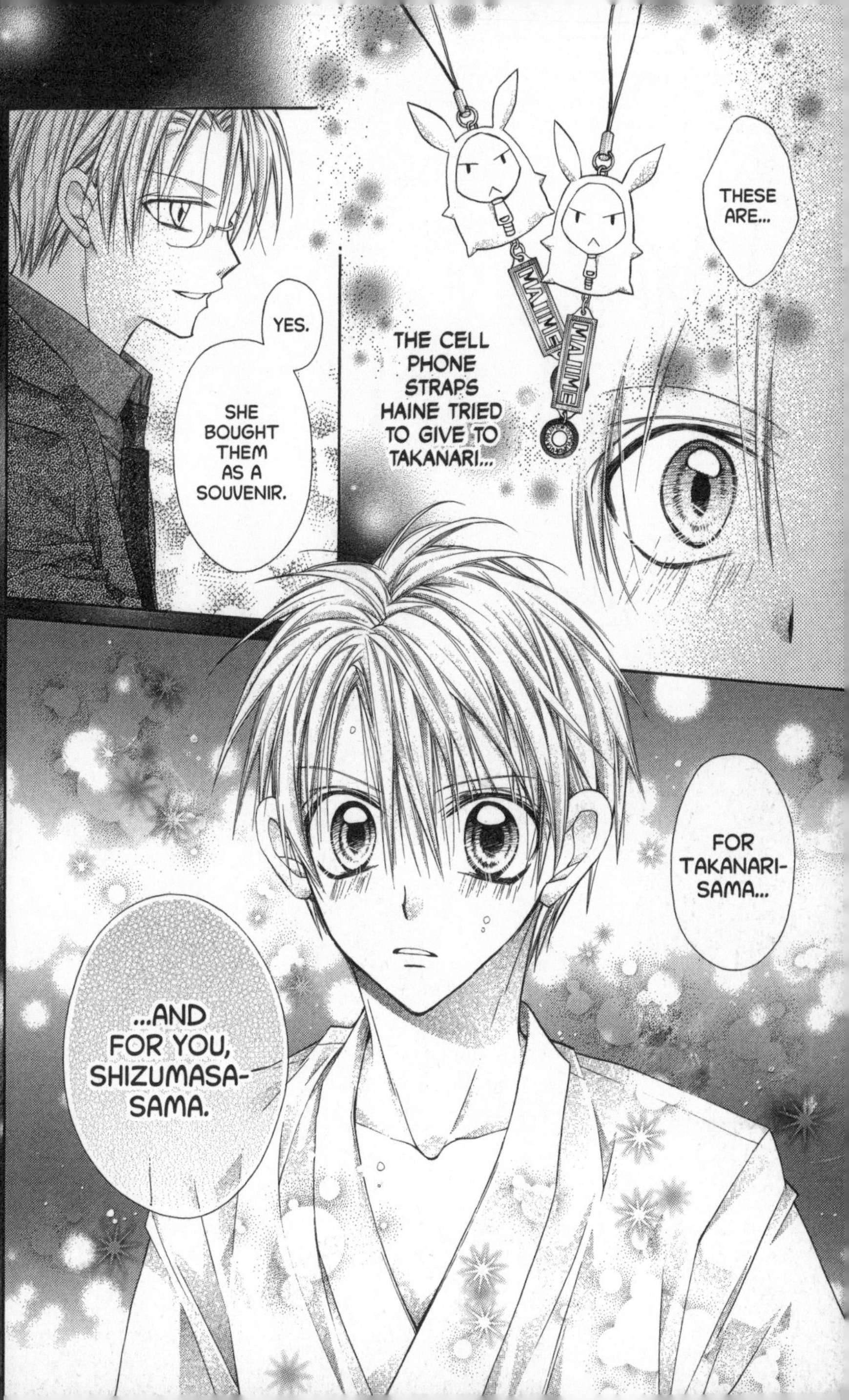
THESE ARE...
THE CELL PHONE STRAPS HAINE TRIED TO GIVE TO TAKANARI...
YES.
SHE BOUGHT THEM AS A SOUVENIR.
FOR TAKANARI-SAMA...
...AND FOR YOU, SHIZUMASA-SAMA.

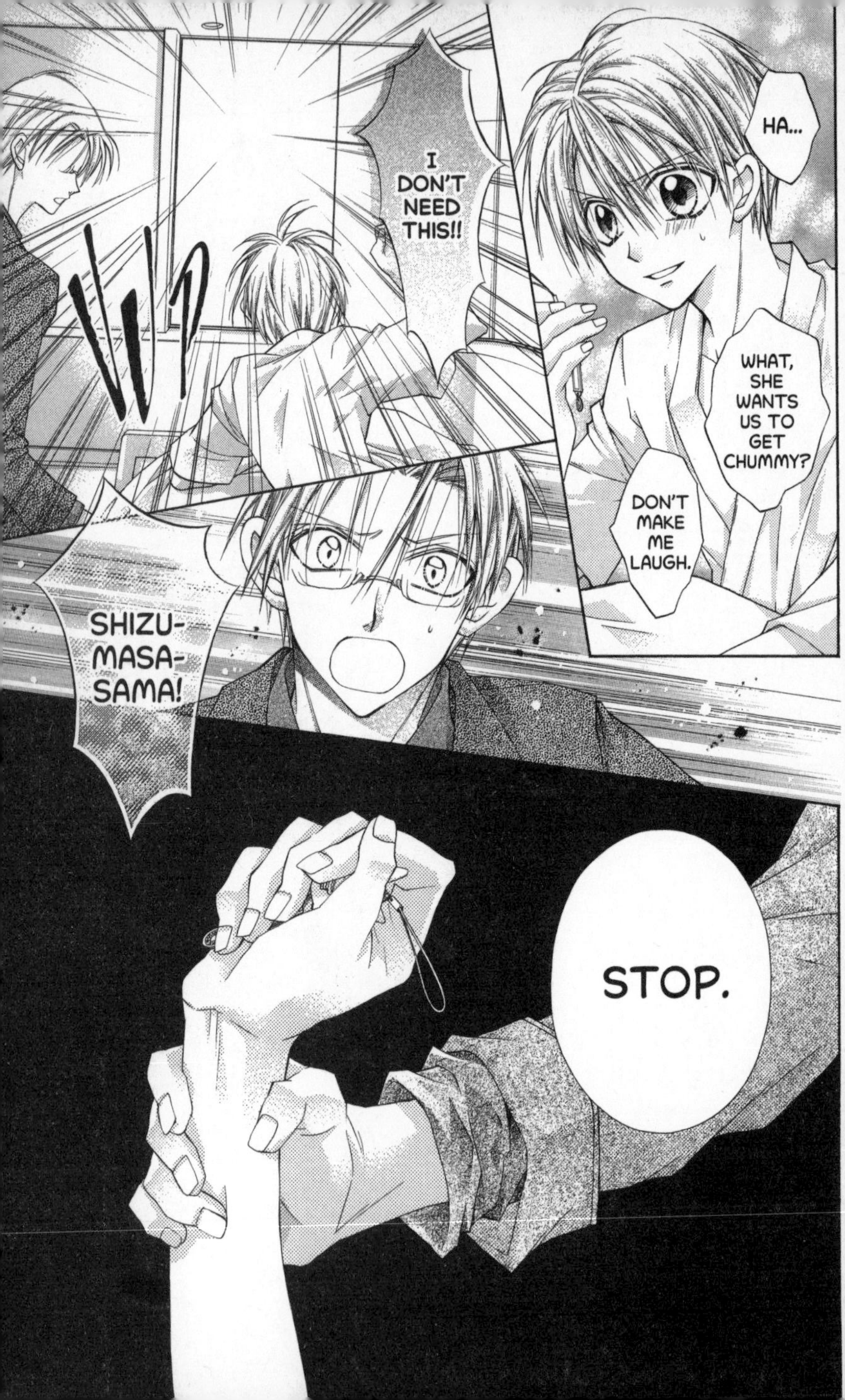
HA...
WHAT, SHE WANTS US TO GET CHUMMY?
DON'T MAKE ME LAUGH.
I DON'T NEED THIS!!
SHIZU-MASA-SAMA!
STOP.

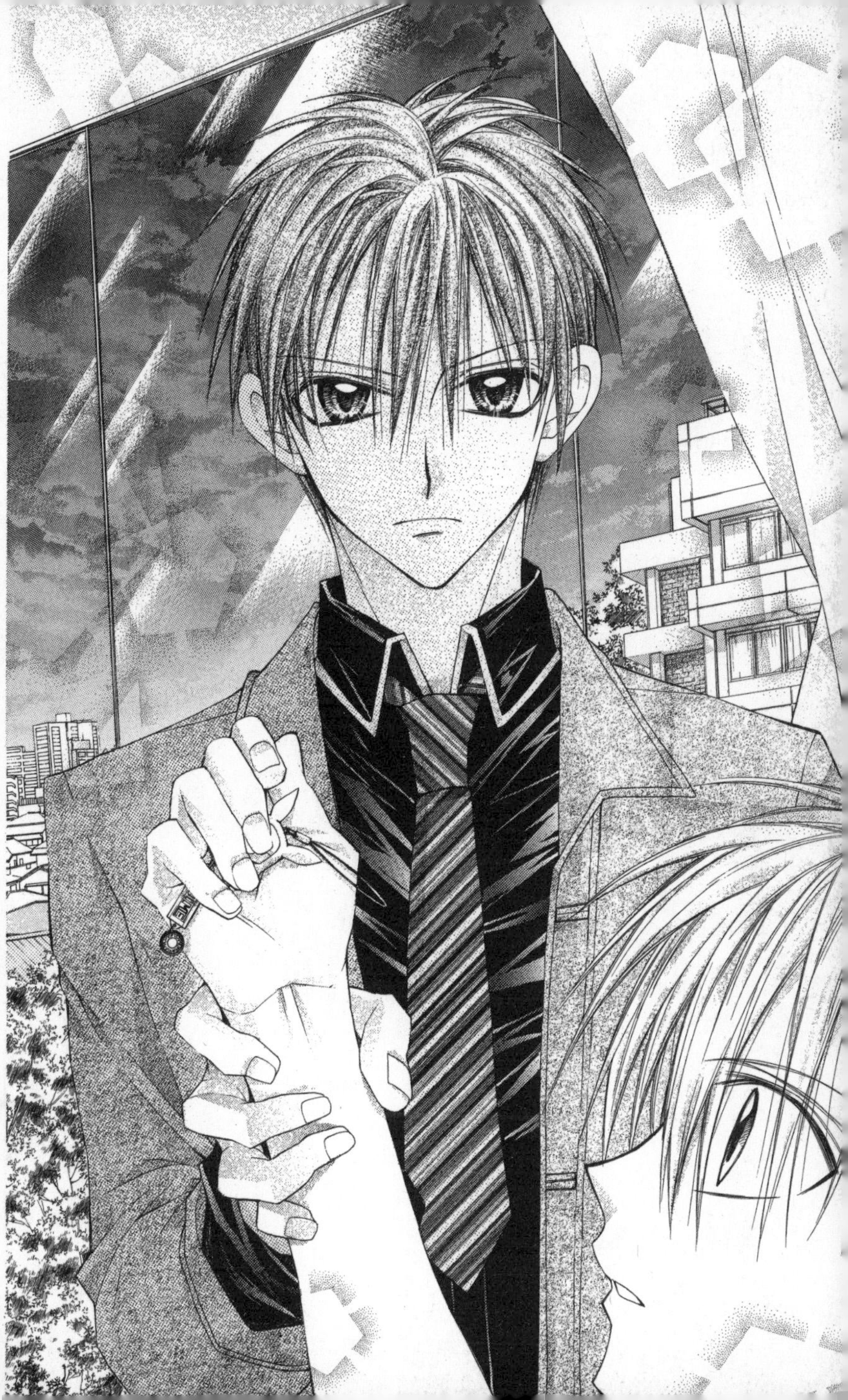

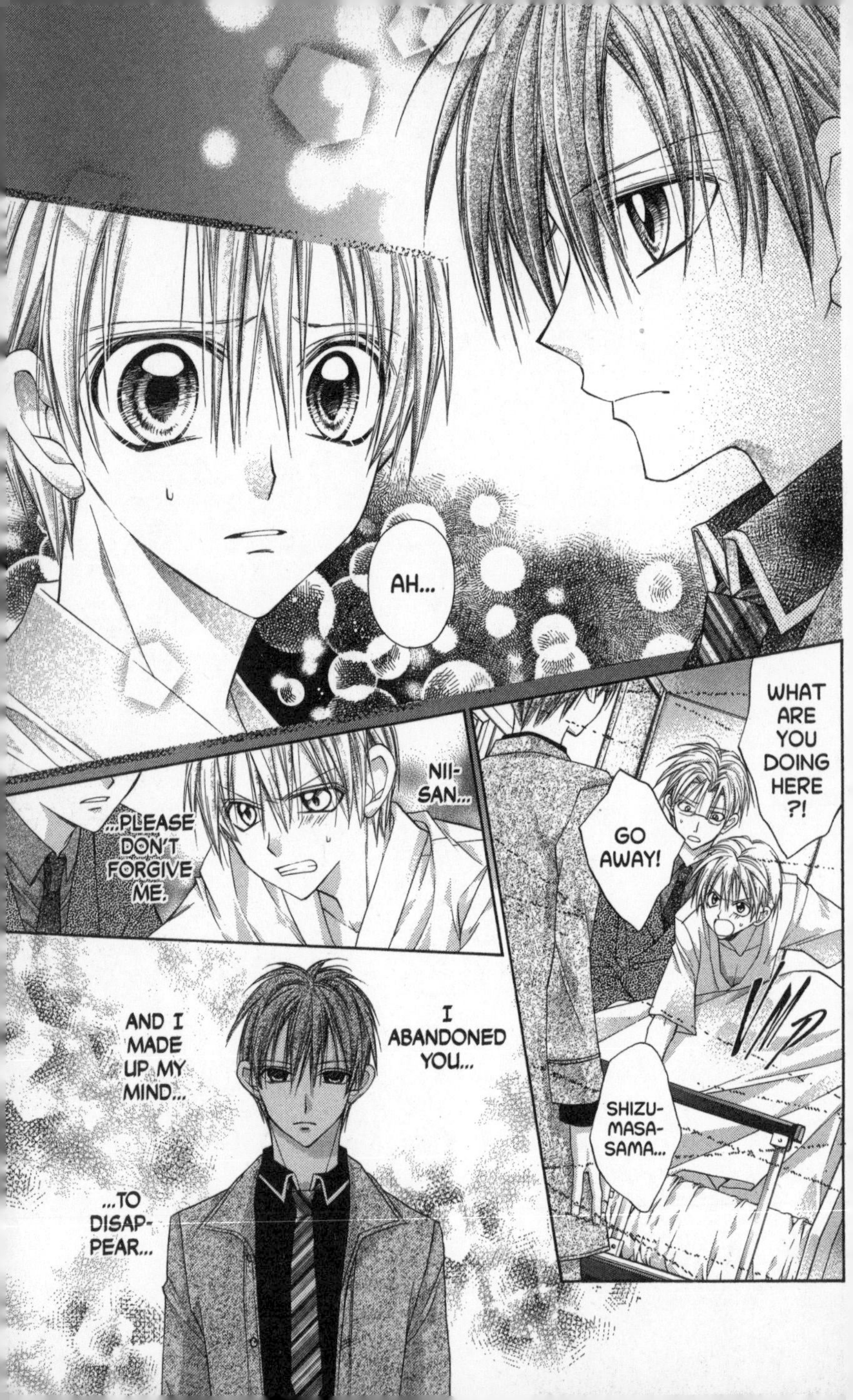
AH...
WHAT ARE YOU DOING HERE?!
GO AWAY!
SHIZU-MASA-SAMA...
NII-SAN...
...PLEASE DON'T FORGIVE ME.
I ABANDONED YOU...
AND I MADE UP MY MIND...
...TO DISAP-PEAR...

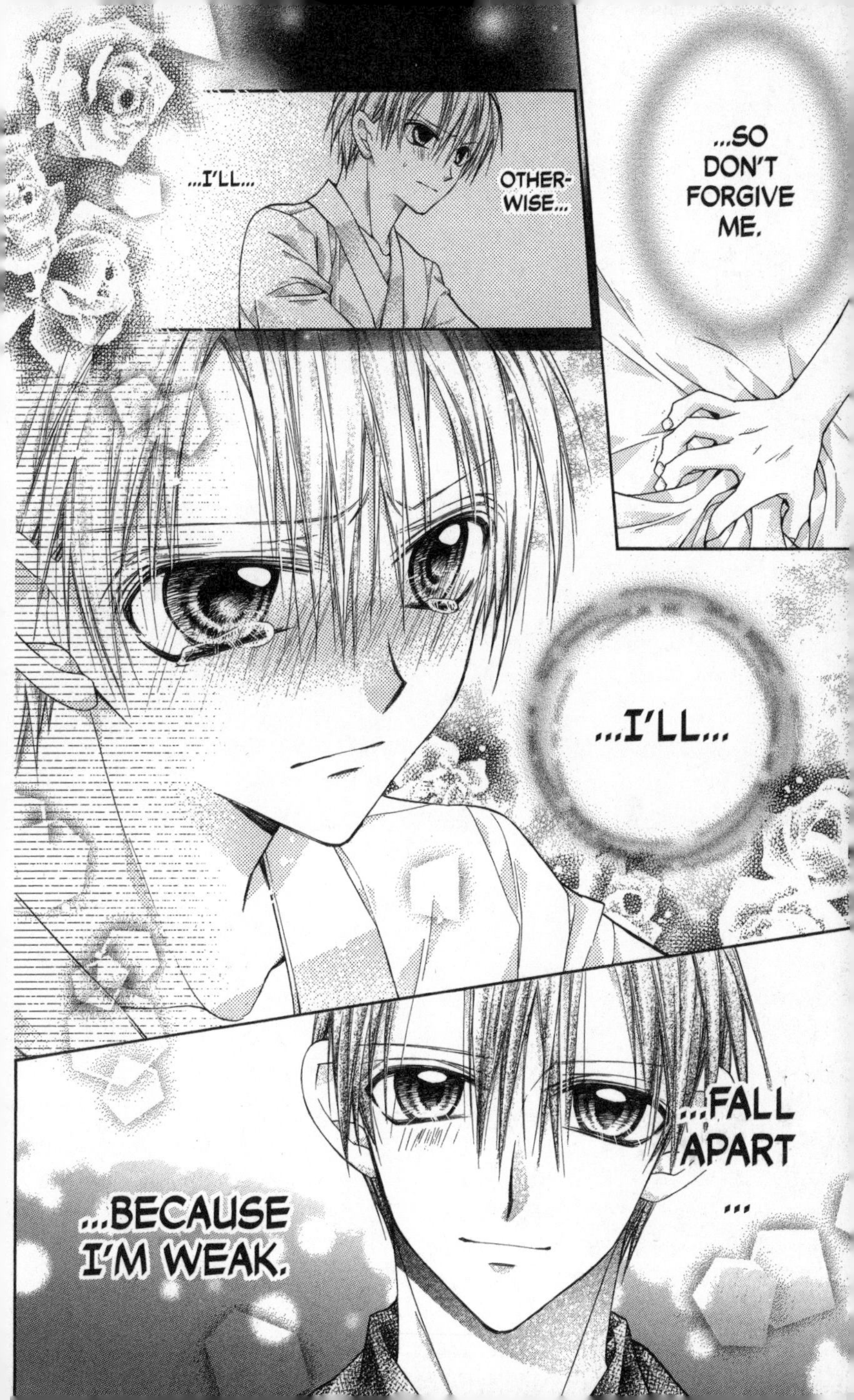
...SO DON'T FORGIVE ME.
OTHER-WISE...
...I'LL...
...I'LL...
...FALL APART ...
...BECAUSE I'M WEAK.

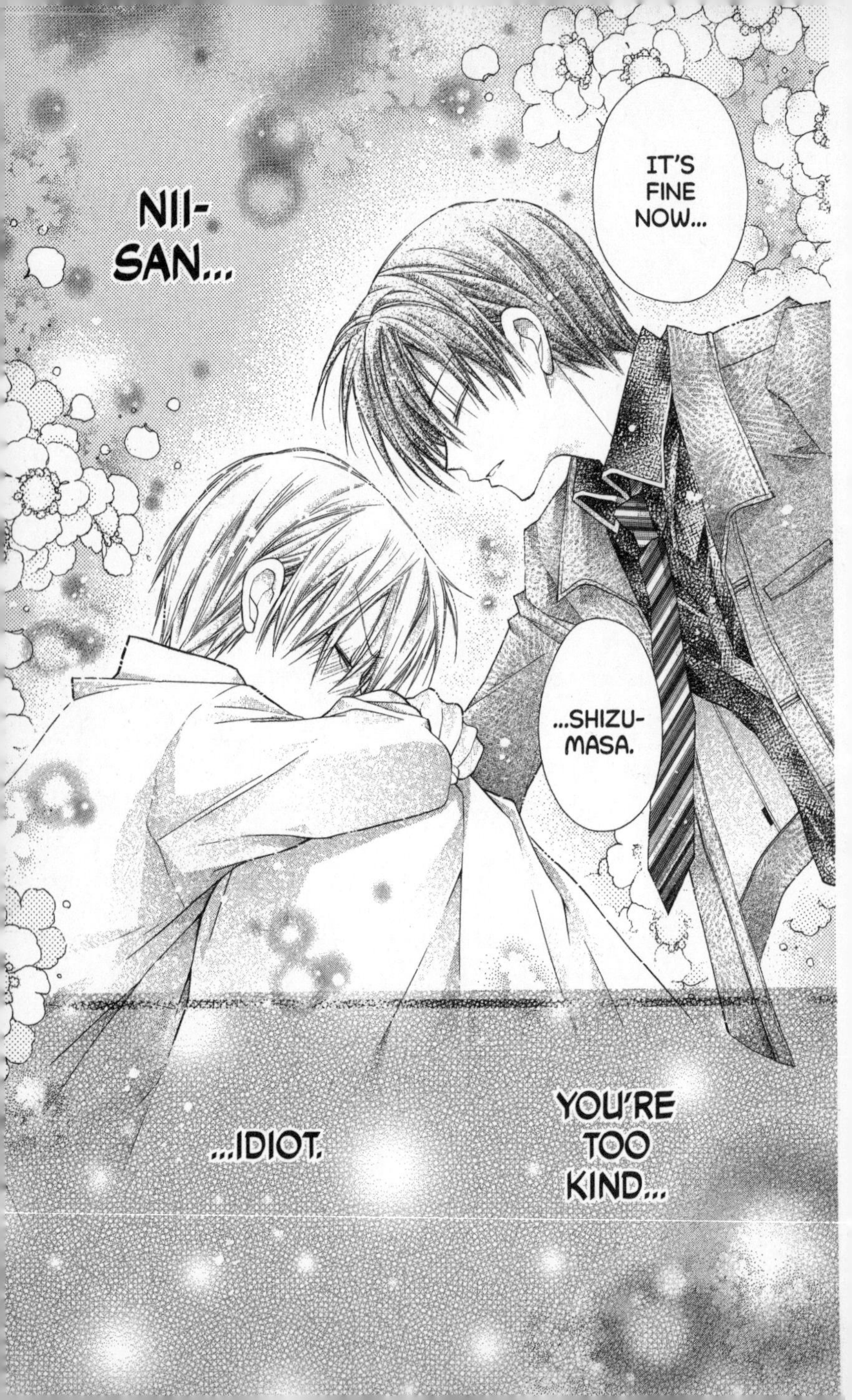
IT'S FINE NOW...
NII-SAN...
...SHIZU-MASA.
YOU'RE TOO KIND...
...IDIOT.

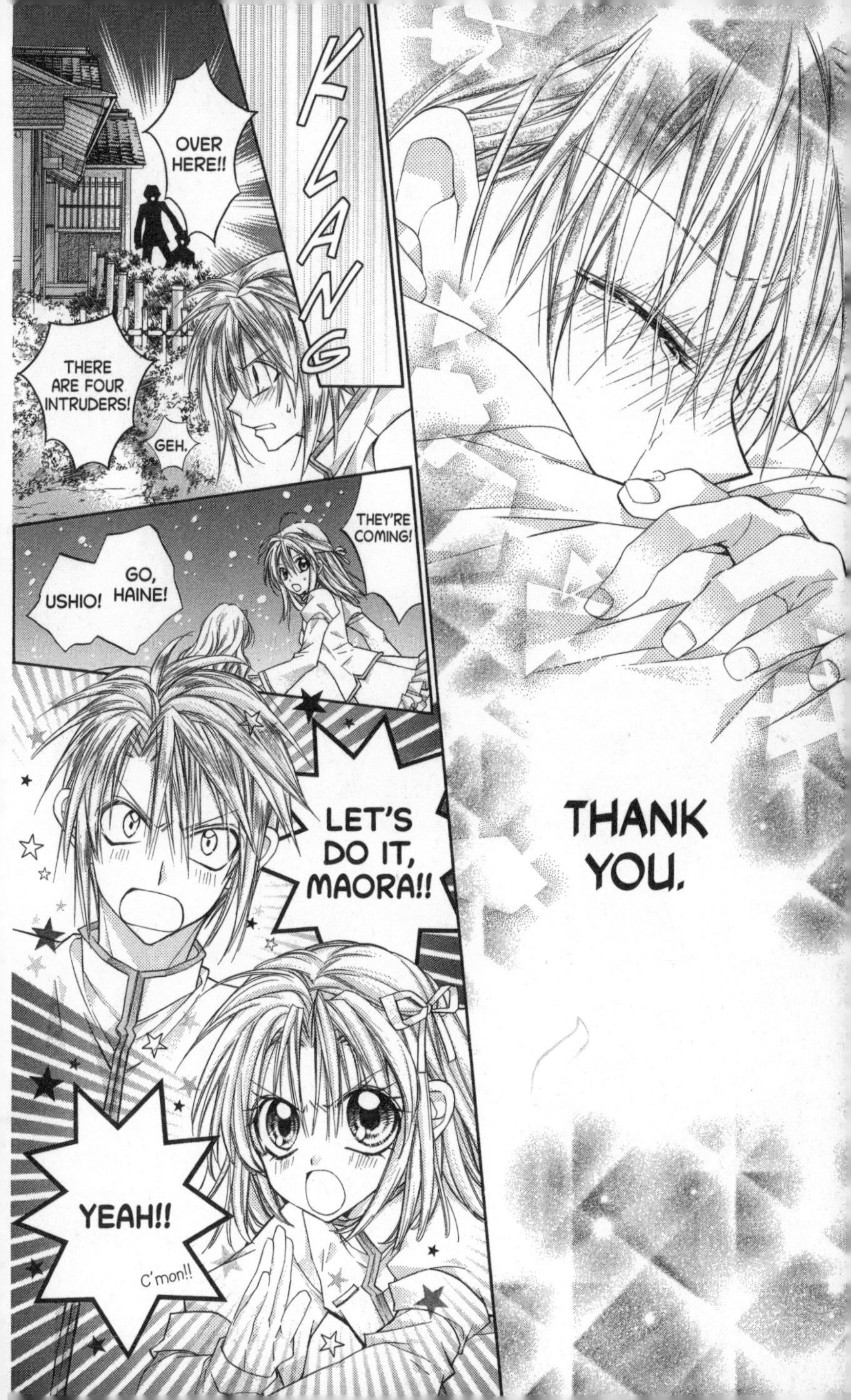
THANK YOU.
KLANG
OVER HERE!!
THERE ARE FOUR INTRUDERS!
GEH.
THEY'RE COMING!
GO, HAINE!
USHIO!
LET'S DO IT, MAORA!!
YEAH!!
C'mon!!

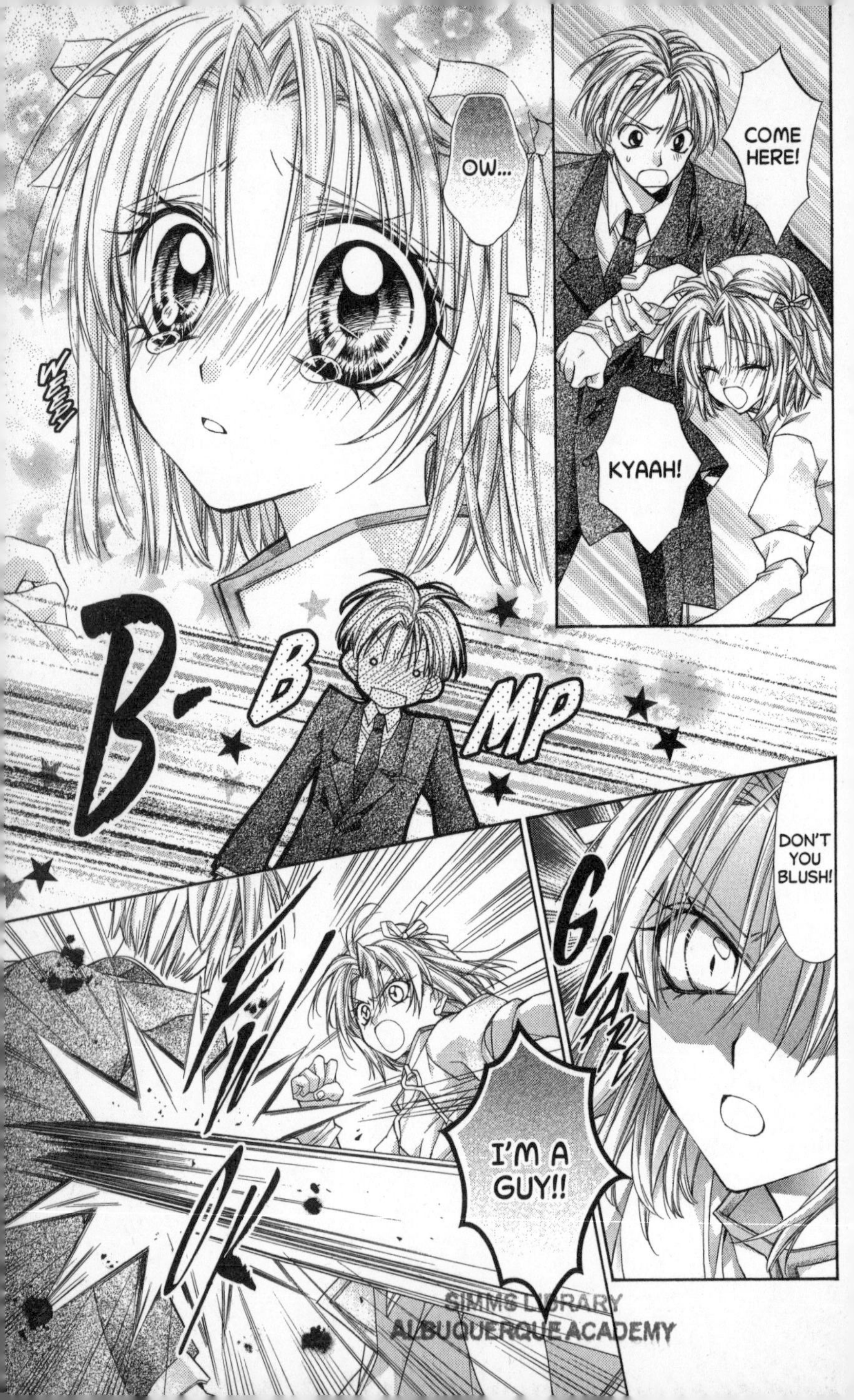
COME HERE!
KYAAH!
OW...
DON'T YOU BLUSH!
I'M A GUY!!

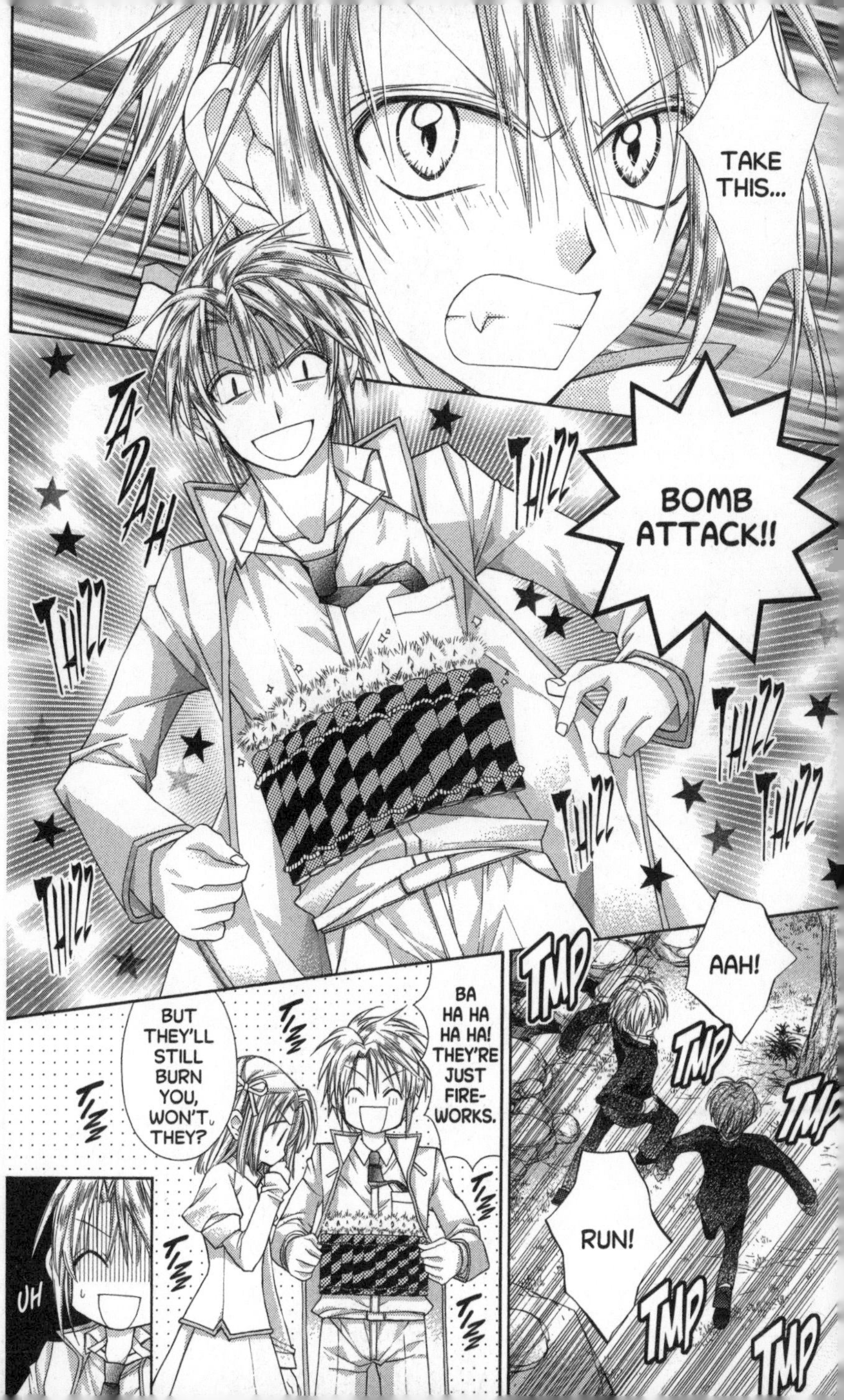
TAKE THIS...
BOMB ATTACK!!
TA-DAAH
THIZZ
THIZZ
THIZZ
THIZZ
THIZZ
THIZZ
AAH!
TMP
TMP
TMP
RUN!
TMP
TMP
BA HA HA HA HA! THEY'RE JUST FIRE-WORKS.
BUT THEY'LL STILL BURN YOU, WON'T THEY?
UH

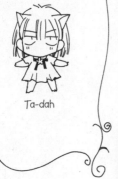

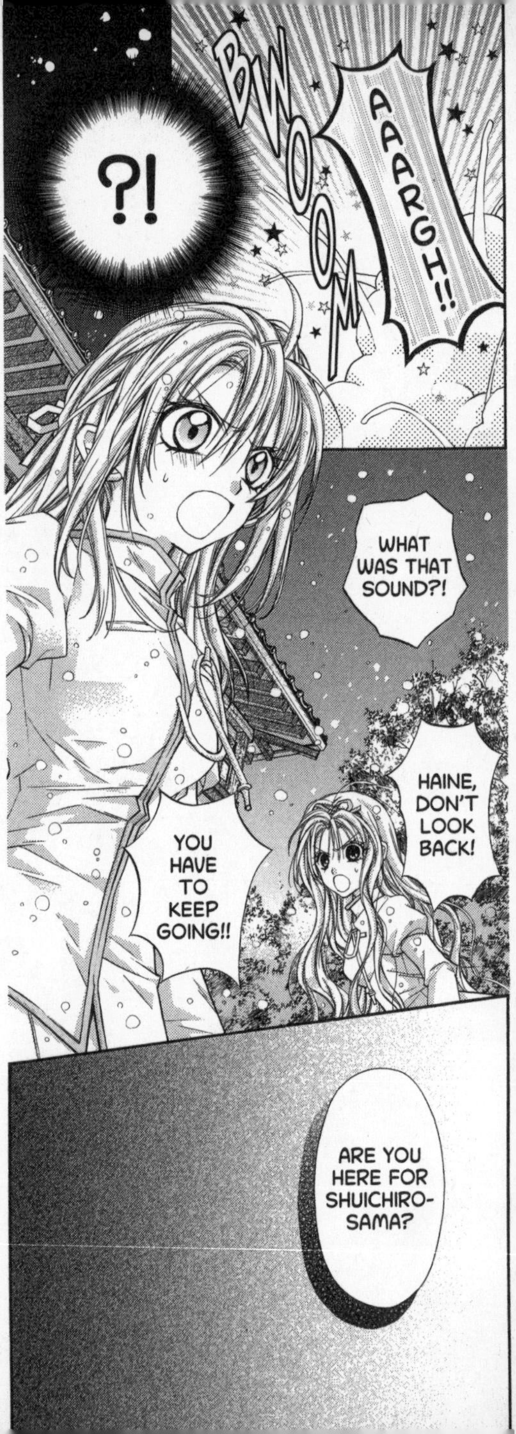
AAARGH!!
BWOOOM
?!
WHAT WAS THAT SOUND?!
HAINE, DON'T LOOK BACK!
YOU HAVE TO KEEP GOING!!
ARE YOU HERE FOR SHUICHIRO-SAMA?

Greetings

Hello, Arina Tanemura here. How are you all doing? I bring forth volume 11 for you, the last volume of *The Gentlemen's Alliance †* series.

This series, which has continued for four years, has finally come to a close. It's a series that has been supported by your love. Thank you very much.

For the sidebars in this volume, I'd like to write about my thoughts on this series.

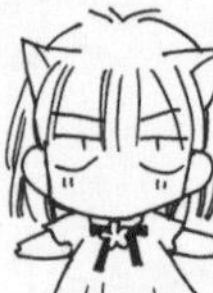

Ta-dah

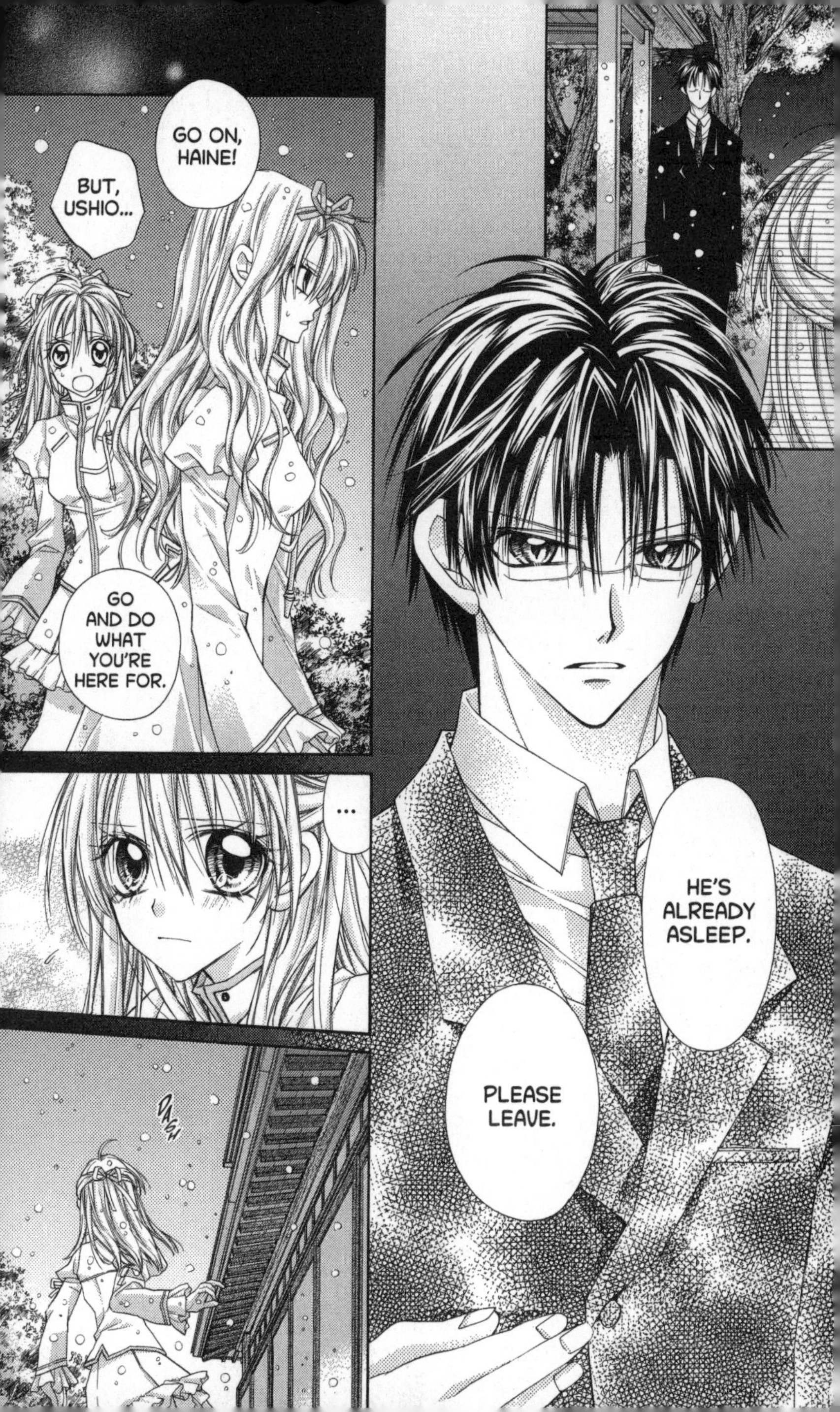
HE'S ALREADY ASLEEP.
PLEASE LEAVE.
GO ON, HAINE!
BUT, USHIO...
GO AND DO WHAT YOU'RE HERE FOR.
...
DASH

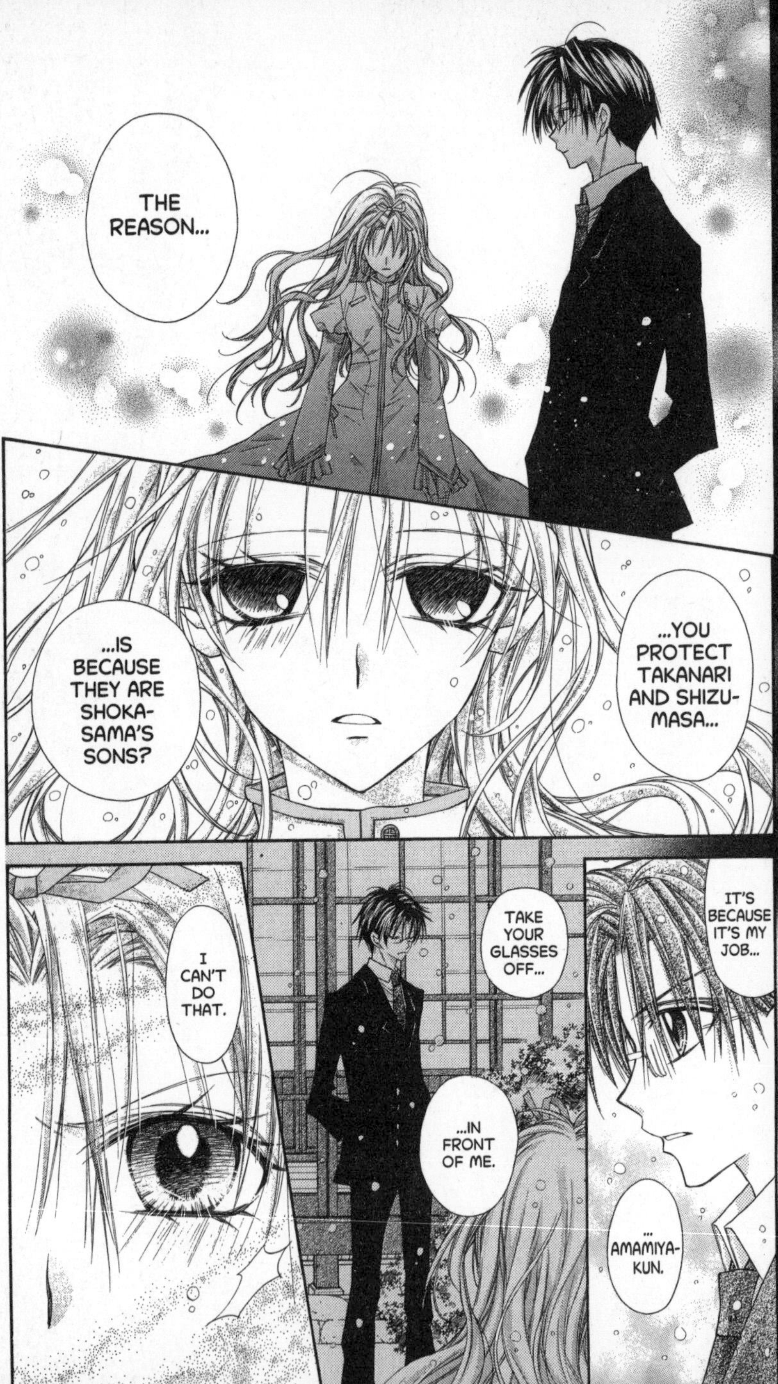
THE REASON...
...YOU PROTECT TAKANARI AND SHIZU-MASA...
...IS BECAUSE THEY ARE SHOKA-SAMA'S SONS?
IT'S BECAUSE IT'S MY JOB...
... AMAMIYA-KUN.
TAKE YOUR GLASSES OFF...
...IN FRONT OF ME.
I CAN'T DO THAT.

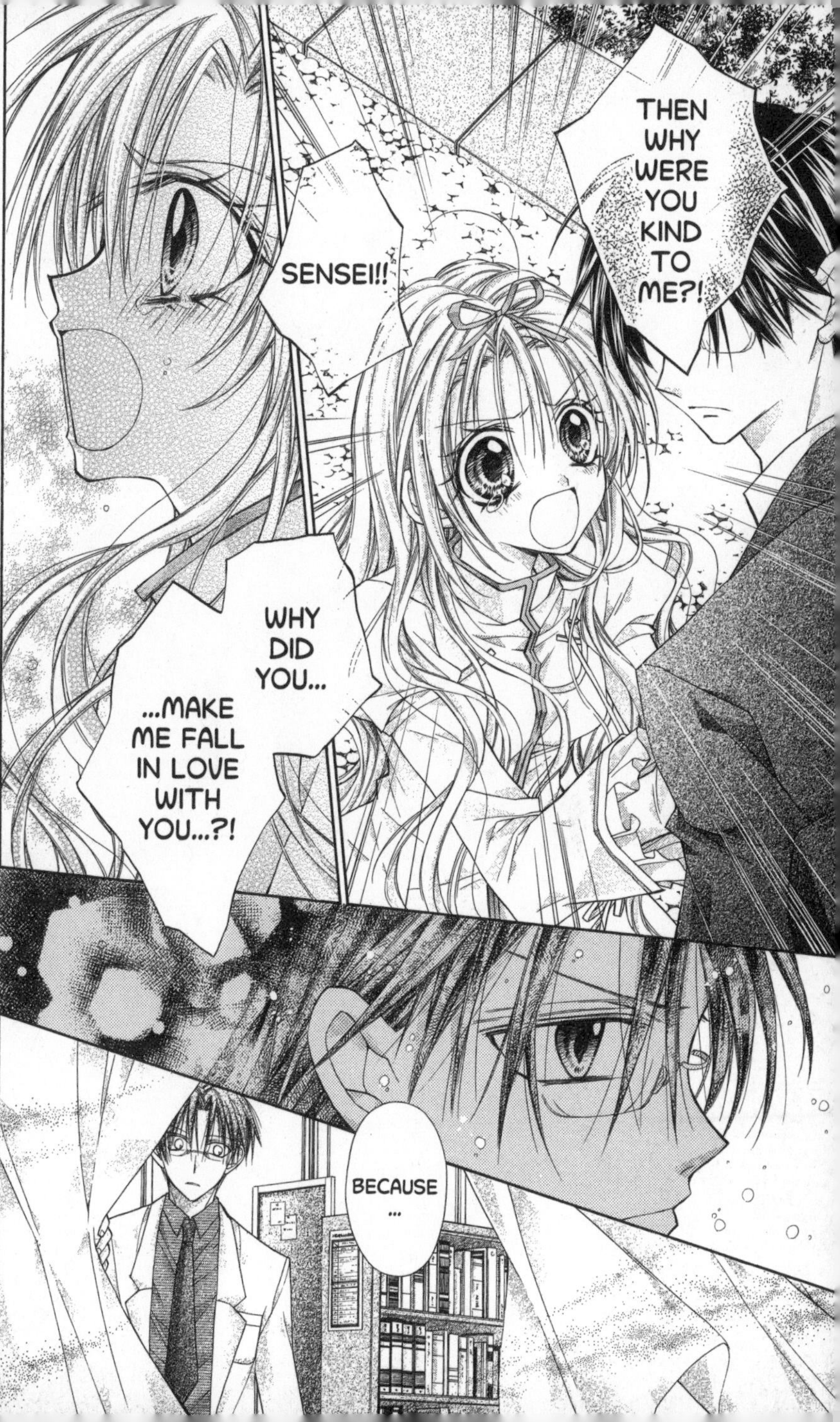
THEN WHY WERE YOU KIND TO ME?!
SENSEI!!
WHY DID YOU...
...MAKE ME FALL IN LOVE WITH YOU...?!
BECAUSE ...

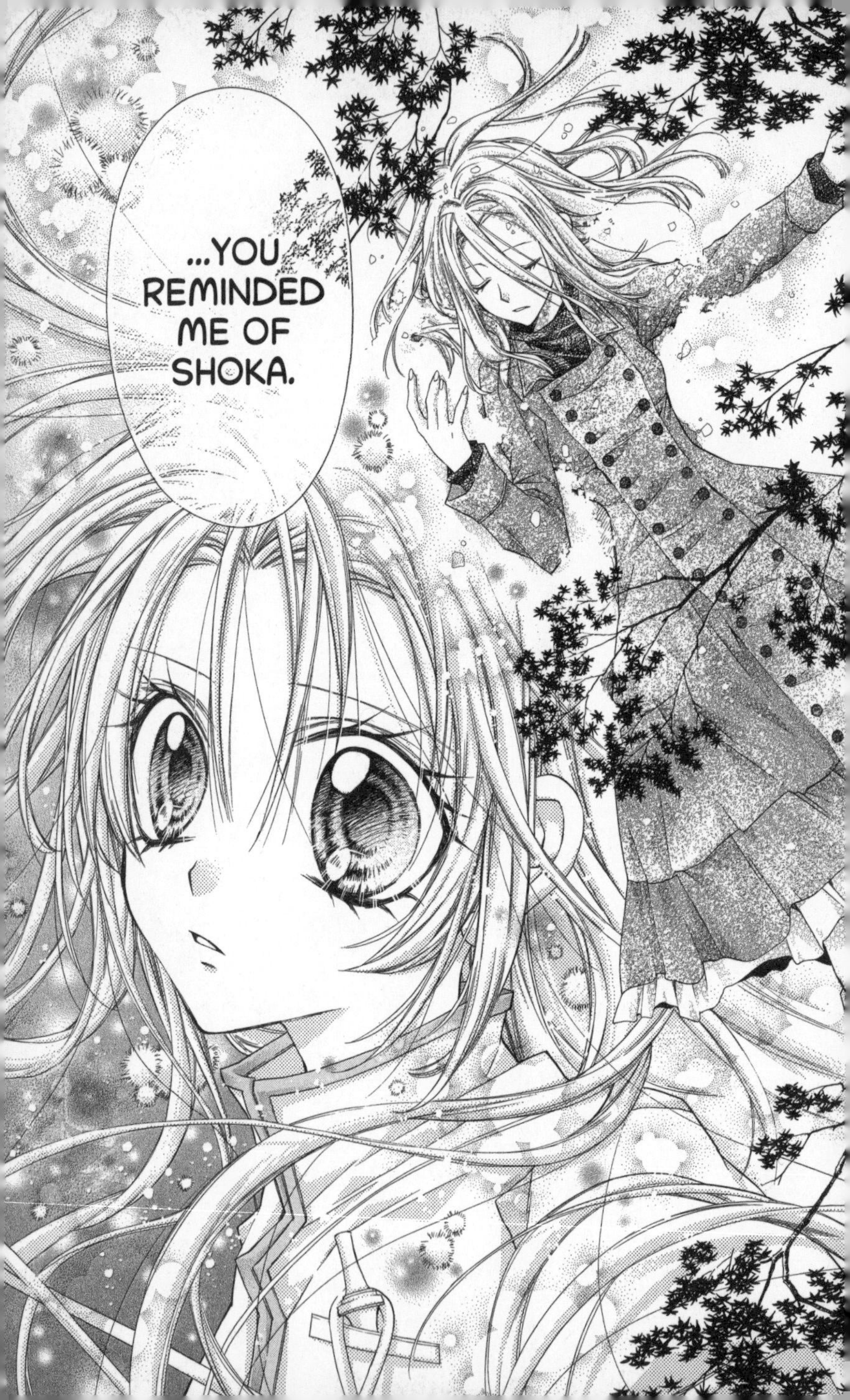
...YOU REMINDED ME OF SHOKA.

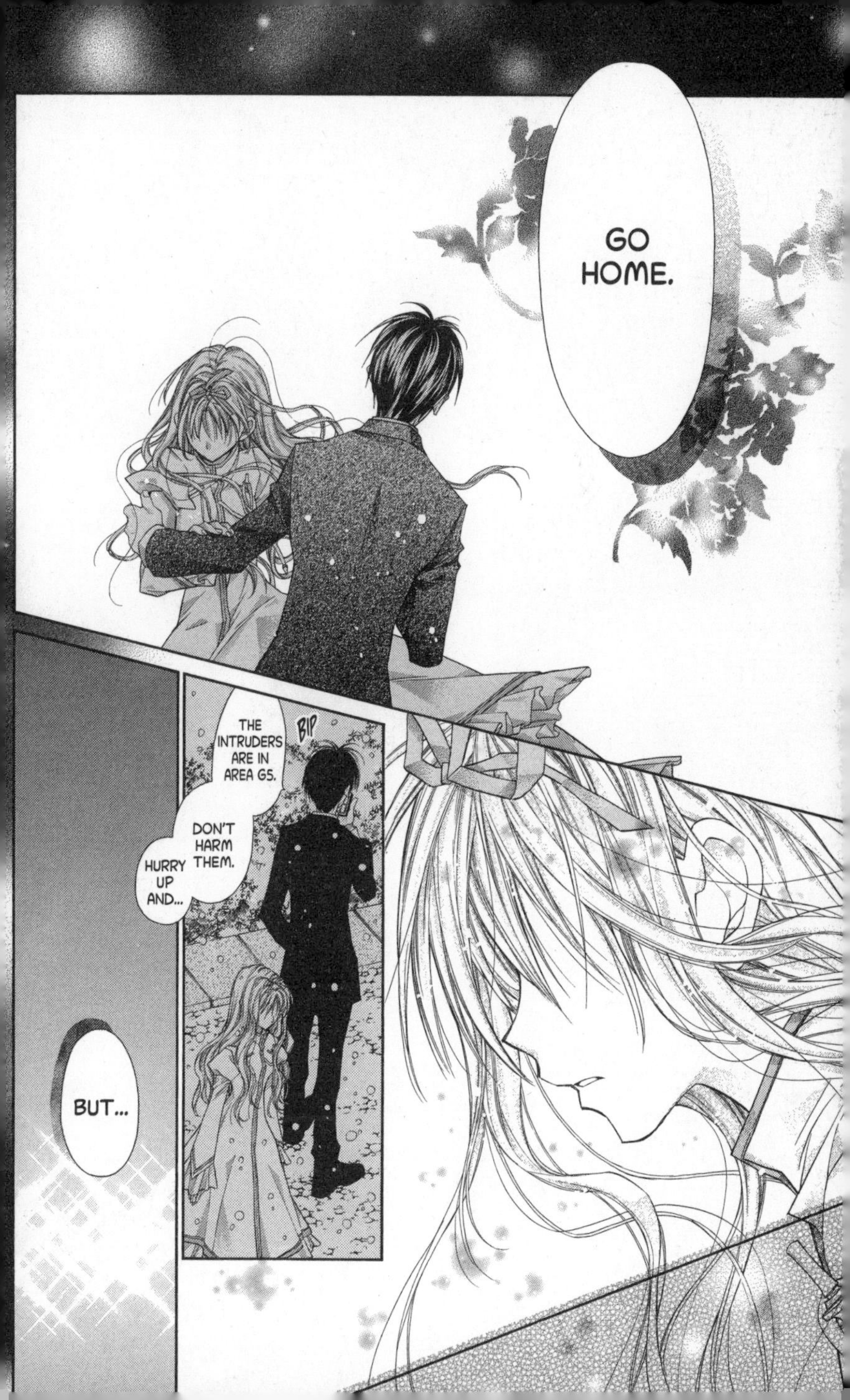
GO HOME.
THE INTRUDERS ARE IN AREA G5.
BIP
DON'T HARM THEM.
HURRY UP AND...
BUT...

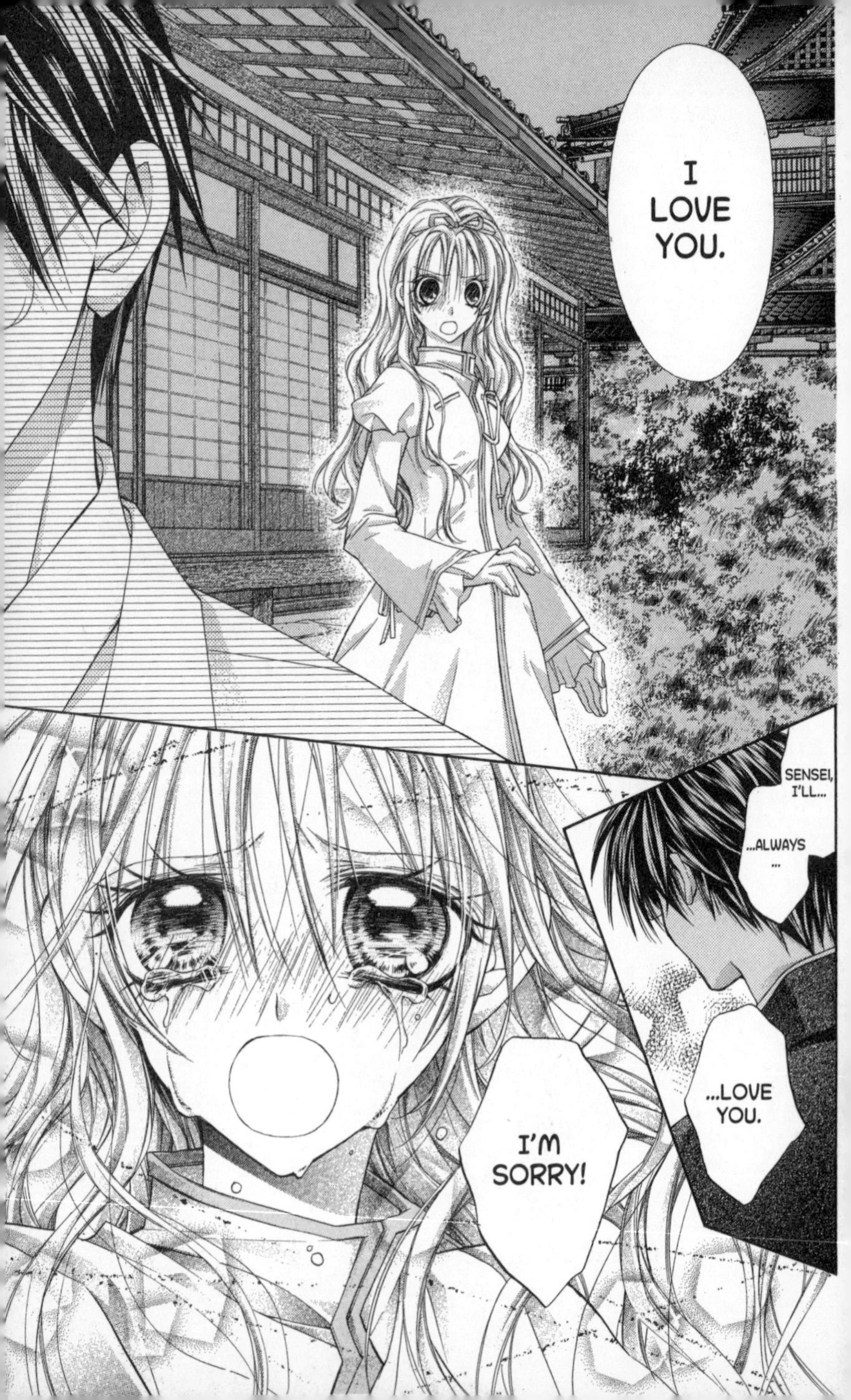
I LOVE YOU.
SENSEI, I'LL...
...ALWAYS...
...LOVE YOU.
I'M SORRY!

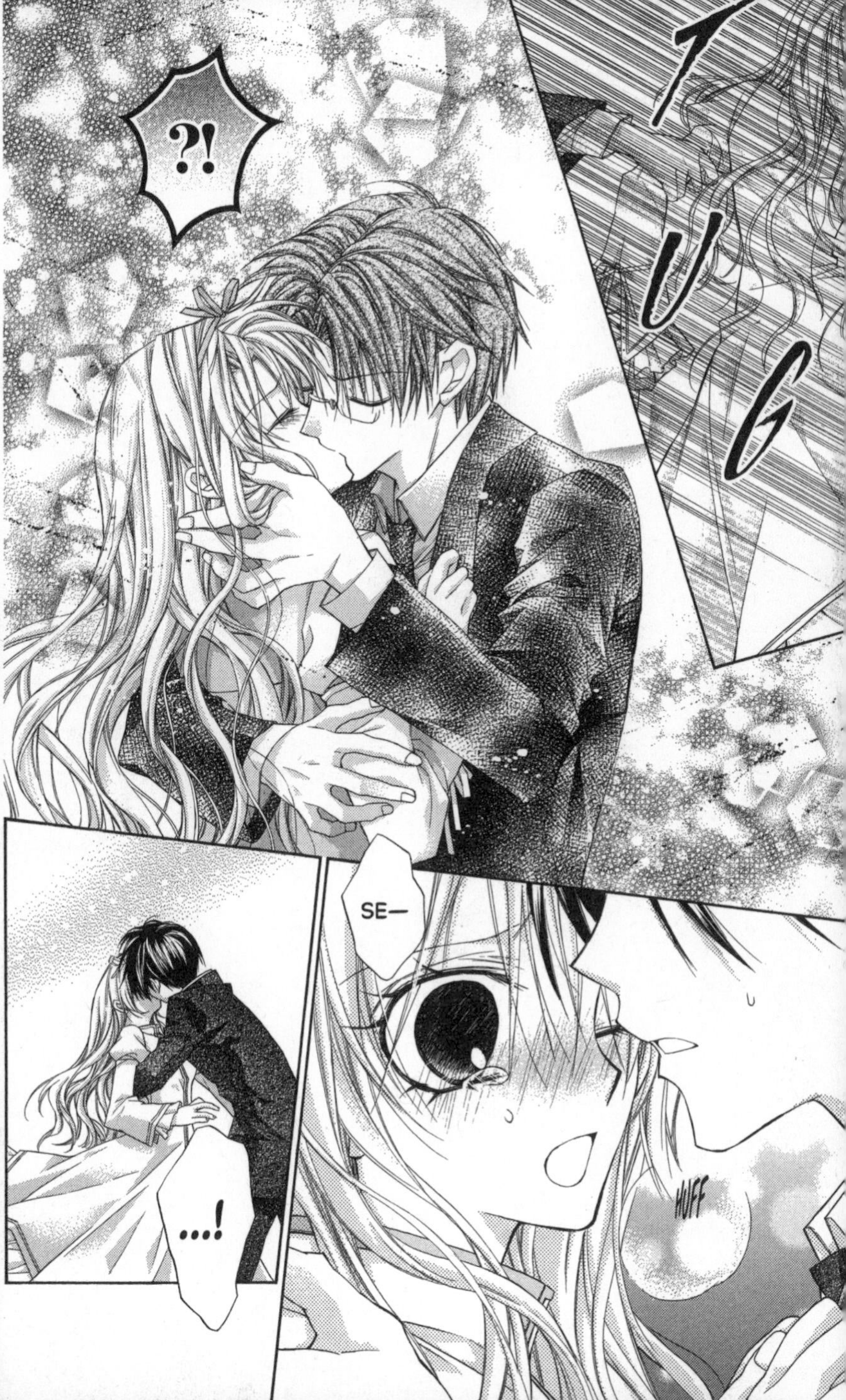
TUG
?!
SE—
HUFF
...!

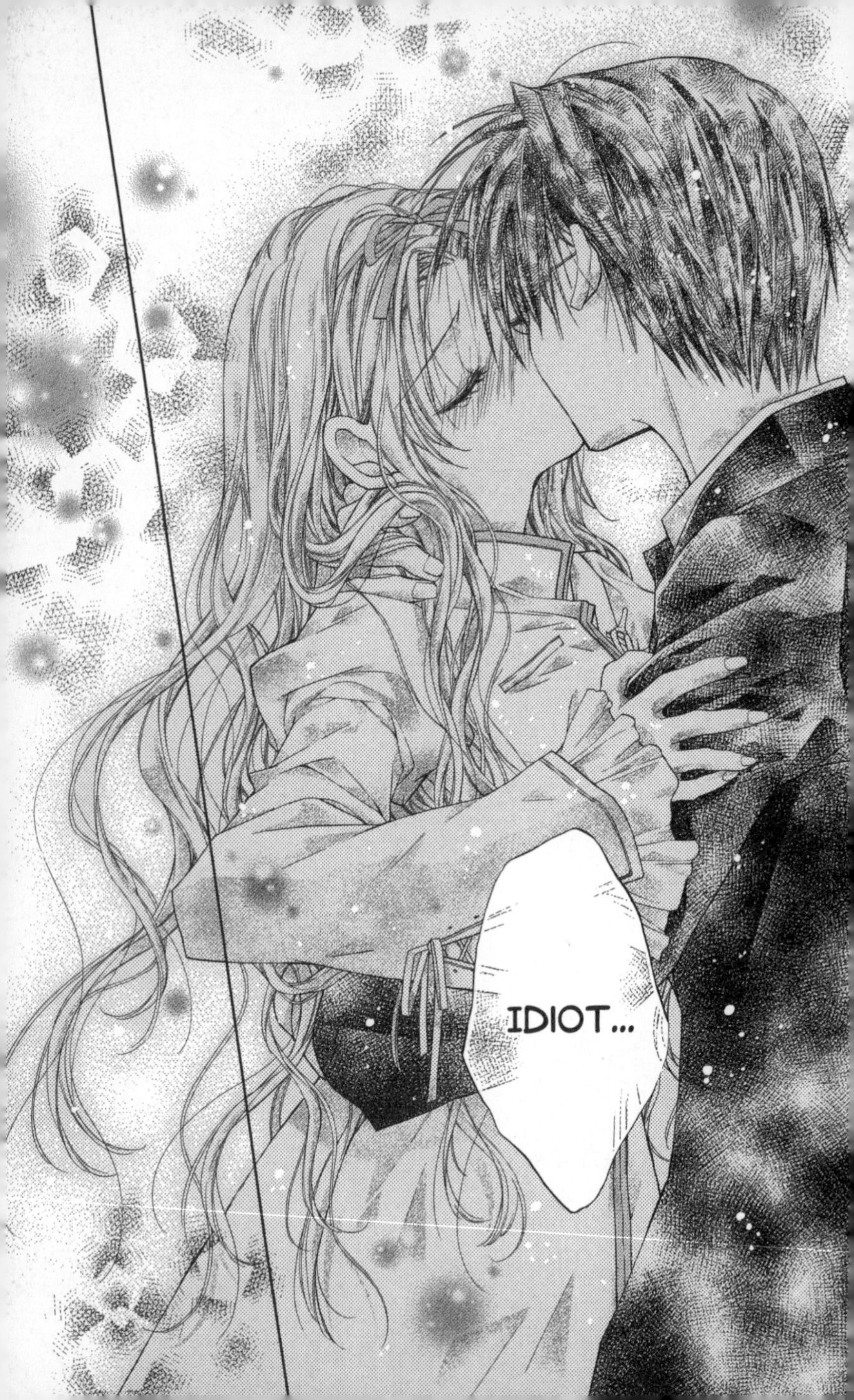
IDIOT...

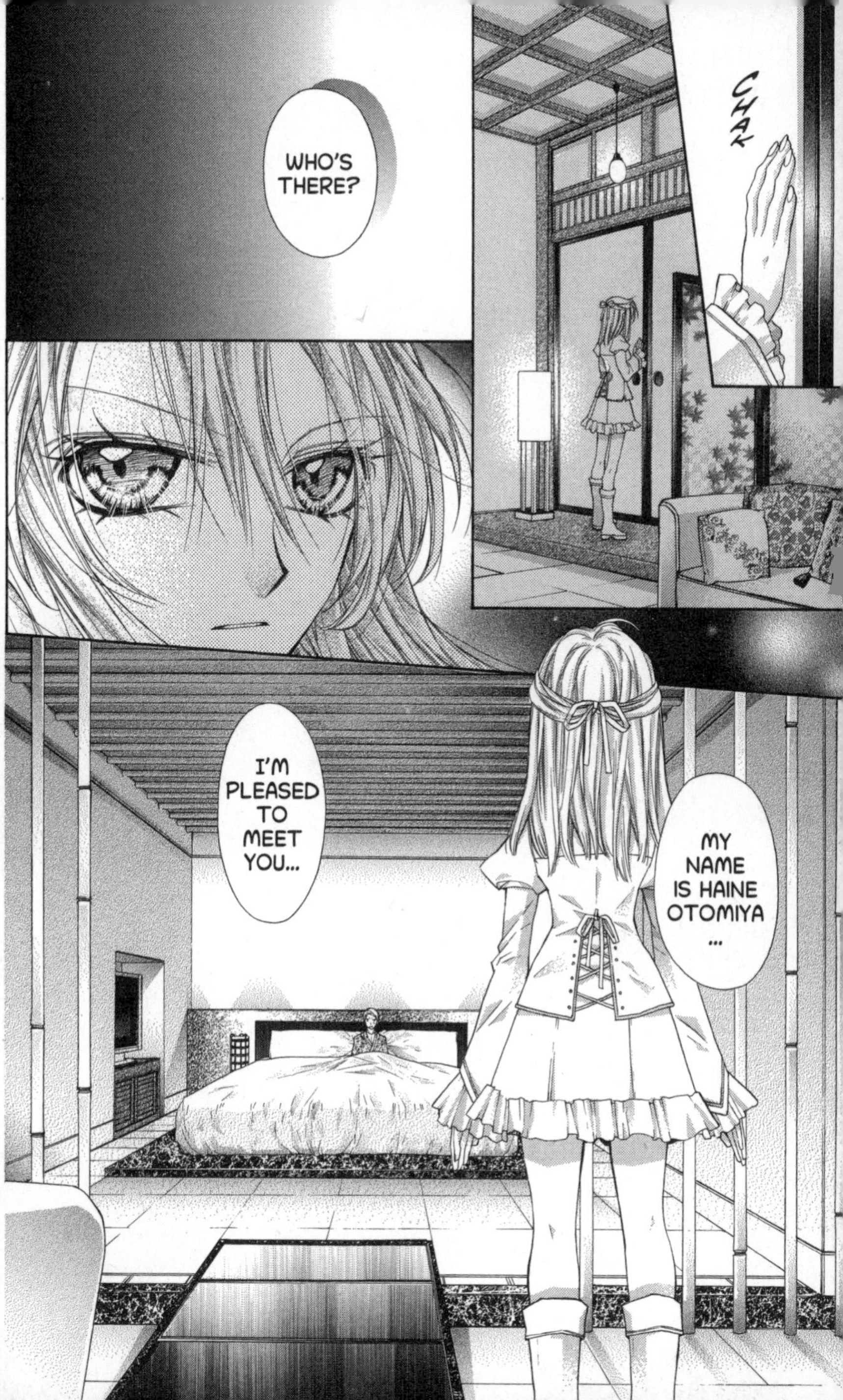
CHAK
WHO'S THERE?
MY NAME IS HAINE OTOMIYA ...
I'M PLEASED TO MEET YOU...

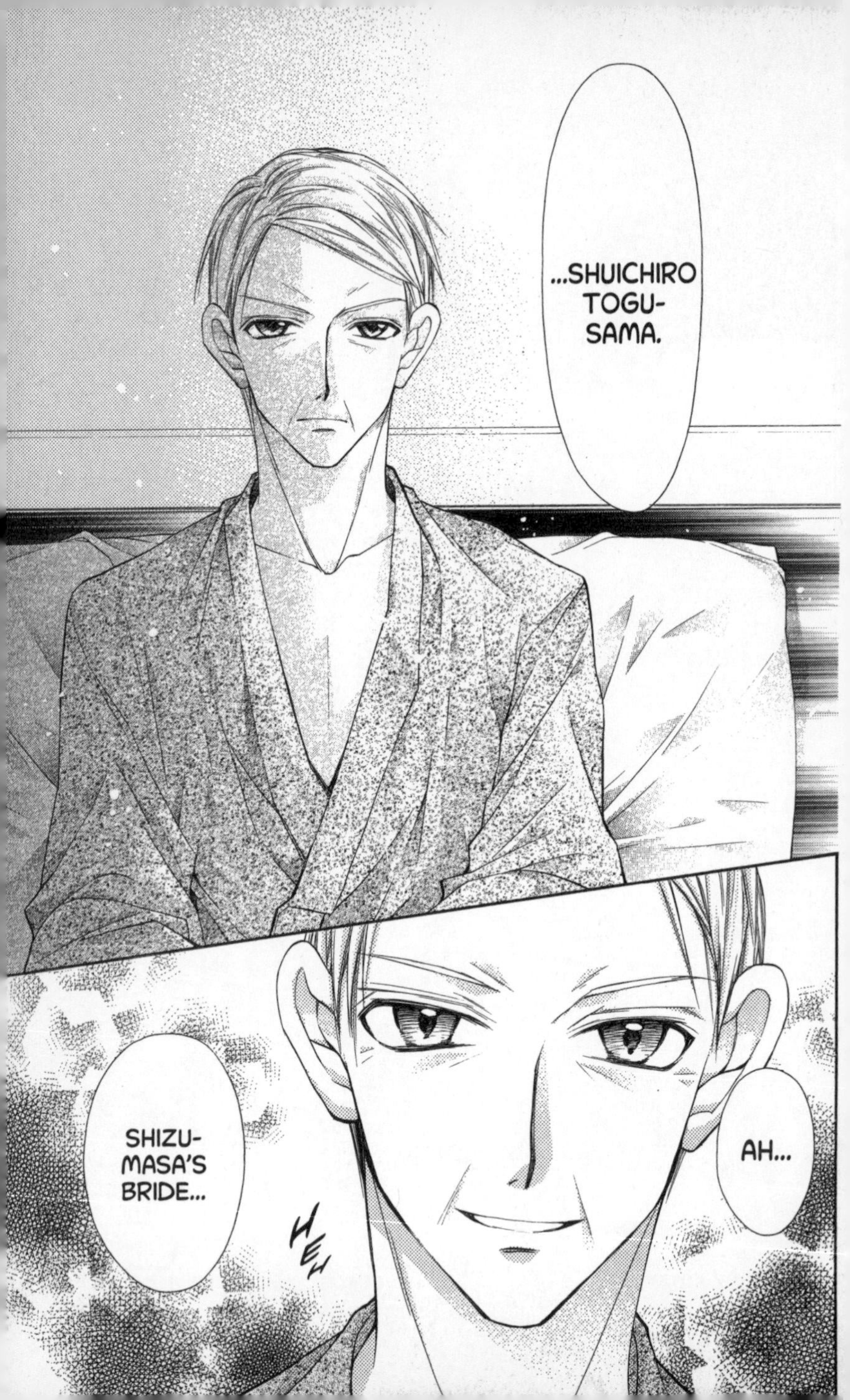
...SHUICHIRO TOGU-SAMA.
AH...
SHIZU-MASA'S BRIDE...
HEH

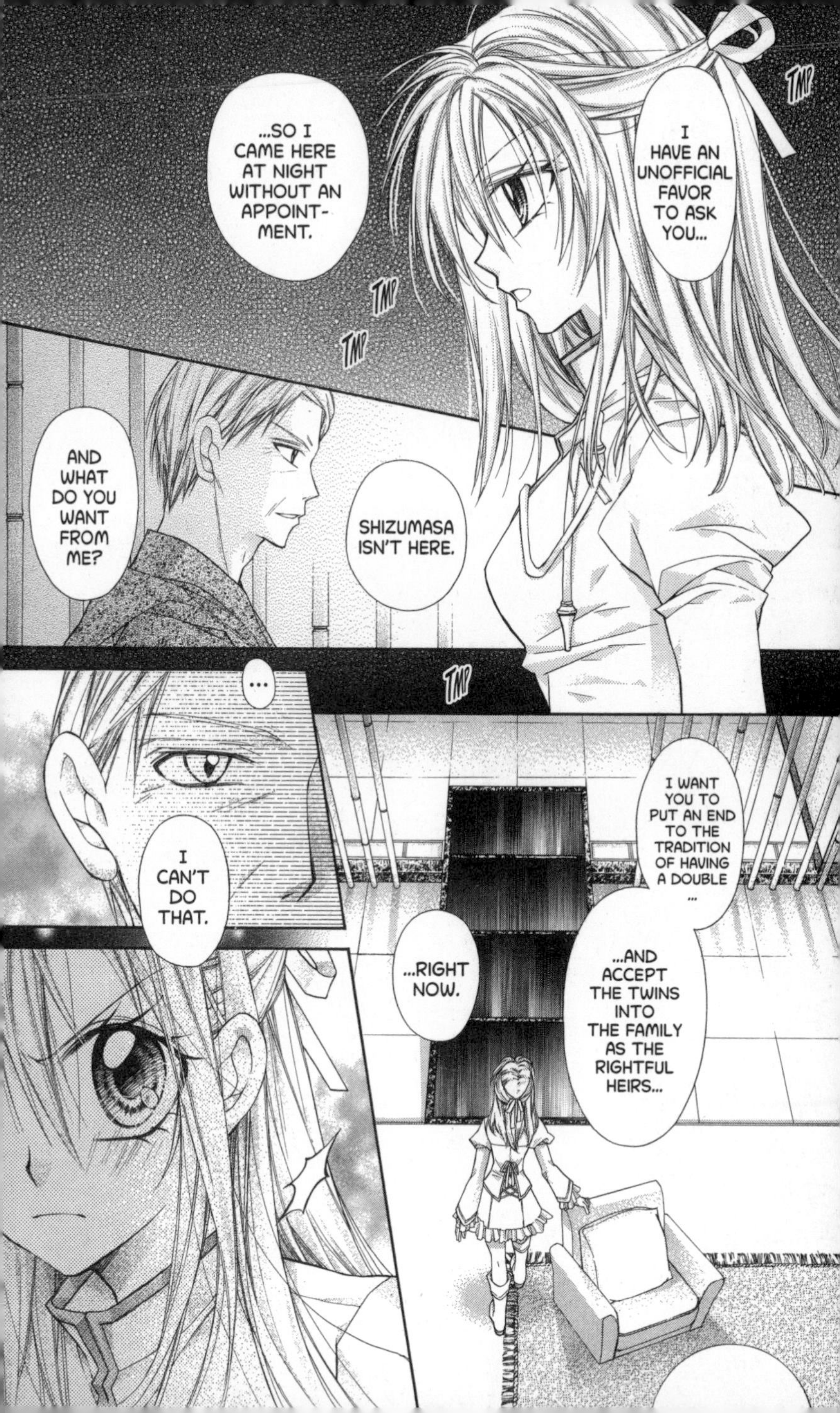
TMP
I HAVE AN UNOFFICIAL FAVOR TO ASK YOU...
...SO I CAME HERE AT NIGHT WITHOUT AN APPOINT-MENT.
TMP
TMP
SHIZUMASA ISN'T HERE.
AND WHAT DO YOU WANT FROM ME?
TMP
I WANT YOU TO PUT AN END TO THE TRADITION OF HAVING A DOUBLE ...
...AND ACCEPT THE TWINS INTO THE FAMILY AS THE RIGHTFUL HEIRS...
...RIGHT NOW.
...
I CAN'T DO THAT.

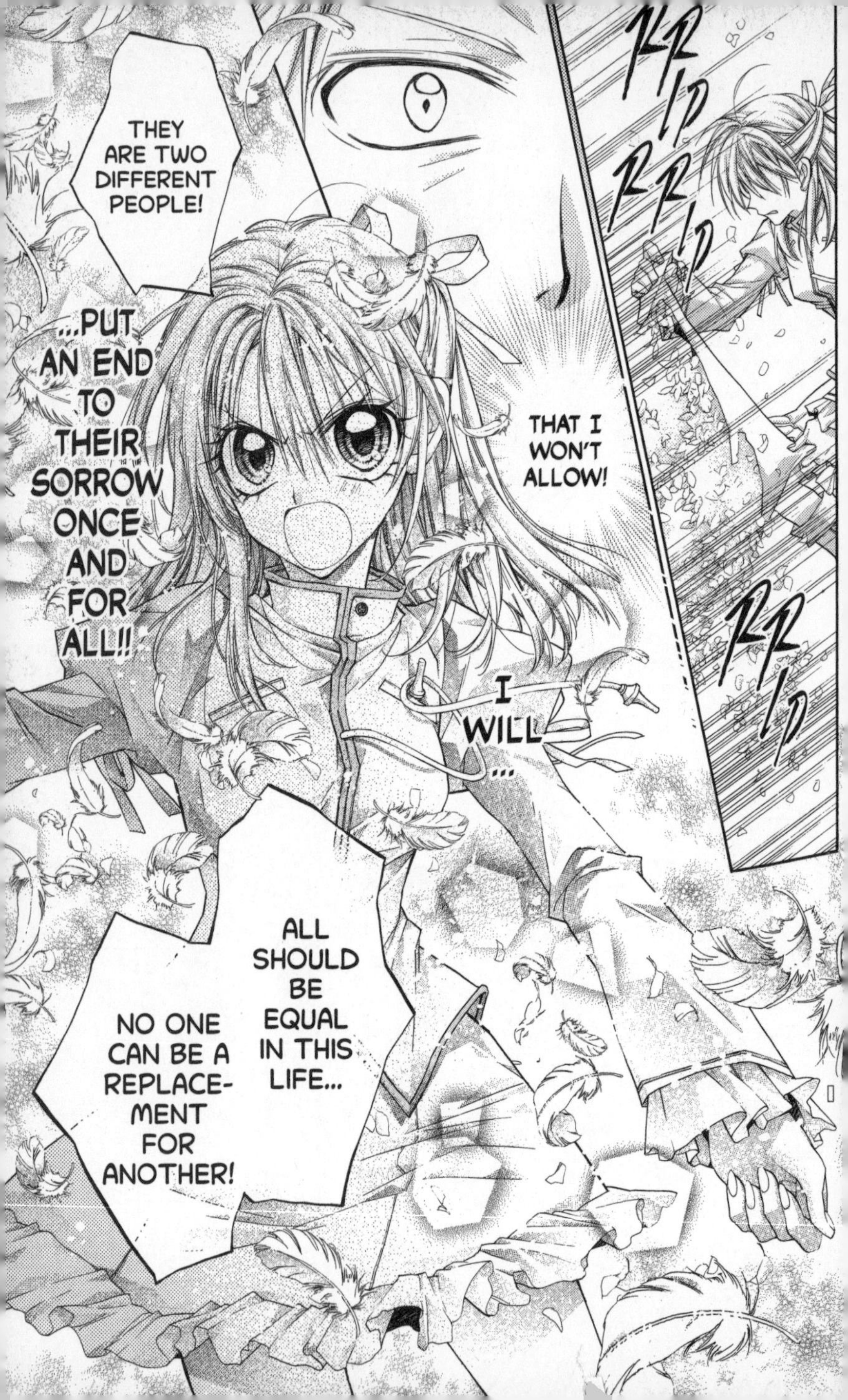
RRIP
RRIP
RRIP
THEY ARE TWO DIFFERENT PEOPLE!
THAT I WON'T ALLOW!
I WILL...
...PUT AN END TO THEIR SORROW ONCE AND FOR ALL!!
ALL SHOULD BE EQUAL IN THIS LIFE...
NO ONE CAN BE A REPLACE-MENT FOR ANOTHER!

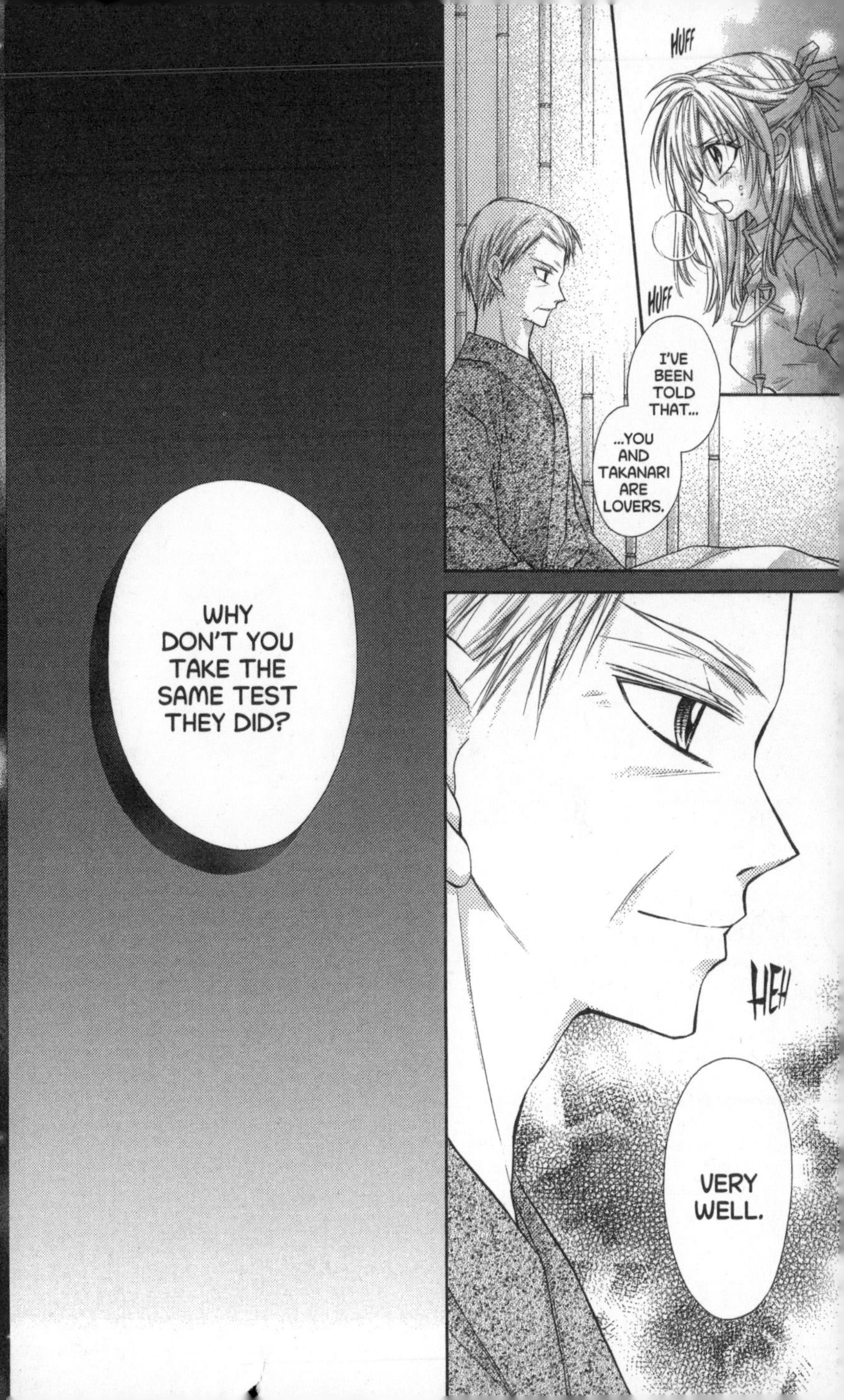
HUFF
HUFF
I'VE BEEN TOLD THAT...
...YOU AND TAKANARI ARE LOVERS.
HEH
VERY WELL.
WHY DON'T YOU TAKE THE SAME TEST THEY DID?

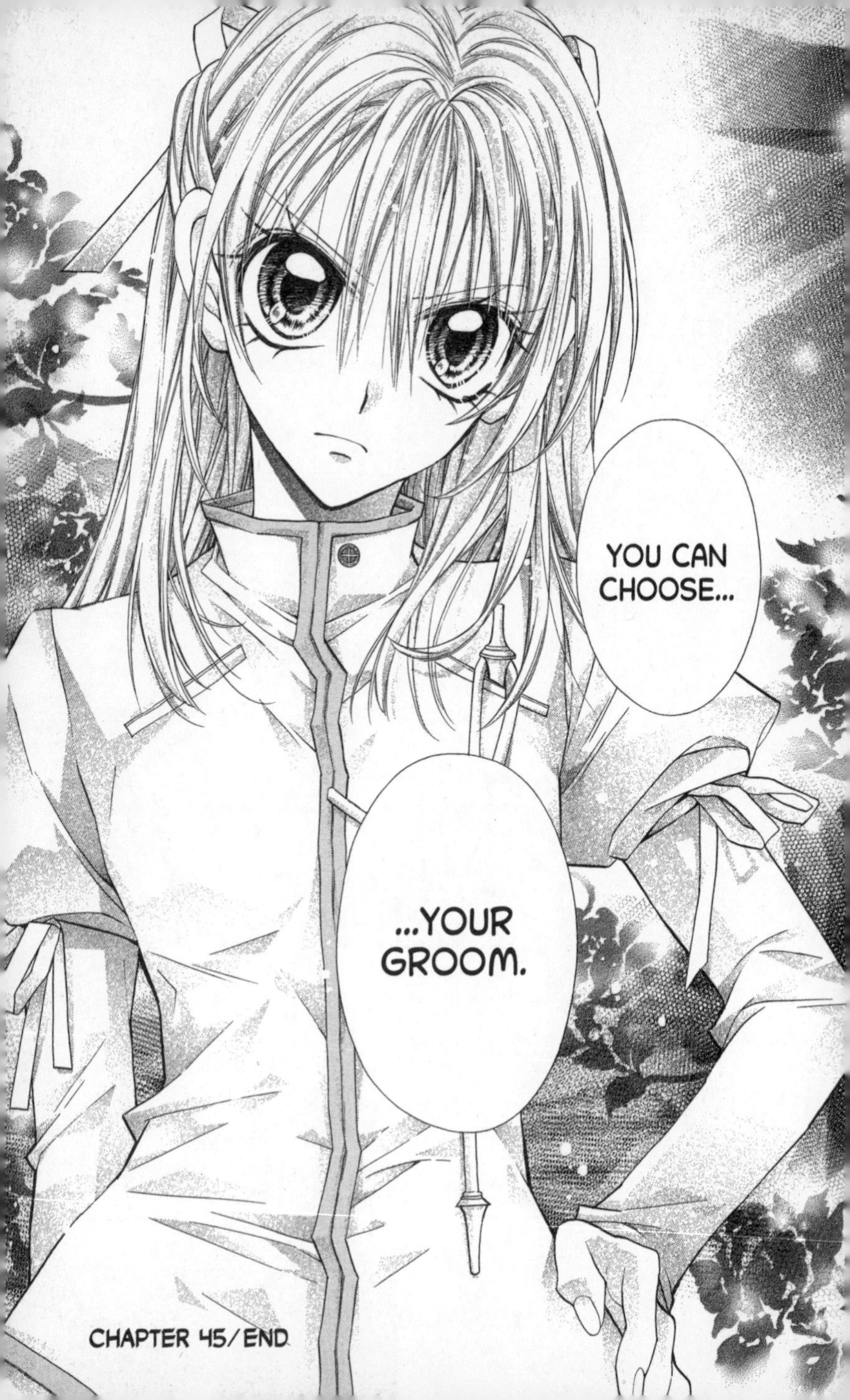
YOU CAN CHOOSE...
...YOUR GROOM.
CHAPTER 45/END

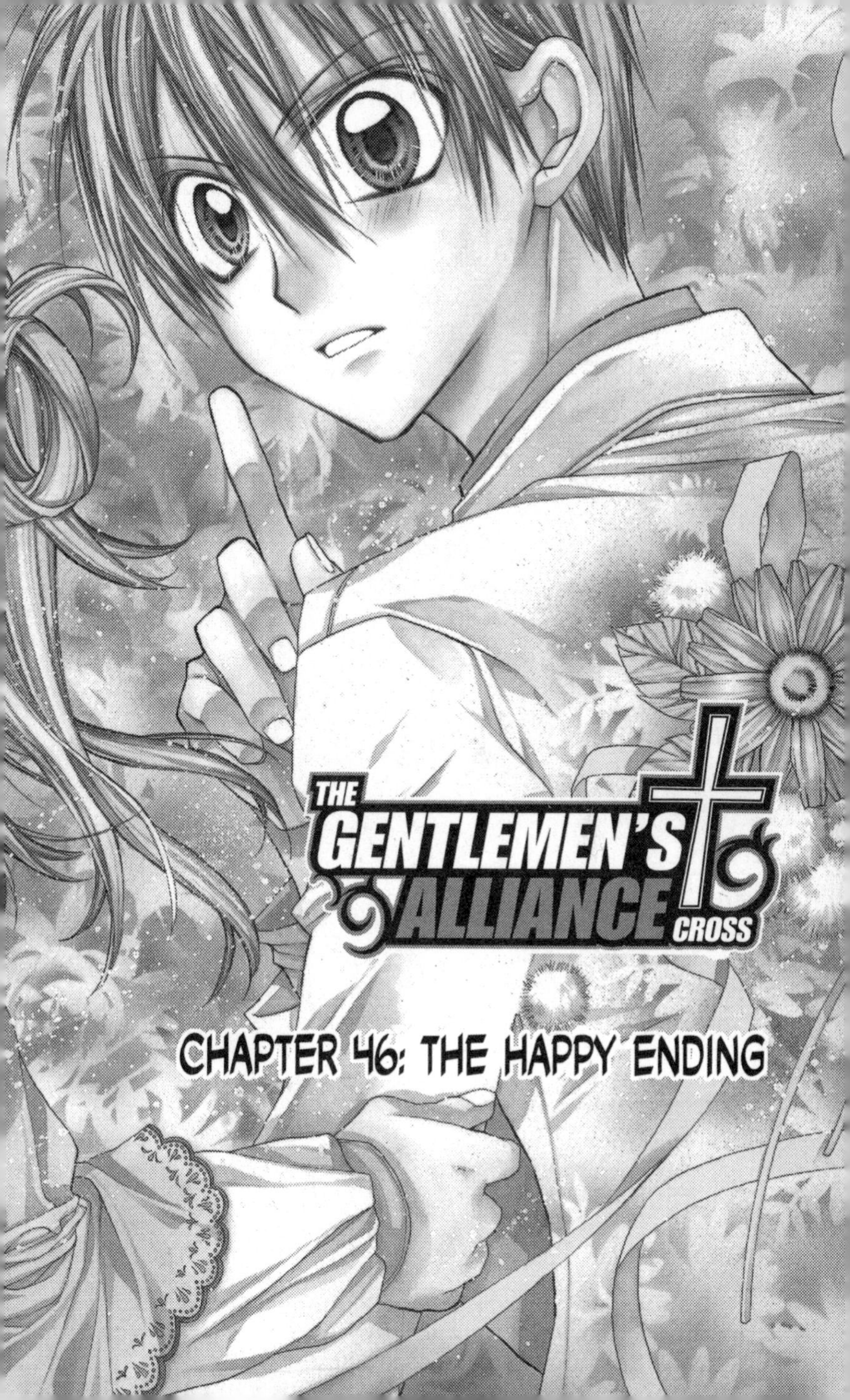
THE GENTLEMEN'S ALLIANCE CROSS
CHAPTER 46: THE HAPPY ENDING

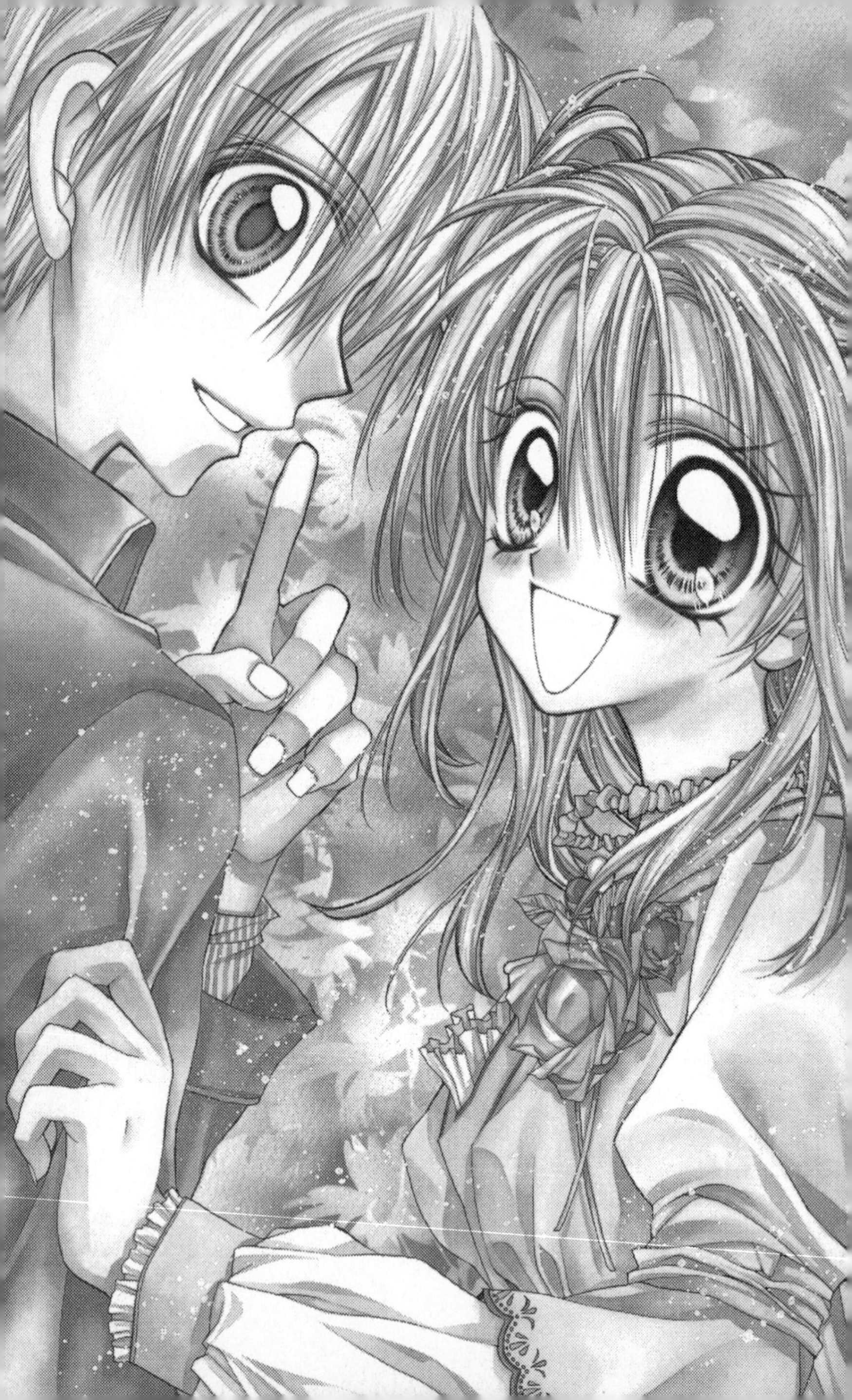

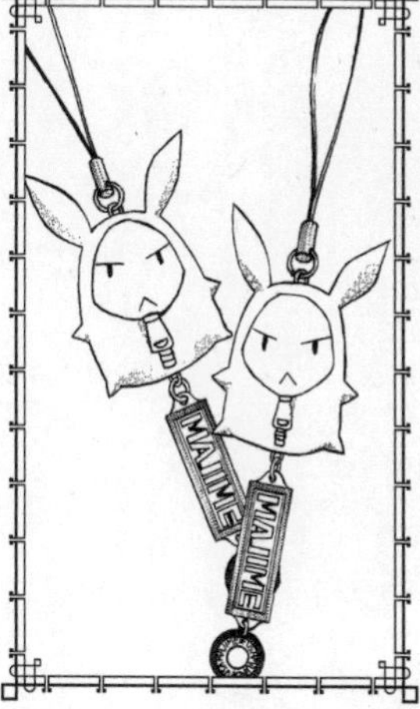
MAJIME
MAJIME

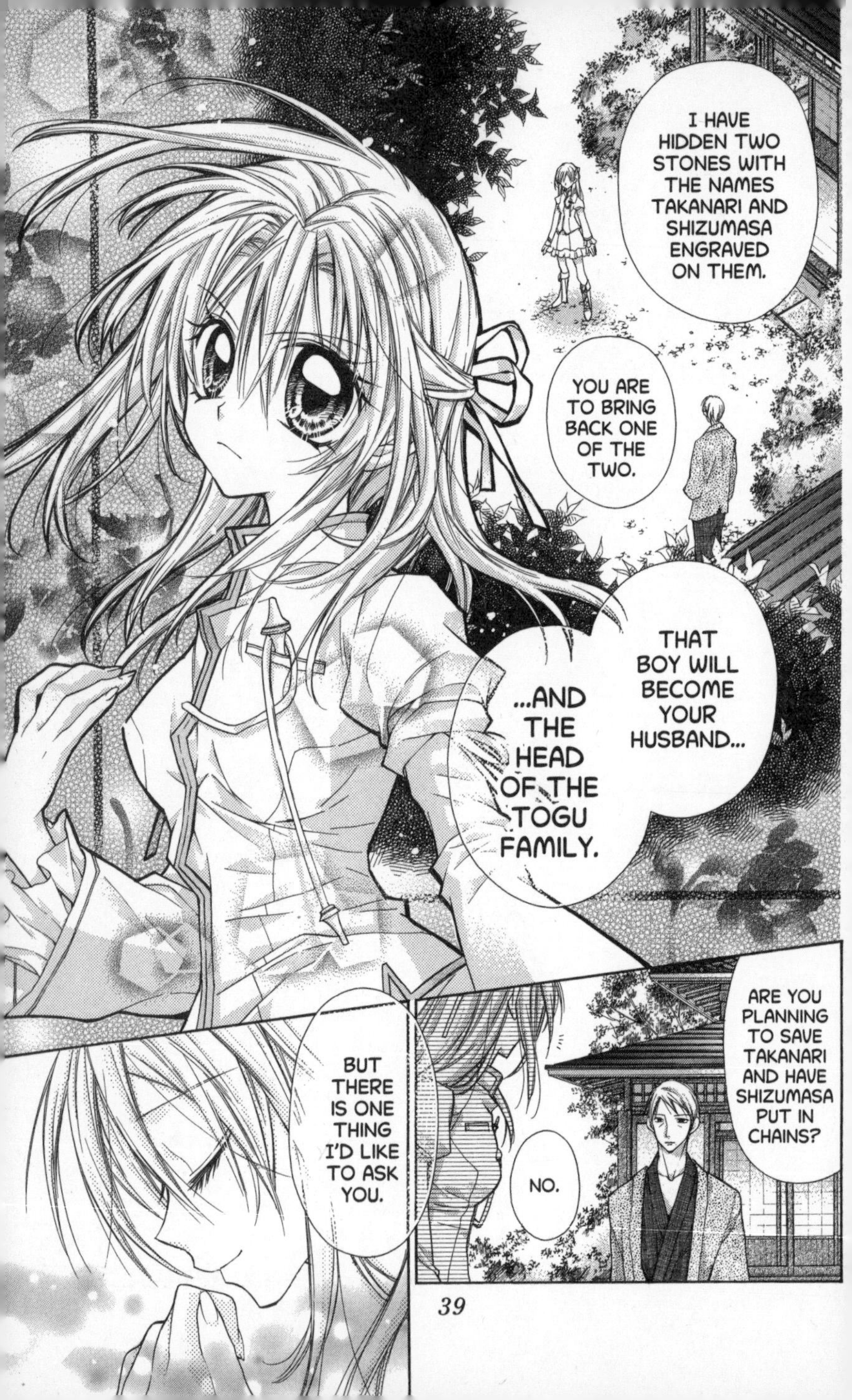
I HAVE HIDDEN TWO STONES WITH THE NAMES TAKANARI AND SHIZUMASA ENGRAVED ON THEM.
YOU ARE TO BRING BACK ONE OF THE TWO.
THAT BOY WILL BECOME YOUR HUSBAND...
...AND THE HEAD OF THE TOGU FAMILY.
ARE YOU PLANNING TO SAVE TAKANARI AND HAVE SHIZUMASA PUT IN CHAINS?
NO.
BUT THERE IS ONE THING I'D LIKE TO ASK YOU.

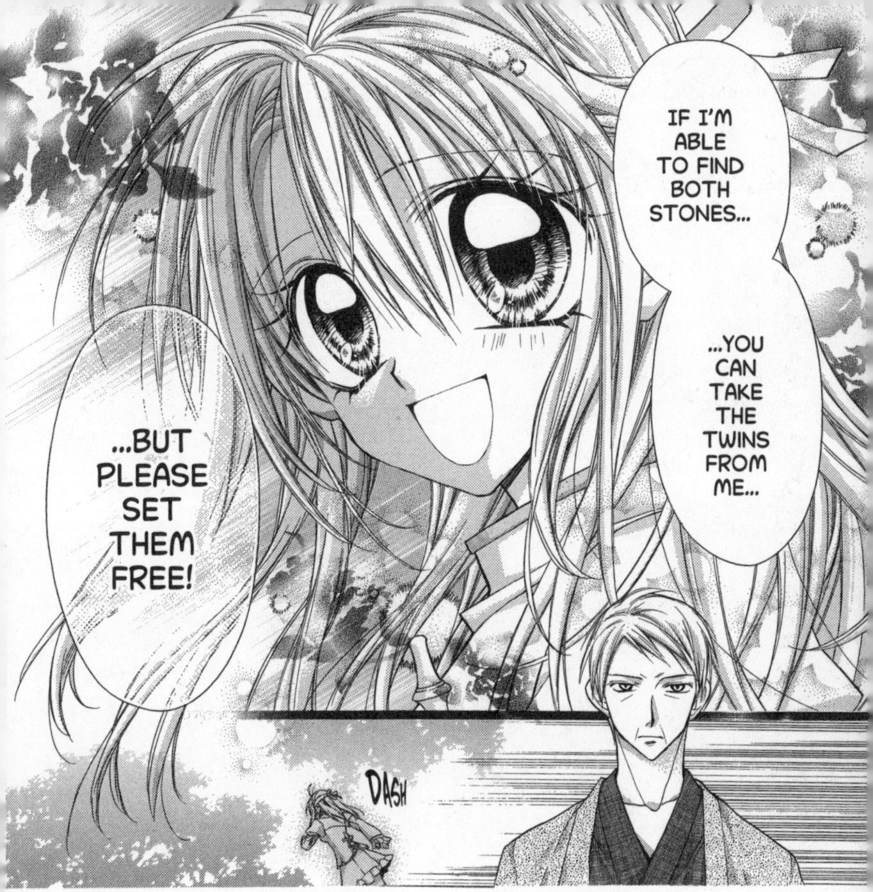
IF I'M ABLE TO FIND BOTH STONES...
...YOU CAN TAKE THE TWINS FROM ME...
...BUT PLEASE SET THEM FREE!
DASH

## Chapter 46: The Happy Ending

※ I'm giving away the story.
Please read this after finishing the chapter.

Lead-in
Goodbye...!
*The Gentlemen's Alliance †*...

It had been three years since I last drew a color illustration for the title page at the very front of the magazine. I drew it thinking that I hadn't done a lot of illustrations with these three together. Takanari seems to have the "elder brother" look on his face when they're together.

Toya is the main character in this chapter... But I wasn't able to do a very good job...so although it's not right, I'd like to do what I was aiming for in my next series. I wanted to show Takanari and Toya-kun's relationship—or bond, shall I say. The scene I wanted to draw most in this chapter is where Haine says, "Thank you!" There are many ways to evaluate people, and there are those who say that Haine is a philanthropist, while others say she just tries to please everybody. The reason Haine said something like that to Toya-kun is because she unwittingly wanted Toya-kun to tell her, "That's not true at all!" (Haine must have realized that when she said it...) And whether he realized it or not, Toya-kun answers her. Haine thanks Toya-kun, but deep inside, she's glad that he was still the Toya-kun she had always known.

By the way, one of the reasons Toya-kun is so surprised when Haine jumps in the water is because he knows Haine-chan can't swim...

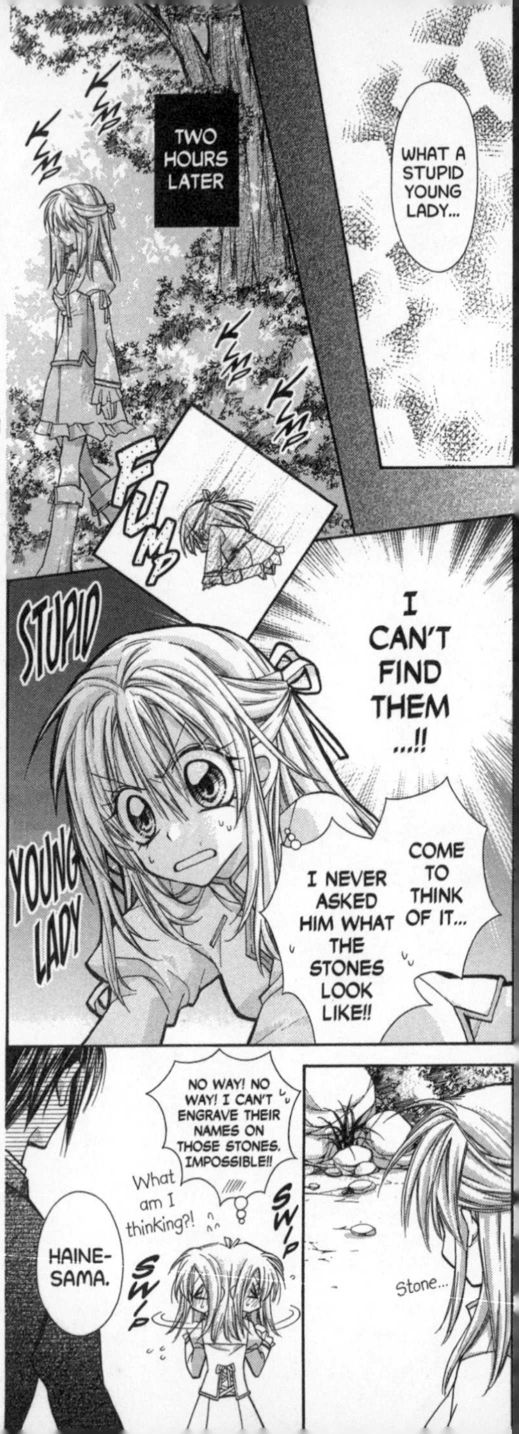
WHAT A STUPID YOUNG LADY...
TWO HOURS LATER
KLMP KLMP
KLMP KLMP
FUMP
I CAN'T FIND THEM ...!!
COME TO THINK OF IT...
I NEVER ASKED HIM WHAT THE STONES LOOK LIKE!!
STUPID YOUNG LADY
Stone...
NO WAY! NO WAY! I CAN'T ENGRAVE THEIR NAMES ON THOSE STONES. IMPOSSIBLE!!
What am I thinking?!
SWIP
HAINE-SAMA.
SWIP

Radio and Whatnot

"Arina Tanemura's Rajio De Shakin ☆," which I'm hosting, is being distributed on Shueisha's Internet site, S-Raji!

You'll find video on how to draw manga as well! You also get to hear the rare voices of Shueisha's editors, and there will be guest mangaka!!

I love talking with people, so I have a lot of fun doing it!

I'm waiting for everyone's messages via post or email! And everyone who has sent me a message will receive a "mumbling standby screen image" for your cell phone as a present! (An illustration of myself that mumbles—and every time you open your cell phone, the illustration and words I mumble will change!)

http://www.s-cast.net/radio/shakin/

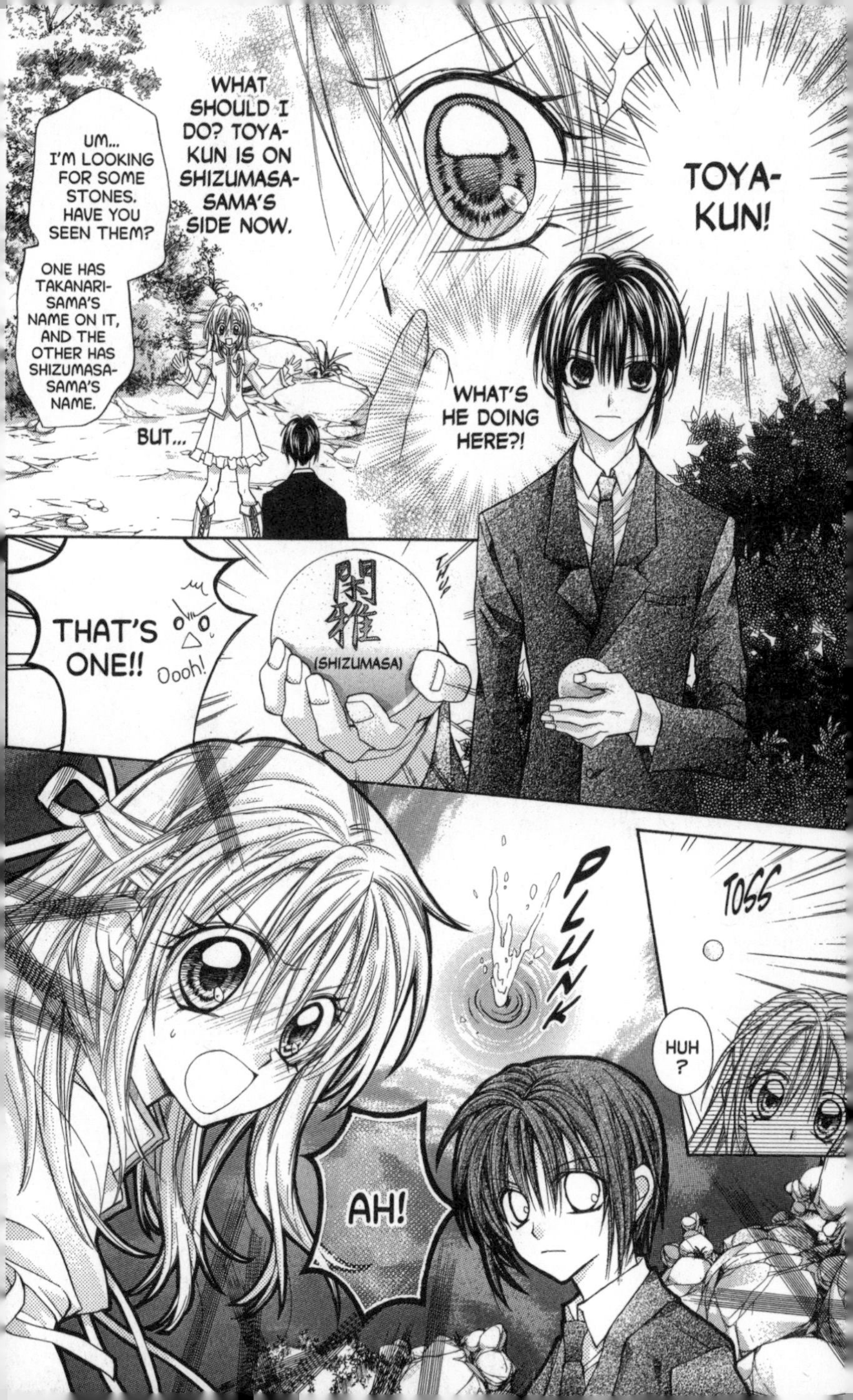
TOYA-KUN!
WHAT'S HE DOING HERE?!
WHAT SHOULD I DO? TOYA-KUN IS ON SHIZUMASA-SAMA'S SIDE NOW.
UM... I'M LOOKING FOR SOME STONES. HAVE YOU SEEN THEM?
ONE HAS TAKANARI-SAMA'S NAME ON IT, AND THE OTHER HAS SHIZUMASA-SAMA'S NAME.
BUT...
閑雅
(SHIZUMASA)
THAT'S ONE!!
Oooh!
TOSS
HUH?
PLUNK
AH!

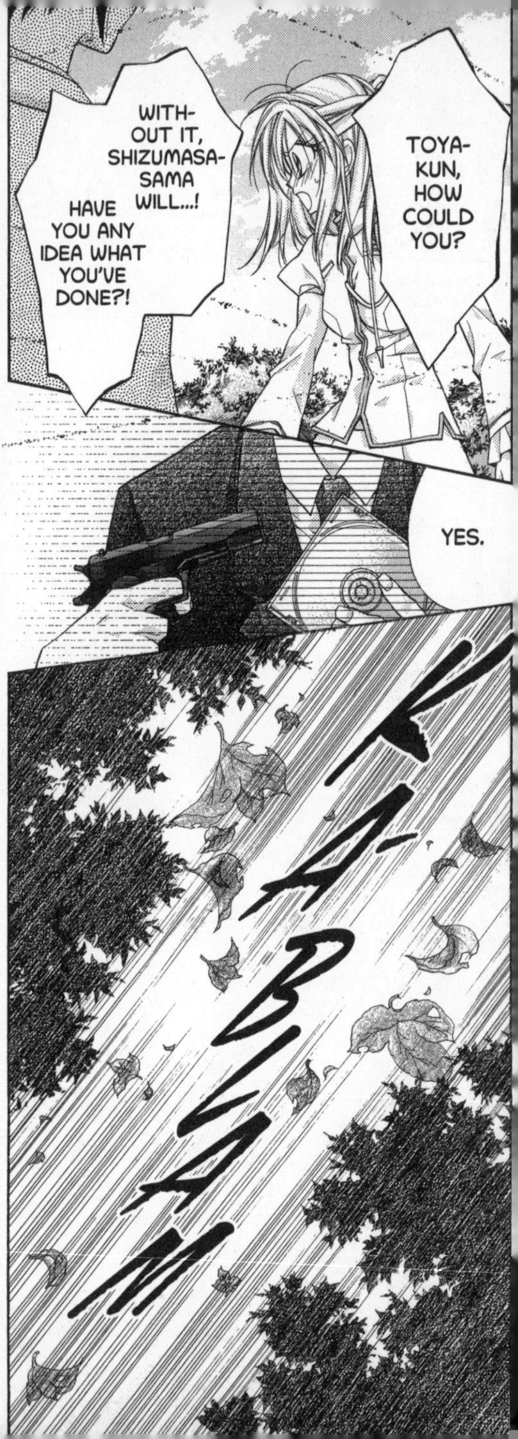
TOYA-KUN, HOW COULD YOU?
WITH-OUT IT, SHIZUMASA-SAMA WILL...!
HAVE YOU ANY IDEA WHAT YOU'VE DONE?!
YES.
KABLAM

My Thoughts on *Gentlemen's Alliance* ①

※ I go pretty deep into the subject, so if you don't like things like that, please don't read this.

When I started this series, I thought, "I'll do a 'freestyle' love story in which the readers won't be able to tell who will end up together!"

The reason I thought that is because I was getting tired of the ordinary shojo manga, and a lot of old shojo manga were like that, so I thought it would be interesting to do something different.

I don't know how the readers feel, but I've never been very fond of reading...guy x guy and girl x girl relationships. But that was another reason for me to have done this series. I thought the series would have a nice twist to it if I tried to draw something I didn't really like.

I regularly challenge myself to eat things I don't like. I don't like the idea of having dislikes, so it became an opportunity for me to get over that.

And the result was...I still couldn't get myself to be interested in it. So it'll probably be a topic I'll never write about again. But I think it was still worth it that I found that out.

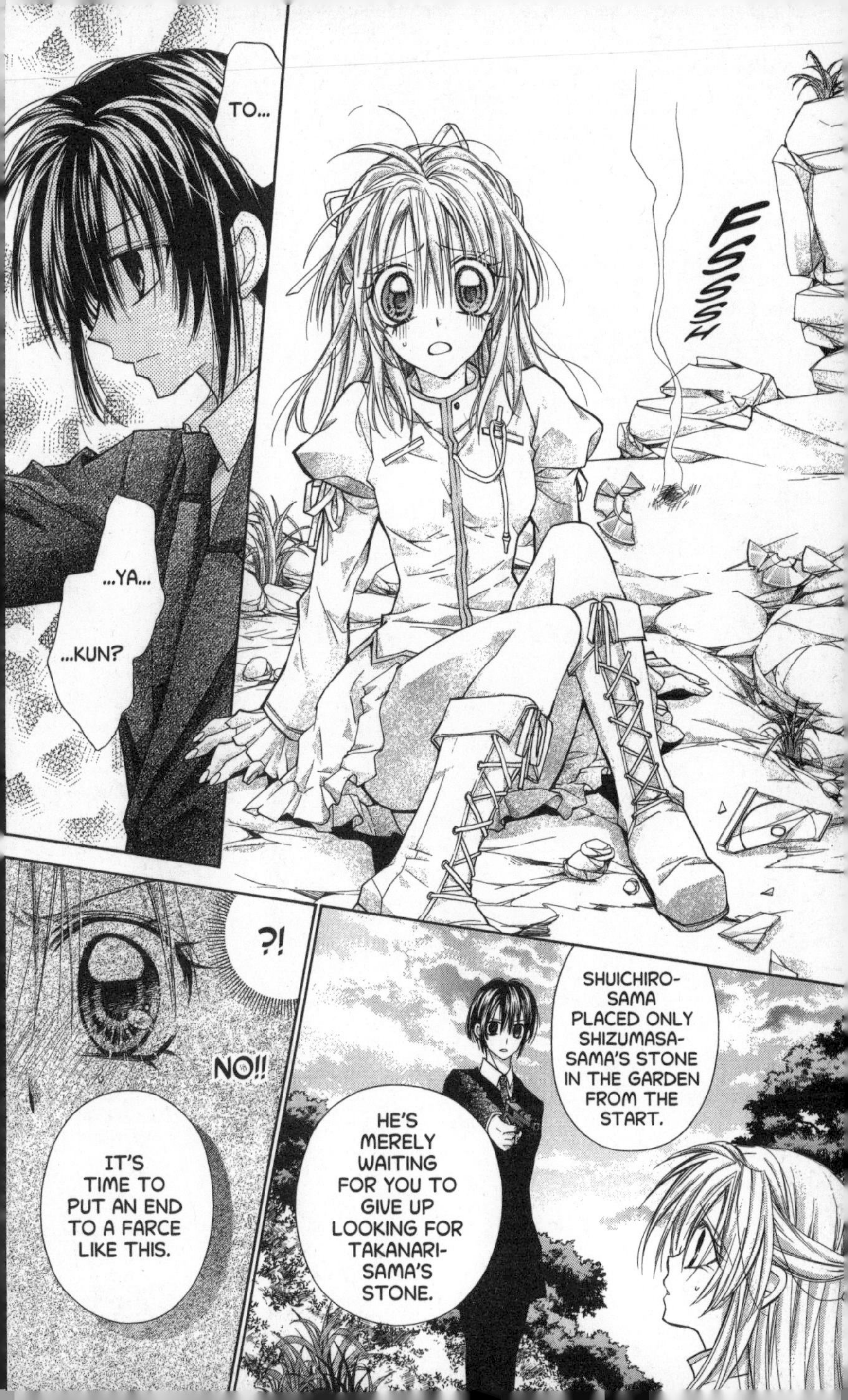
FSSSSH
TO...
...YA...
...KUN?
SHUICHIRO-SAMA PLACED ONLY SHIZUMASA-SAMA'S STONE IN THE GARDEN FROM THE START.
HE'S MERELY WAITING FOR YOU TO GIVE UP LOOKING FOR TAKANARI-SAMA'S STONE.
?!
NO!!
IT'S TIME TO PUT AN END TO A FARCE LIKE THIS.

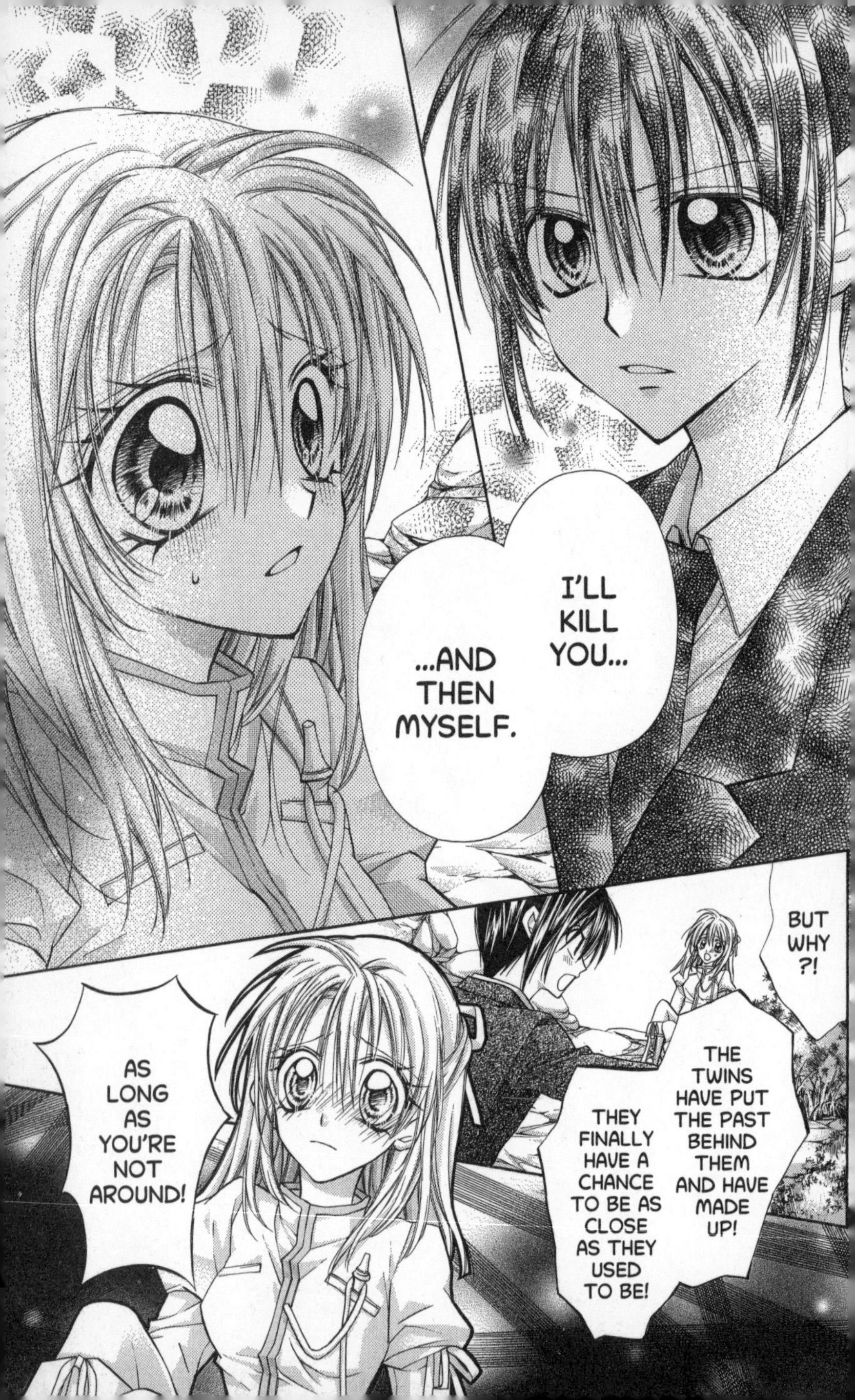
I'LL KILL YOU...
...AND THEN MYSELF.
BUT WHY?!
THE TWINS HAVE PUT THE PAST BEHIND THEM AND HAVE MADE UP!
THEY FINALLY HAVE A CHANCE TO BE AS CLOSE AS THEY USED TO BE!
AS LONG AS YOU'RE NOT AROUND!

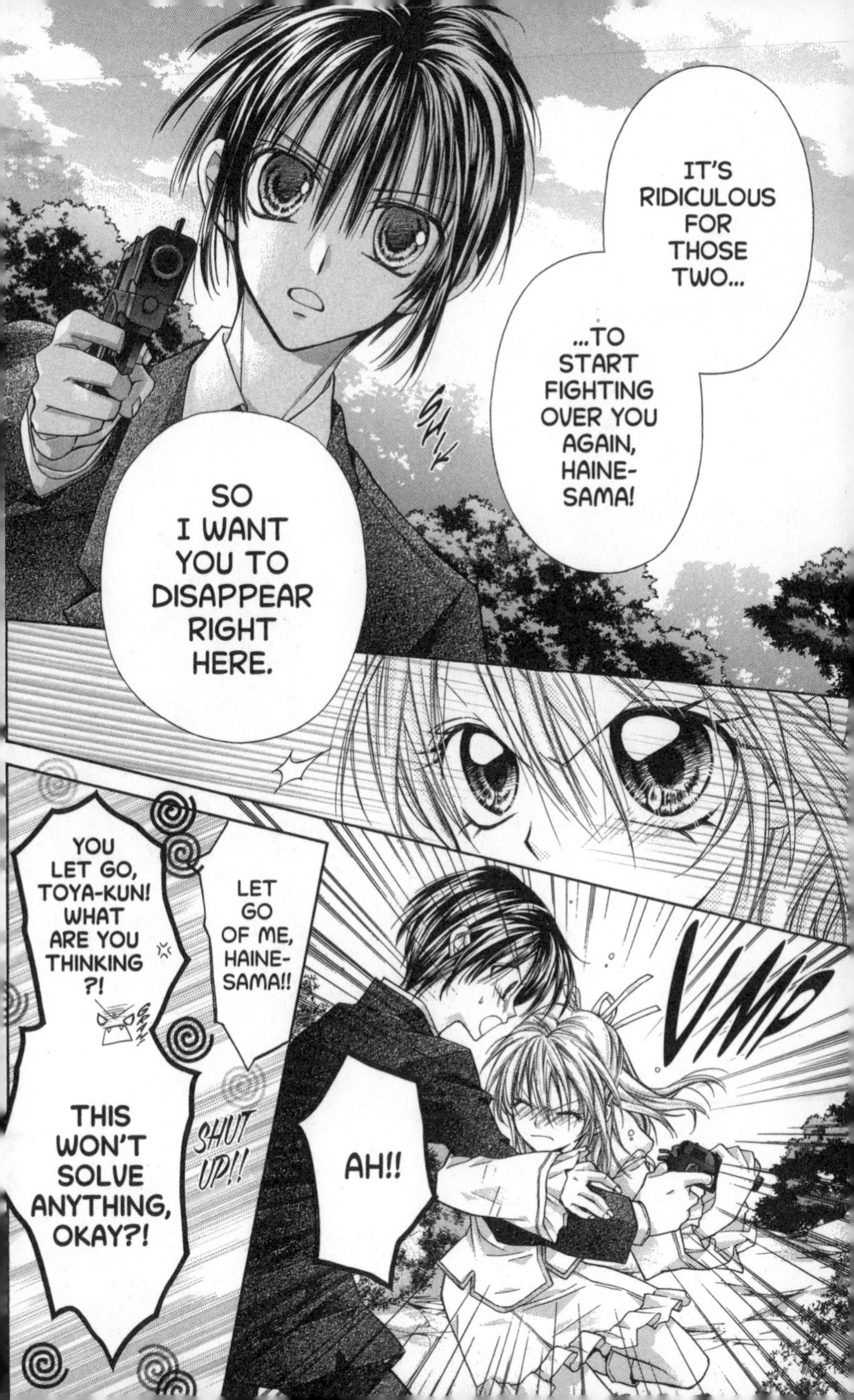
IT'S RIDICULOUS FOR THOSE TWO...
...TO START FIGHTING OVER YOU AGAIN, HAINE-SAMA!
SO I WANT YOU TO DISAPPEAR RIGHT HERE.
LET GO OF ME, HAINE-SAMA!!
YOU LET GO, TOYA-KUN! WHAT ARE YOU THINKING?!
AH!!
SHUT UP!!
THIS WON'T SOLVE ANYTHING, OKAY?!

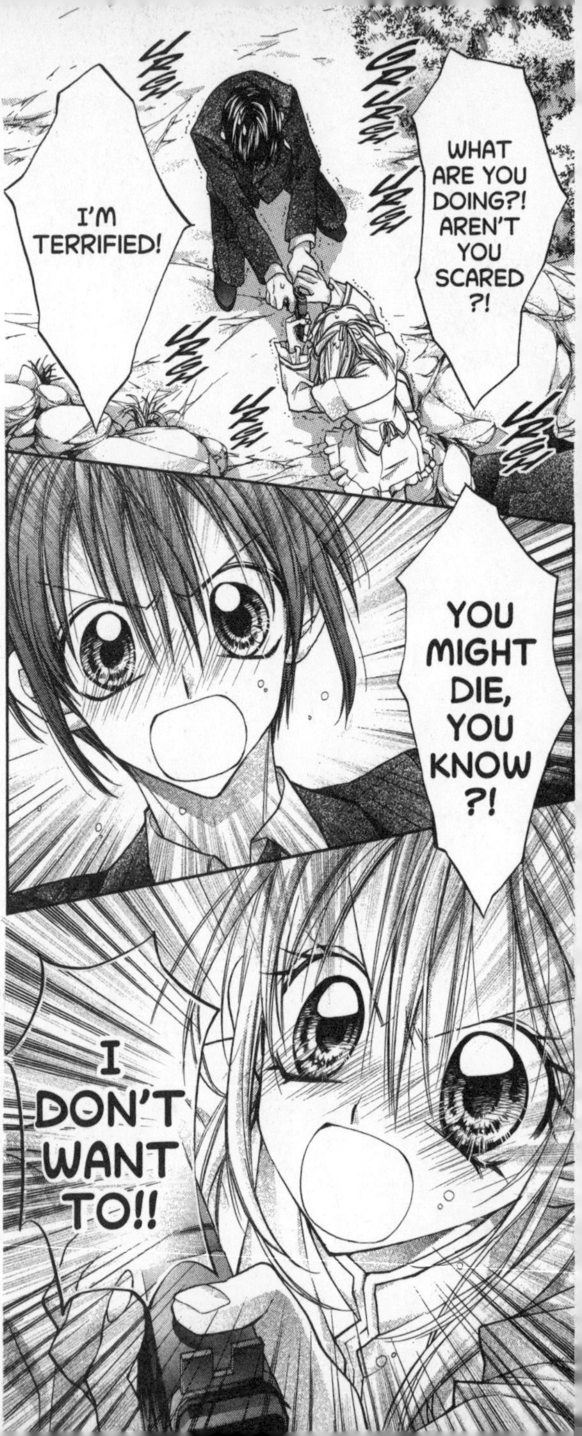
WHAT ARE YOU DOING?! AREN'T YOU SCARED ?!
I'M TERRIFIED!
YOU MIGHT DIE, YOU KNOW ?!
I DON'T WANT TO!!

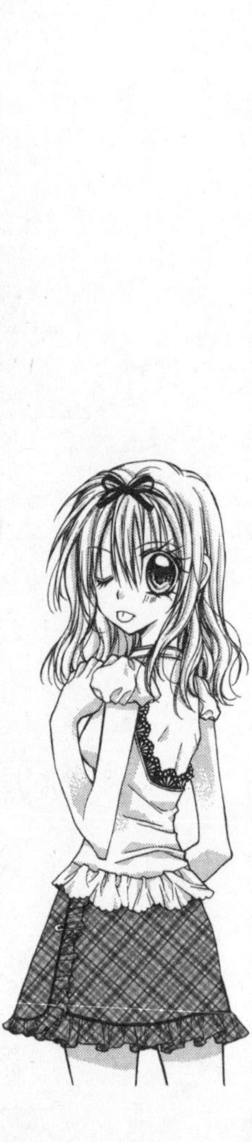

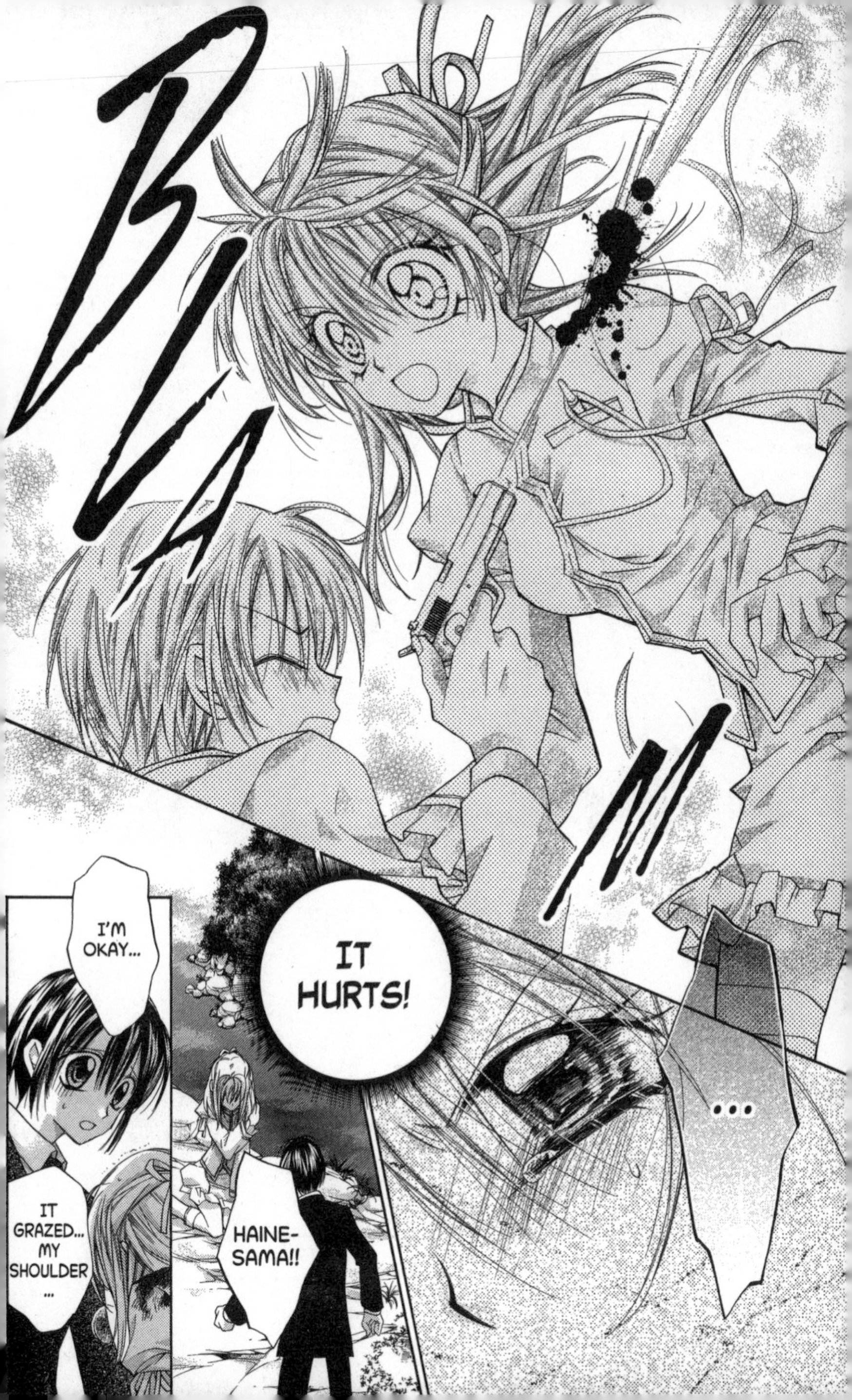
IT HURTS!
...
HAINE-SAMA!!
I'M OKAY...
IT GRAZED... MY SHOULDER ...

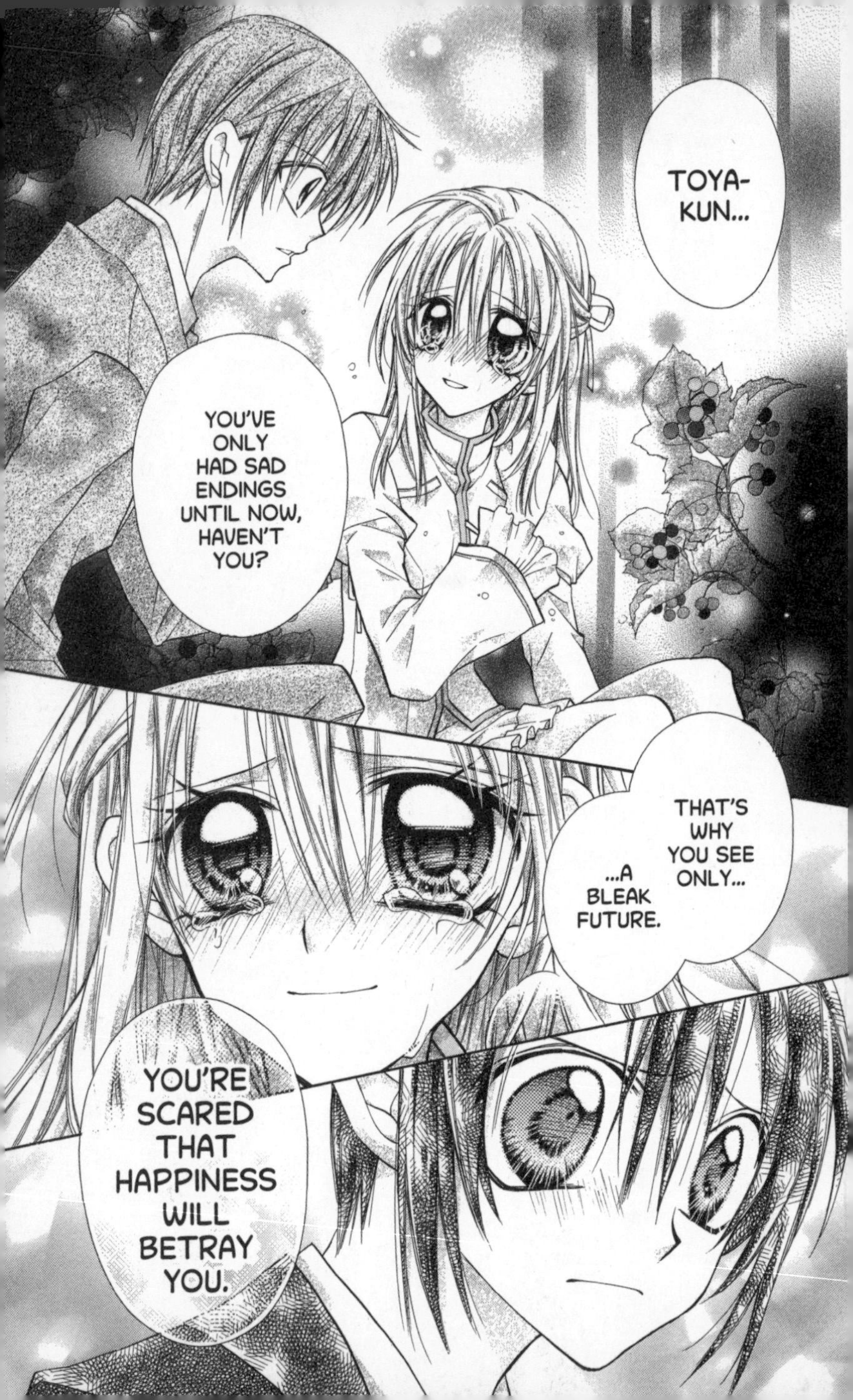
TOYA-KUN...
YOU'VE ONLY HAD SAD ENDINGS UNTIL NOW, HAVEN'T YOU?
THAT'S WHY YOU SEE ONLY...
...A BLEAK FUTURE.
YOU'RE SCARED THAT HAPPINESS WILL BETRAY YOU.

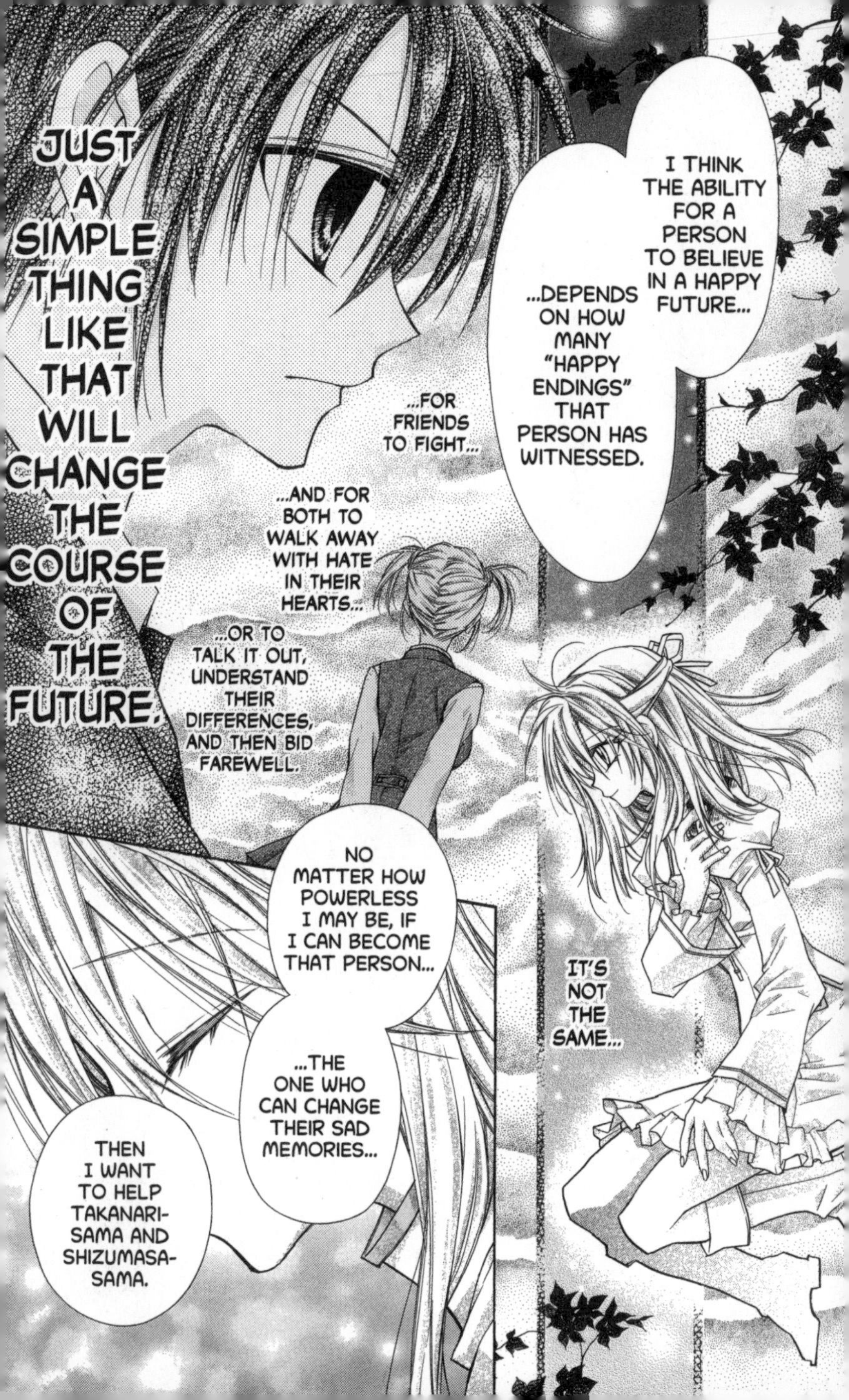
I THINK THE ABILITY FOR A PERSON TO BELIEVE IN A HAPPY FUTURE...
...DEPENDS ON HOW MANY "HAPPY ENDINGS" THAT PERSON HAS WITNESSED.
...FOR FRIENDS TO FIGHT...
...AND FOR BOTH TO WALK AWAY WITH HATE IN THEIR HEARTS...
...OR TO TALK IT OUT, UNDERSTAND THEIR DIFFERENCES, AND THEN BID FAREWELL.
JUST A SIMPLE THING LIKE THAT WILL CHANGE THE COURSE OF THE FUTURE.
IT'S NOT THE SAME...
NO MATTER HOW POWERLESS I MAY BE, IF I CAN BECOME THAT PERSON...
...THE ONE WHO CAN CHANGE THEIR SAD MEMORIES...
THEN I WANT TO HELP TAKANARI-SAMA AND SHIZUMASA-SAMA.

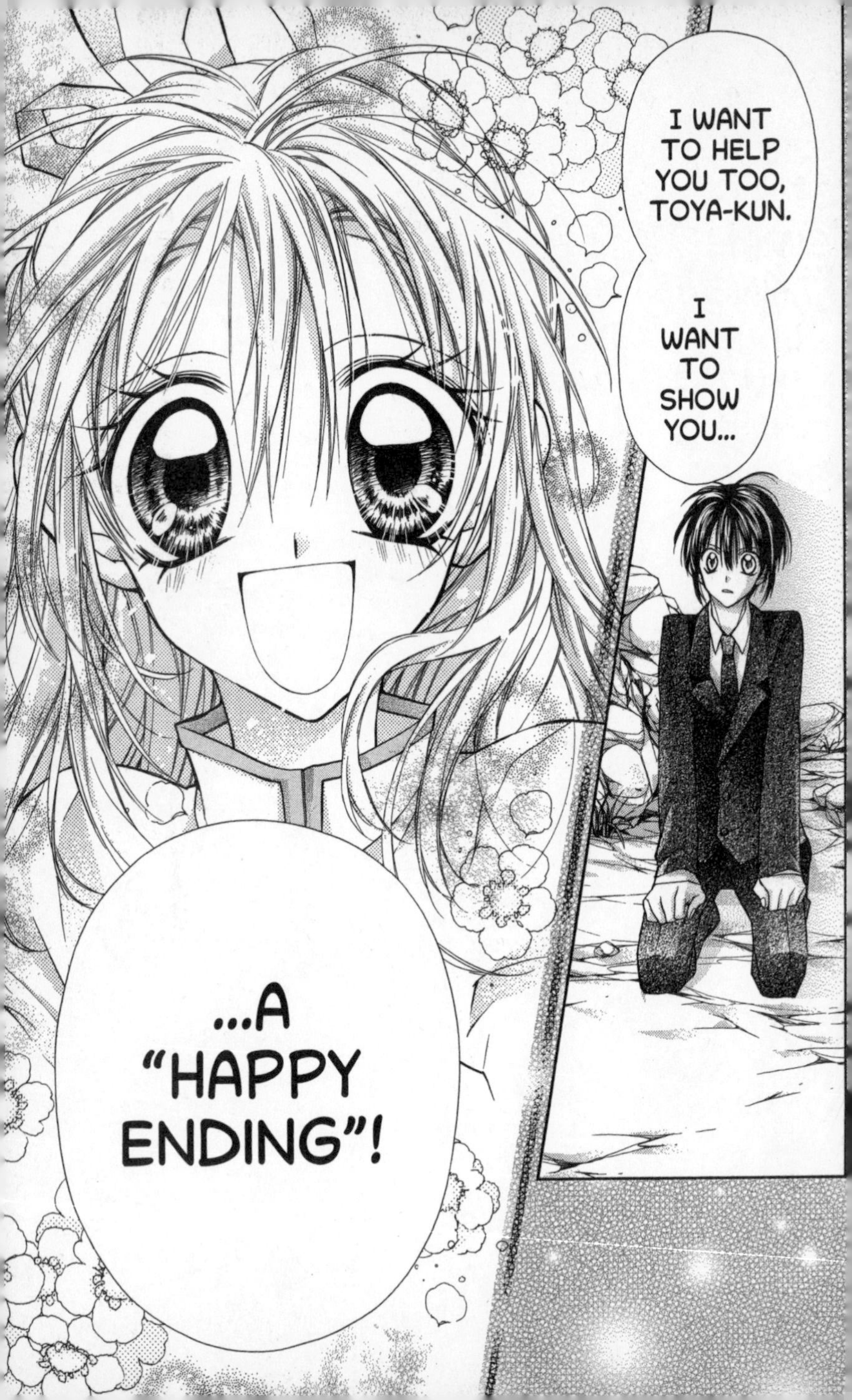
I WANT TO HELP YOU TOO, TOYA-KUN.
I WANT TO SHOW YOU...
...A "HAPPY ENDING"!

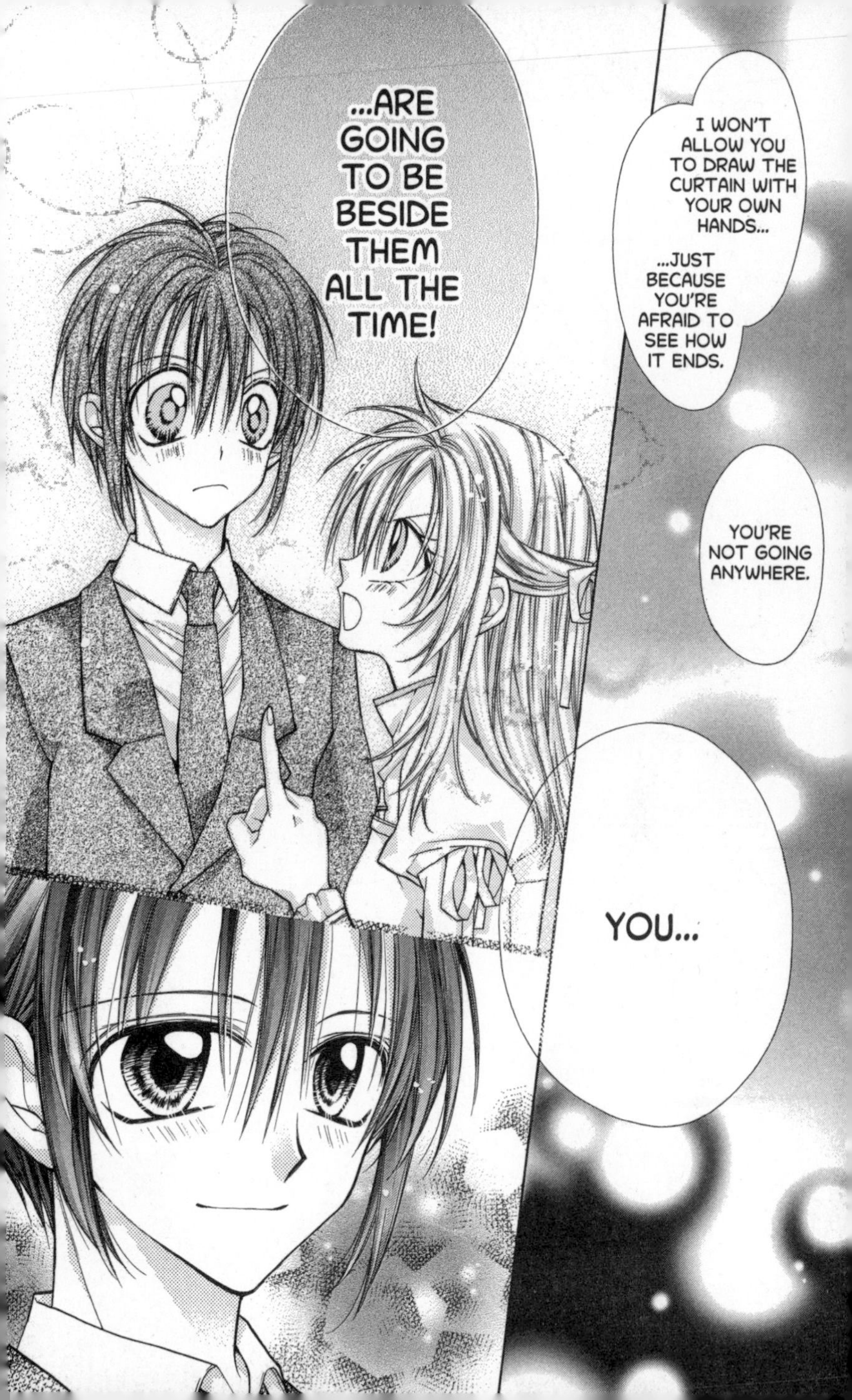
...ARE GOING TO BE BESIDE THEM ALL THE TIME!
I WON'T ALLOW YOU TO DRAW THE CURTAIN WITH YOUR OWN HANDS...
...JUST BECAUSE YOU'RE AFRAID TO SEE HOW IT ENDS.
YOU'RE NOT GOING ANYWHERE.
YOU...

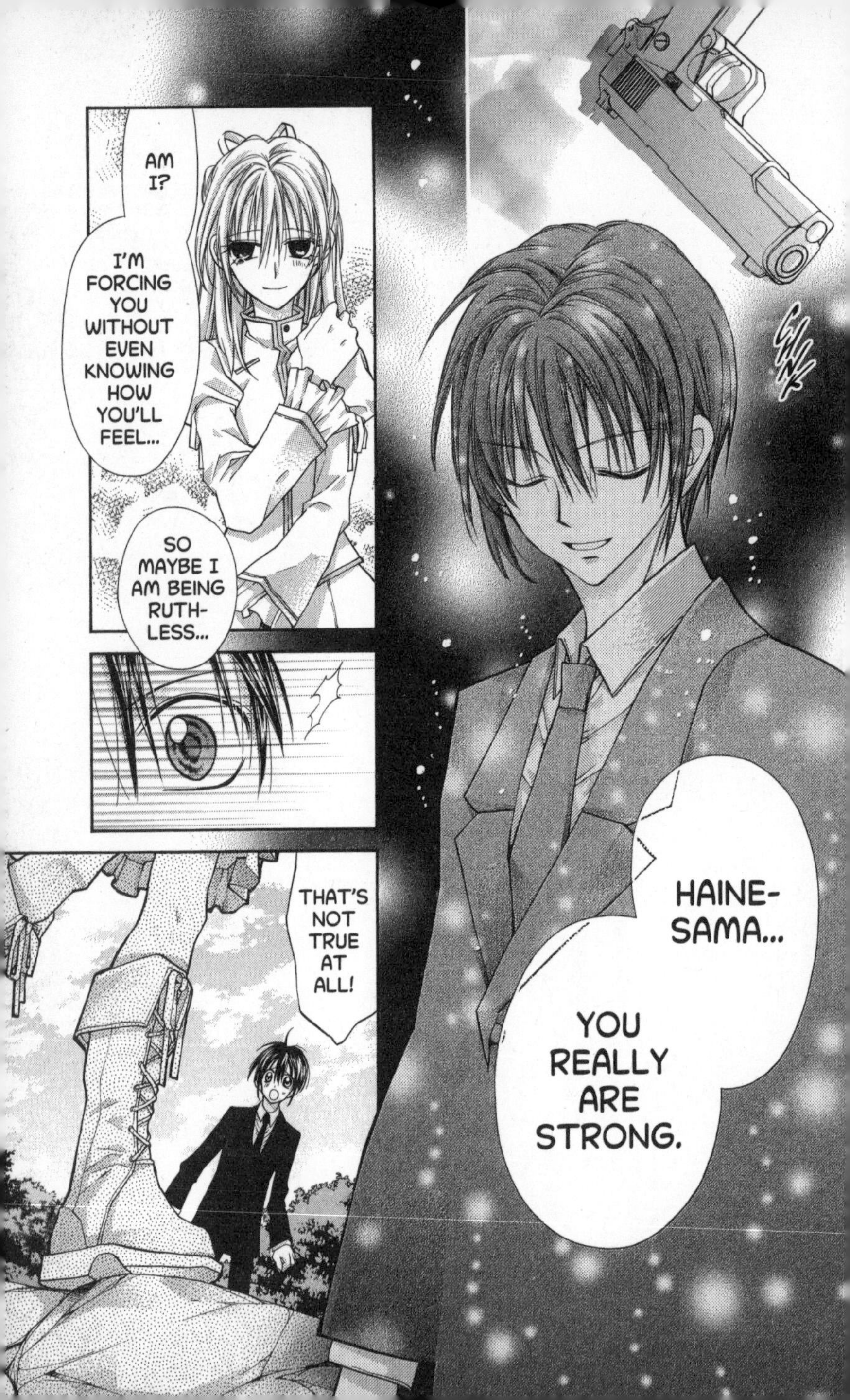
HAINE-SAMA...
YOU REALLY ARE STRONG.
AM I?
I'M FORCING YOU WITHOUT EVEN KNOWING HOW YOU'LL FEEL...
SO MAYBE I AM BEING RUTH-LESS...
THAT'S NOT TRUE AT ALL!

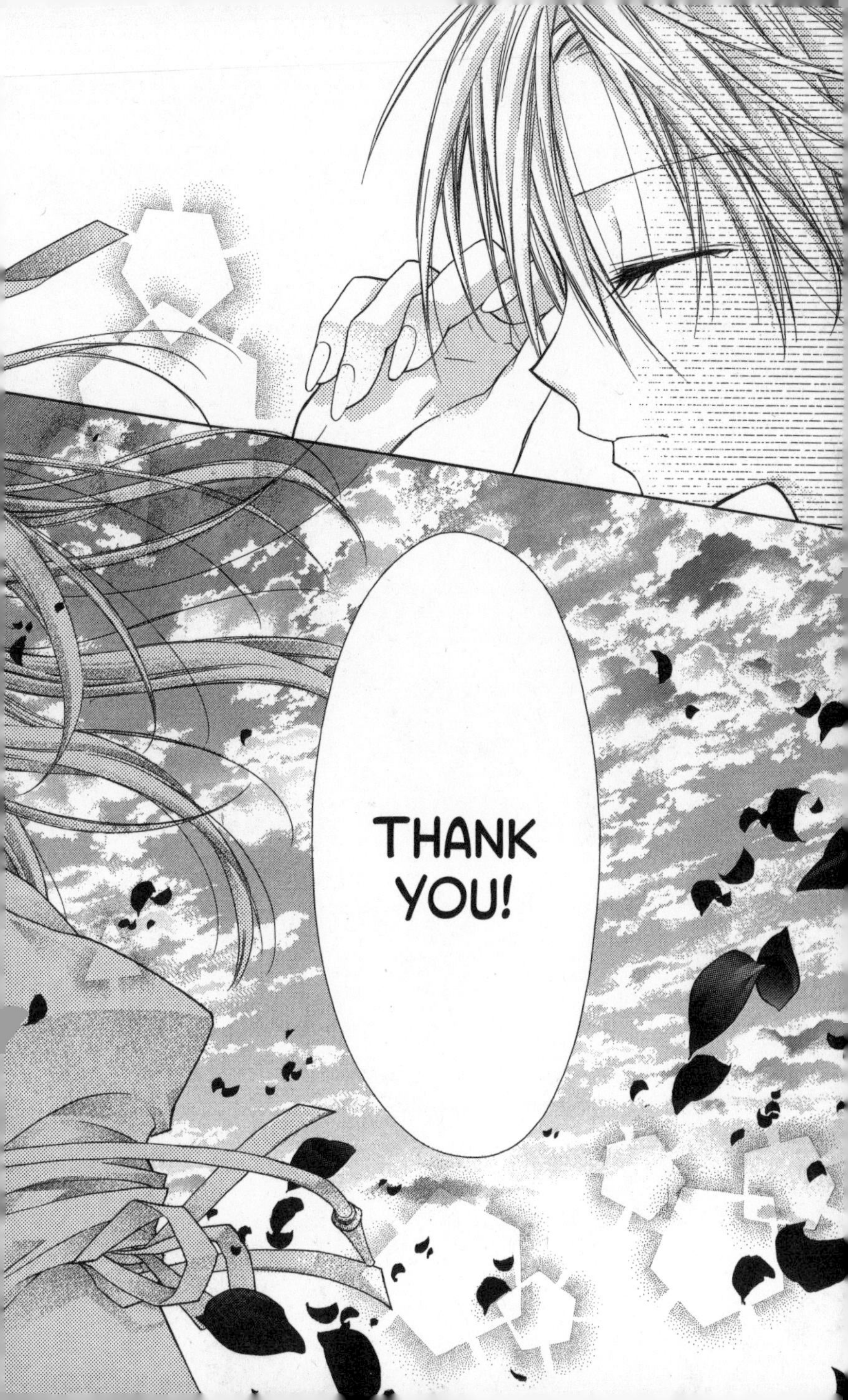
THANK YOU!

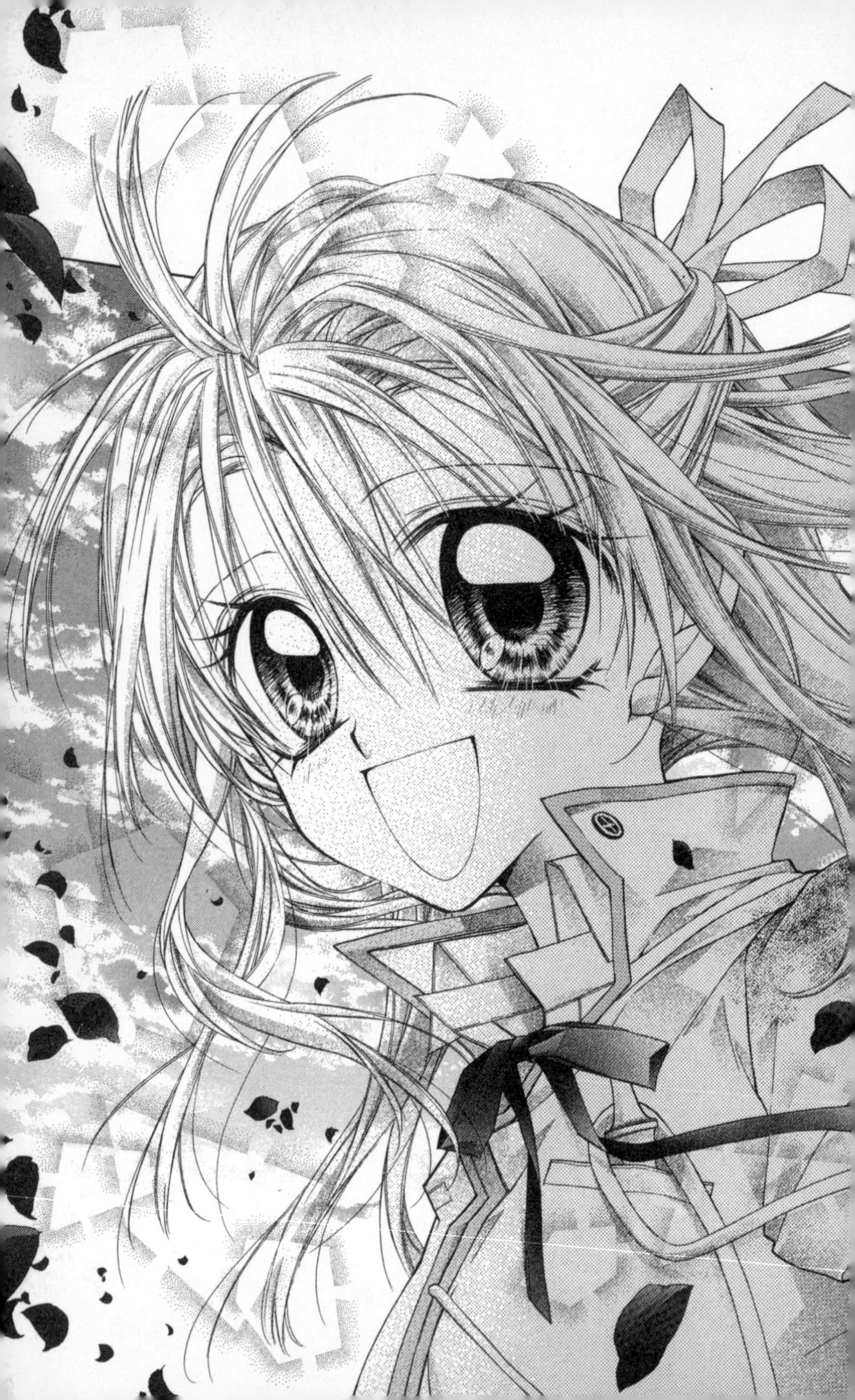

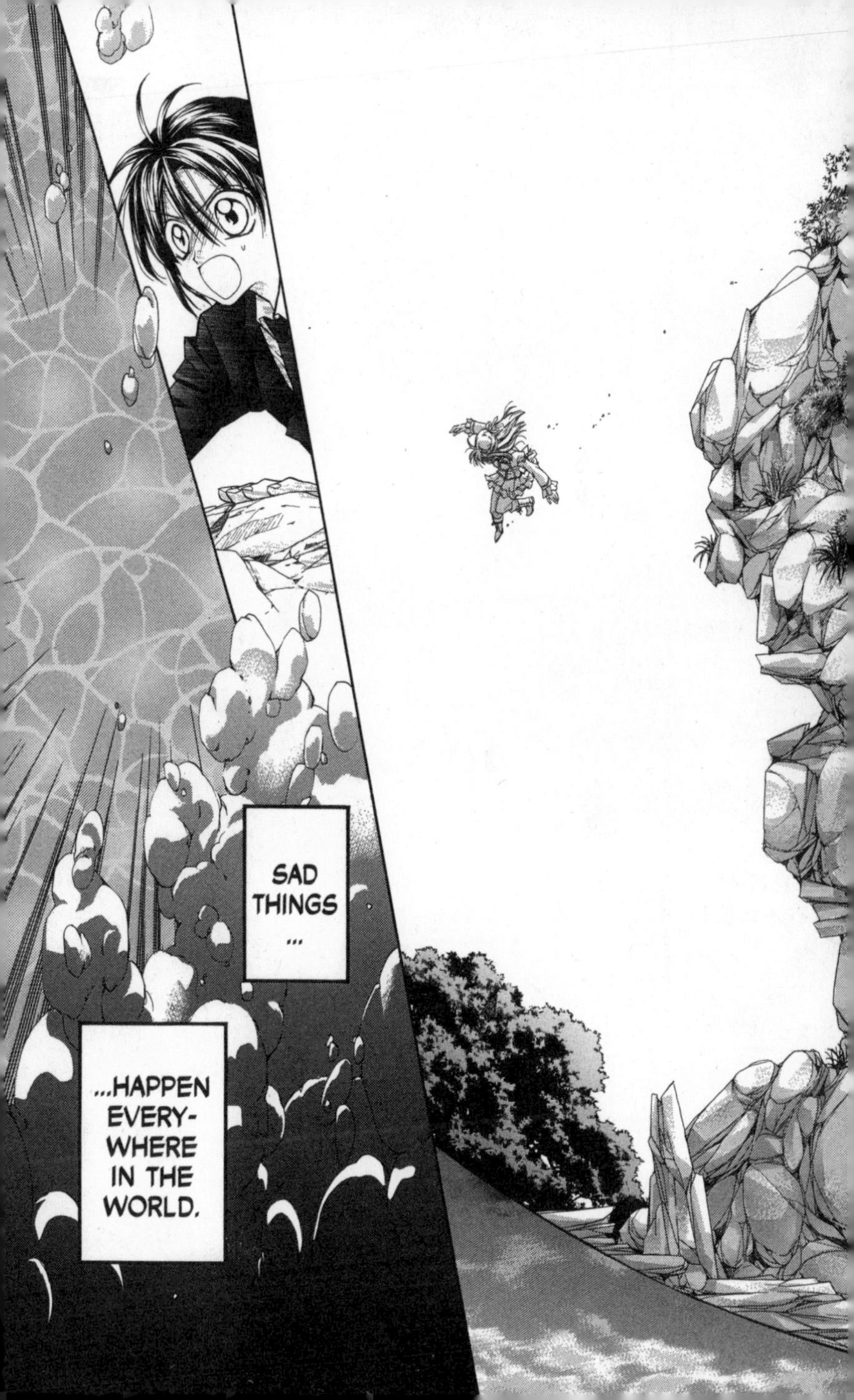
SAD THINGS ...
...HAPPEN EVERY-WHERE IN THE WORLD.

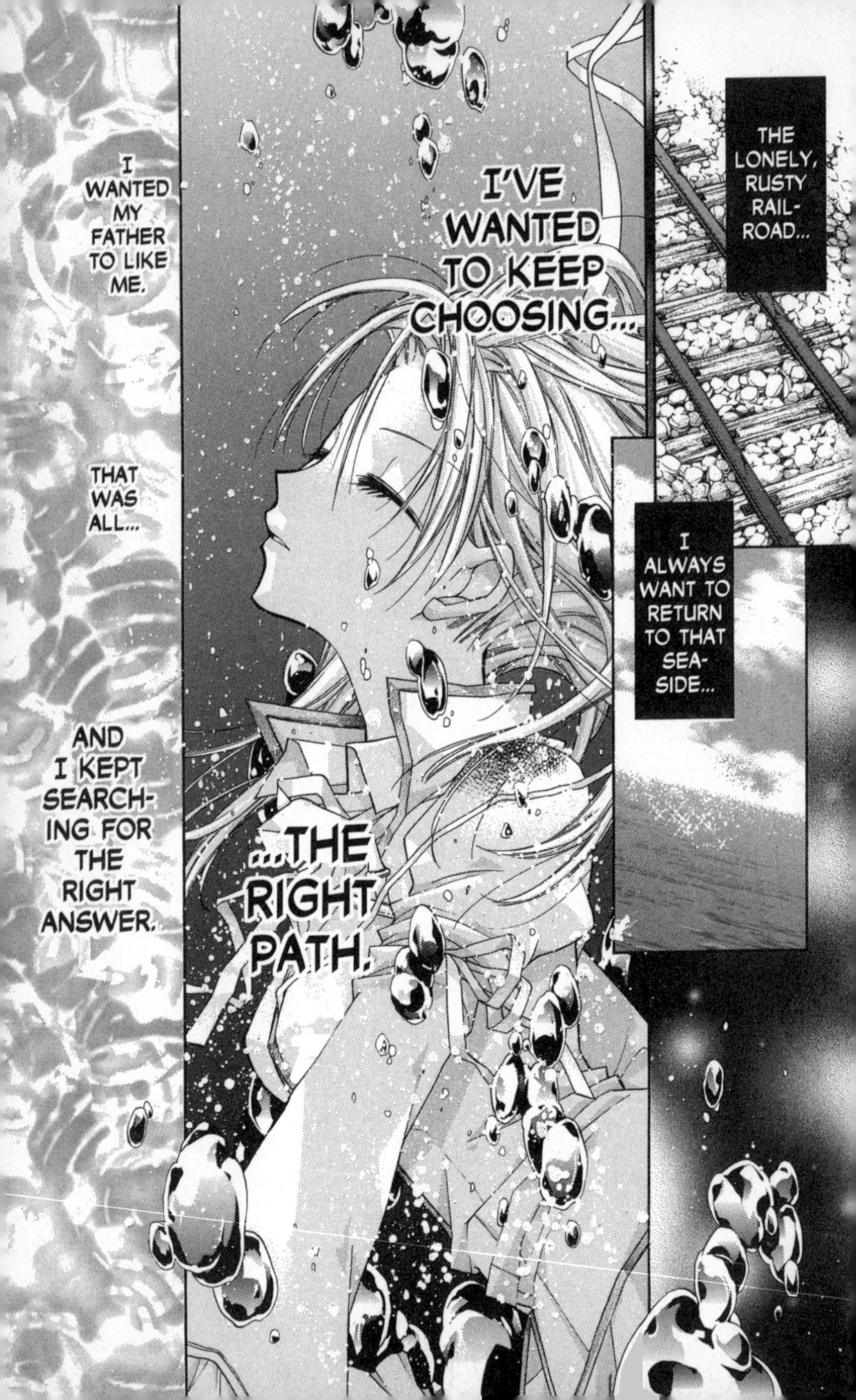
THE LONELY, RUSTY RAILROAD...
I ALWAYS WANT TO RETURN TO THAT SEASIDE...
I'VE WANTED TO KEEP CHOOSING...
...THE RIGHT PATH.
I WANTED MY FATHER TO LIKE ME.
THAT WAS ALL...
AND I KEPT SEARCHING FOR THE RIGHT ANSWER.

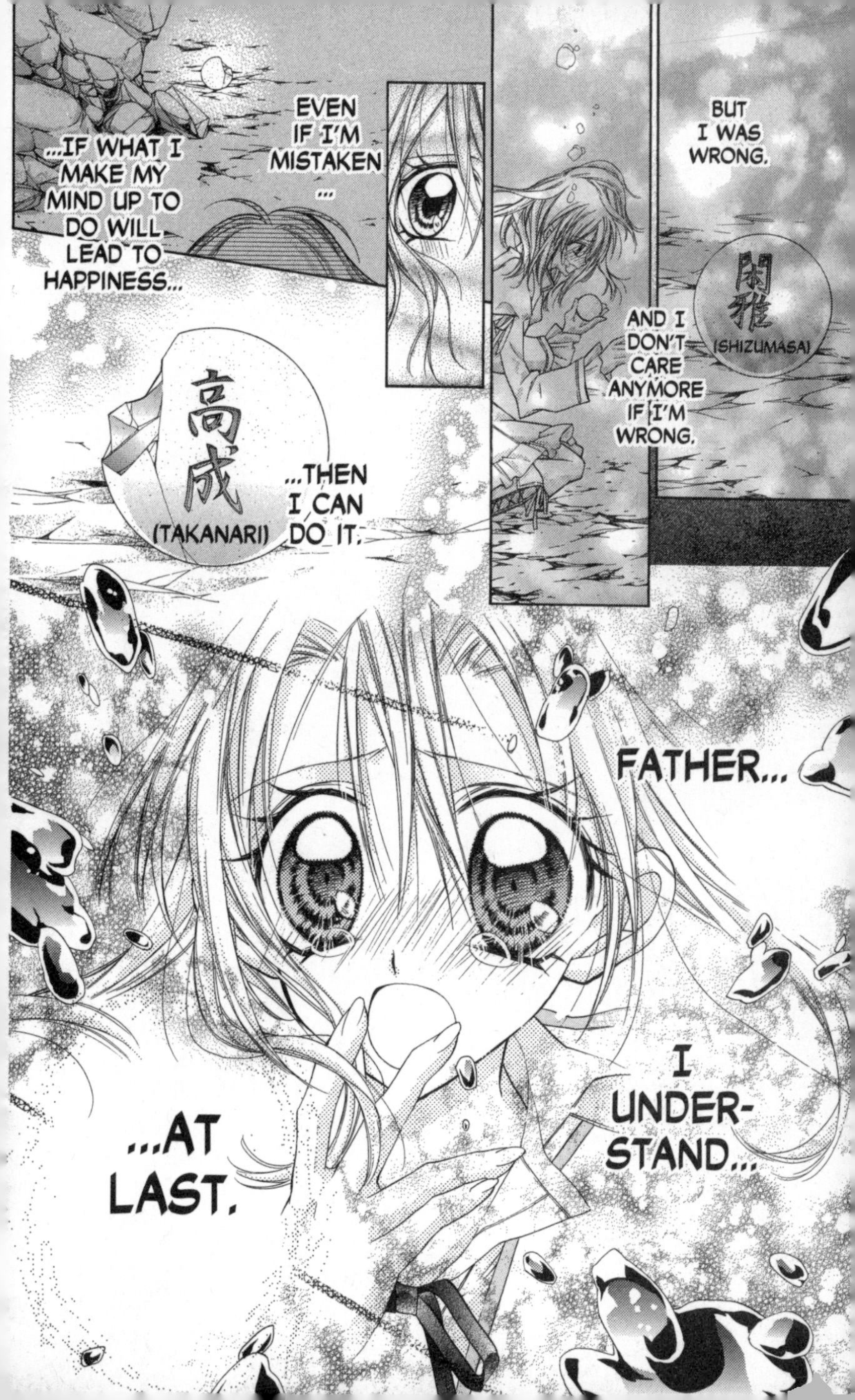
BUT I WAS WRONG.
閑雅
(ISHIZUMASA)
AND I DON'T CARE ANYMORE IF I'M WRONG.
EVEN IF I'M MISTAKEN ...
...IF WHAT I MAKE MY MIND UP TO DO WILL LEAD TO HAPPINESS...
高成
(TAKANARI)
...THEN I CAN DO IT.
FATHER...
I UNDER-STAND...
...AT LAST.

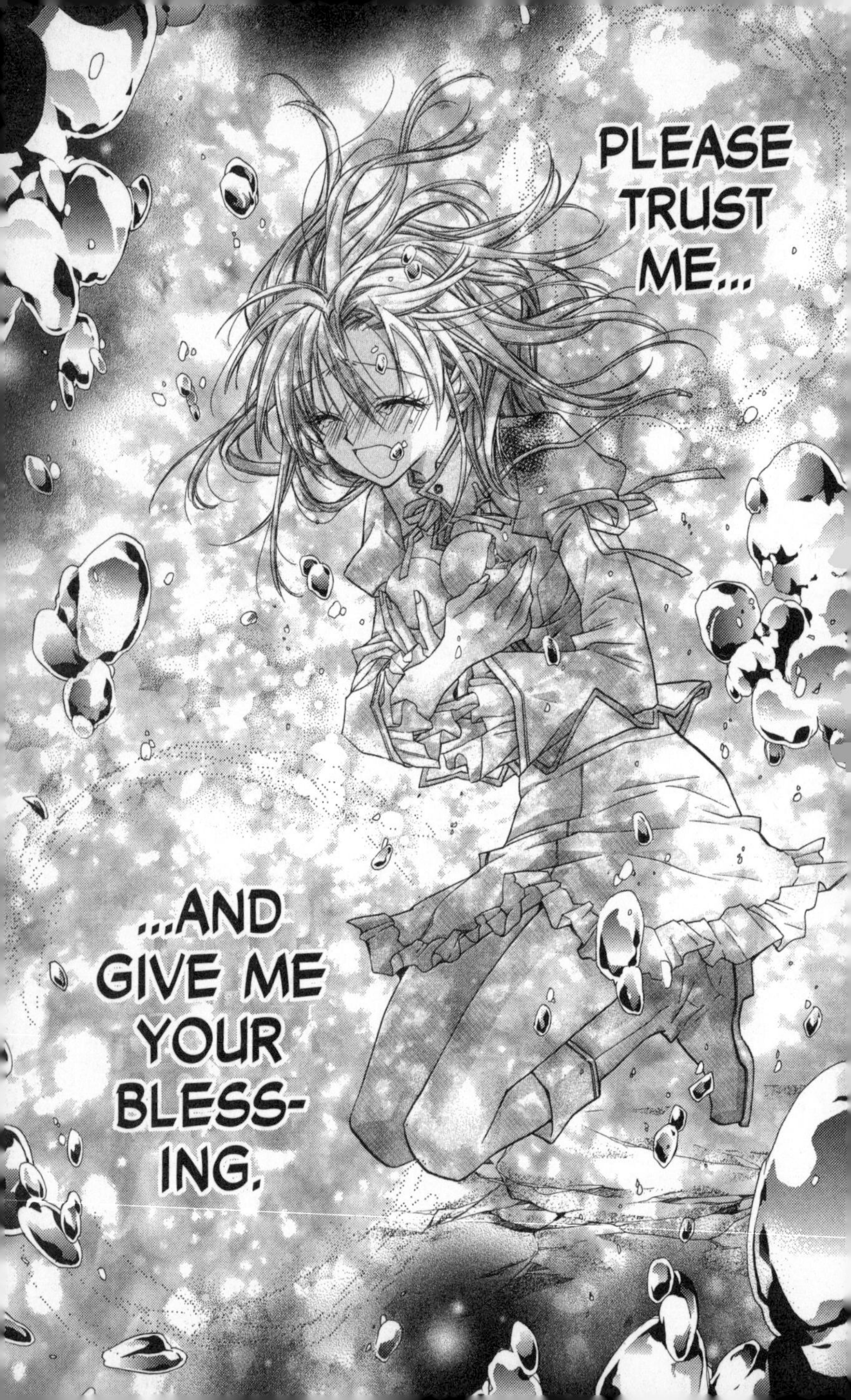
PLEASE TRUST ME...
...AND GIVE ME YOUR BLESS-ING.

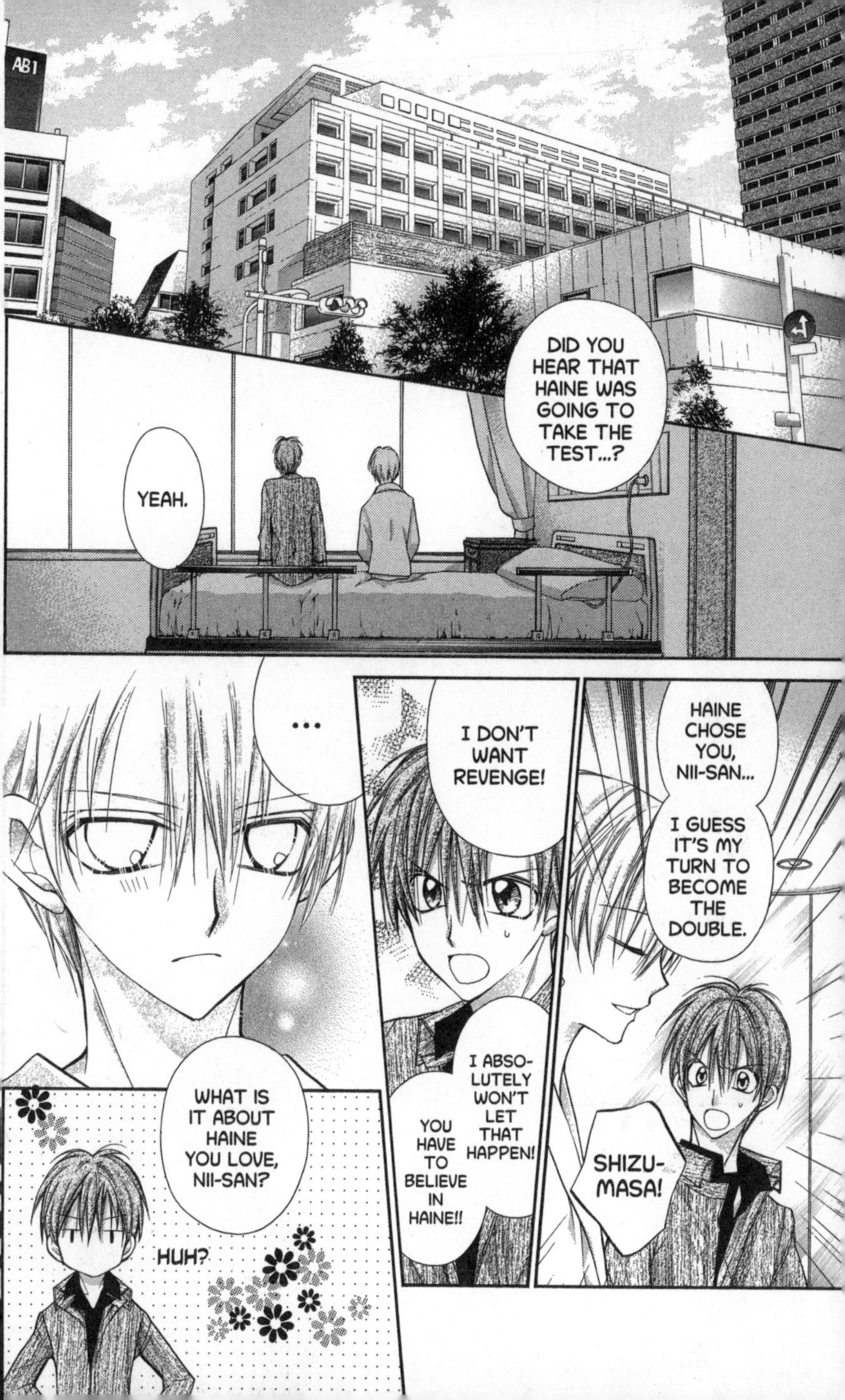
AB1
DID YOU HEAR THAT HAINE WAS GOING TO TAKE THE TEST...?
YEAH.
HAINE CHOSE YOU, NII-SAN...
I GUESS IT'S MY TURN TO BECOME THE DOUBLE.
SHIZU-MASA!
I DON'T WANT REVENGE!
I ABSO-LUTELY WON'T LET THAT HAPPEN!
YOU HAVE TO BELIEVE IN HAINE!!
...
WHAT IS IT ABOUT HAINE YOU LOVE, NII-SAN?
HUH?

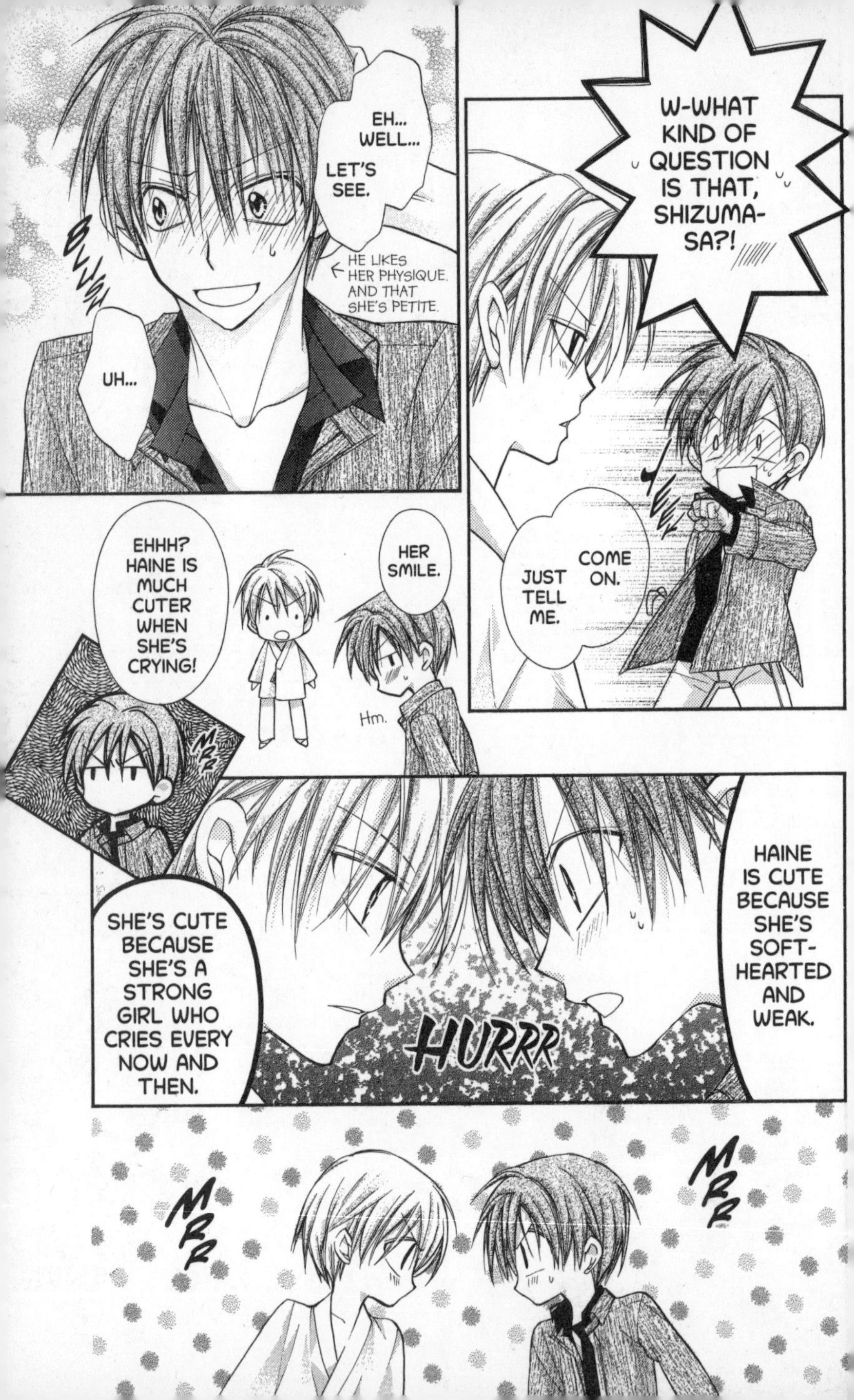
W-WHAT KIND OF QUESTION IS THAT, SHIZUMA-SA?!
COME ON.
JUST TELL ME.
EH... WELL...
LET'S SEE.
HE LIKES HER PHYSIQUE. AND THAT SHE'S PETITE.
UH...
HER SMILE.
Hm.
EHHH? HAINE IS MUCH CUTER WHEN SHE'S CRYING!
MRR
HAINE IS CUTE BECAUSE SHE'S SOFT-HEARTED AND WEAK.
HURRR
SHE'S CUTE BECAUSE SHE'S A STRONG GIRL WHO CRIES EVERY NOW AND THEN.
MRR
MRR

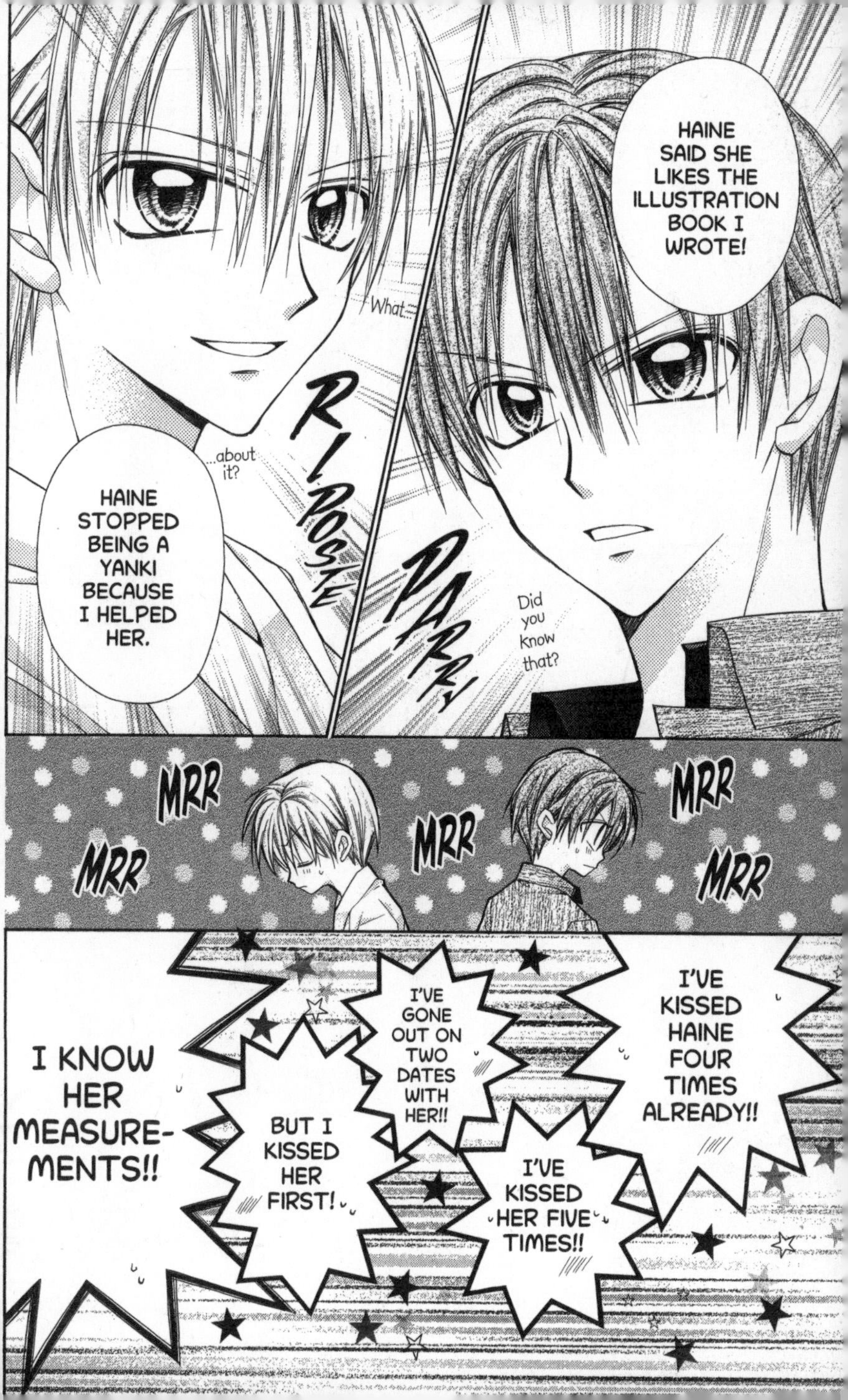
HAINE SAID SHE LIKES THE ILLUSTRATION BOOK I WROTE!
Did you know that?
PARRY
What...
...about it?
HAINE STOPPED BEING A YANKI BECAUSE I HELPED HER.
RIPOSTE
MRR
MRR
MRR
MRR
MRR
I'VE KISSED HAINE FOUR TIMES ALREADY!!
I'VE GONE OUT ON TWO DATES WITH HER!!
I'VE KISSED HER FIVE TIMES!!
BUT I KISSED HER FIRST!
I KNOW HER MEASUREMENTS!!

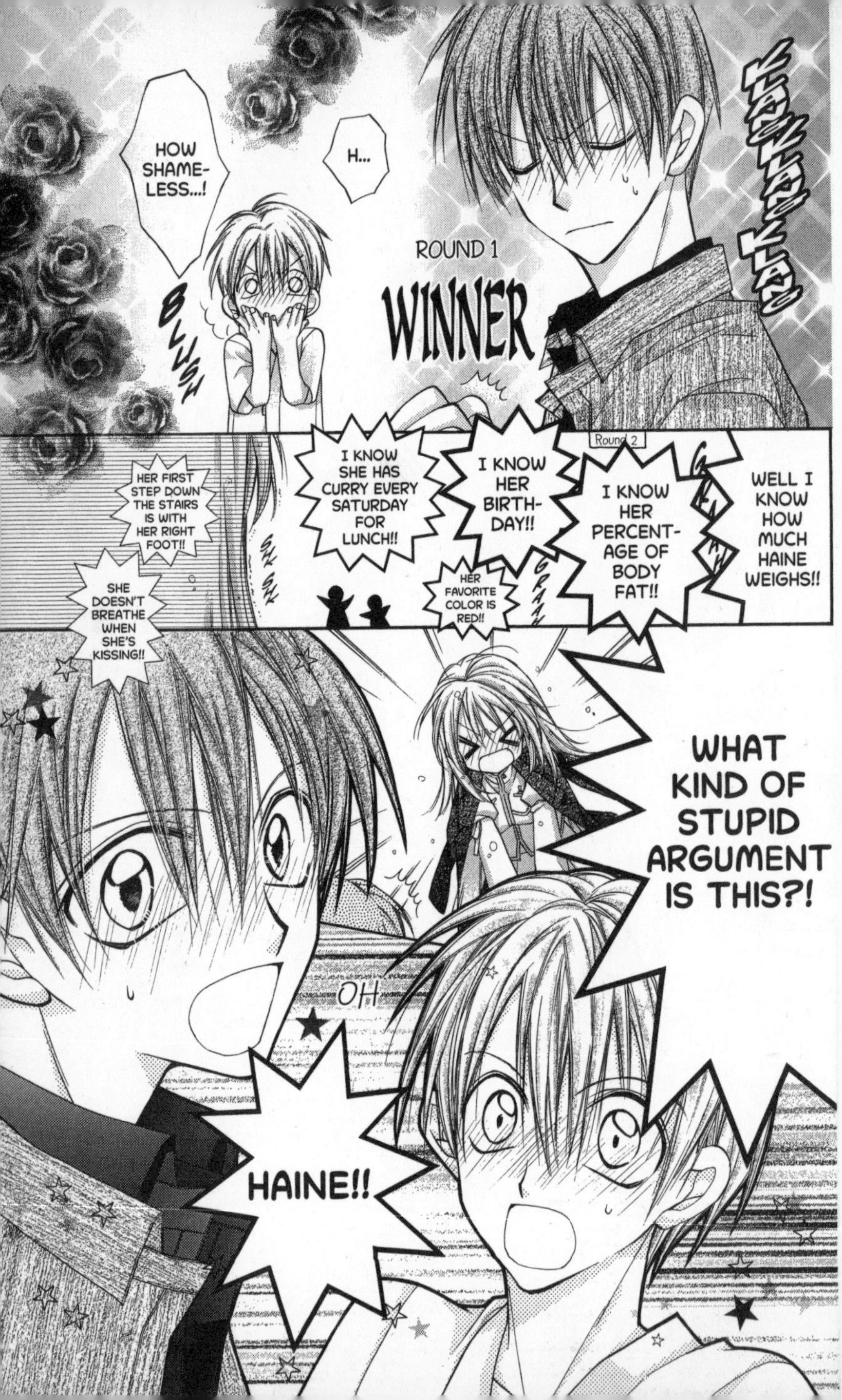
ROUND 1
WINNER
H...
HOW SHAME-LESS...!
BLUSH
WELL I KNOW HOW MUCH HAINE WEIGHS!!
Round 2
I KNOW HER PERCENT-AGE OF BODY FAT!!
HER FAVORITE COLOR IS RED!!
I KNOW HER BIRTH-DAY!!
I KNOW SHE HAS CURRY EVERY SATURDAY FOR LUNCH!!
HER FIRST STEP DOWN THE STAIRS IS WITH HER RIGHT FOOT!!
SHE DOESN'T BREATHE WHEN SHE'S KISSING!!
WHAT KIND OF STUPID ARGUMENT IS THIS?!
OH
HAINE!!

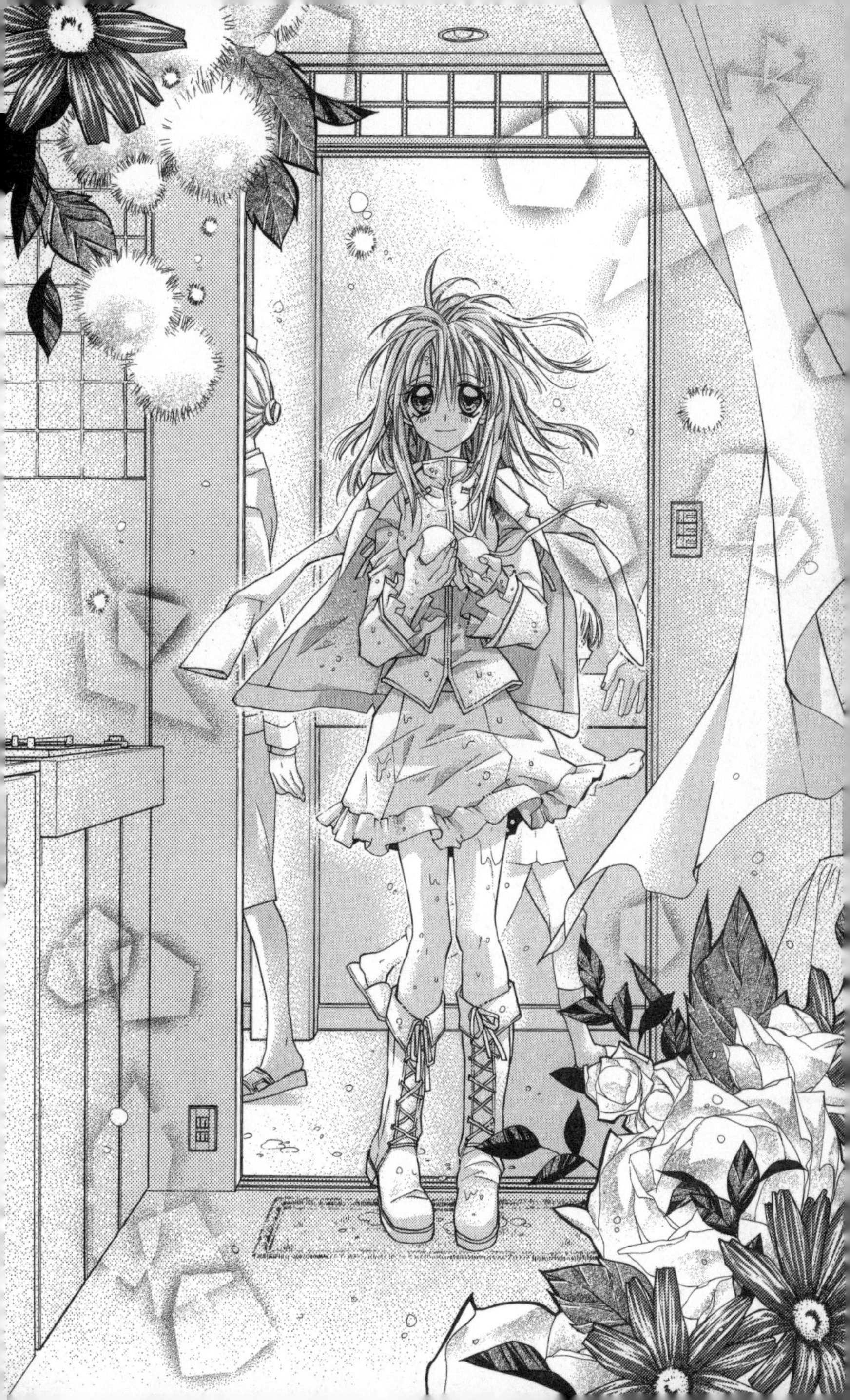

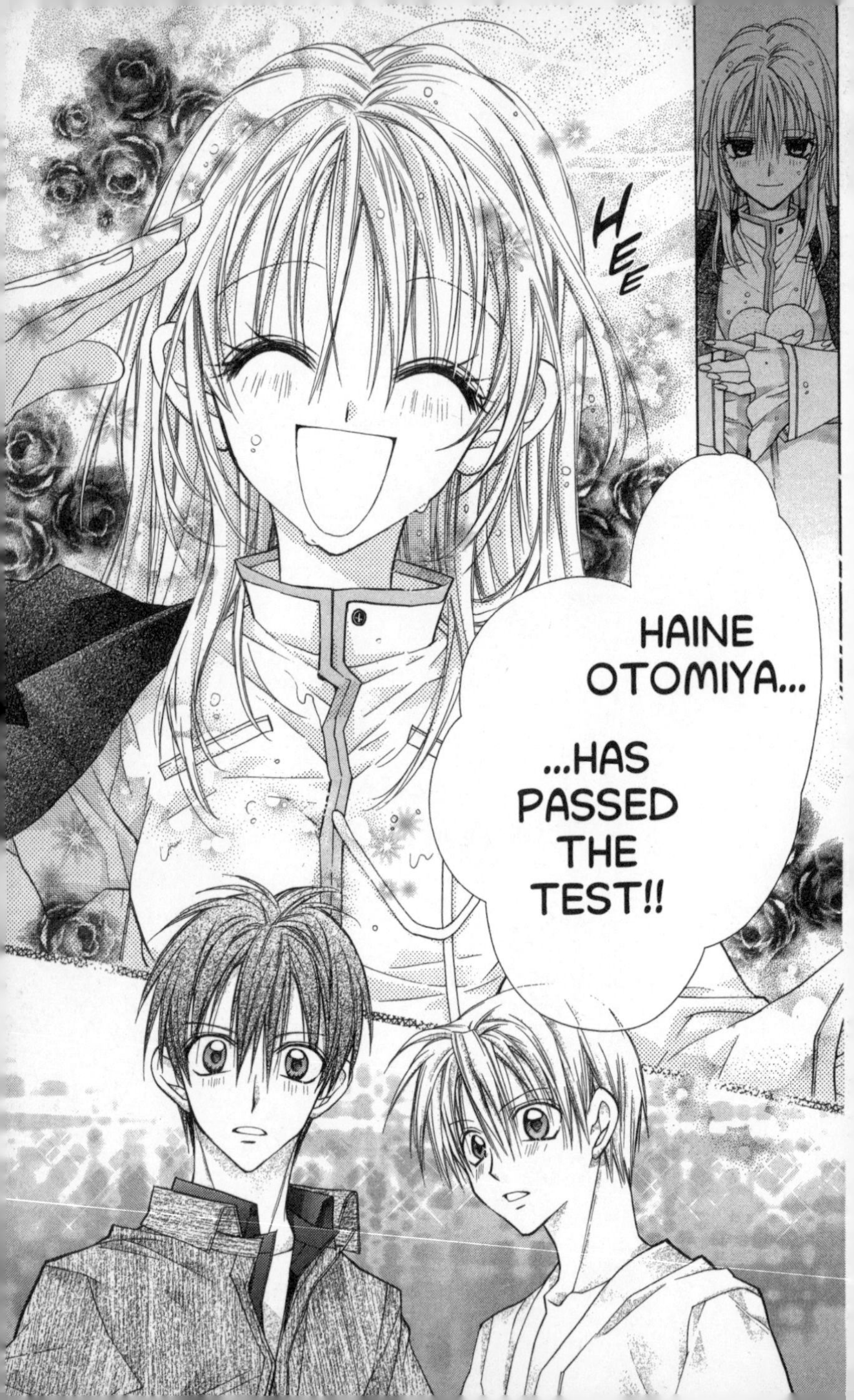
HEE
HAINE OTOMIYA...
...HAS PASSED THE TEST!!

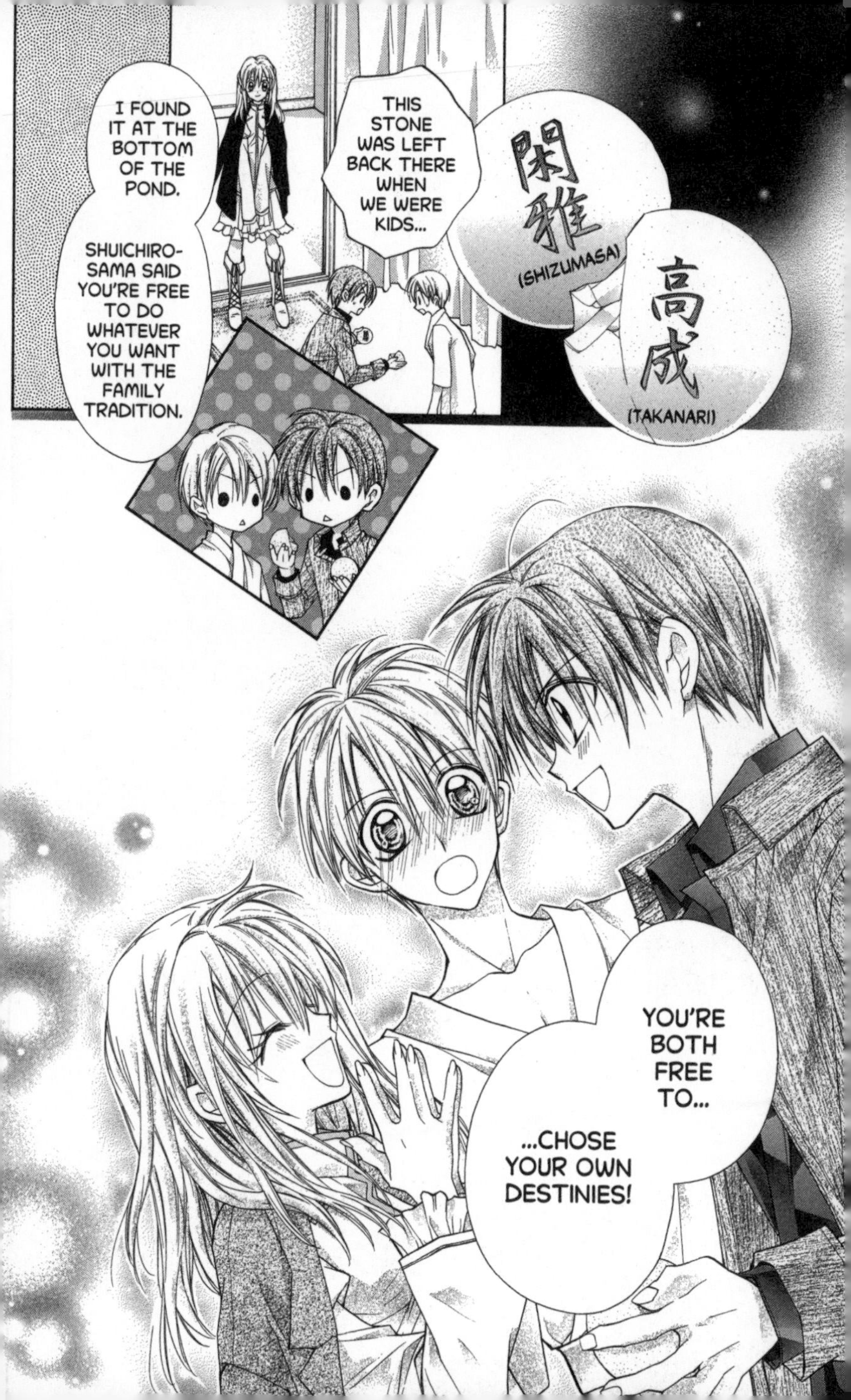
閑雅
(SHIZUMASA)
高成
(TAKANARI)
THIS STONE WAS LEFT BACK THERE WHEN WE WERE KIDS...
I FOUND IT AT THE BOTTOM OF THE POND.
SHUICHIRO-SAMA SAID YOU'RE FREE TO DO WHATEVER YOU WANT WITH THE FAMILY TRADITION.
YOU'RE BOTH FREE TO...
...CHOSE YOUR OWN DESTINIES!

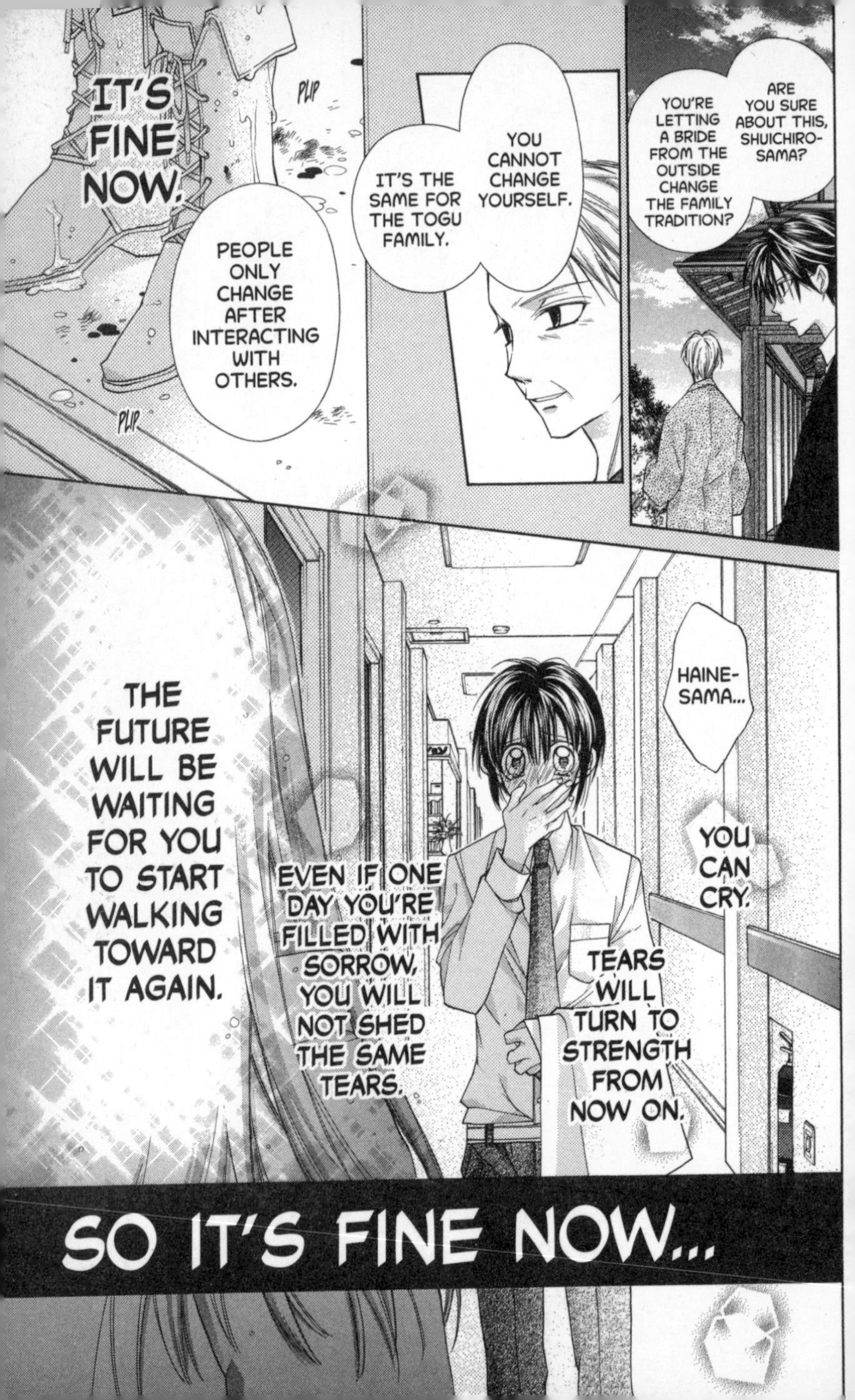
ARE YOU SURE ABOUT THIS, SHUICHIRO-SAMA?
YOU'RE LETTING A BRIDE FROM THE OUTSIDE CHANGE THE FAMILY TRADITION?
YOU CANNOT CHANGE YOURSELF.
IT'S THE SAME FOR THE TOGU FAMILY.
PEOPLE ONLY CHANGE AFTER INTERACTING WITH OTHERS.
PLIP
IT'S FINE NOW.
PLIP
HAINE-SAMA...
YOU CAN CRY.
TEARS WILL TURN TO STRENGTH FROM NOW ON.
EVEN IF ONE DAY YOU'RE FILLED WITH SORROW, YOU WILL NOT SHED THE SAME TEARS.
THE FUTURE WILL BE WAITING FOR YOU TO START WALKING TOWARD IT AGAIN.
SO IT'S FINE NOW...

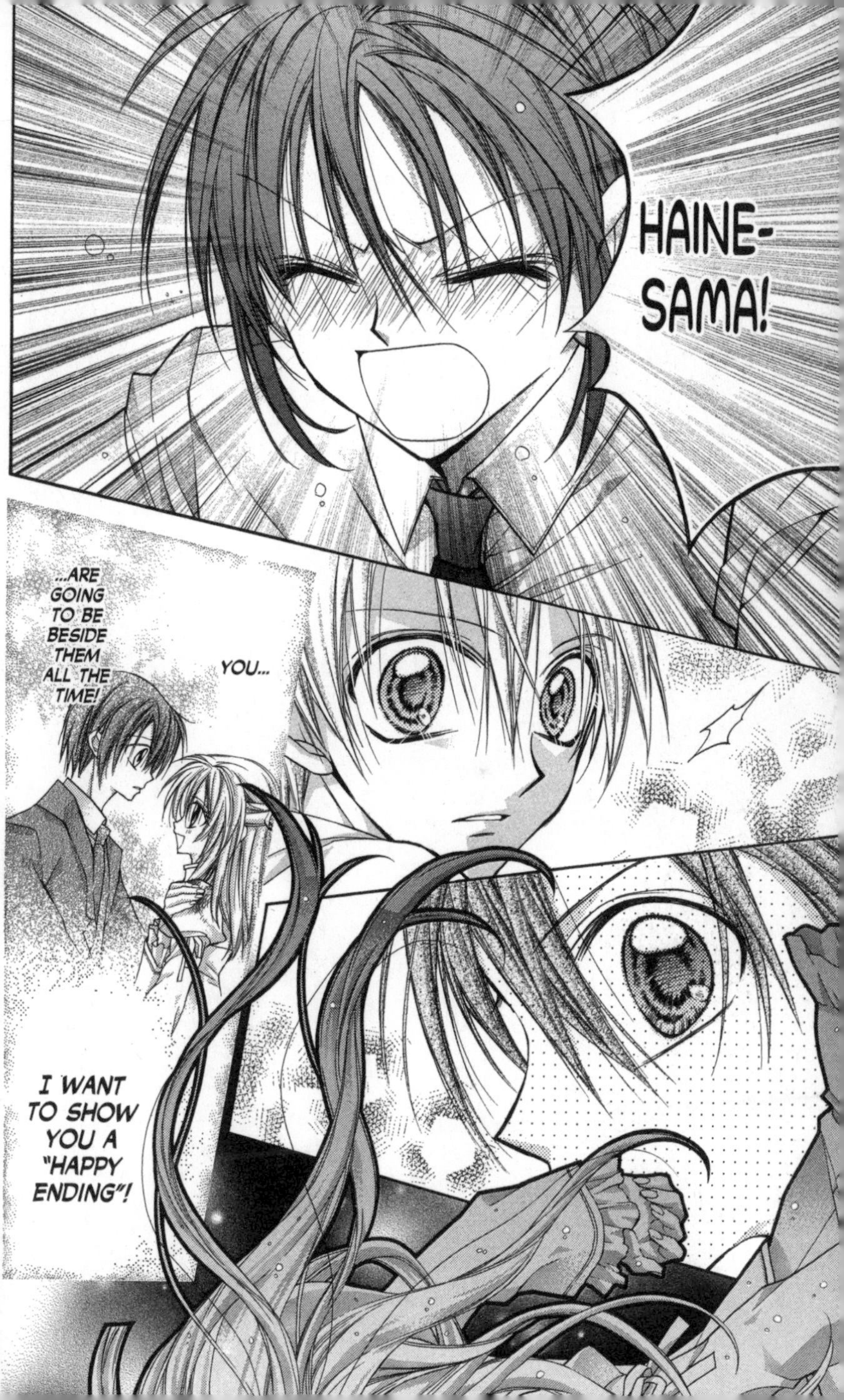
HAINE-SAMA!
YOU...
...ARE GOING TO BE BESIDE THEM ALL THE TIME!
I WANT TO SHOW YOU A "HAPPY ENDING"!

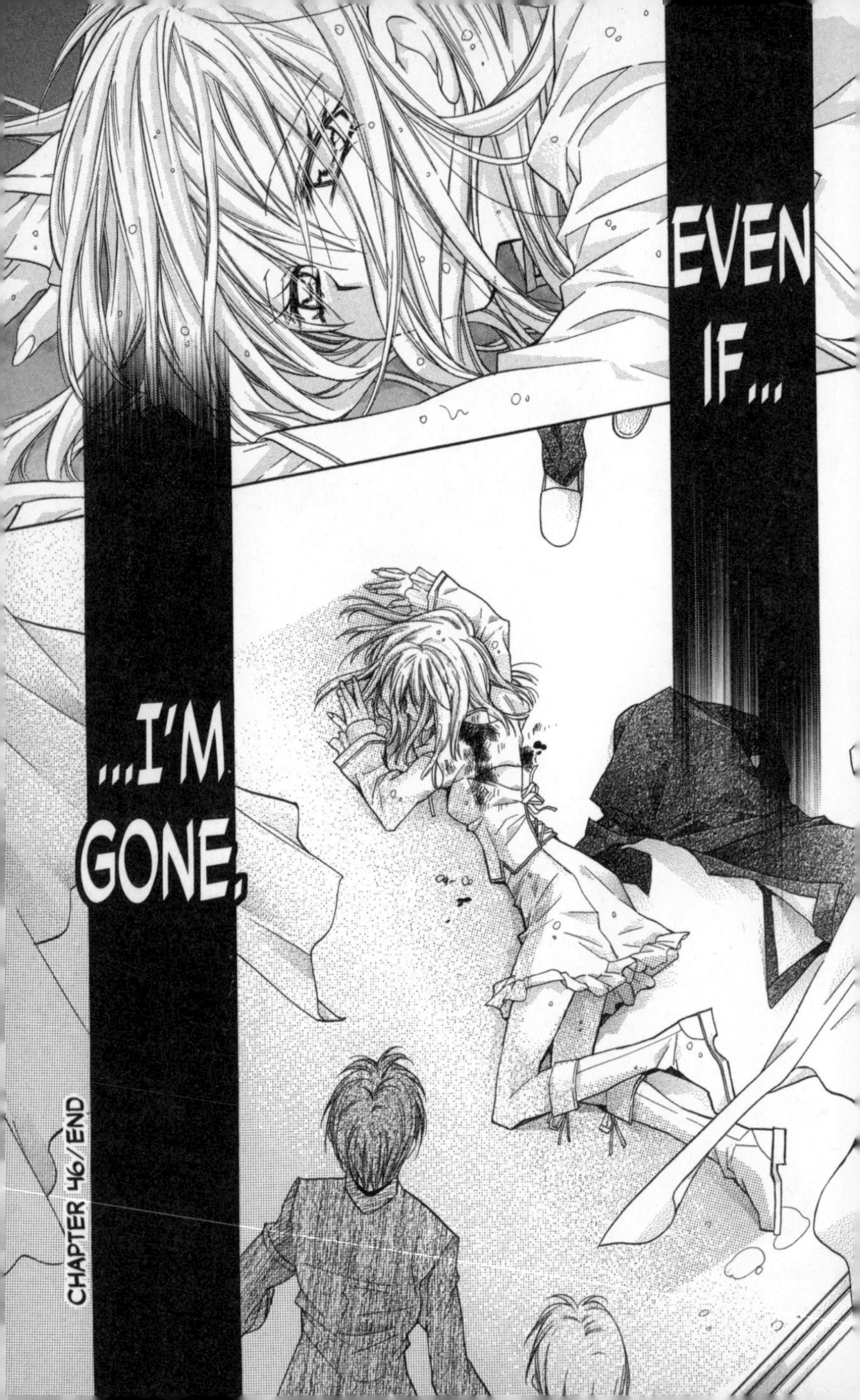
EVEN IF...
...I'M GONE.
CHAPTER 46/END

A full view of Imperial Academy

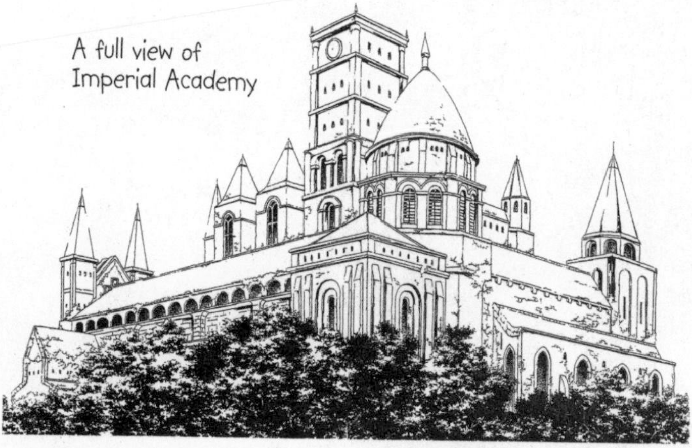

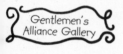

Gentlemen's Alliance Gallery

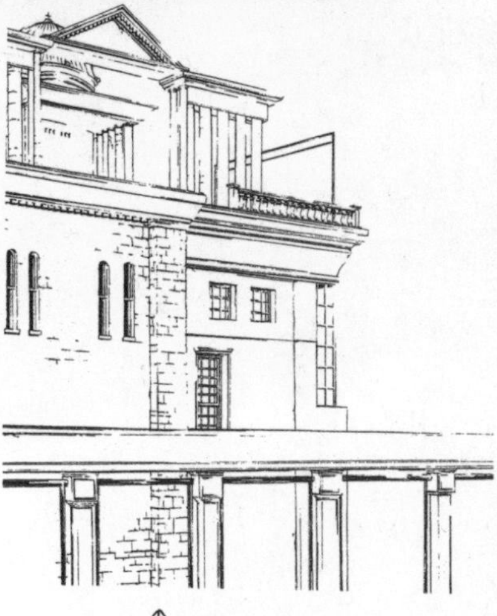

↑ Rooftop

This is where Haine and Ushio were talking on the phone in volume 2.

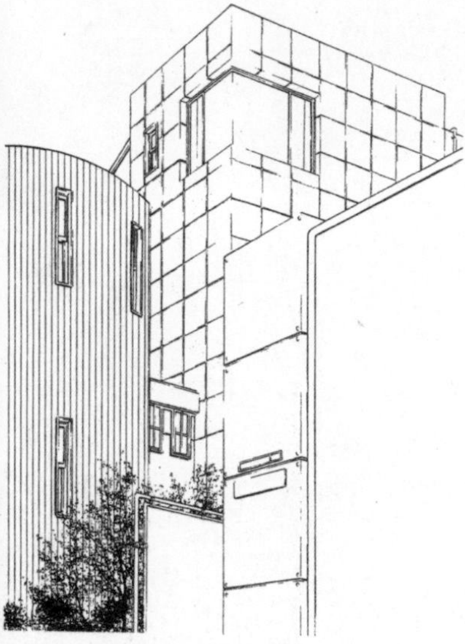

← Otomiya Family House

It's a really large house.
(The backgrounds were basically all my original design.)

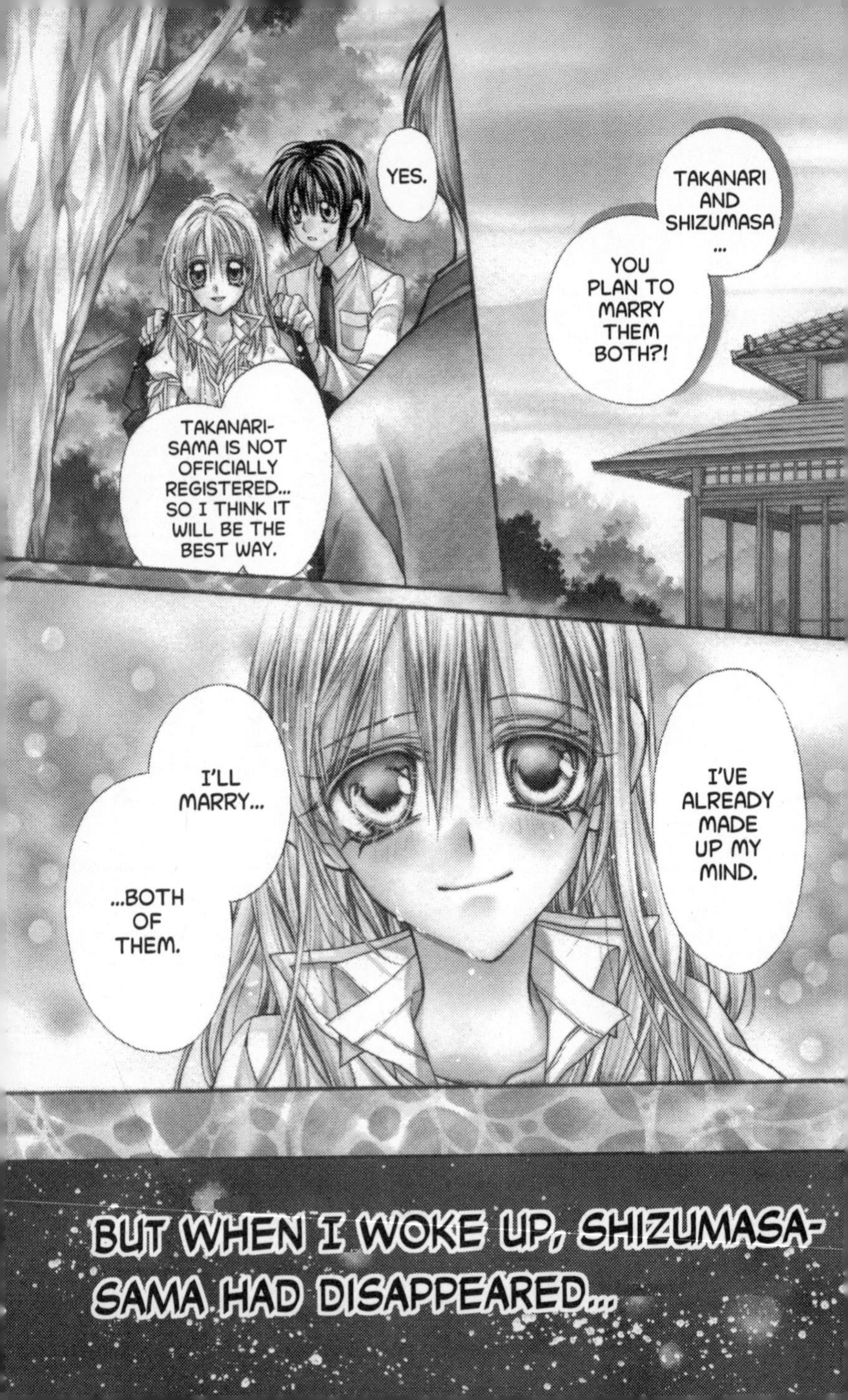
TAKANARI AND SHIZUMASA...
YOU PLAN TO MARRY THEM BOTH?!
YES.
TAKANARI-SAMA IS NOT OFFICIALLY REGISTERED... SO I THINK IT WILL BE THE BEST WAY.
I'VE ALREADY MADE UP MY MIND.
I'LL MARRY...
...BOTH OF THEM.
BUT WHEN I WOKE UP, SHIZUMASA-SAMA HAD DISAPPEARED...

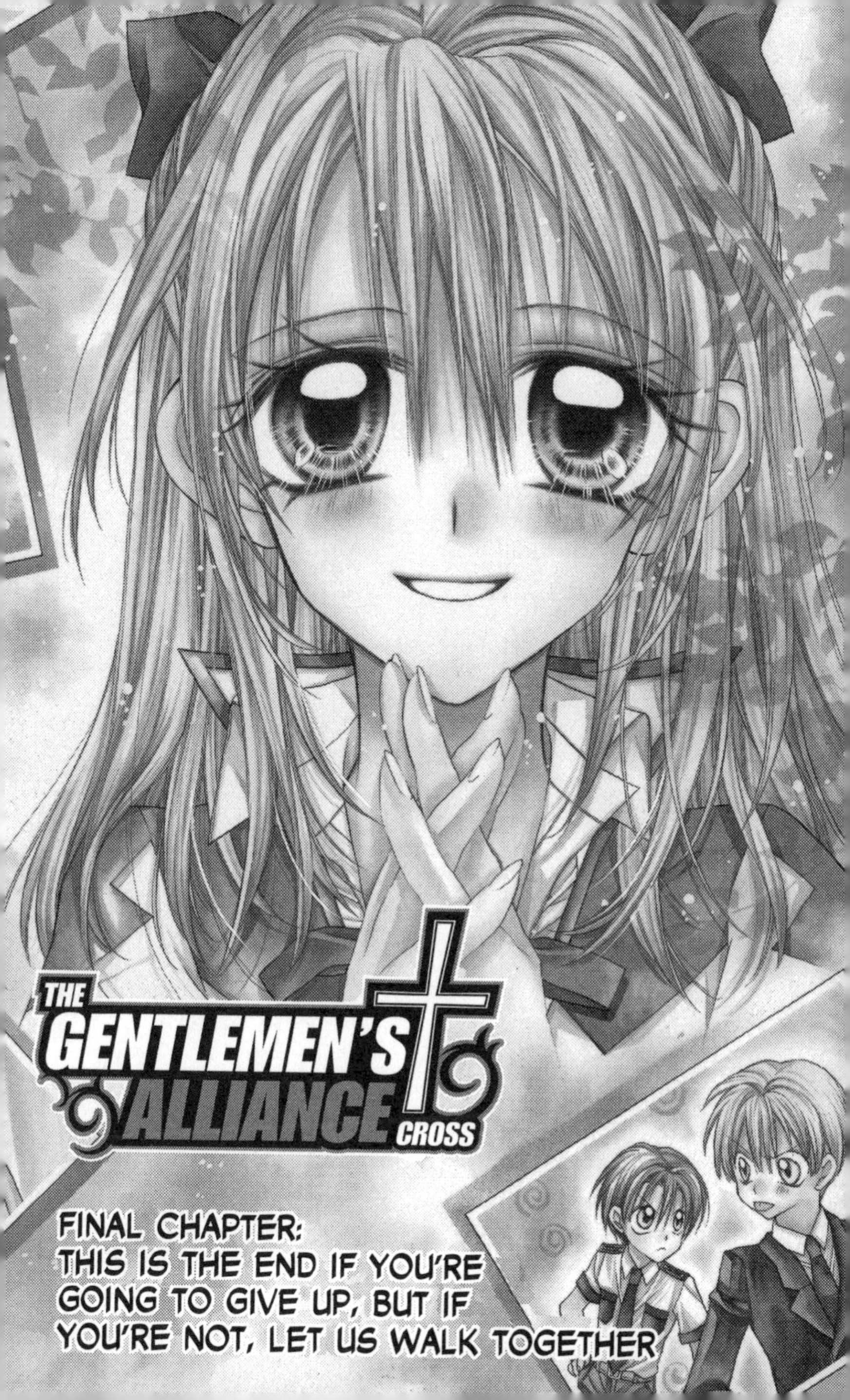
THE GENTLEMEN'S ALLIANCE CROSS
FINAL CHAPTER:
THIS IS THE END IF YOU'RE GOING TO GIVE UP, BUT IF YOU'RE NOT, LET US WALK TOGETHER

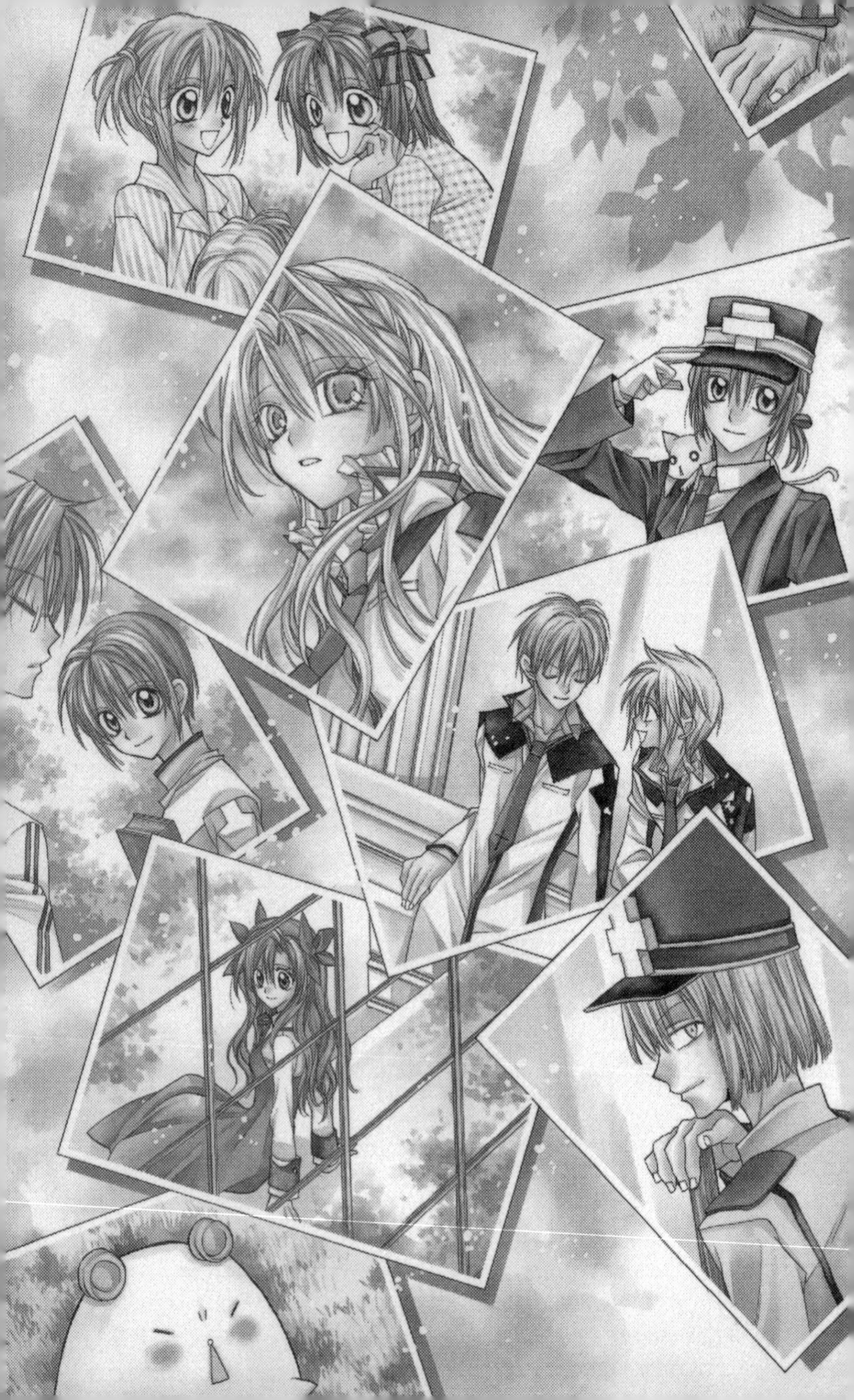

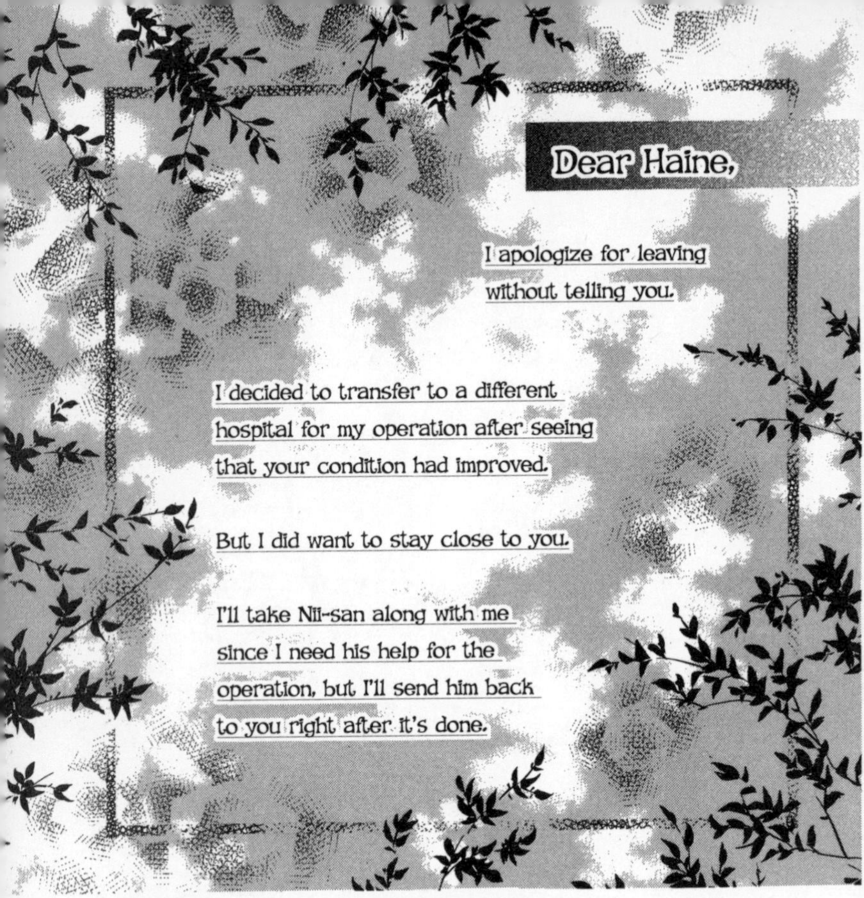
Dear Haine,
I apologize for leaving without telling you.
I decided to transfer to a different hospital for my operation after seeing that your condition had improved.
But I did want to stay close to you.
I'll take Nii-san along with me since I need his help for the operation, but I'll send him back to you right after it's done.

Final Chapter (Chapter 47)
※ I'm giving away the story.

This Is the End if You're Going to Give Up, but if You're Not, Let Us Walk Together

(Lead-in) I'll forever be thinking, "Thank you"...

I realized at the very end that the title of this chapter was probably the overall theme behind *The Gentlemen's Alliance* †. The members of the student council and Shizumasa were all people who had "given up." Both Haine-chan and I are rather impatient people, so it was very tough for me to keep watching them. I kept thinking about why they wouldn't try a little harder... I was really contemplating having these three get married in the end. Ever since the first chapter! That was actually the only thing I had decided on from the start. I was still thinking about doing it, and the editorial department had given me the go-ahead, but when it came down to doing it... Hmm. I thought it made Shizumasa look like a really pitiful, hopeless guy, so I changed it at the very end. I'm glad I changed it now, but that's why the first page of the last chapter ended up like this.

The very last thing Takanari thinks is also what everyone else is feeling.
It is also his reply to Haine's love confession to him four years ago.

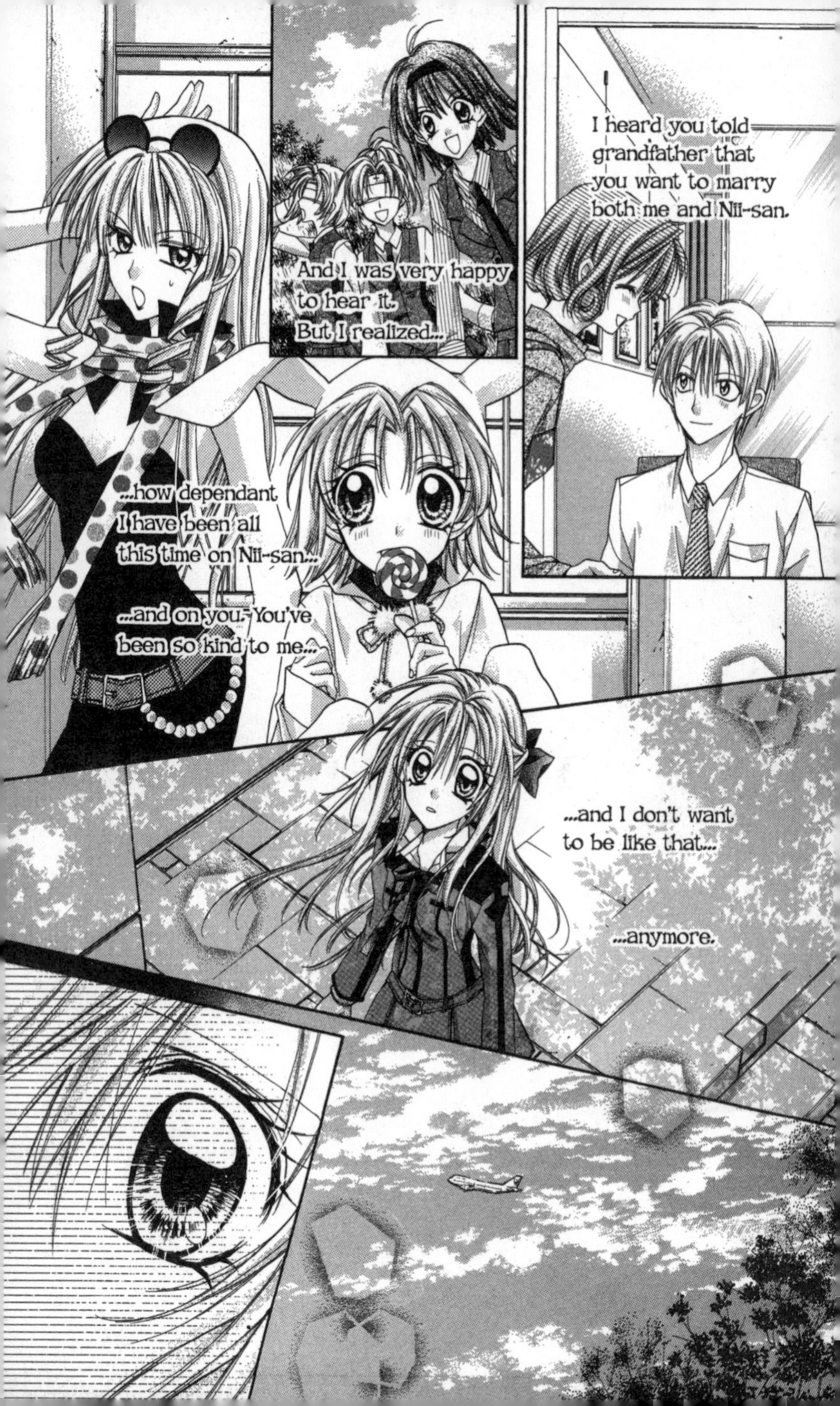
I heard you told grandfather that you want to marry both me and Nii-san.
And I was very happy to hear it. But I realized...
...how dependant I have been all this time on Nii-san...
...and on you. You've been so kind to me...
...and I don't want to be like that...
...anymore.

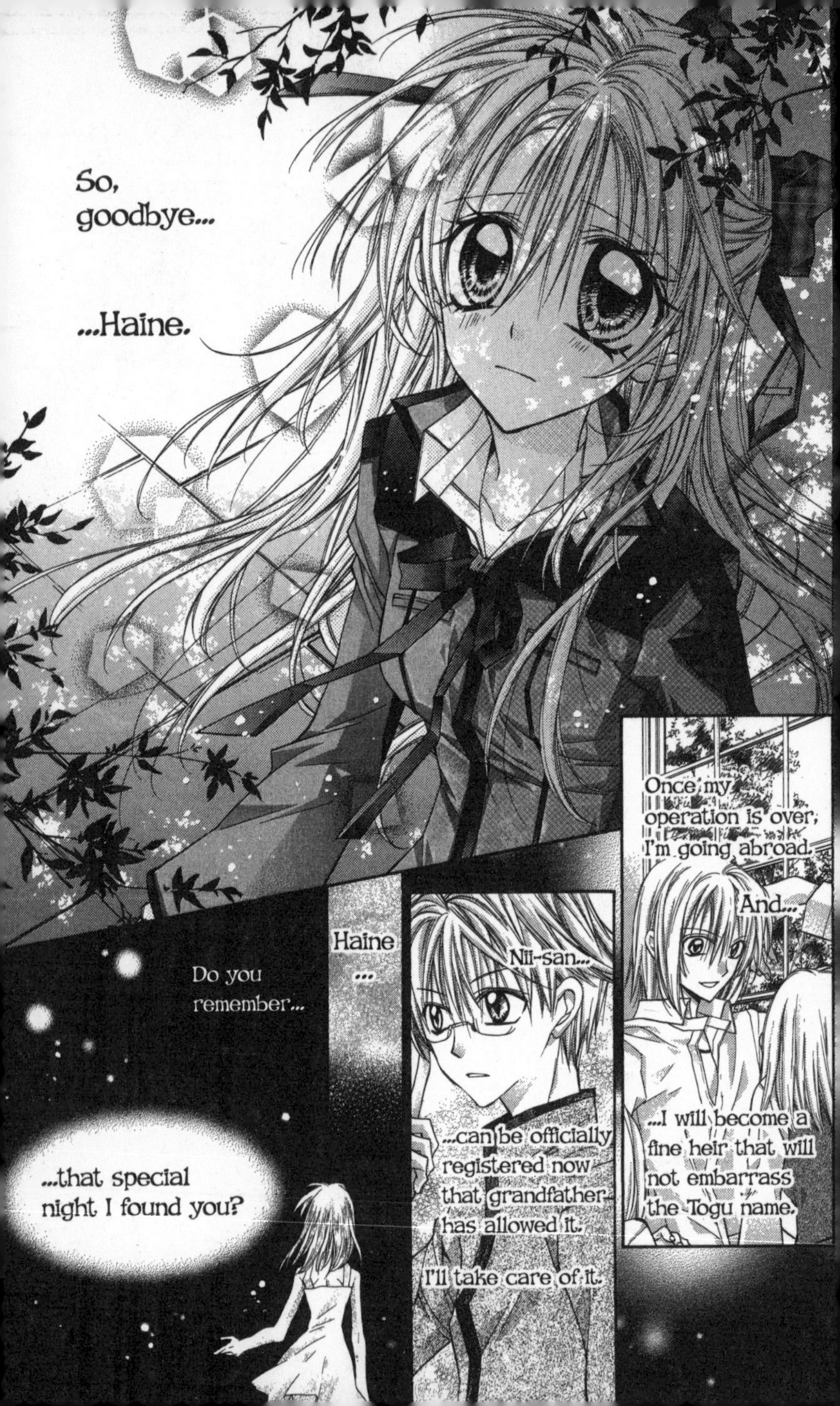
So, goodbye...
...Haine.
Once my operation is over, I'm going abroad.
And...
...I will become a fine heir that will not embarrass the Togu name.
Nii-san...
...can be officially registered now that grandfather has allowed it.
I'll take care of it.
Haine...
Do you remember...
...that special night I found you?

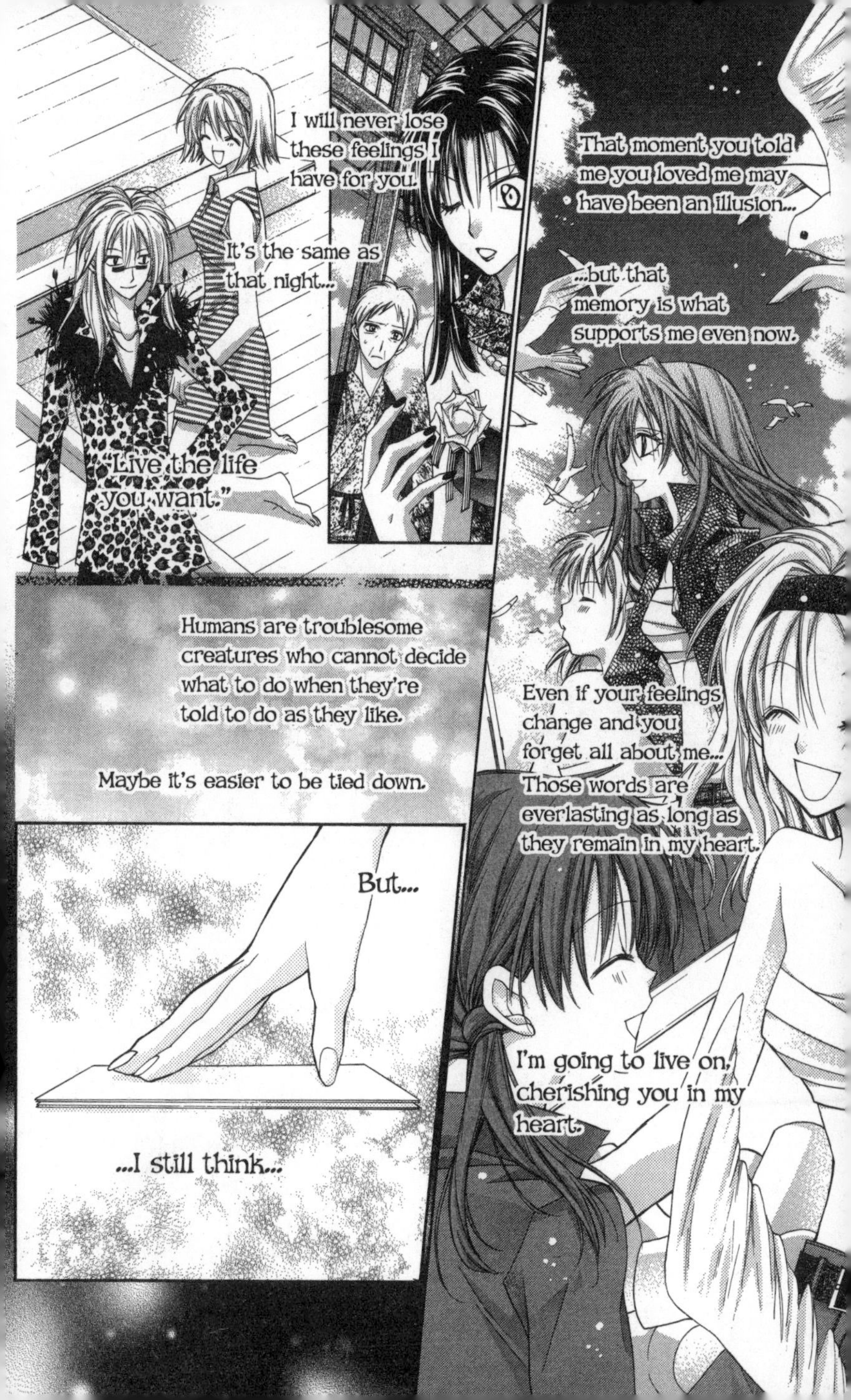
That moment you told me you loved me may have been an illusion...
...but that memory is what supports me even now.
Even if your feelings change and you forget all about me... Those words are everlasting as long as they remain in my heart.
I'm going to live on, cherishing you in my heart.
I will never lose these feelings I have for you.
It's the same as that night...
"Live the life you want."
Humans are troublesome creatures who cannot decide what to do when they're told to do as they like.
Maybe it's easier to be tied down.
But...
...I still think...

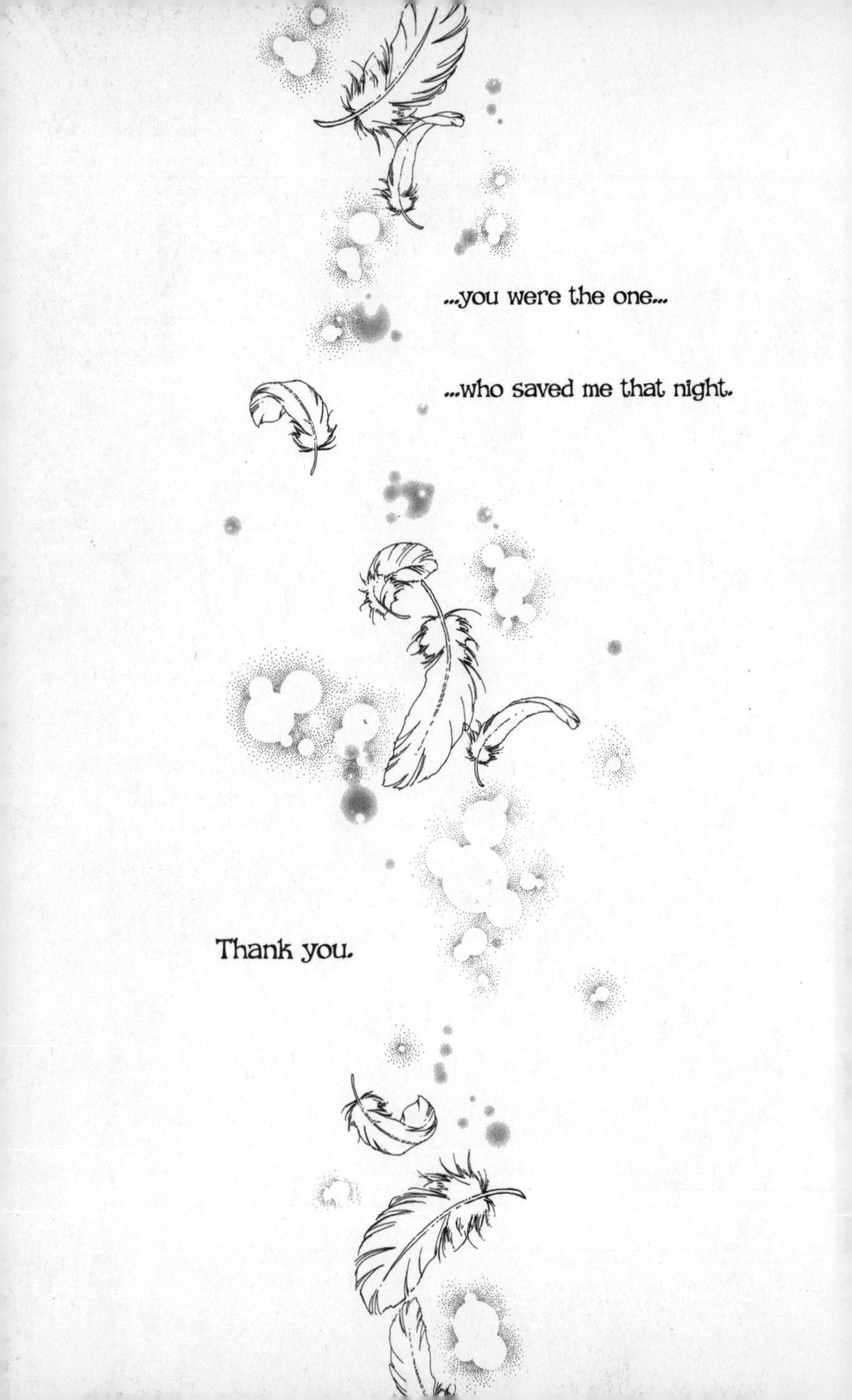
...you were the one...
...who saved me that night.
Thank you.

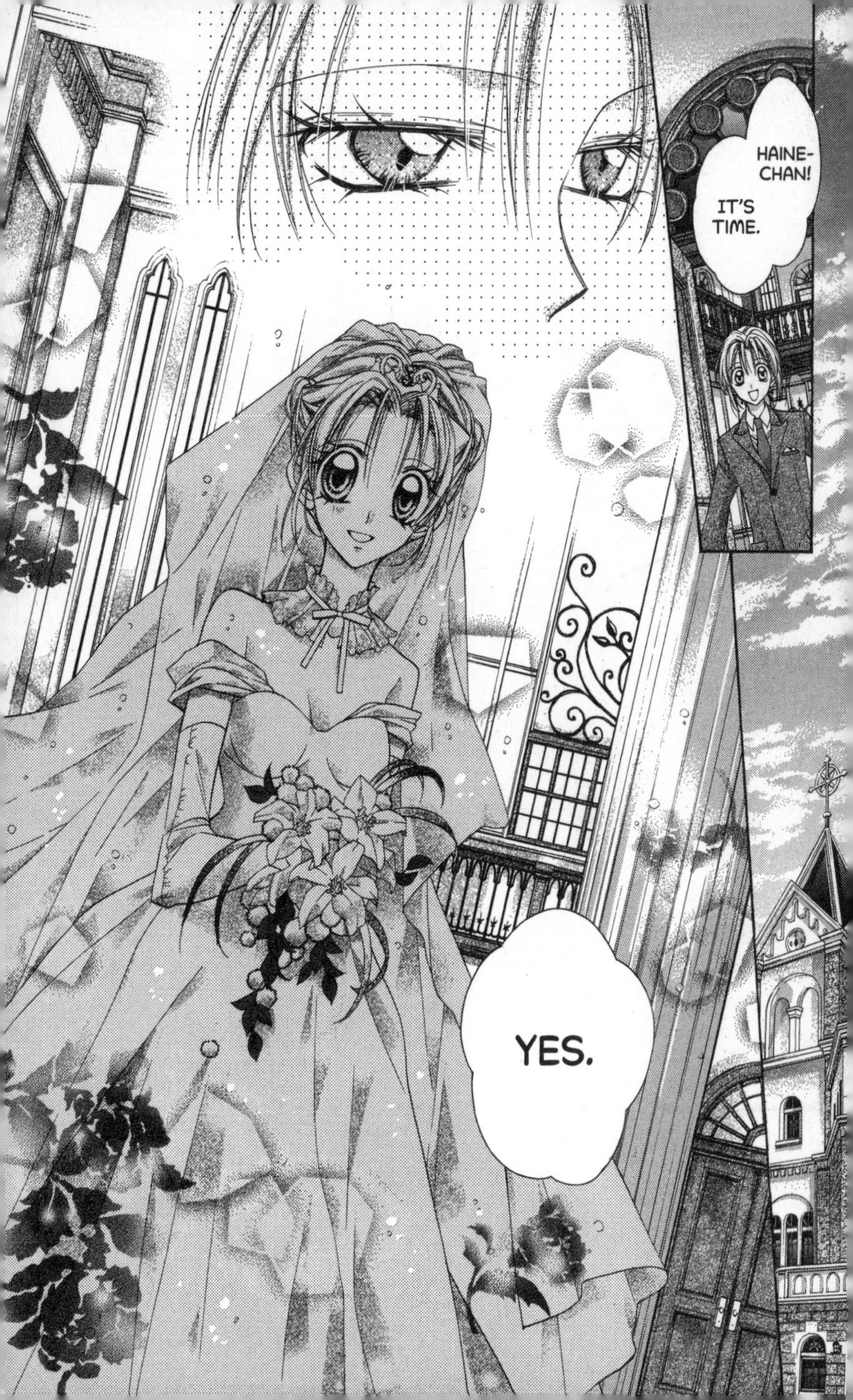
HAINE-CHAN!
IT'S TIME.
YES.

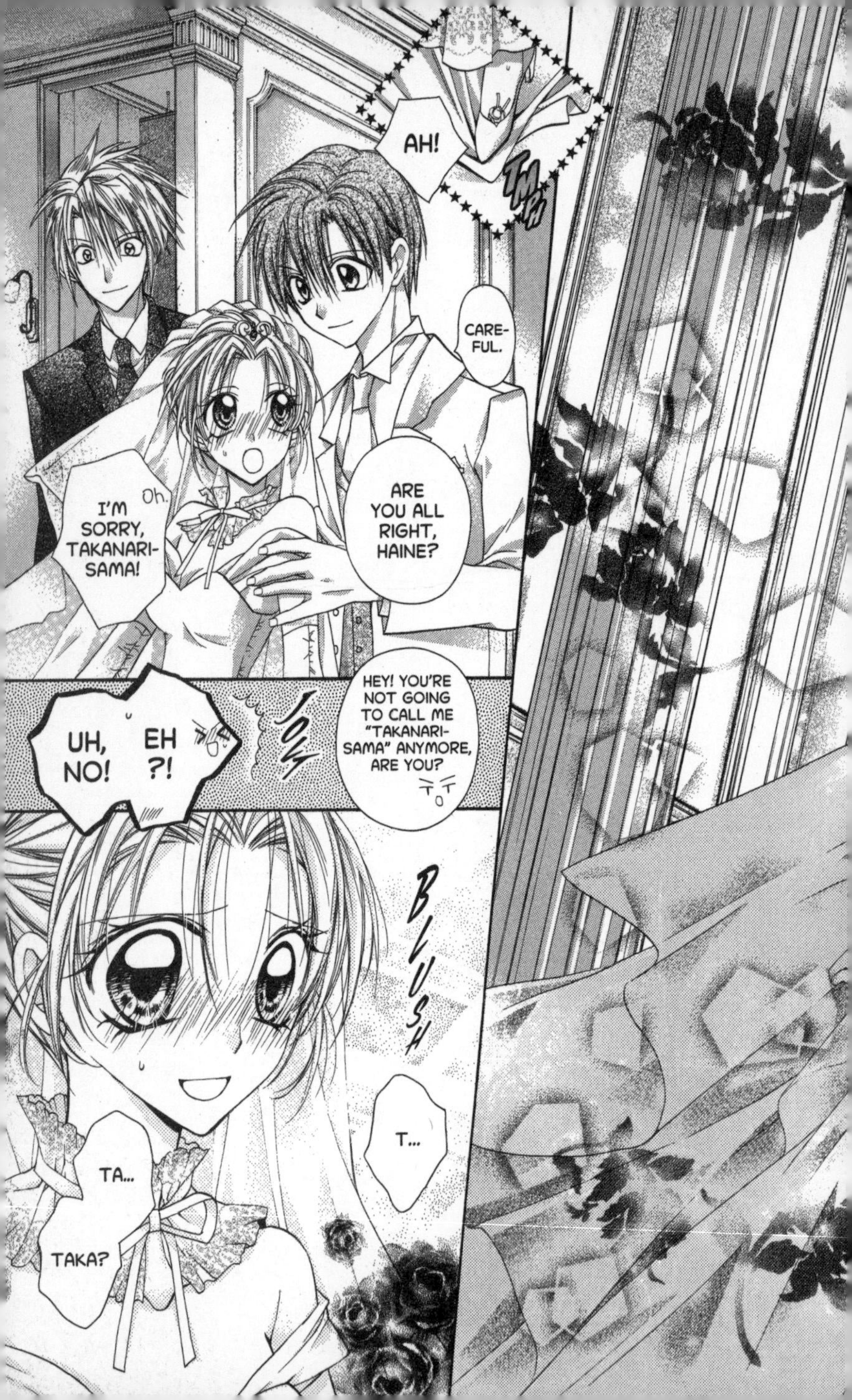
AH!
TMP
CARE-FUL.
ARE YOU ALL RIGHT, HAINE?
Oh.
I'M SORRY, TAKANARI-SAMA!
HEY! YOU'RE NOT GOING TO CALL ME "TAKANARI-SAMA" ANYMORE, ARE YOU?
JOLT
EH?!
UH, NO!
BLUSH
T...
TA...
TAKA?

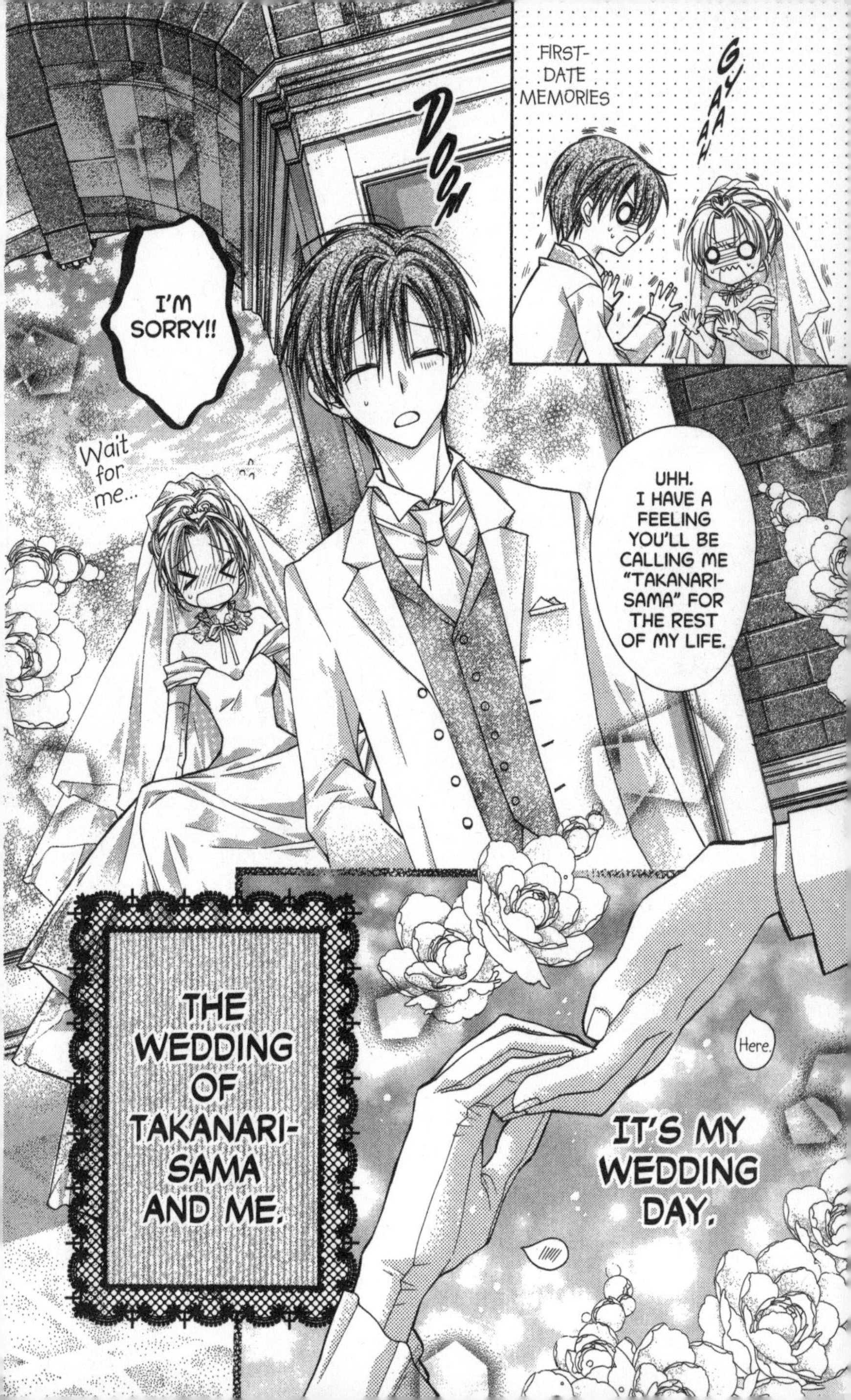
FIRST-DATE MEMORIES
GYAAAH
DOOM
I'M SORRY!!
UHH. I HAVE A FEELING YOU'LL BE CALLING ME "TAKANARI-SAMA" FOR THE REST OF MY LIFE.
Wait for me...
Here.
IT'S MY WEDDING DAY.
THE WEDDING OF TAKANARI-SAMA AND ME.

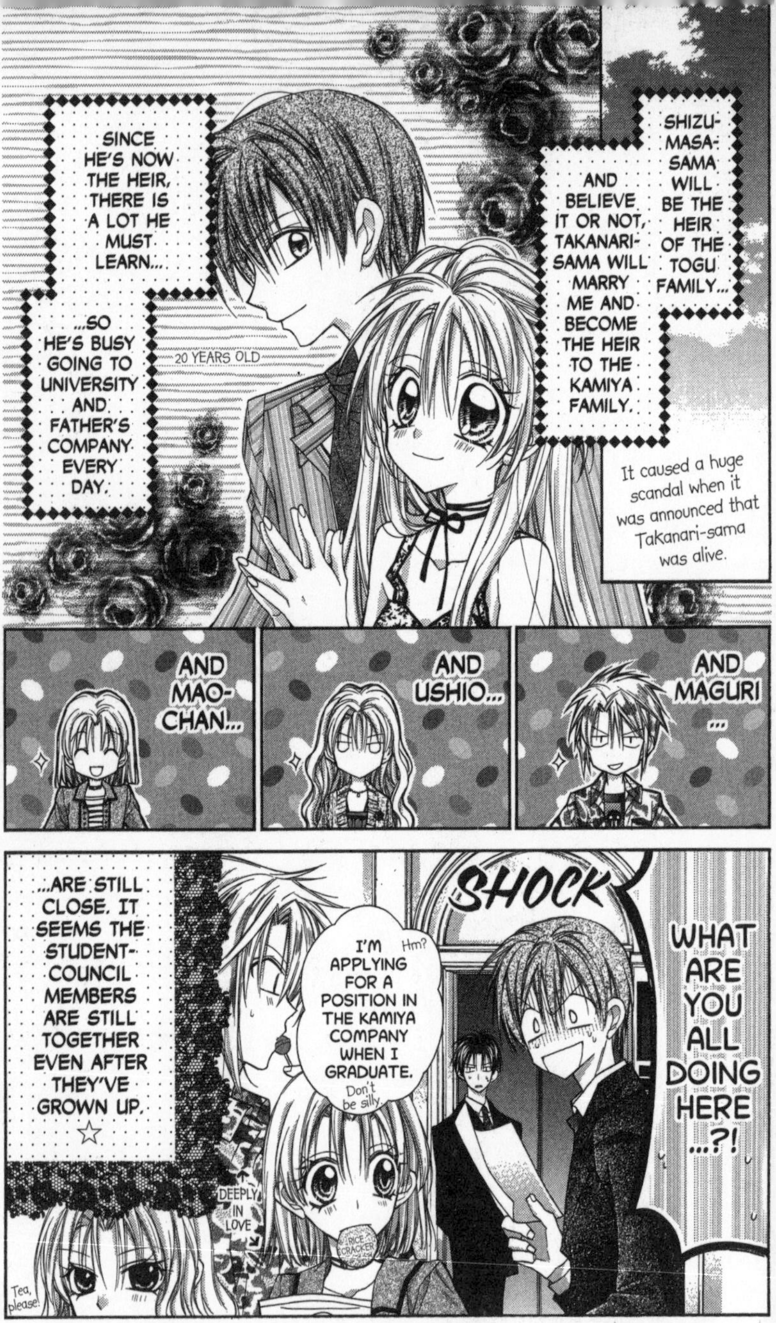
SHIZU-MASA-SAMA WILL BE THE HEIR OF THE TOGU FAMILY...
AND BELIEVE IT OR NOT, TAKANARI-SAMA WILL MARRY ME AND BECOME THE HEIR TO THE KAMIYA FAMILY.
It caused a huge scandal when it was announced that Takanari-sama was alive.
SINCE HE'S NOW THE HEIR, THERE IS A LOT HE MUST LEARN...
20 YEARS OLD
...SO HE'S BUSY GOING TO UNIVERSITY AND FATHER'S COMPANY EVERY DAY.
AND MAGURI...
AND USHIO...
AND MAO-CHAN...
SHOCK
WHAT ARE YOU ALL DOING HERE...?!
I'M APPLYING FOR A POSITION IN THE KAMIYA COMPANY WHEN I GRADUATE.
Hm?
Don't be silly.
...ARE STILL CLOSE. IT SEEMS THE STUDENT-COUNCIL MEMBERS ARE STILL TOGETHER EVEN AFTER THEY'VE GROWN UP. ☆
DEEPLY IN LOVE
RICE CRACKER
Tea, please!

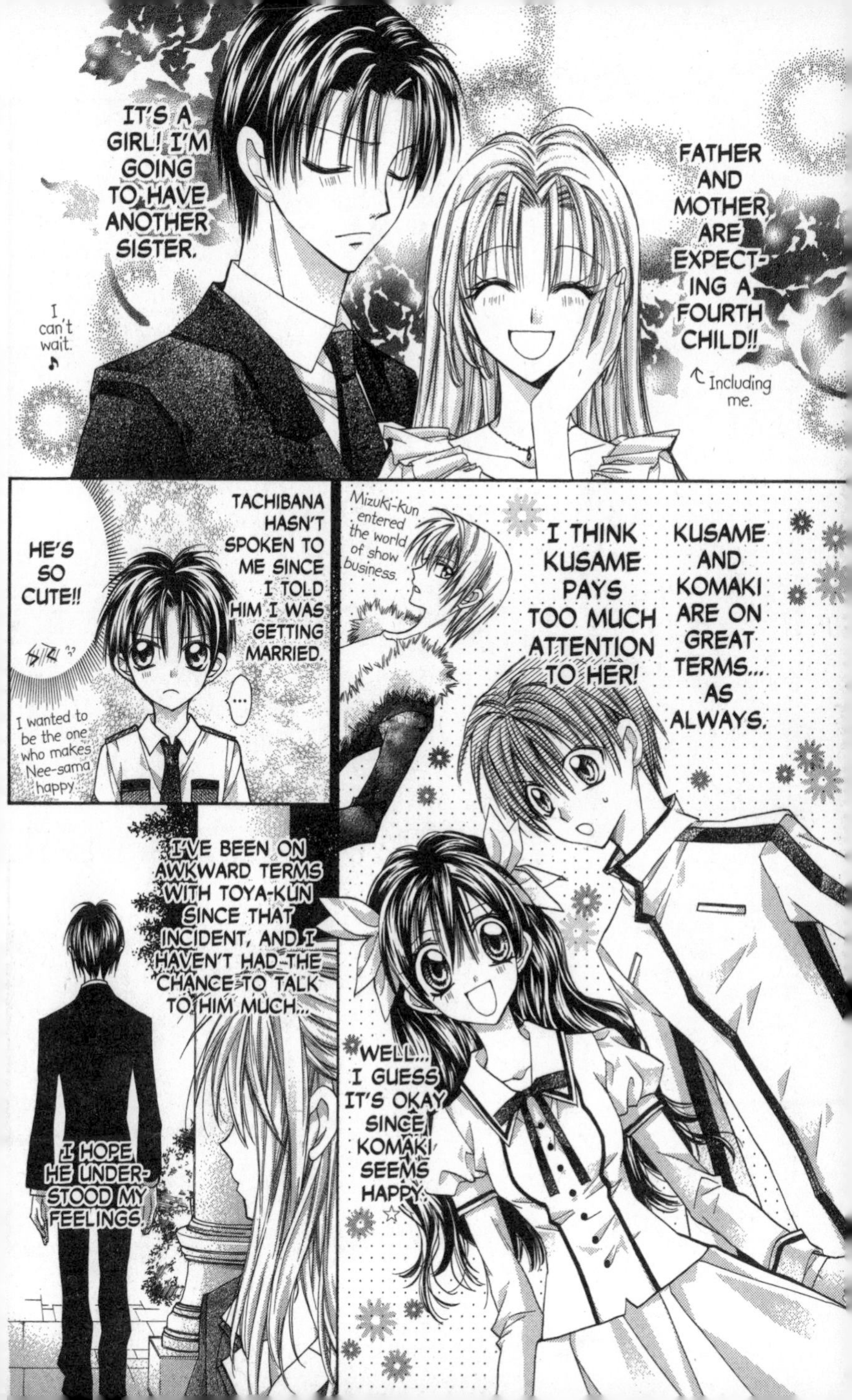
FATHER AND MOTHER ARE EXPECTING A FOURTH CHILD!!
Including me.
IT'S A GIRL! I'M GOING TO HAVE ANOTHER SISTER.
I can't wait. ♪
KUSAME AND KOMAKI ARE ON GREAT TERMS... AS ALWAYS.
I THINK KUSAME PAYS TOO MUCH ATTENTION TO HER!
Mizuki-kun entered the world of show business.
WELL... I GUESS IT'S OKAY SINCE KOMAKI SEEMS HAPPY. ☆
TACHIBANA HASN'T SPOKEN TO ME SINCE I TOLD HIM I WAS GETTING MARRIED.
HE'S SO CUTE!!
...
I wanted to be the one who makes Nee-sama happy.
I'VE BEEN ON AWKWARD TERMS WITH TOYA-KUN SINCE THAT INCIDENT, AND I HAVEN'T HAD THE CHANCE TO TALK TO HIM MUCH...
I HOPE HE UNDER-STOOD MY FEELINGS.

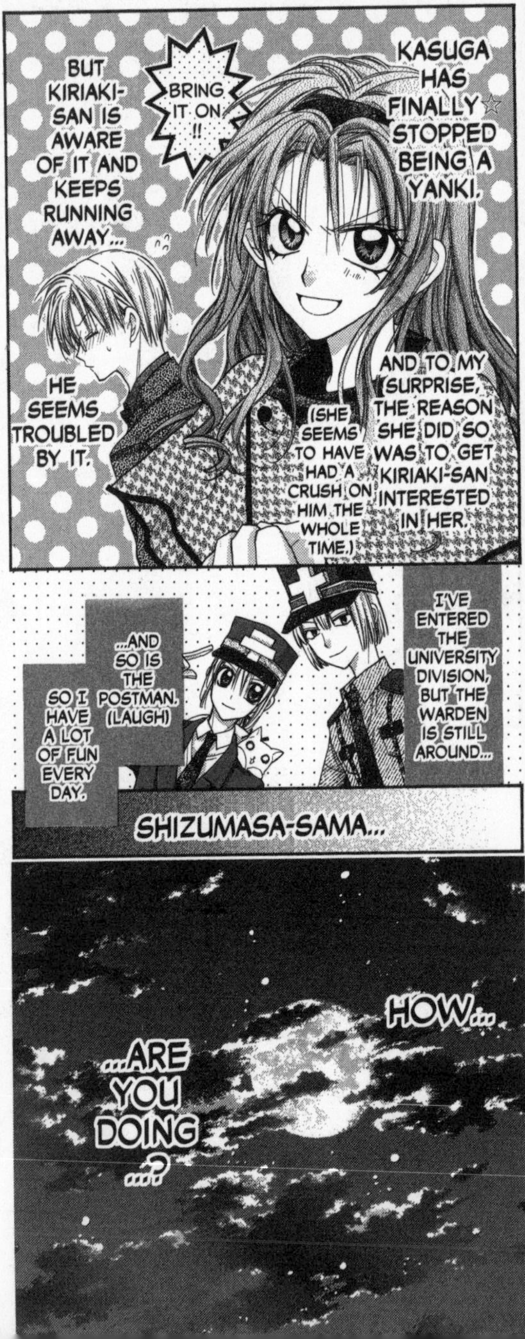
KASUGA HAS FINALLY☆ STOPPED BEING A YANKI.
BRING IT ON!!
BUT KIRIAKI-SAN IS AWARE OF IT AND KEEPS RUNNING AWAY...
AND TO MY SURPRISE, THE REASON SHE DID SO WAS TO GET KIRIAKI-SAN INTERESTED IN HER.
(SHE SEEMS TO HAVE HAD A CRUSH ON HIM THE WHOLE TIME.)
HE SEEMS TROUBLED BY IT.
I'VE ENTERED THE UNIVERSITY DIVISION, BUT THE WARDEN IS STILL AROUND...
...AND SO IS THE POSTMAN. (LAUGH)
SO I HAVE A LOT OF FUN EVERY DAY.
SHIZUMASA-SAMA...
HOW...
...ARE YOU DOING ...?

My Thoughts on *Gentlemen's Alliance*
②

I've always wanted to draw twins, but actually drawing them was different from what I had thought it would be. I wanted to make them more sociable with each other, but they were on uneasy terms till the very end.

At the beginning of the series, I used similar screentones for Takanari's and Shizumasa's hair since I didn't want people to realize that they had switched. And when I announced that they were two different people, I gradually made Shizumasa's hair whiter so the readers could easily distinguish between the two.

But there were about five stages of change, and that was partly for my self-satisfaction, so I was expecting most of the readers not to notice it.

I was wrong to assume that! The readers had all quickly caught on! ◎◎
The affection of the fans is really amazing, isn't it?
I take my hat off to you.

As for me, I would want Takanari to be my lover while I'd rather have Shizumasa as my son.

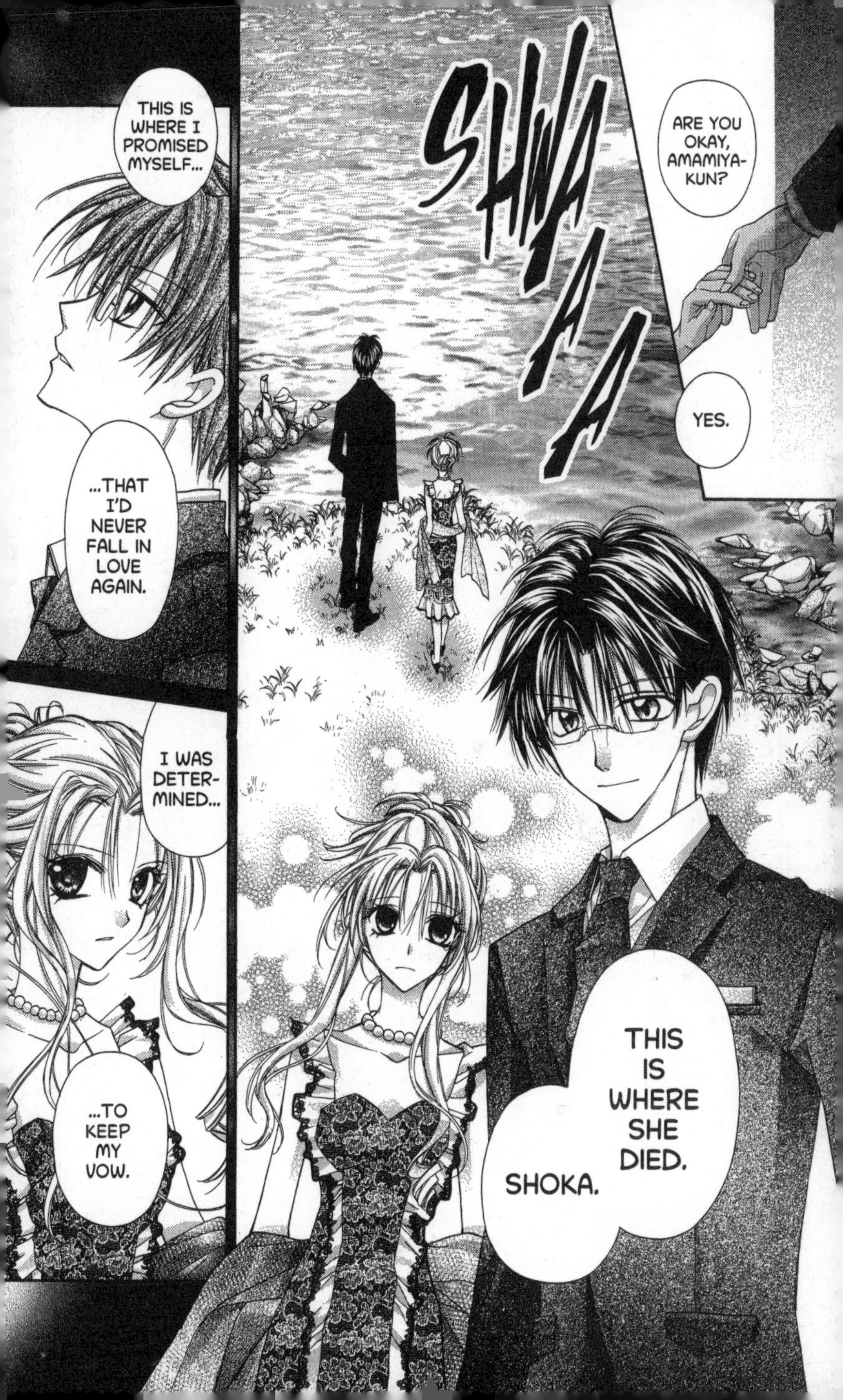
ARE YOU OKAY, AMAMIYA-KUN?
YES.
SHWAAA
THIS IS WHERE SHE DIED.
SHOKA.
THIS IS WHERE I PROMISED MYSELF...
...THAT I'D NEVER FALL IN LOVE AGAIN.
I WAS DETERMINED...
...TO KEEP MY VOW.

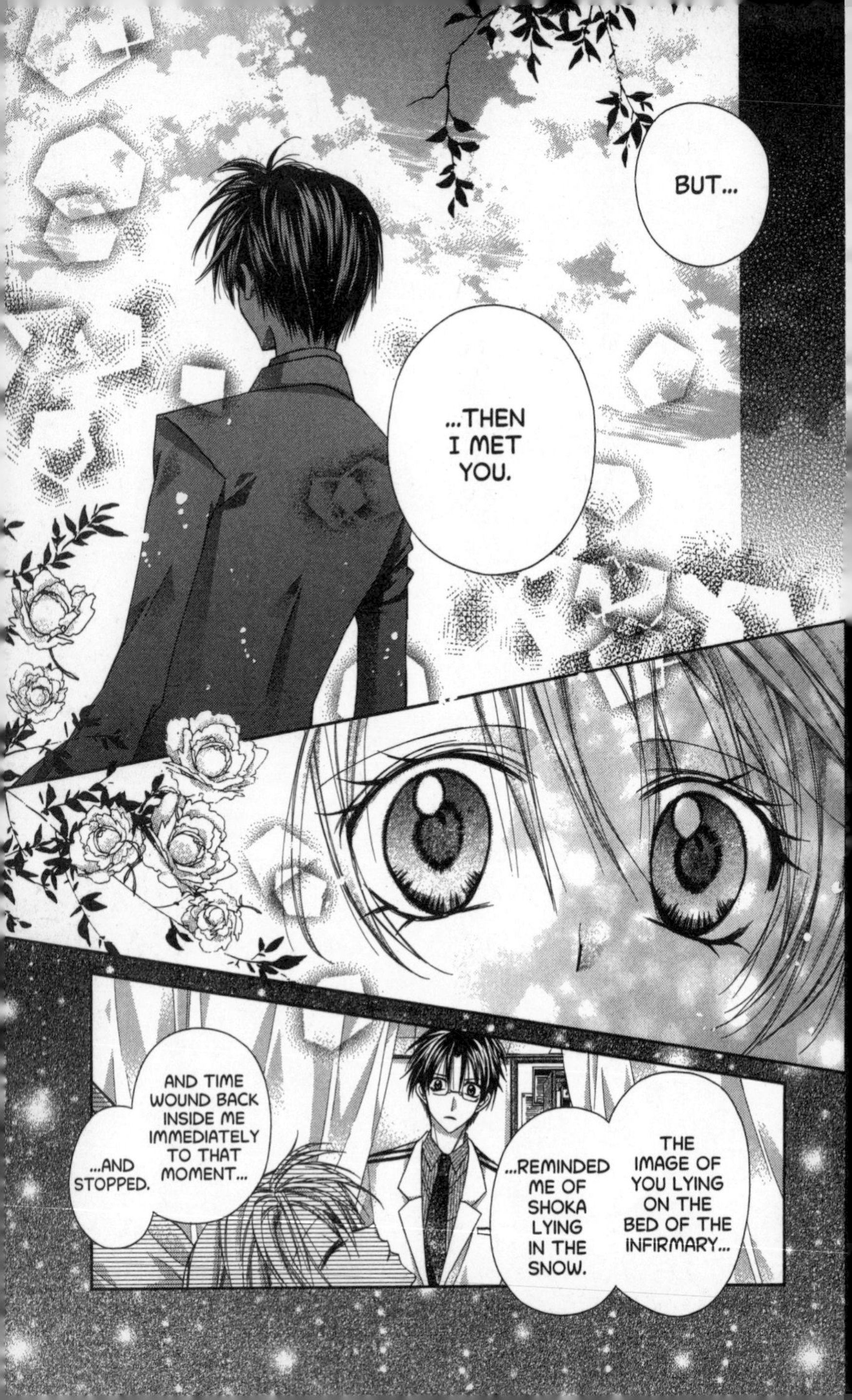
BUT...
...THEN I MET YOU.
THE IMAGE OF YOU LYING ON THE BED OF THE INFIRMARY...
...REMINDED ME OF SHOKA LYING IN THE SNOW.
AND TIME WOUND BACK INSIDE ME IMMEDIATELY TO THAT MOMENT...
...AND STOPPED.

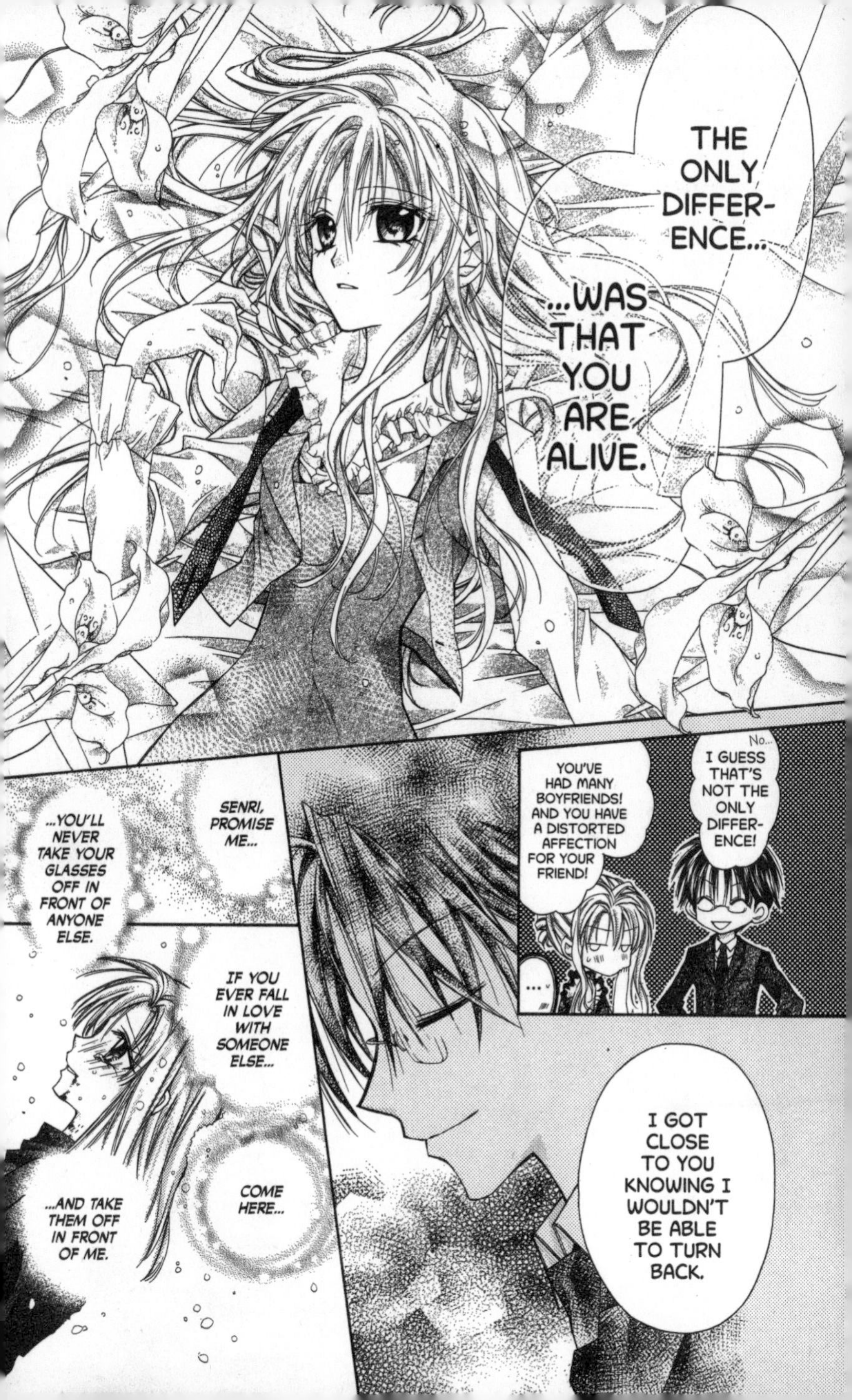
THE ONLY DIFFERENCE...
...WAS THAT YOU ARE ALIVE.
No... I GUESS THAT'S NOT THE ONLY DIFFERENCE!
YOU'VE HAD MANY BOYFRIENDS! AND YOU HAVE A DISTORTED AFFECTION FOR YOUR FRIEND!
...
I GOT CLOSE TO YOU KNOWING I WOULDN'T BE ABLE TO TURN BACK.
SENRI, PROMISE ME...
...YOU'LL NEVER TAKE YOUR GLASSES OFF IN FRONT OF ANYONE ELSE.
IF YOU EVER FALL IN LOVE WITH SOMEONE ELSE...
COME HERE...
...AND TAKE THEM OFF IN FRONT OF ME.

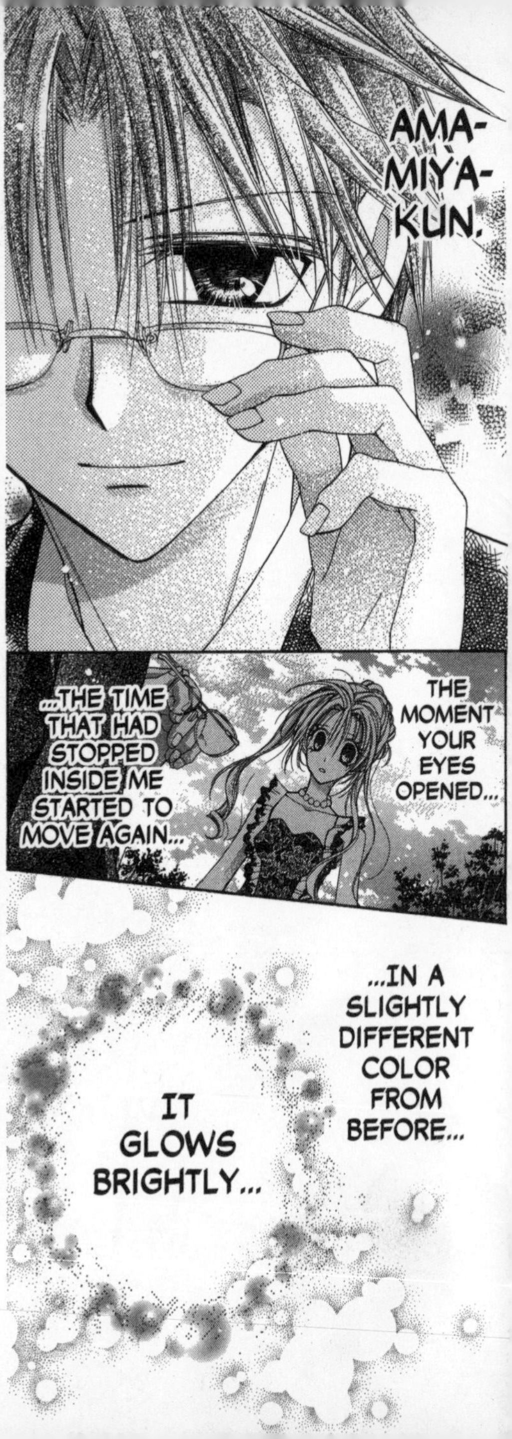
AMA-MIYA-KUN.
THE MOMENT YOUR EYES OPENED...
...THE TIME THAT HAD STOPPED INSIDE ME STARTED TO MOVE AGAIN...
...IN A SLIGHTLY DIFFERENT COLOR FROM BEFORE...
IT GLOWS BRIGHTLY...

My Thoughts on
*Gentlemen's Alliance*

I wanted to have many characters appear in the story! So even before I thought about the story, I drew up a whole series of characters to try my luck(?) for this series.

The toughest part was their names. There are close to 40 characters, so it really was a headache... I knew what their first names would be as I designed them, but their surnames...
So I decided to use the character "宮" for all of their surnames! It was mostly read as "miya," but for the characters I had special feelings for, I gave it a different reading, like Togu (東宮) and Rikyu (離宮).

There really wasn't a specific reason as to why I had so many characters appear in it.

Whenever I start a new series, I usually try to do something that *Ribon* doesn't have at that point. Well, most of the time.

So I'm sure the next series will follow that too...

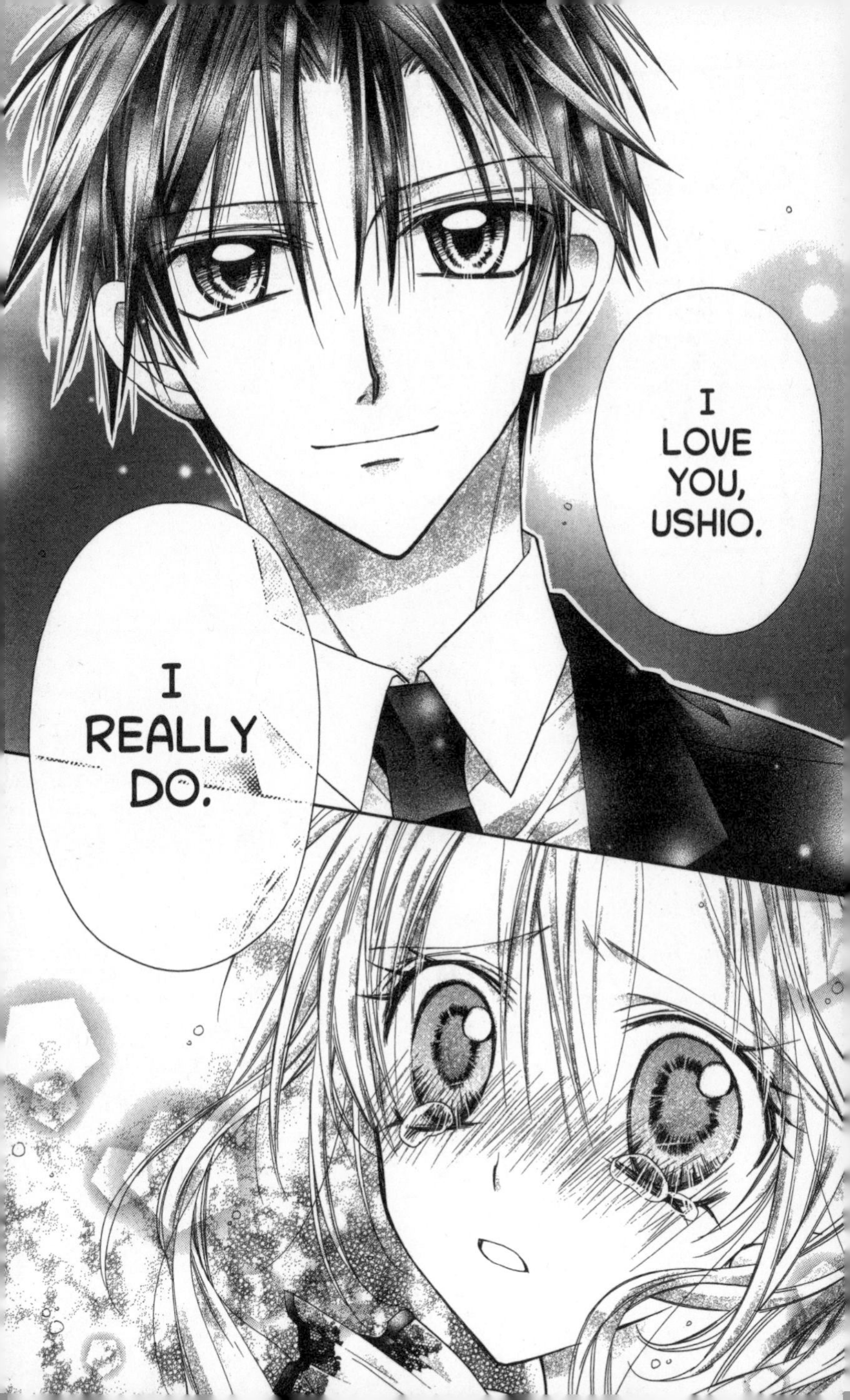
I LOVE YOU, USHIO.
I REALLY DO.

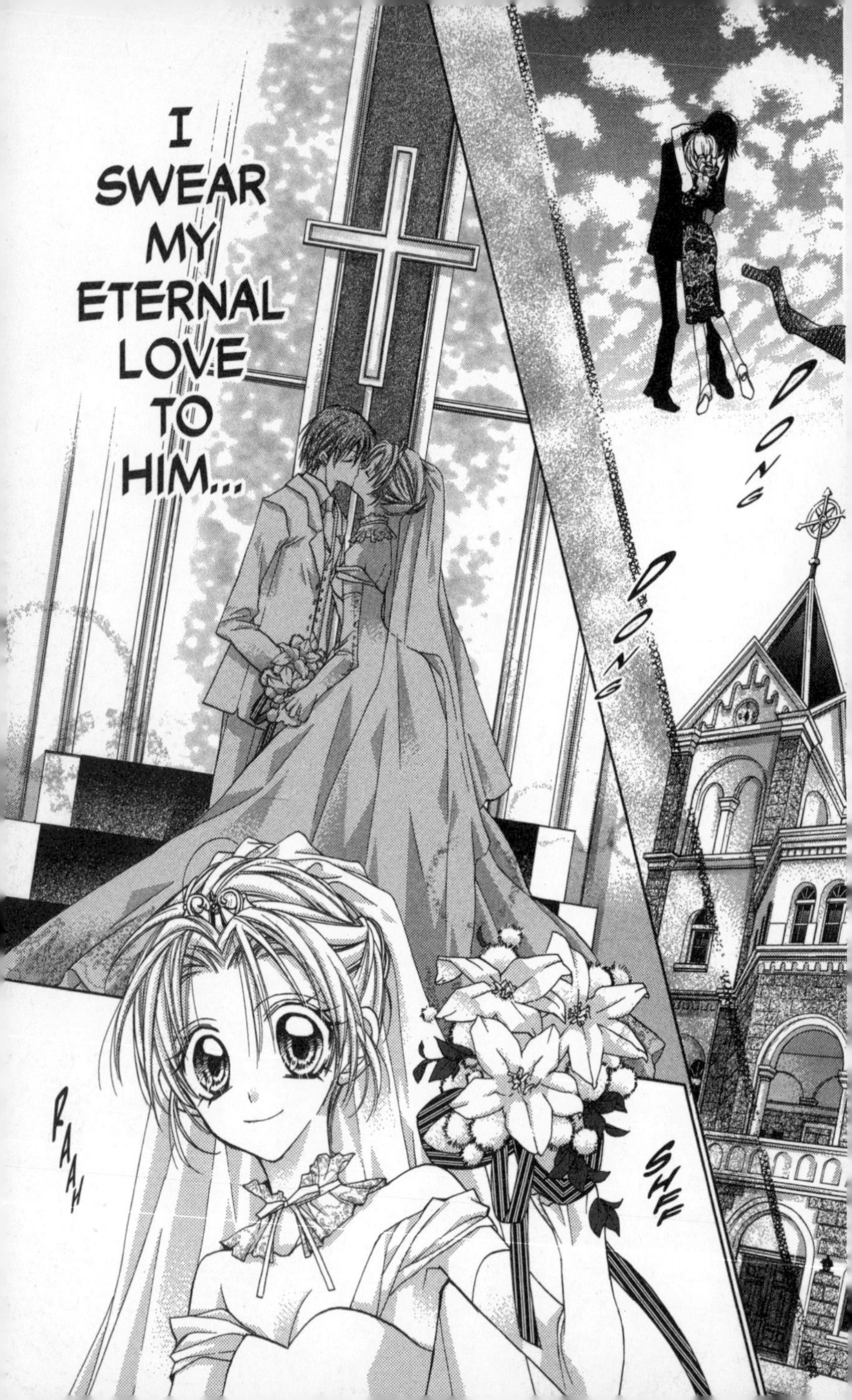
DOONG
DOONG
I SWEAR MY ETERNAL LOVE TO HIM...
SHFF
RAAH

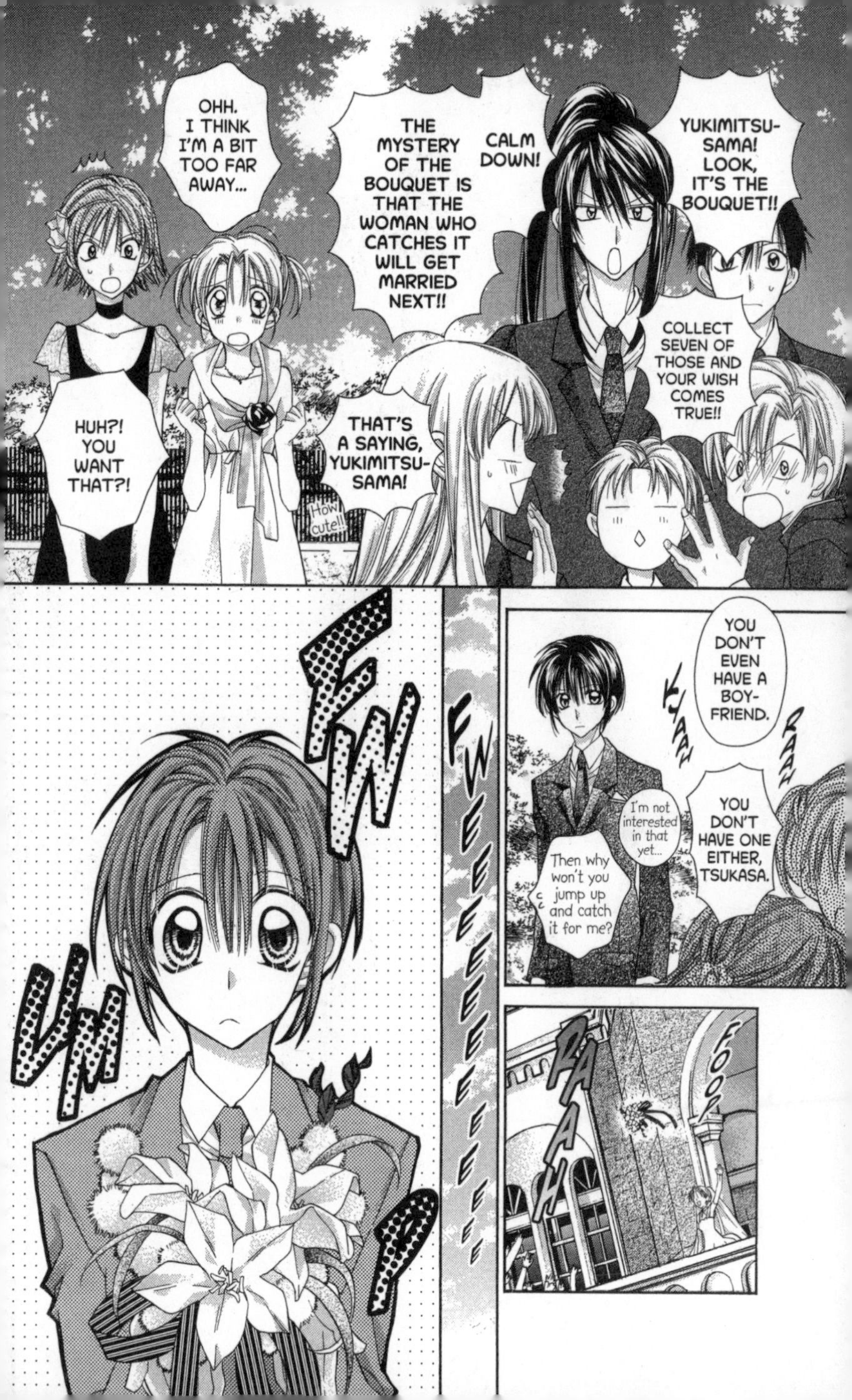
YUKIMITSU-SAMA! LOOK, IT'S THE BOUQUET!!
CALM DOWN!
THE MYSTERY OF THE BOUQUET IS THAT THE WOMAN WHO CATCHES IT WILL GET MARRIED NEXT!!
COLLECT SEVEN OF THOSE AND YOUR WISH COMES TRUE!!
OHH. I THINK I'M A BIT TOO FAR AWAY...
THAT'S A SAYING, YUKIMITSU-SAMA!
How cute!!
HUH?! YOU WANT THAT?!
YOU DON'T EVEN HAVE A BOY-FRIEND.
KYAAH
RAAAH
YOU DON'T HAVE ONE EITHER, TSUKASA.
I'm not interested in that yet...
Then why won't you jump up and catch it for me?
FOOP
RAAAH
FWEEEEEEEEEEEE
FWUMP

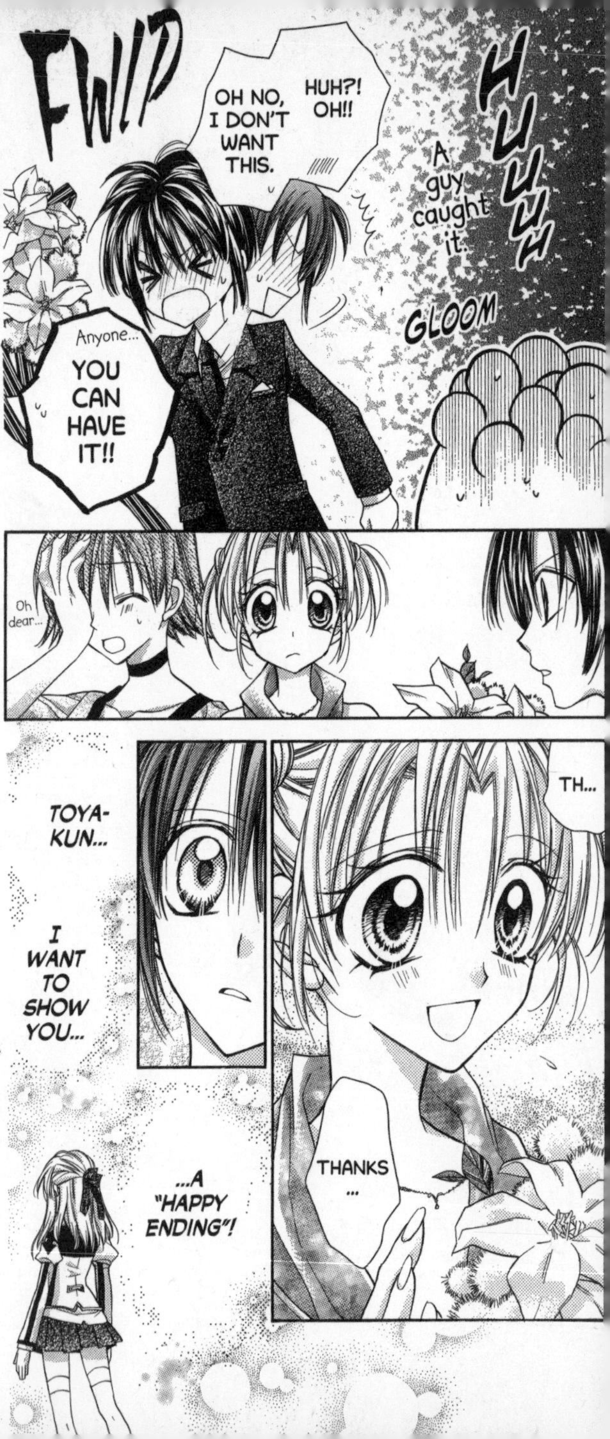
HUUUH
A guy caught it.
GLOOM
HUH?! OH!!
OH NO, I DON'T WANT THIS.
FWIP
Anyone... YOU CAN HAVE IT!!
Oh dear...
TH...
THANKS...
TOYA-KUN...
I WANT TO SHOW YOU...
...A "HAPPY ENDING"!
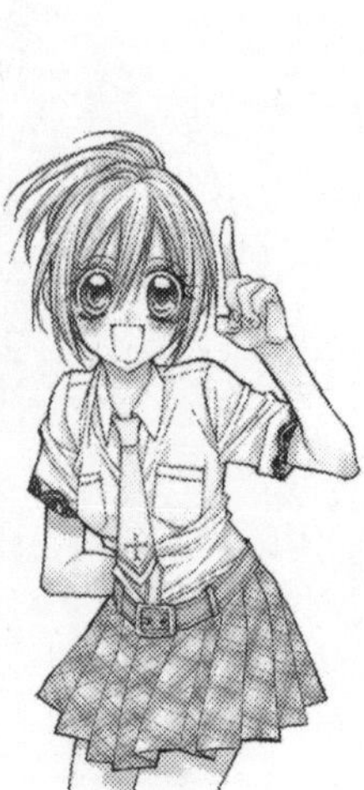

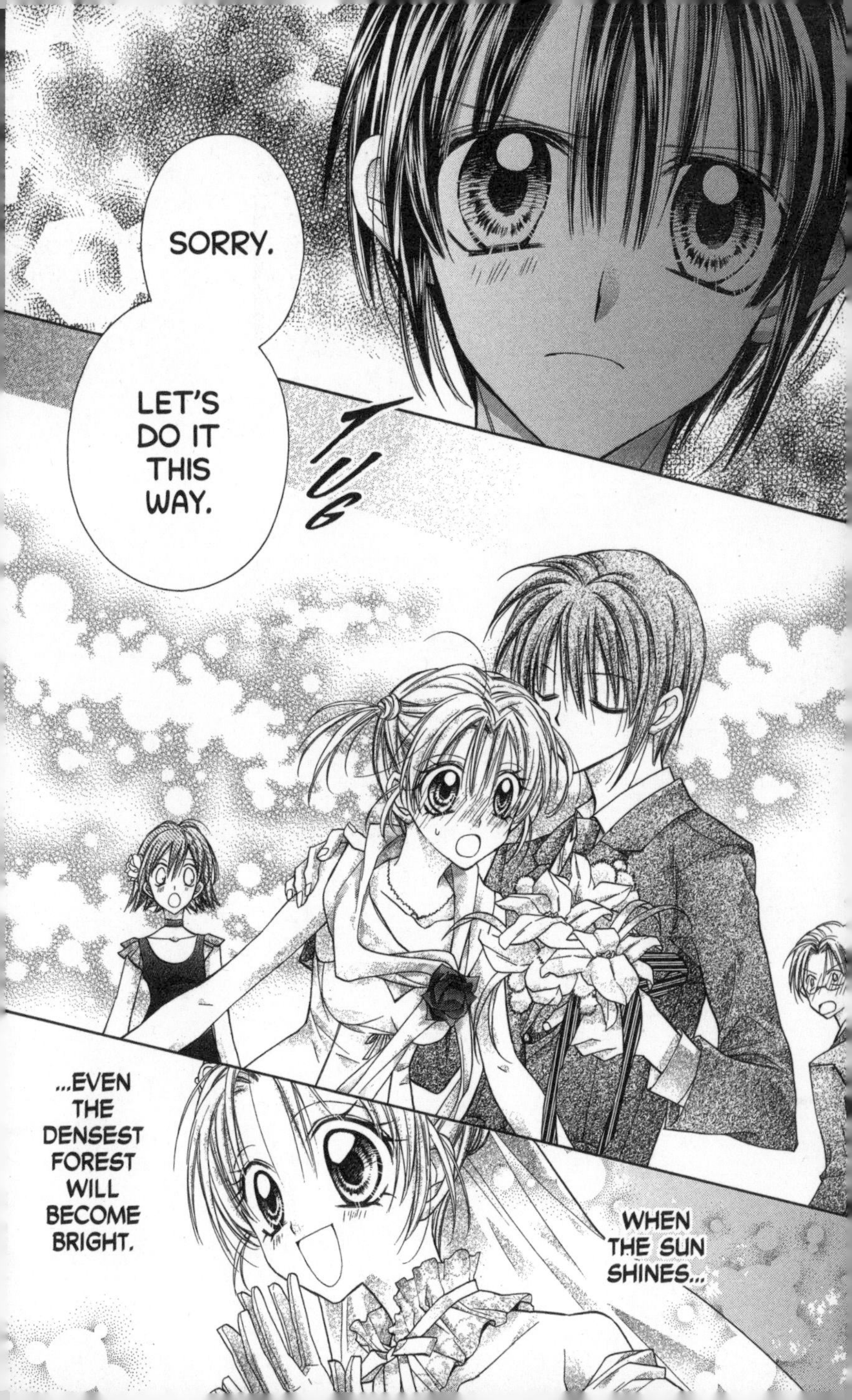
SORRY.
LET'S DO IT THIS WAY.
TUG
WHEN THE SUN SHINES...
...EVEN THE DENSEST FOREST WILL BECOME BRIGHT.

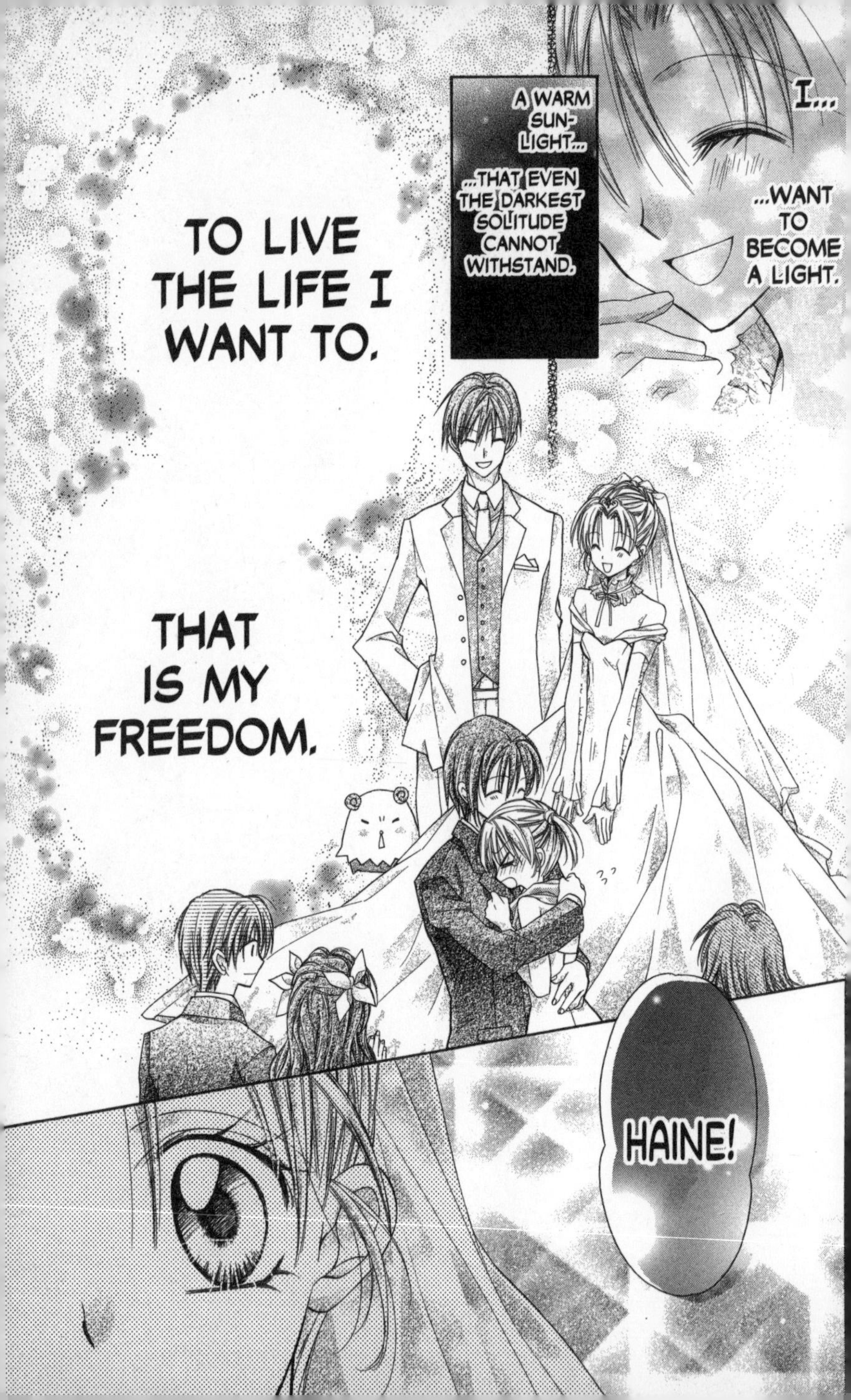
I...
...WANT TO BECOME A LIGHT.
A WARM SUN-LIGHT...
...THAT EVEN THE DARKEST SOLITUDE CANNOT WITHSTAND.
TO LIVE THE LIFE I WANT TO.
THAT IS MY FREEDOM.
HAINE!

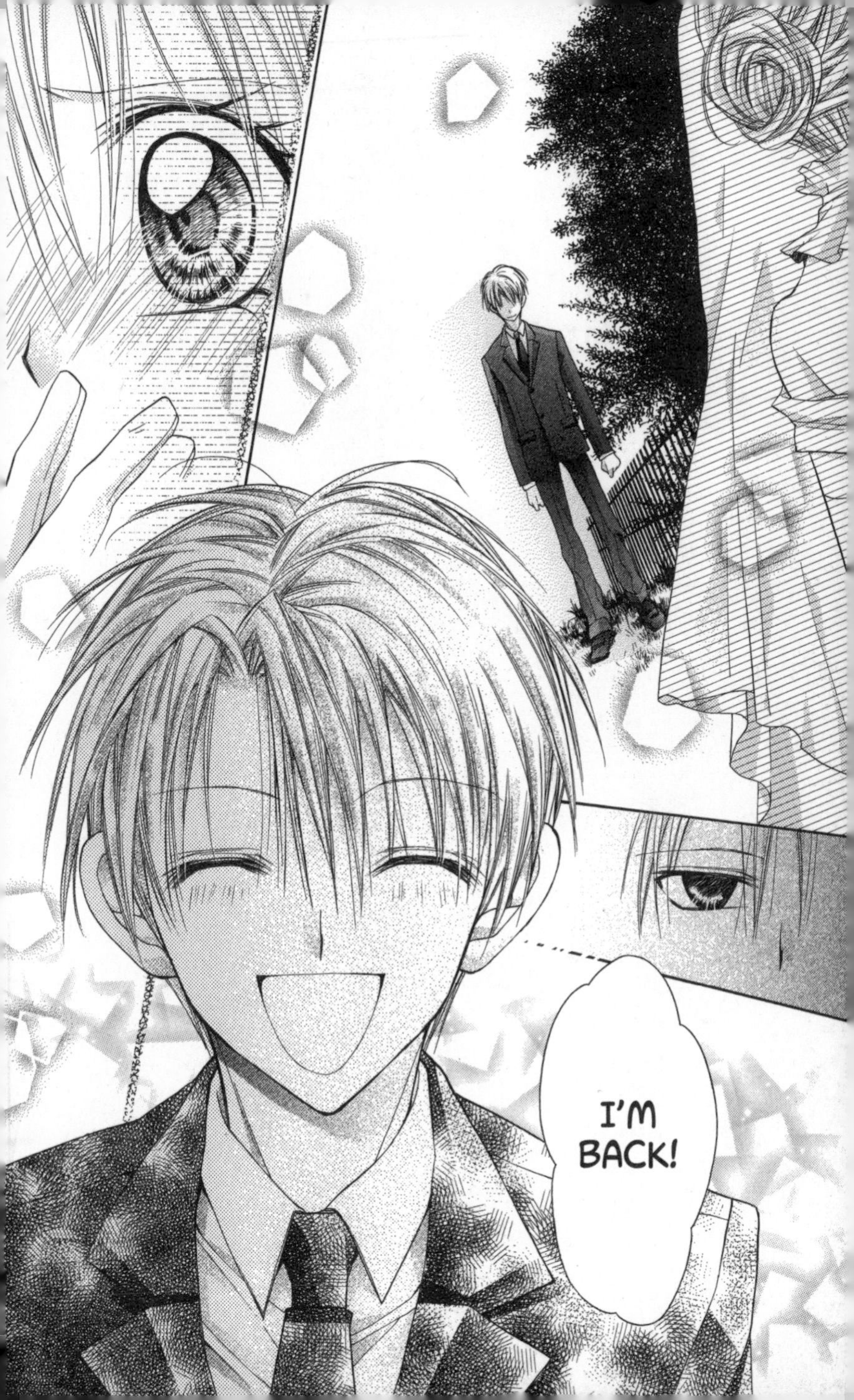
I'M BACK!

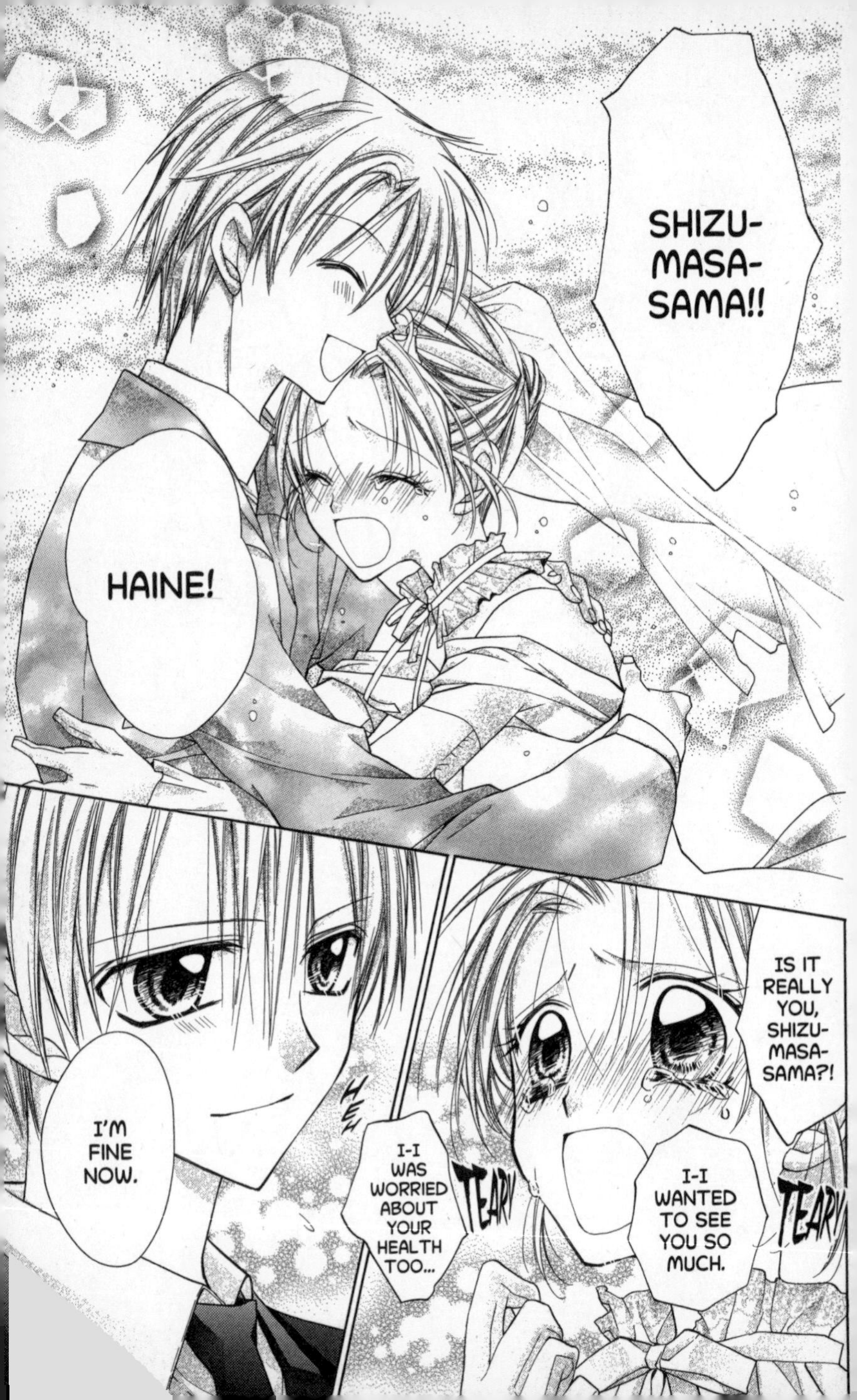
SHIZU-MASA-SAMA!!
HAINE!
IS IT REALLY YOU, SHIZU-MASA-SAMA?!
TEARY
I-I WANTED TO SEE YOU SO MUCH.
TEARY
I-I WAS WORRIED ABOUT YOUR HEALTH TOO...
HEH
I'M FINE NOW.

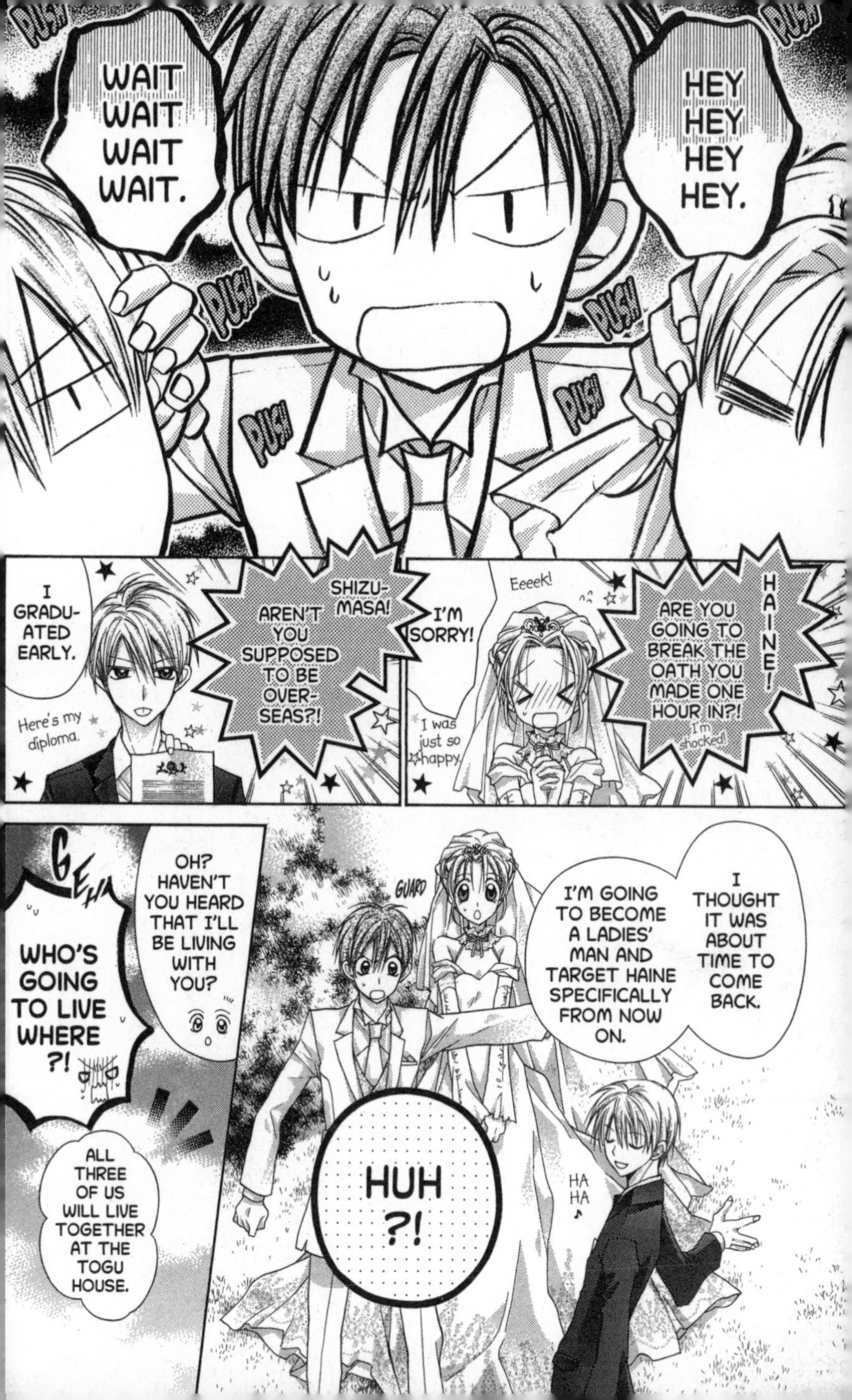

PUSH
HEY HEY HEY HEY.
PUSH
PUSH
PUSH
PUSH
WAIT WAIT WAIT WAIT.
PUSH
HAINE!
ARE YOU GOING TO BREAK THE OATH YOU MADE ONE HOUR IN?!
I'm shocked!
Eeeek!
I'M SORRY!
I was just so happy.
SHIZU-MASA!
AREN'T YOU SUPPOSED TO BE OVER-SEAS?!
I GRADU-ATED EARLY.
Here's my diploma.
I THOUGHT IT WAS ABOUT TIME TO COME BACK.
I'M GOING TO BECOME A LADIES' MAN AND TARGET HAINE SPECIFICALLY FROM NOW ON.
GUARD
OH? HAVEN'T YOU HEARD THAT I'LL BE LIVING WITH YOU?
GEH
WHO'S GOING TO LIVE WHERE?!
HA HA
HUH?!
ALL THREE OF US WILL LIVE TOGETHER AT THE TOGU HOUSE.

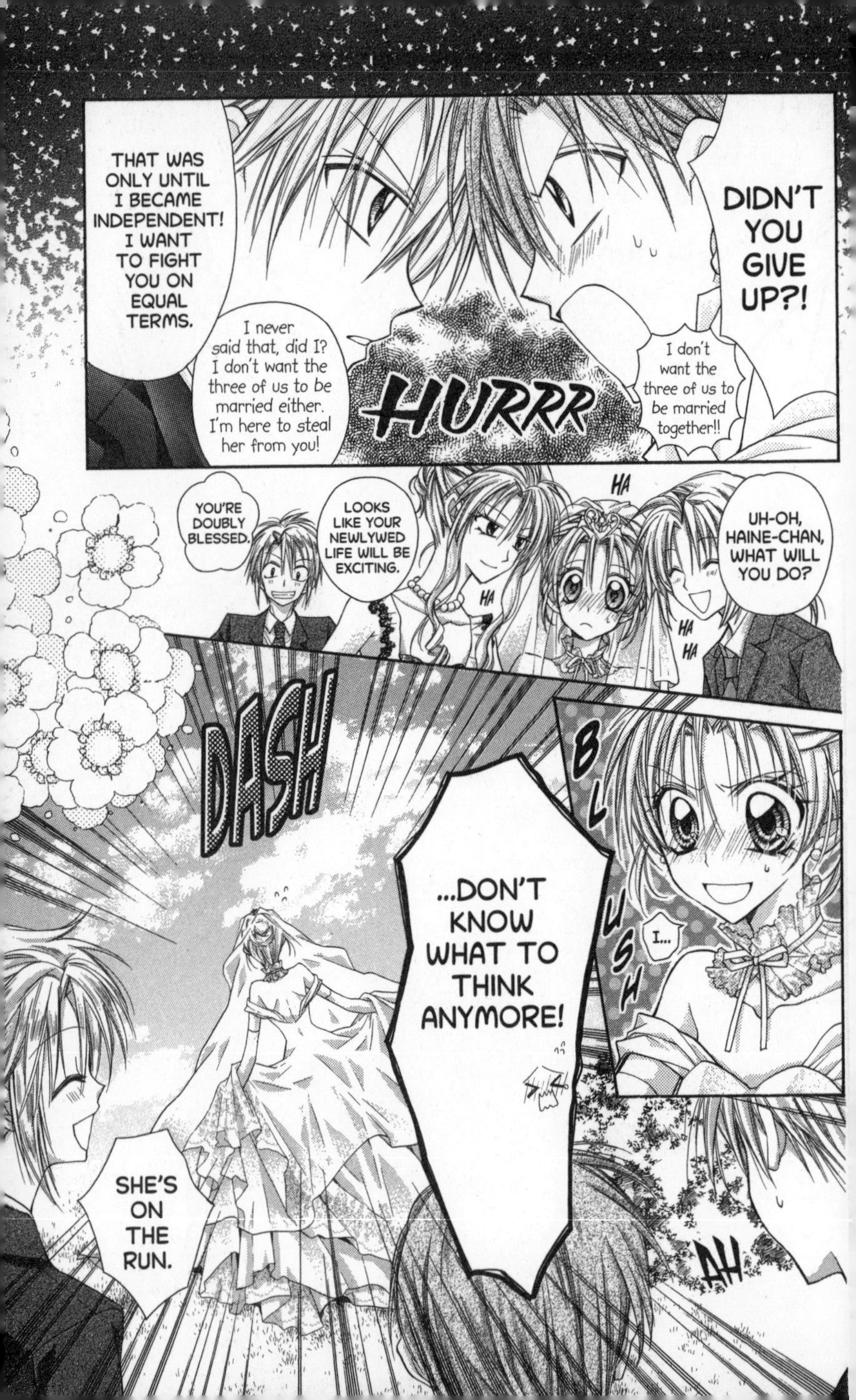
DIDN'T YOU GIVE UP?!
I don't want the three of us to be married together!!
HURRR
THAT WAS ONLY UNTIL I BECAME INDEPENDENT! I WANT TO FIGHT YOU ON EQUAL TERMS.
I never said that, did I? I don't want the three of us to be married either. I'm here to steal her from you!
UH-OH, HAINE-CHAN, WHAT WILL YOU DO?
HA
HA
HA
HA
LOOKS LIKE YOUR NEWLYWED LIFE WILL BE EXCITING.
YOU'RE DOUBLY BLESSED.
BLUSH
I...
...DON'T KNOW WHAT TO THINK ANYMORE!
DASH
AH
SHE'S ON THE RUN.

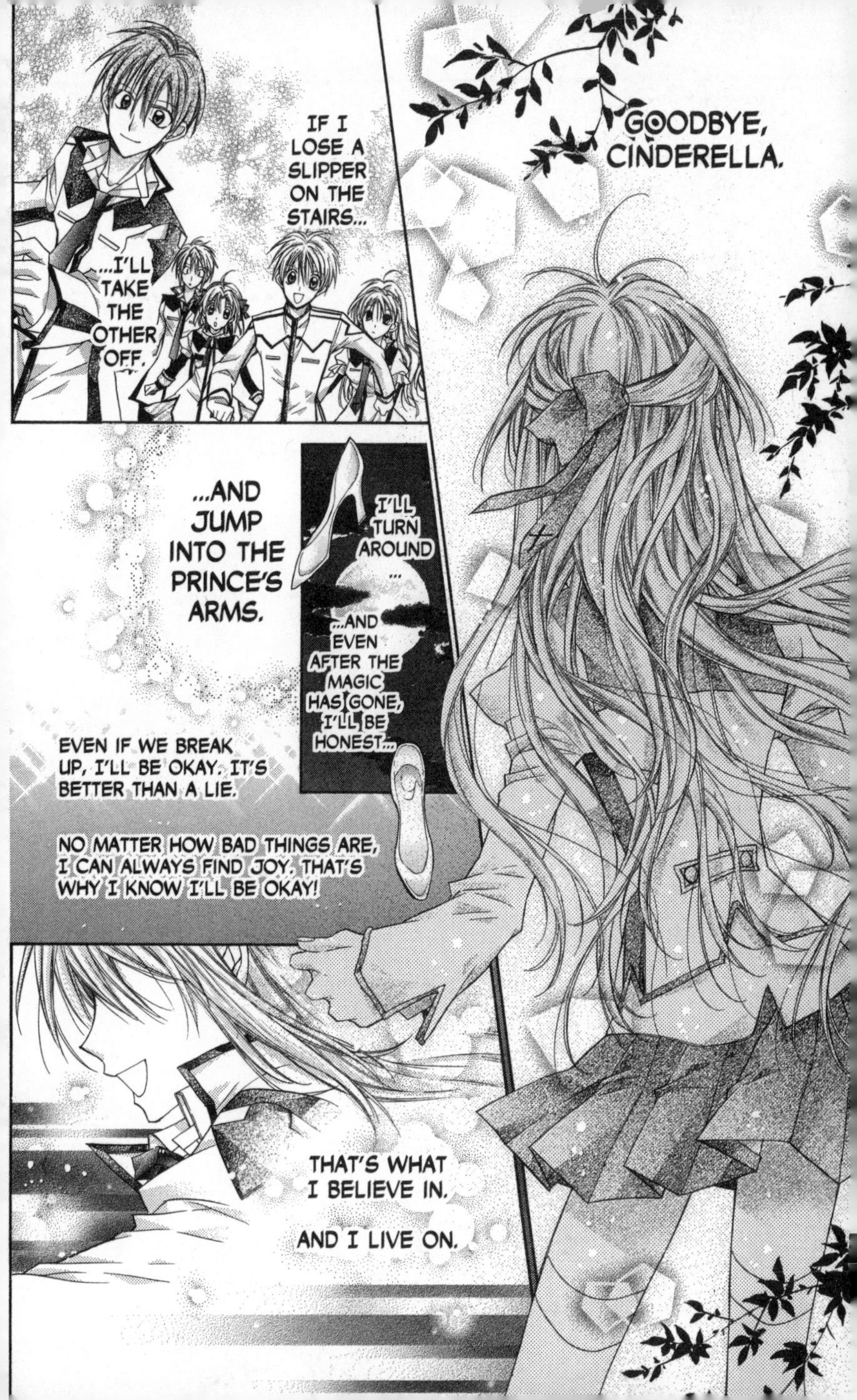
GOODBYE, CINDERELLA.
IF I LOSE A SLIPPER ON THE STAIRS...
...I'LL TAKE THE OTHER OFF.
...AND JUMP INTO THE PRINCE'S ARMS.
I'LL TURN AROUND...
...AND EVEN AFTER THE MAGIC HAS GONE, I'LL BE HONEST...
EVEN IF WE BREAK UP, I'LL BE OKAY. IT'S BETTER THAN A LIE.
NO MATTER HOW BAD THINGS ARE, I CAN ALWAYS FIND JOY. THAT'S WHY I KNOW I'LL BE OKAY!
THAT'S WHAT I BELIEVE IN.
AND I LIVE ON.

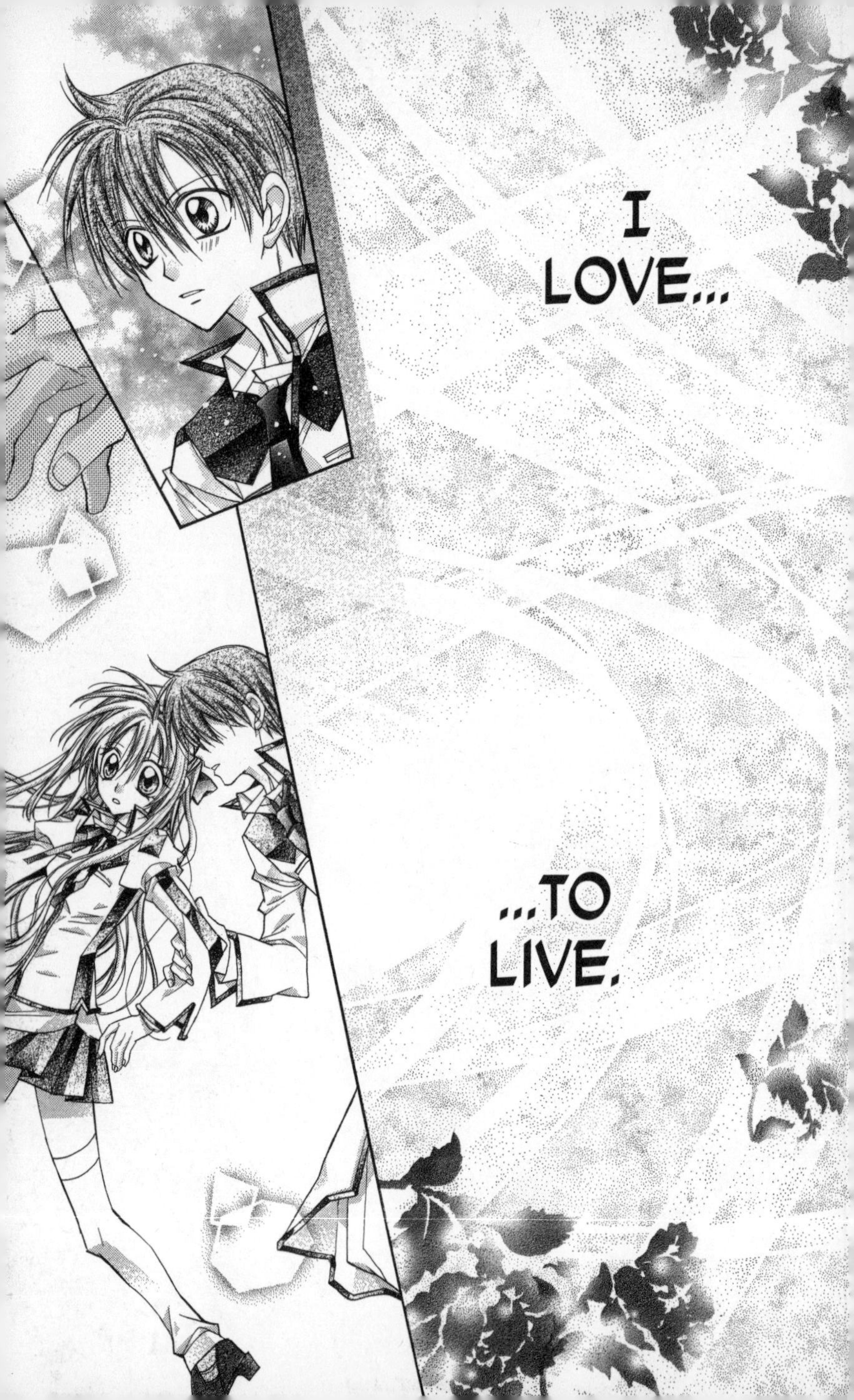
I LOVE...
...TO LIVE.

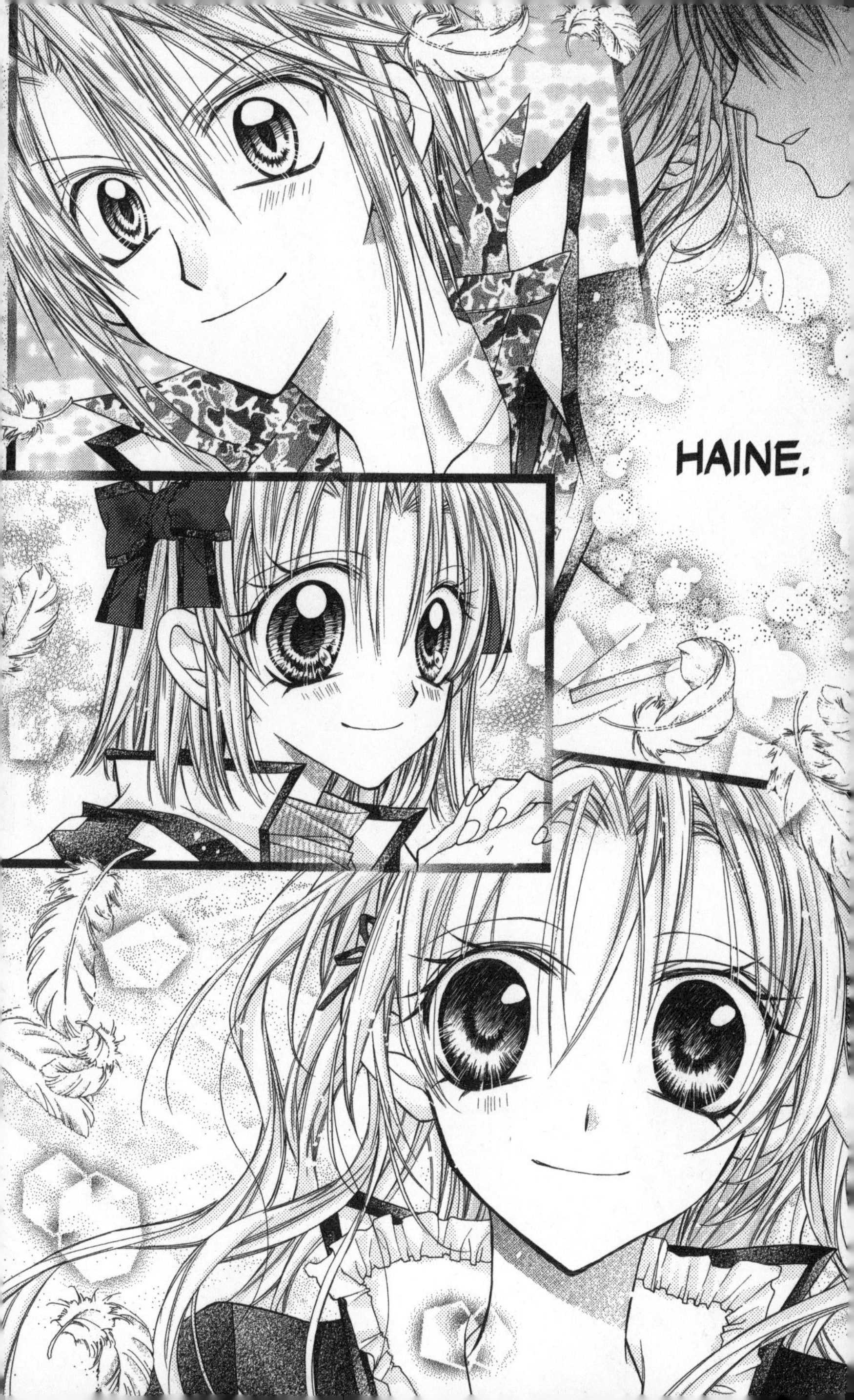
HAINE.

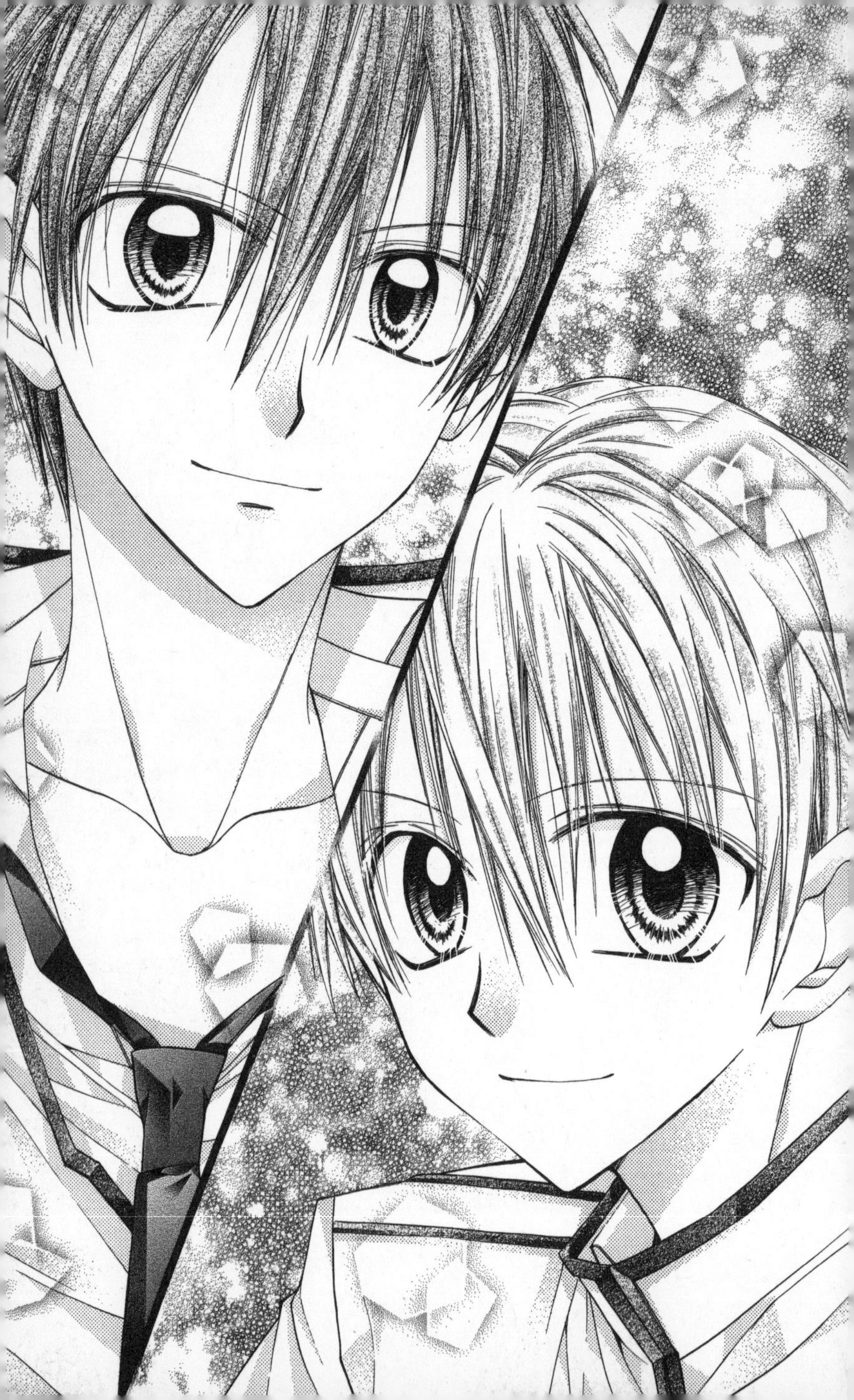

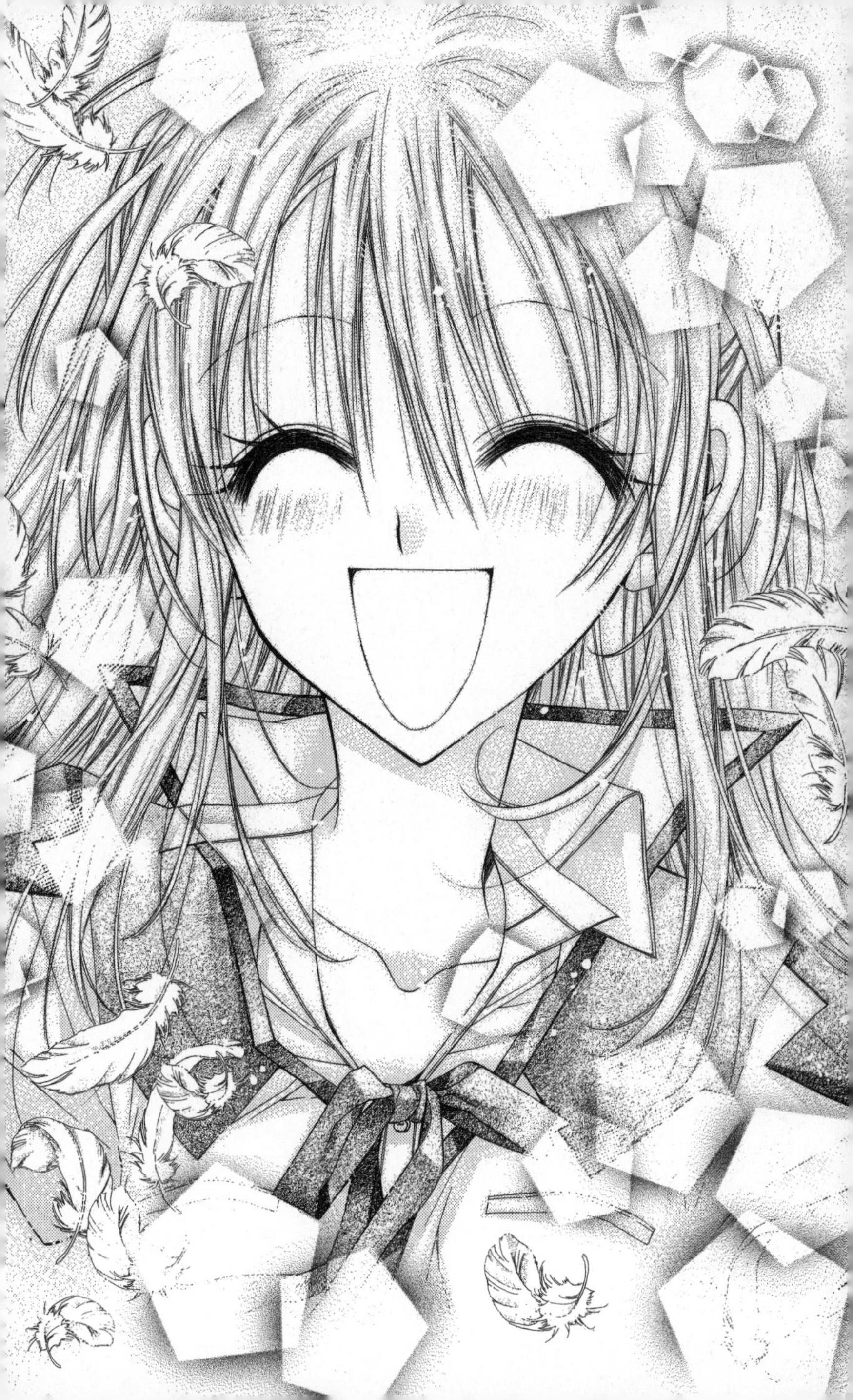

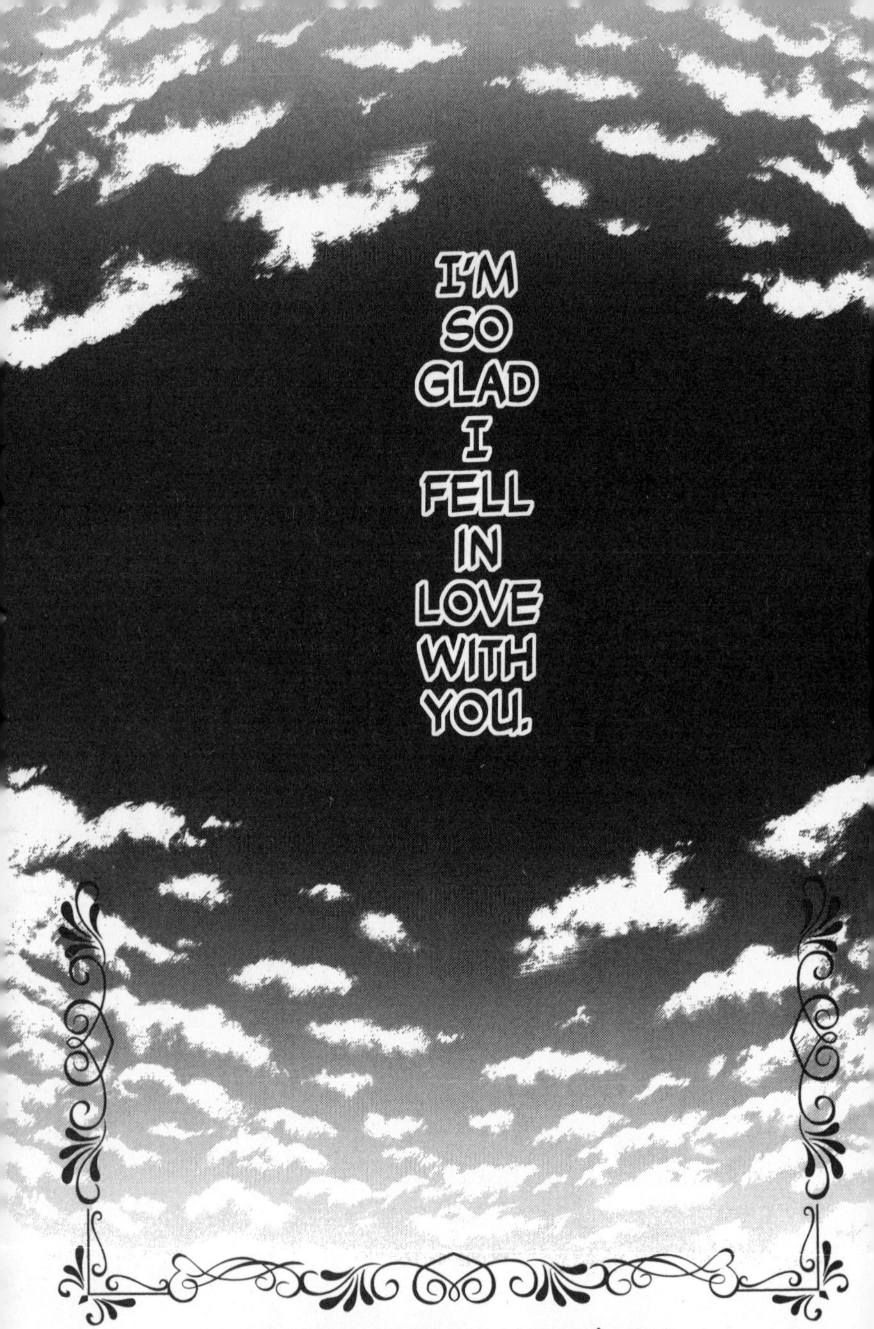
I'M SO GLAD I FELL IN LOVE WITH YOU.

THE GENTLEMEN'S ALLIANCE †/END

Gentlemen's
Alliance Gallery

Student Council
Office Entrance →

I looked at
photos and books
to draw this.

The flag in
the middle isn't
drawn very well.

School Corridor
↓

I looked through
photos and books.

I used this a lot in the
beginning of the series.

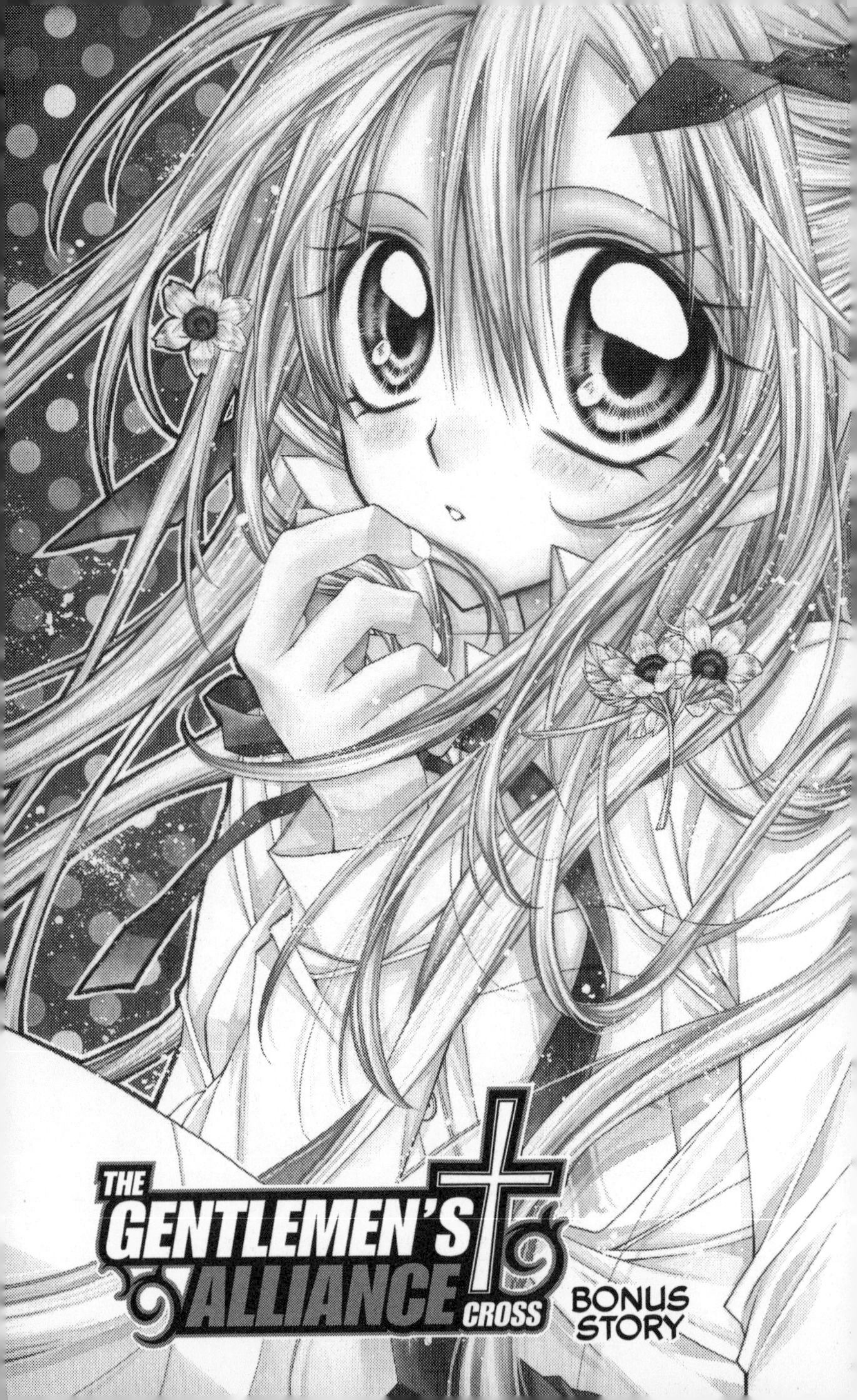
THE GENTLEMEN'S ALLIANCE CROSS
BONUS STORY

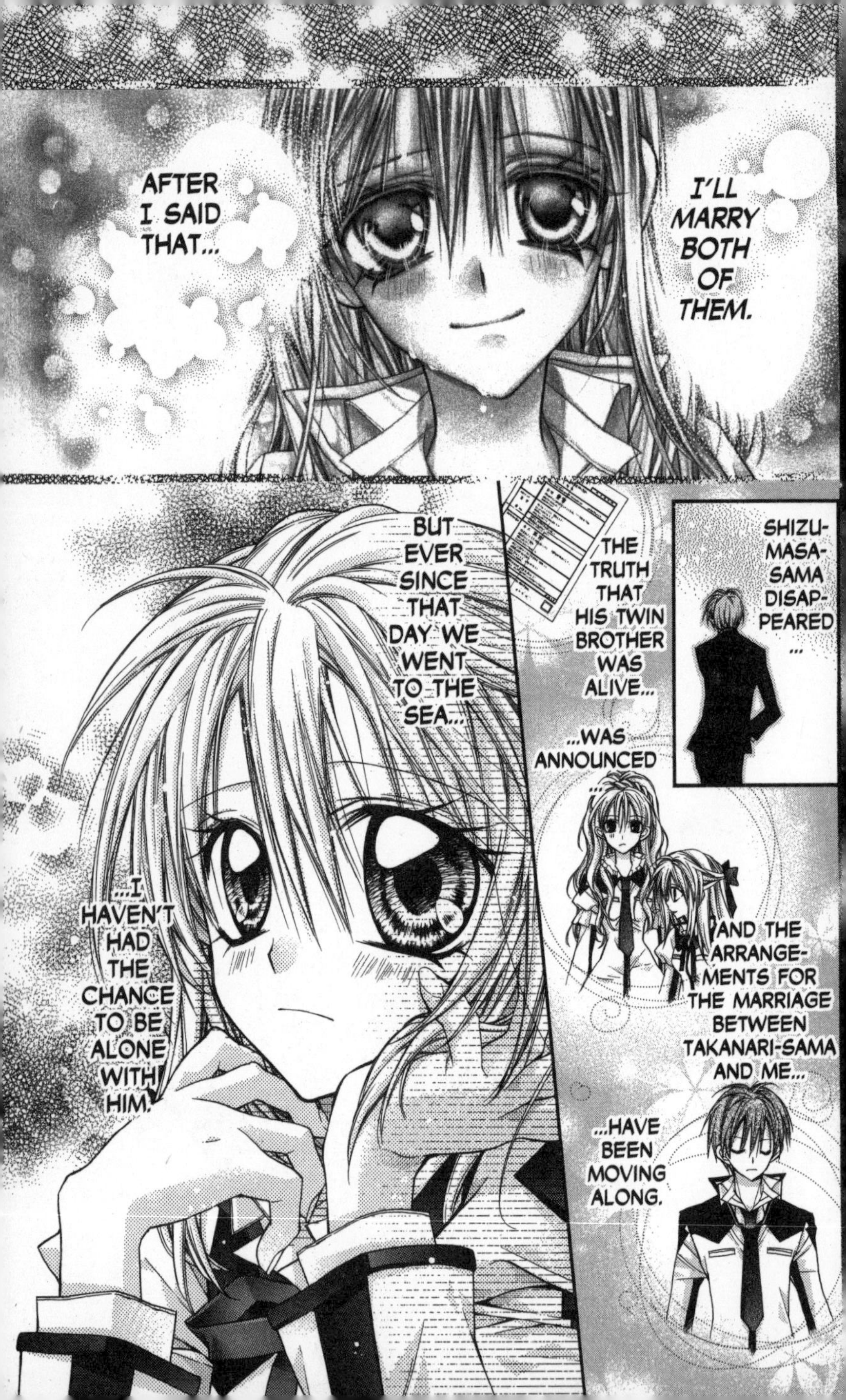
I'LL MARRY BOTH OF THEM.
AFTER I SAID THAT...
SHIZUMASA-SAMA DISAPPEARED...
THE TRUTH THAT HIS TWIN BROTHER WAS ALIVE...
...WAS ANNOUNCED...
AND THE ARRANGEMENTS FOR THE MARRIAGE BETWEEN TAKANARI-SAMA AND ME...
...HAVE BEEN MOVING ALONG.
BUT EVER SINCE THAT DAY WE WENT TO THE SEA...
...I HAVEN'T HAD THE CHANCE TO BE ALONE WITH HIM.

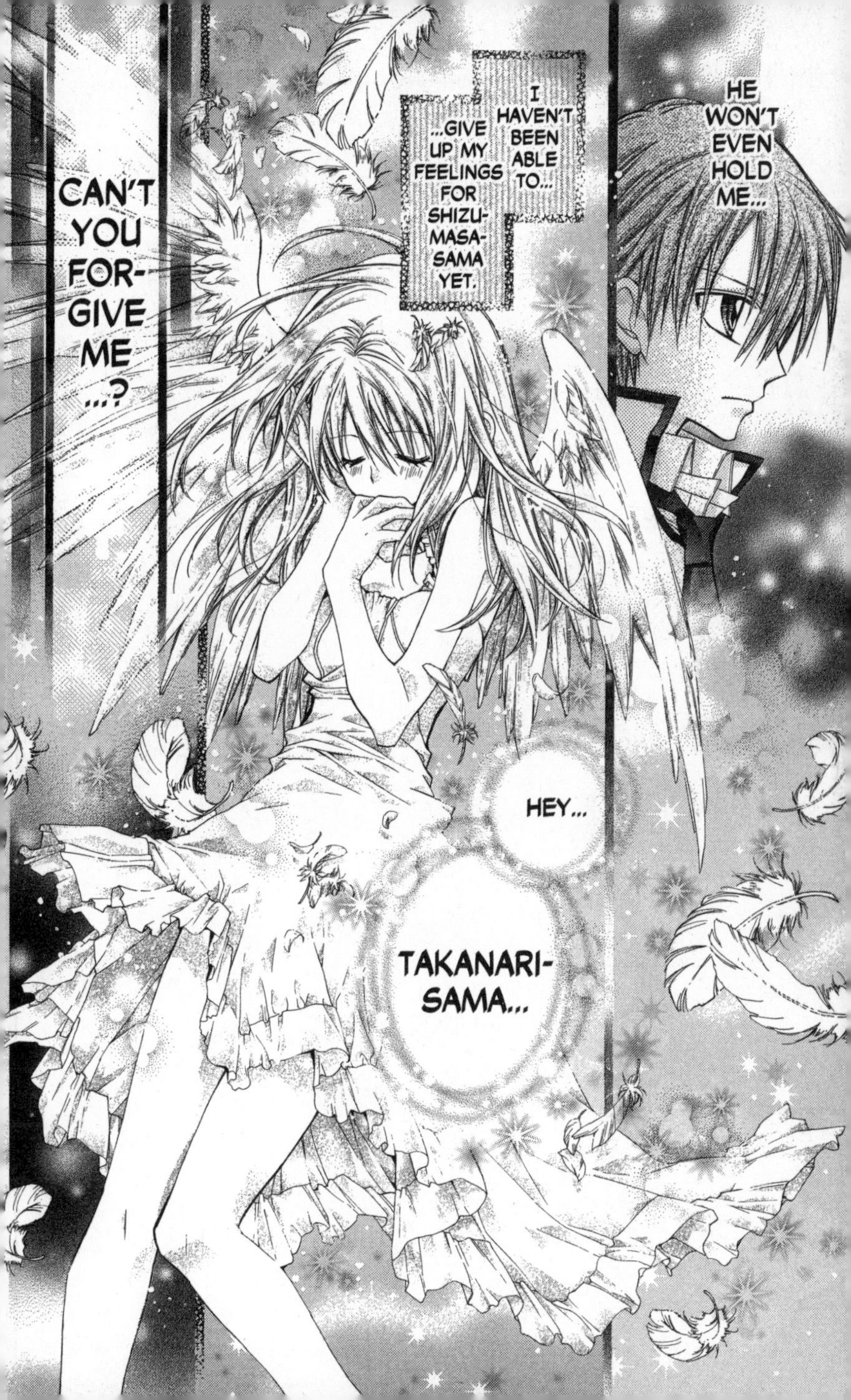
HE WON'T EVEN HOLD ME...
I HAVEN'T BEEN ABLE TO...
...GIVE UP MY FEELINGS FOR SHIZUMASA-SAMA YET.
CAN'T YOU FORGIVE ME...?
HEY...
TAKANARI-SAMA...

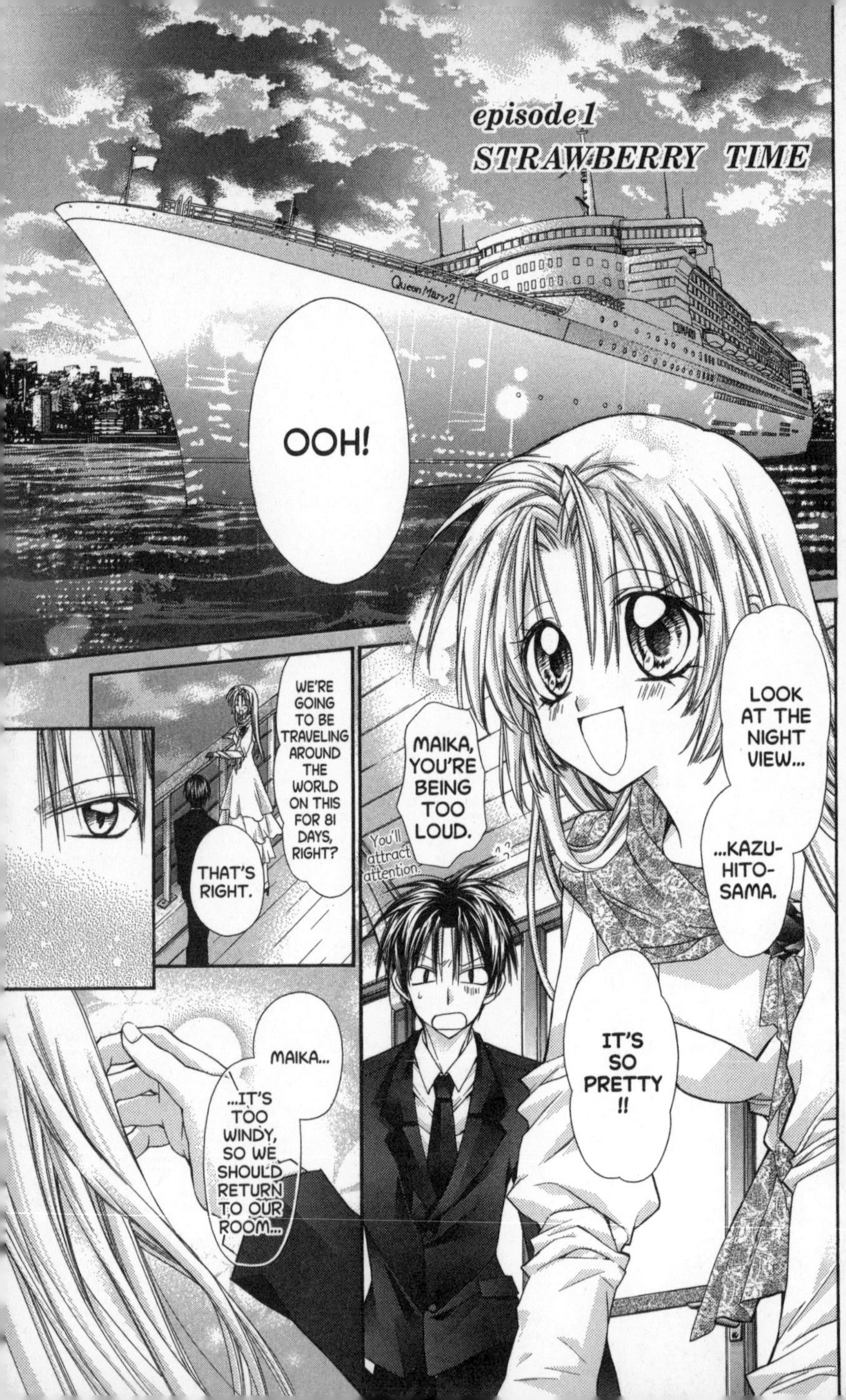
episode 1
STRAWBERRY TIME
Queen Mary 2
OOH!
LOOK AT THE NIGHT VIEW...
...KAZU-HITO-SAMA.
IT'S SO PRETTY !!
MAIKA, YOU'RE BEING TOO LOUD.
You'll attract attention.
WE'RE GOING TO BE TRAVELING AROUND THE WORLD ON THIS FOR 81 DAYS, RIGHT?
THAT'S RIGHT.
MAIKA...
...IT'S TOO WINDY, SO WE SHOULD RETURN TO OUR ROOM...

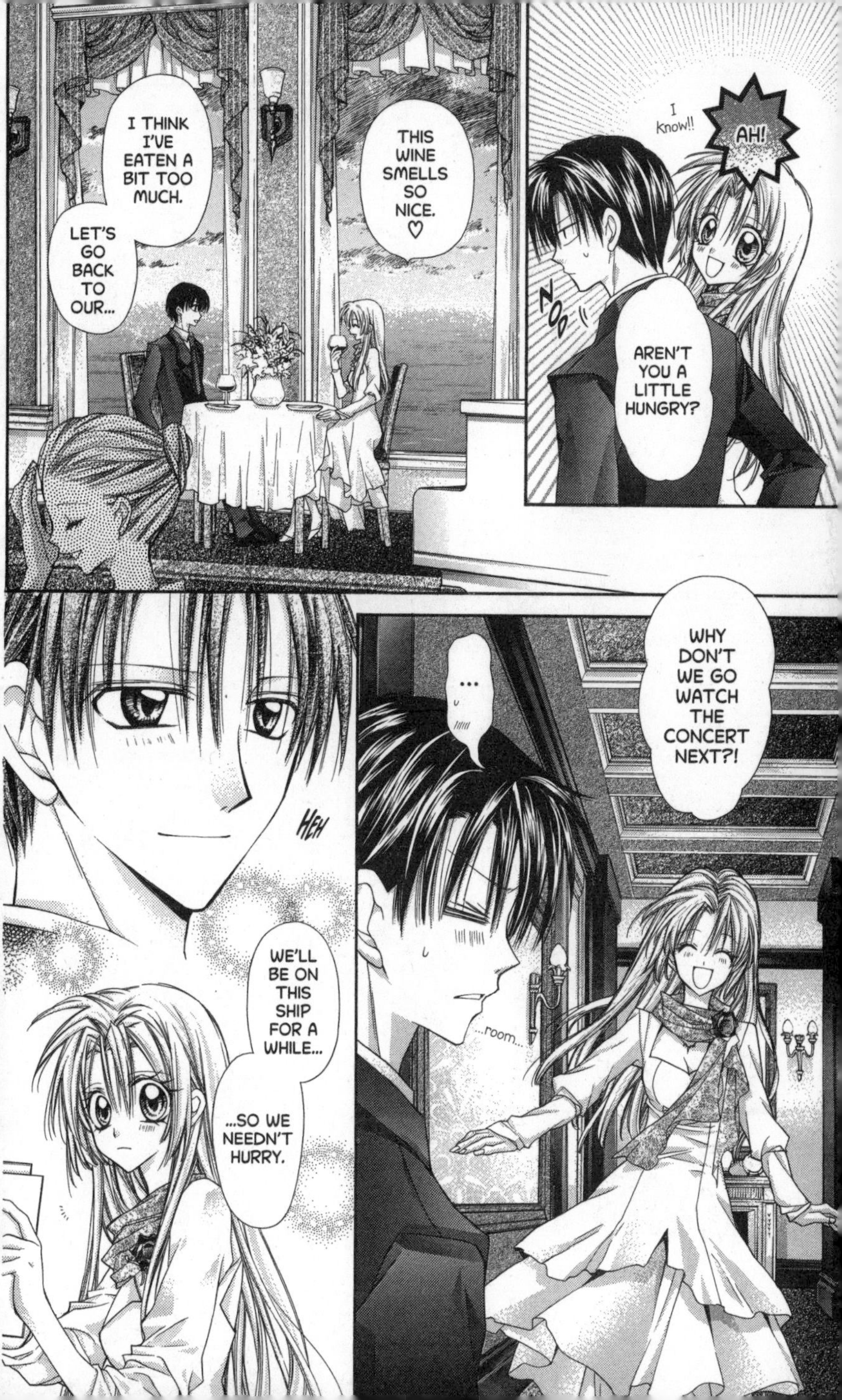
I Know!!
AH!
NOD
AREN'T YOU A LITTLE HUNGRY?
THIS WINE SMELLS SO NICE. ♡
I THINK I'VE EATEN A BIT TOO MUCH.
LET'S GO BACK TO OUR...
WHY DON'T WE GO WATCH THE CONCERT NEXT?!
...
...room...
HEH
WE'LL BE ON THIS SHIP FOR A WHILE...
...SO WE NEEDN'T HURRY.

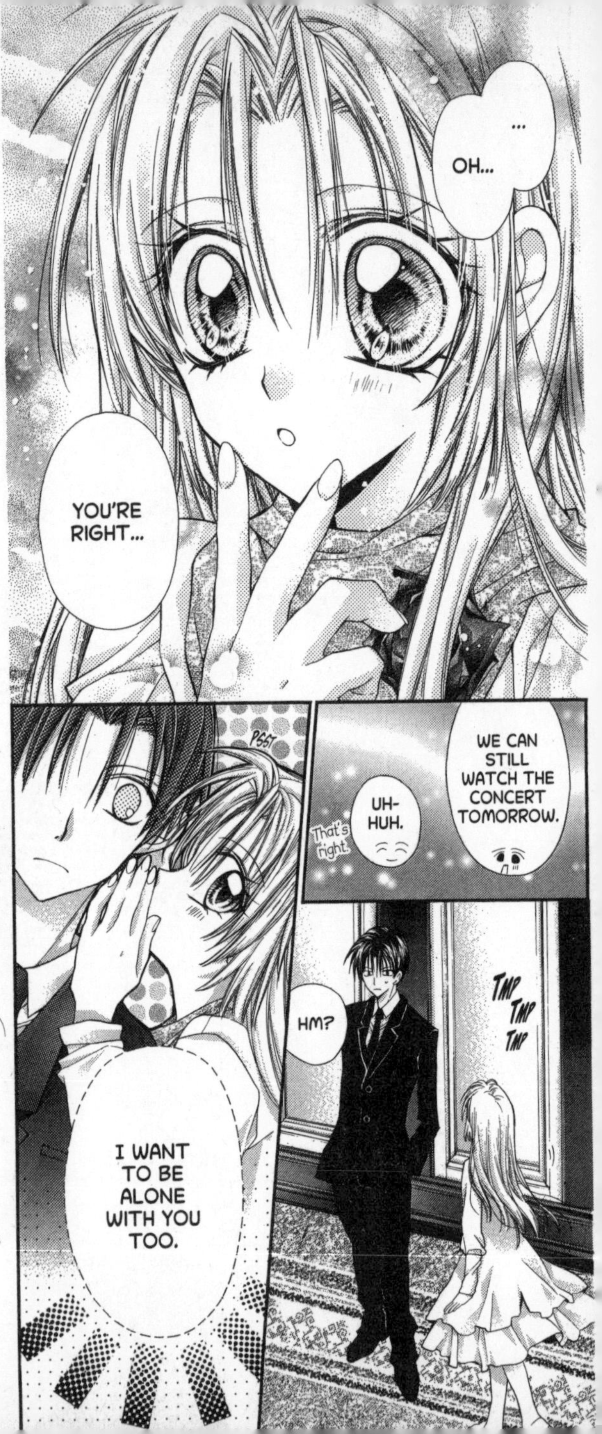
...
OH...
YOU'RE RIGHT...
WE CAN STILL WATCH THE CONCERT TOMORROW.
UH-HUH.
That's right.
TMP TMP TMP
HM?
PSST
I WANT TO BE ALONE WITH YOU TOO.

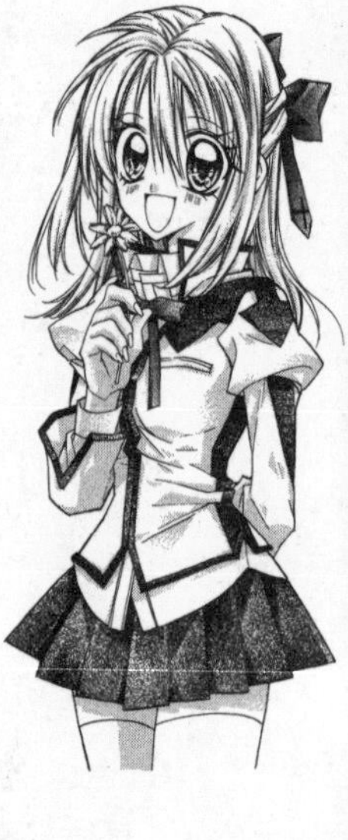

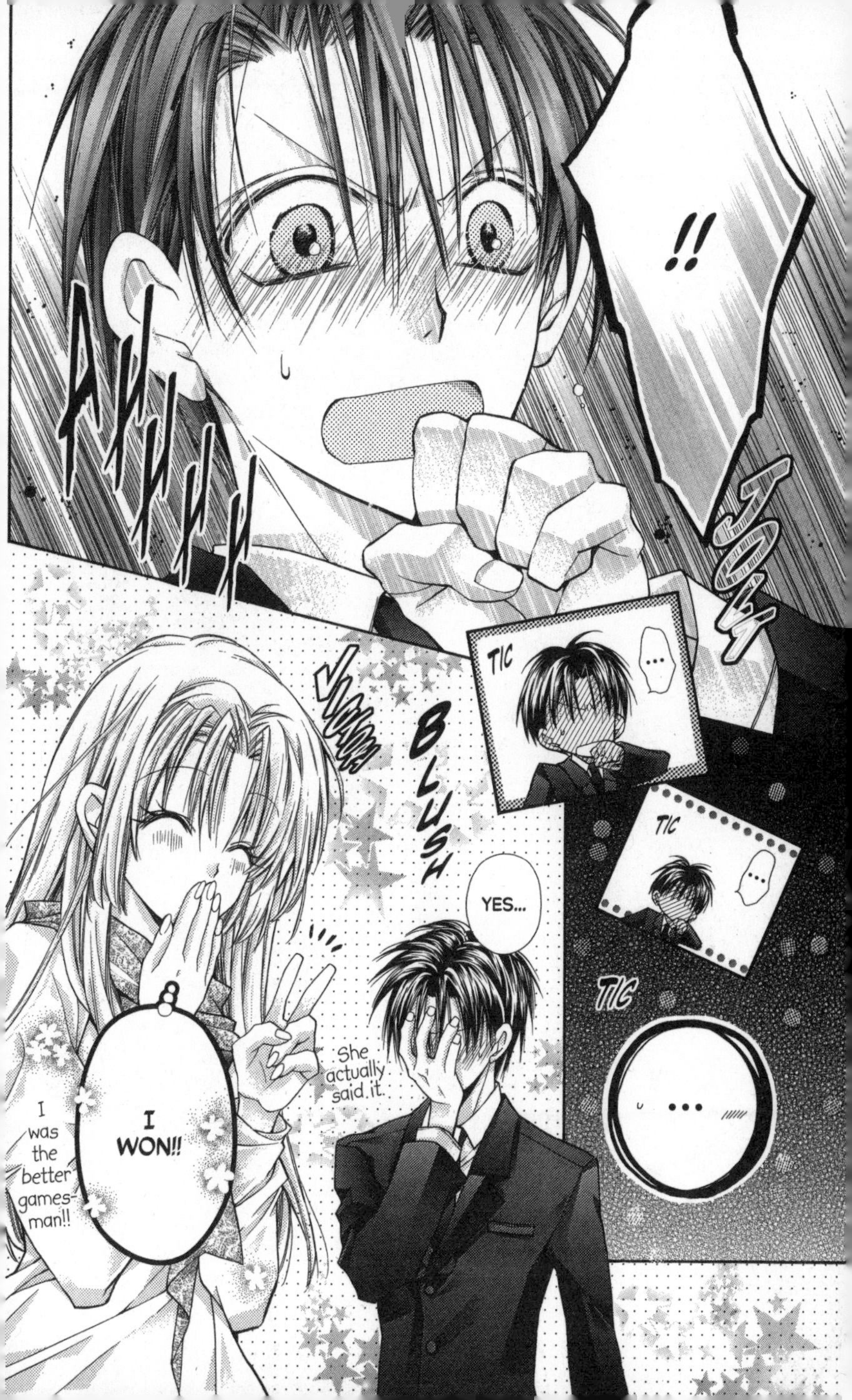

!!
JOLT
TIC
...
TIC
...
TIC
...
YES...
BLUSH
She actually said it.
I WON!!
I was the better games-man!!

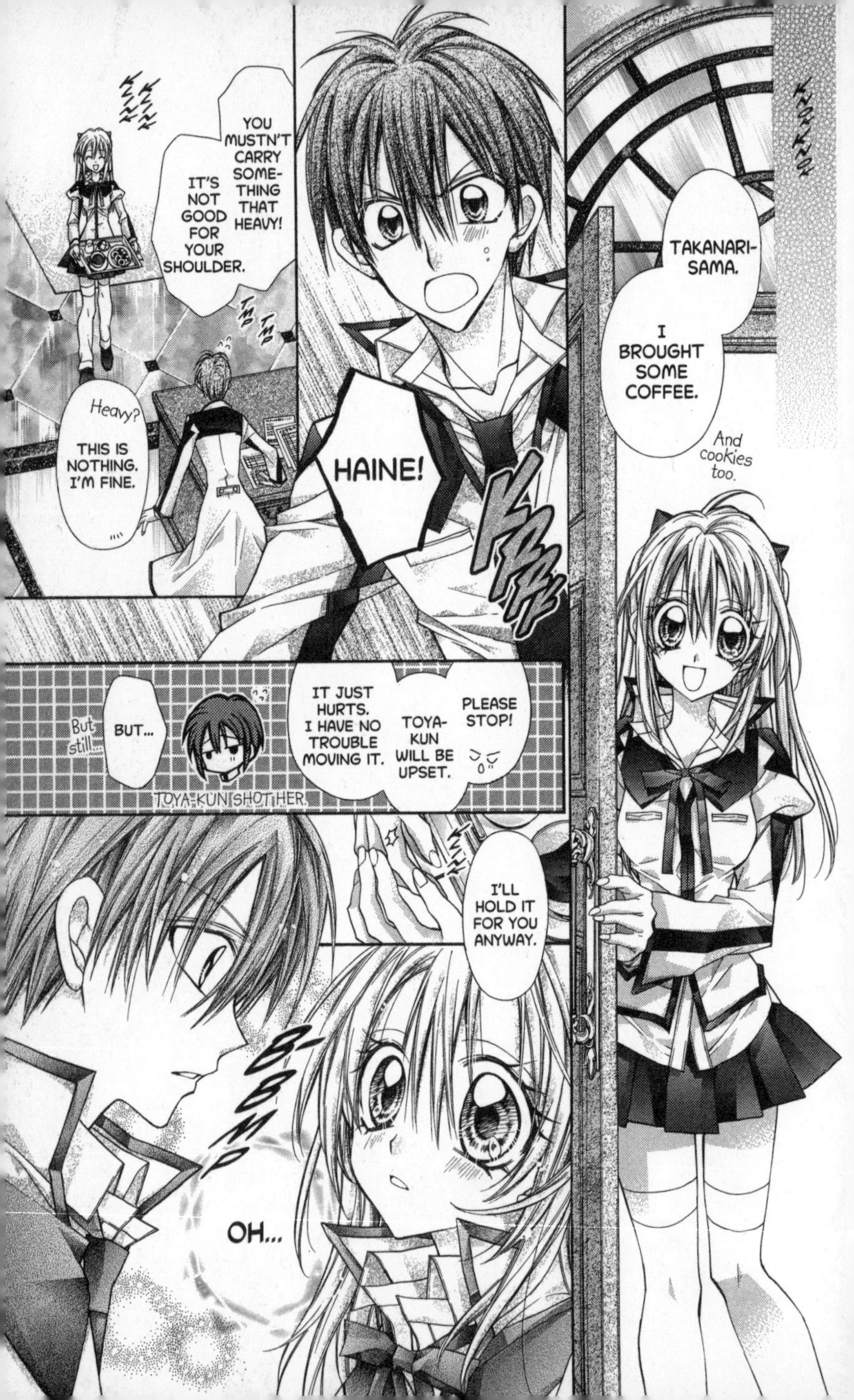
KNOCK KNOCK
TAKANARI-SAMA.
I BROUGHT SOME COFFEE.
And cookies too.
HAINE!
YOU MUSTN'T CARRY SOMETHING THAT HEAVY!
IT'S NOT GOOD FOR YOUR SHOULDER.
Heavy?
THIS IS NOTHING. I'M FINE.
PLEASE STOP!
TOYA-KUN WILL BE UPSET.
IT JUST HURTS. I HAVE NO TROUBLE MOVING IT.
BUT...
But still...
TOYA-KUN SHOT HER.
I'LL HOLD IT FOR YOU ANYWAY.
OH...

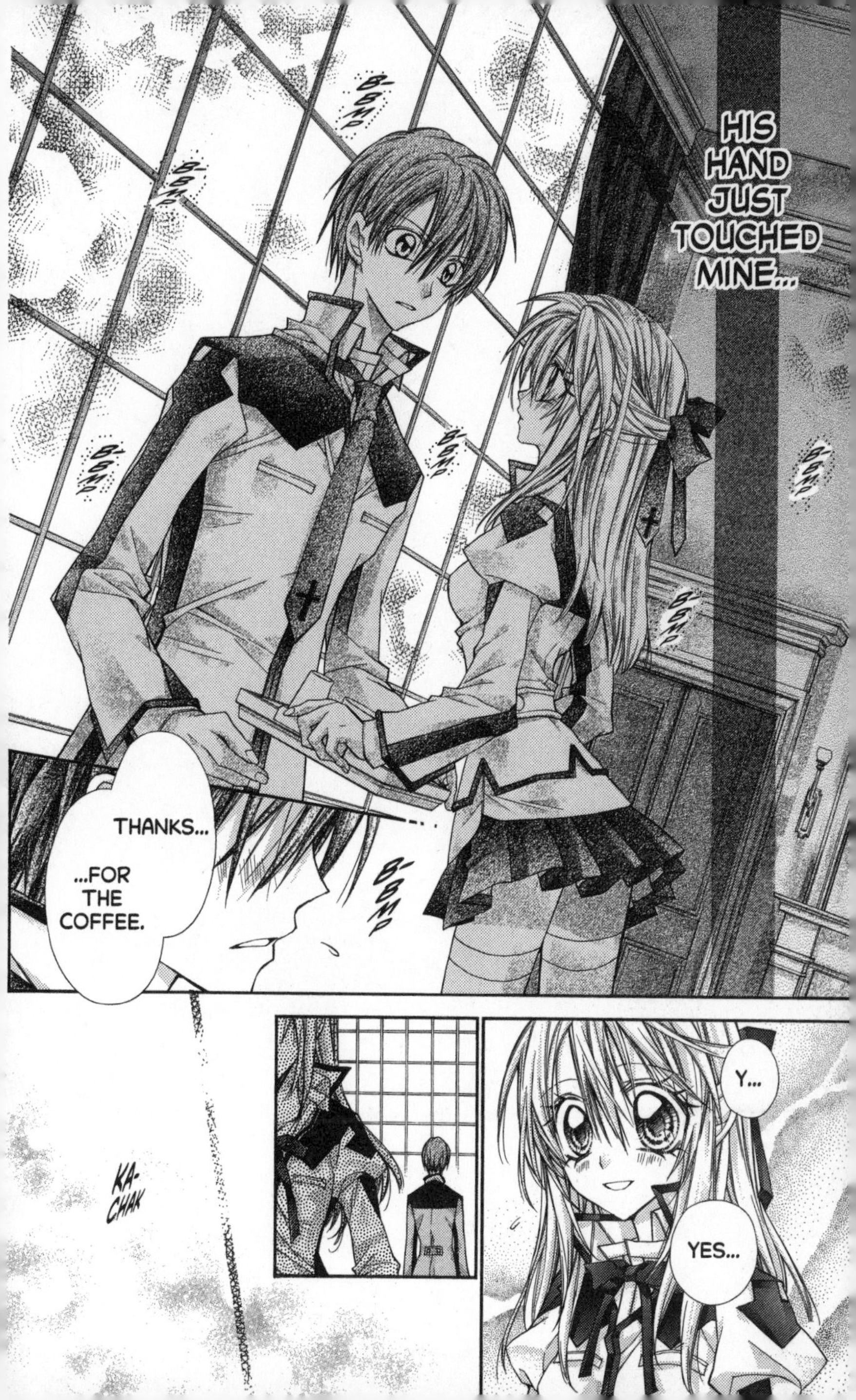
HIS HAND JUST TOUCHED MINE...
B-BMP
B-BMP
B-BMP
B-BMP
B-BMP
B-BMP
THANKS...
...FOR THE COFFEE.
B-BMP
Y...
YES...
KA-CHAK

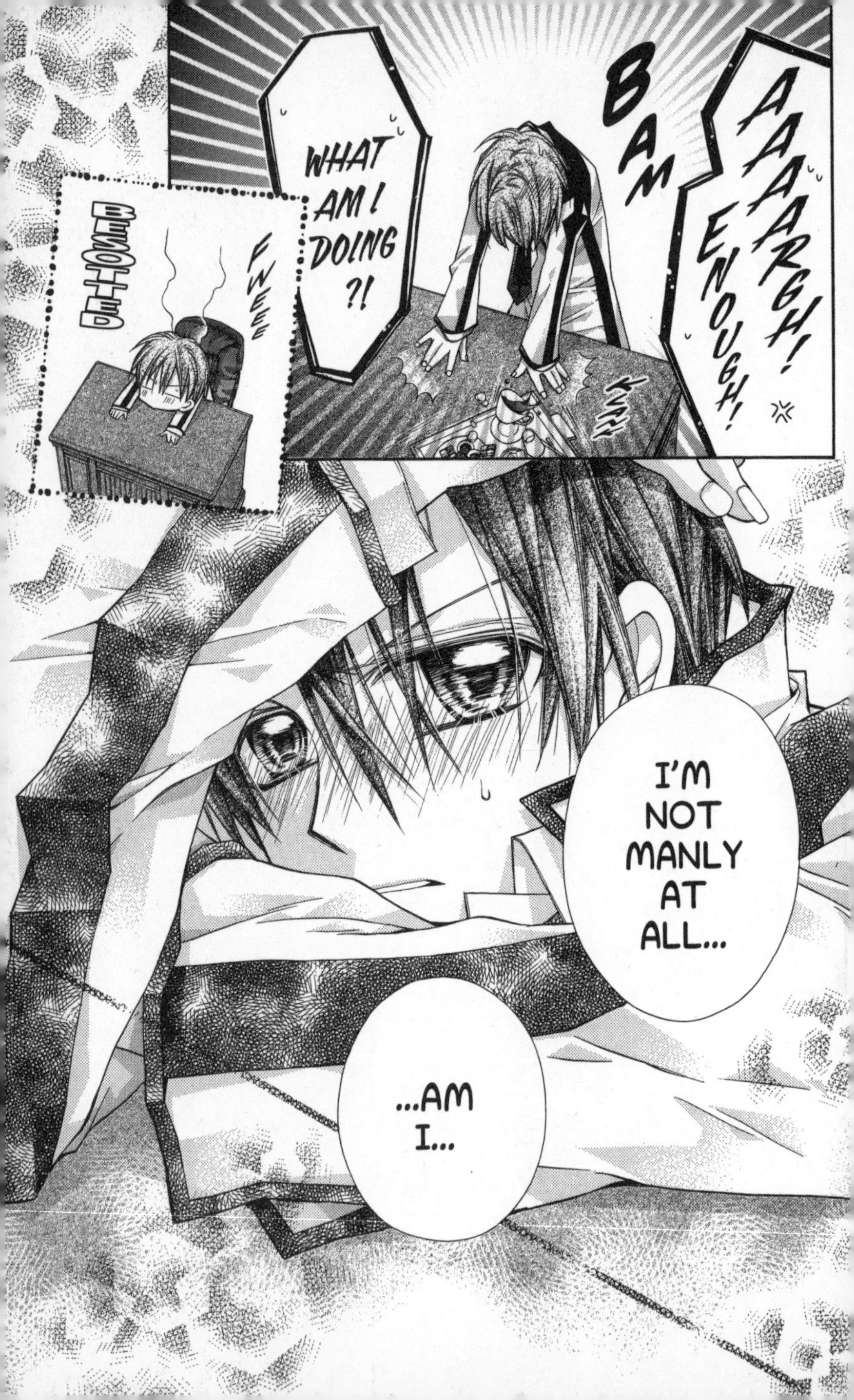
AAAARGH!
ENOUGH!
BAM
WHAT AM I DOING ?!
FWEEE
BESOTTED
I'M NOT MANLY AT ALL...
...AM I...

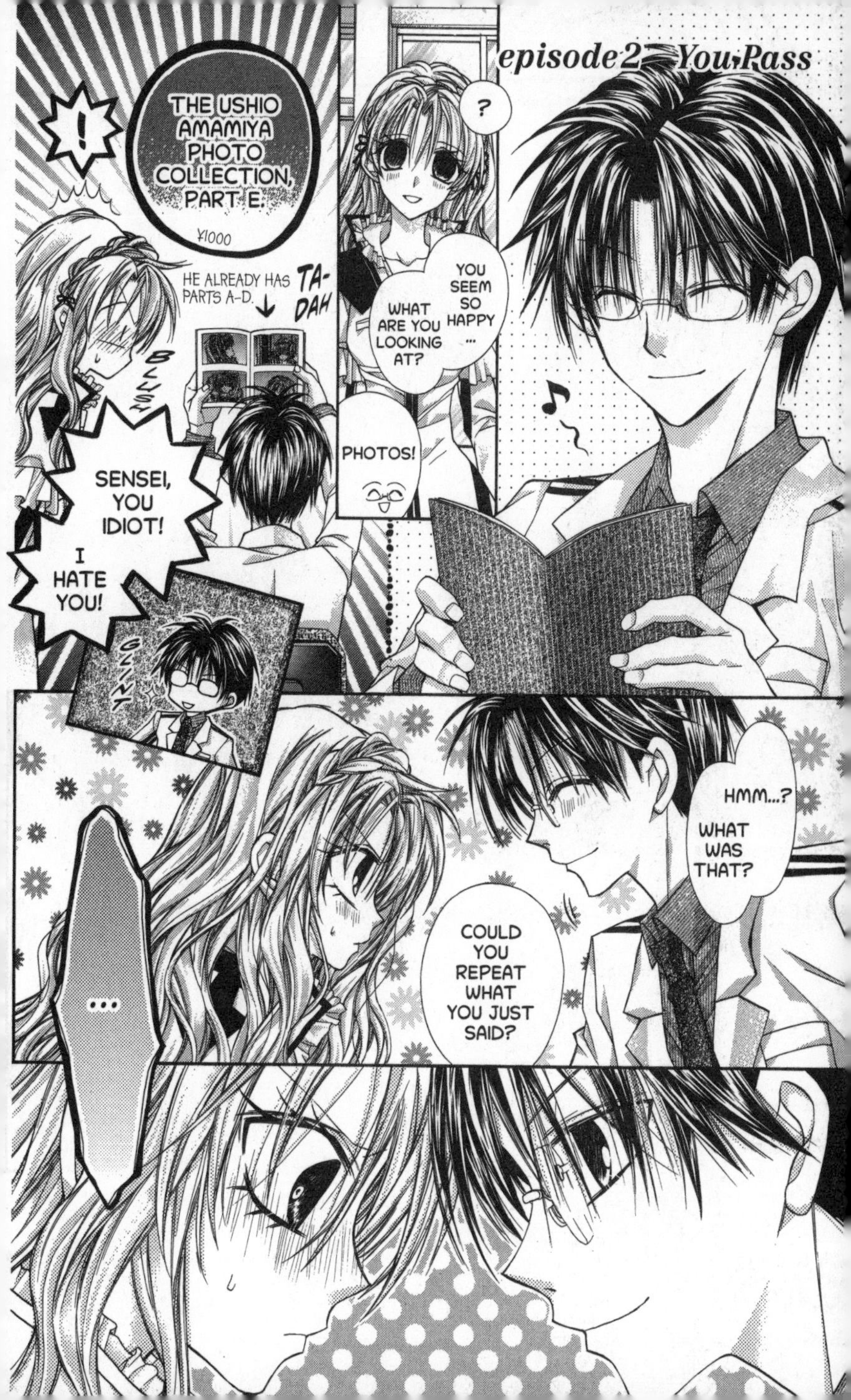
episode 2 You Pass
?
YOU SEEM SO HAPPY ...
WHAT ARE YOU LOOKING AT?
PHOTOS!
!
THE USHIO AMAMIYA PHOTO COLLECTION, PART E.
¥1000
TA-DAH
HE ALREADY HAS PARTS A-D.
BLUSH
SENSEI, YOU IDIOT!
I HATE YOU!
GLINT
HMM...?
WHAT WAS THAT?
COULD YOU REPEAT WHAT YOU JUST SAID?
...

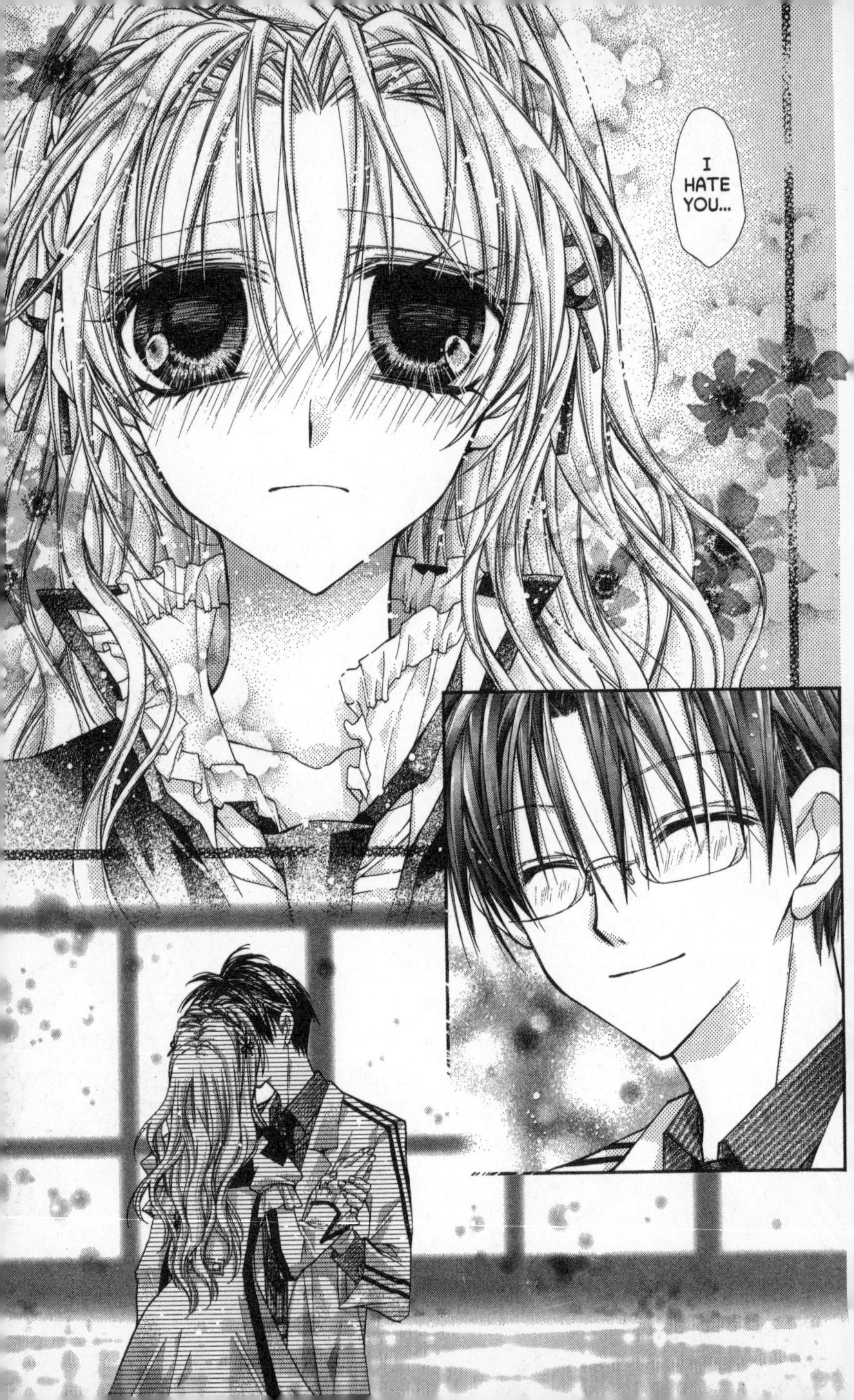
I HATE YOU...

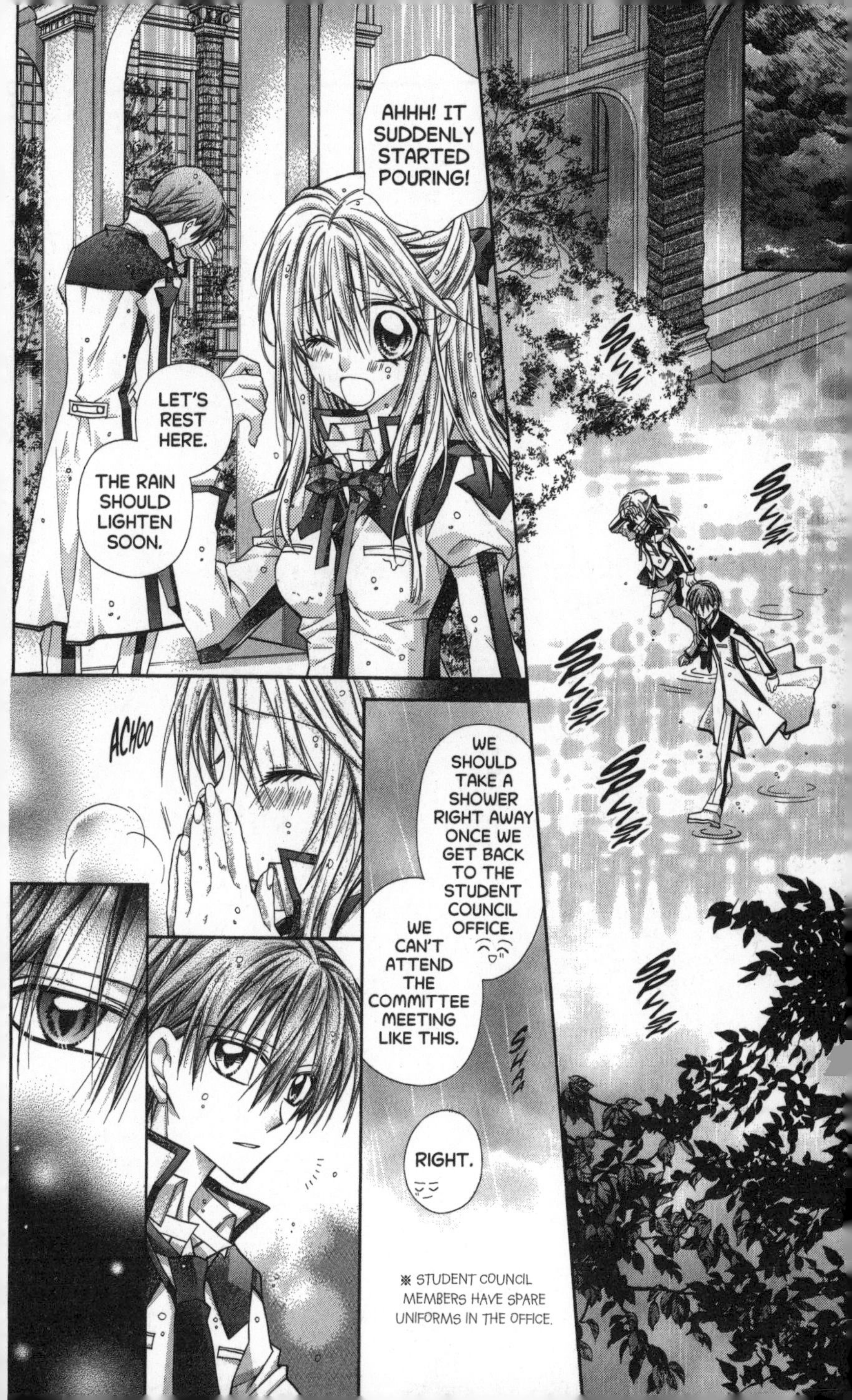
AHHH! IT SUDDENLY STARTED POURING!
LET'S REST HERE.
THE RAIN SHOULD LIGHTEN SOON.
ACHOO
WE SHOULD TAKE A SHOWER RIGHT AWAY ONCE WE GET BACK TO THE STUDENT COUNCIL OFFICE.
WE CAN'T ATTEND THE COMMITTEE MEETING LIKE THIS.
RIGHT.
※ STUDENT COUNCIL MEMBERS HAVE SPARE UNIFORMS IN THE OFFICE.

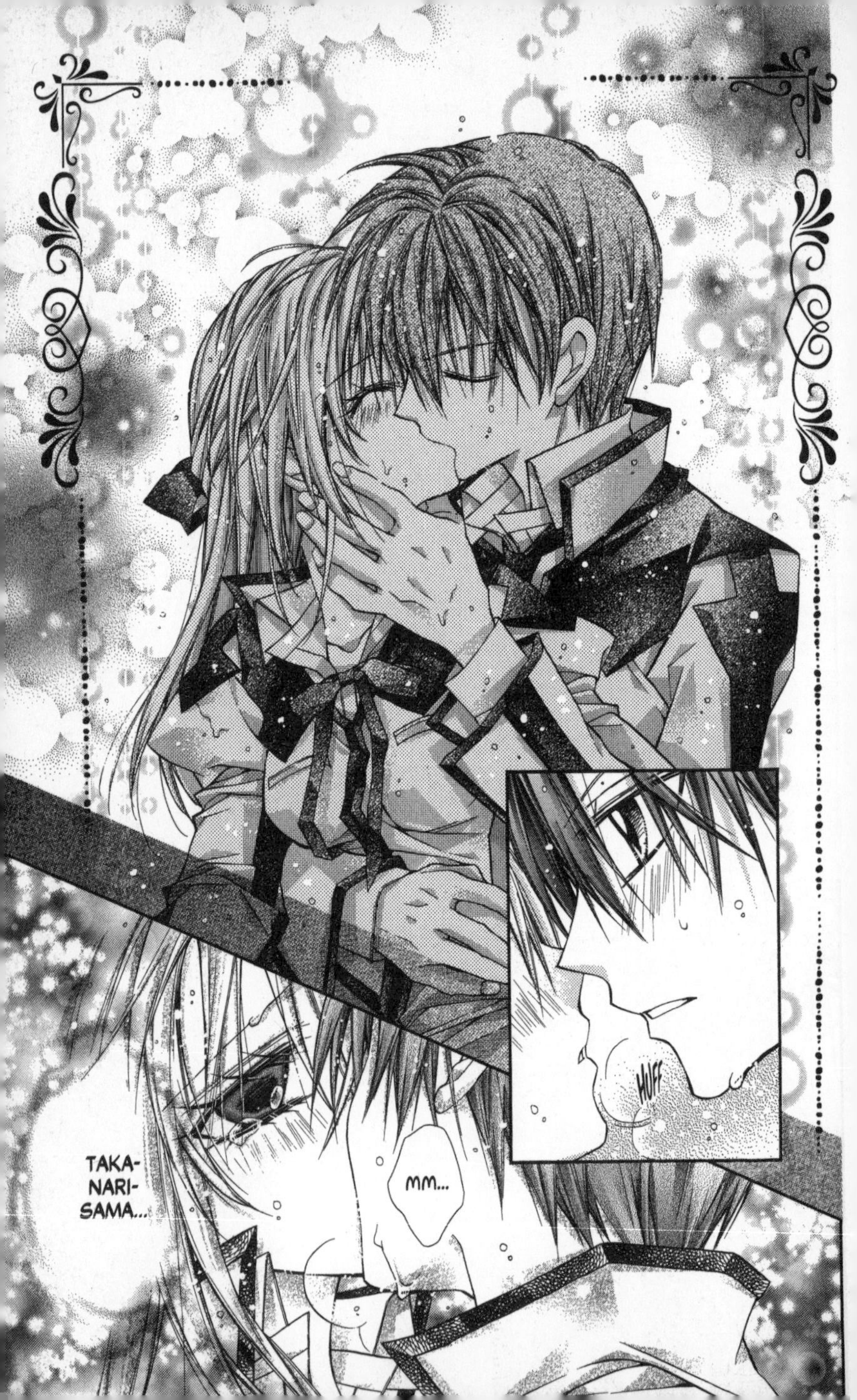
HUFF
MM...
TAKA-NARI-SAMA...

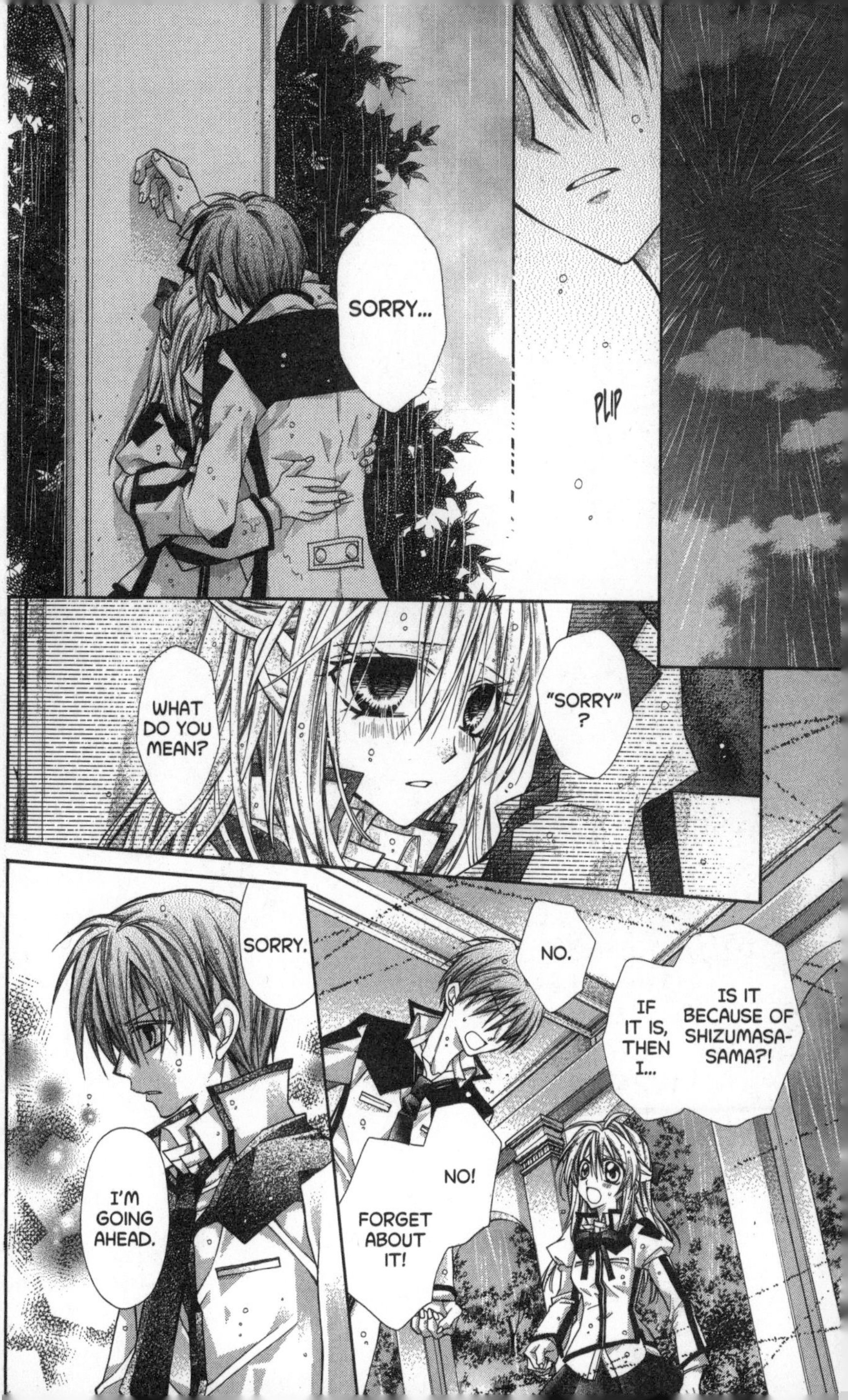
PLIP
SORRY...
"SORRY"?
WHAT DO YOU MEAN?
IS IT BECAUSE OF SHIZUMASA-SAMA?!
IF IT IS, THEN I...
NO.
SORRY.
NO!
FORGET ABOUT IT!
I'M GOING AHEAD.

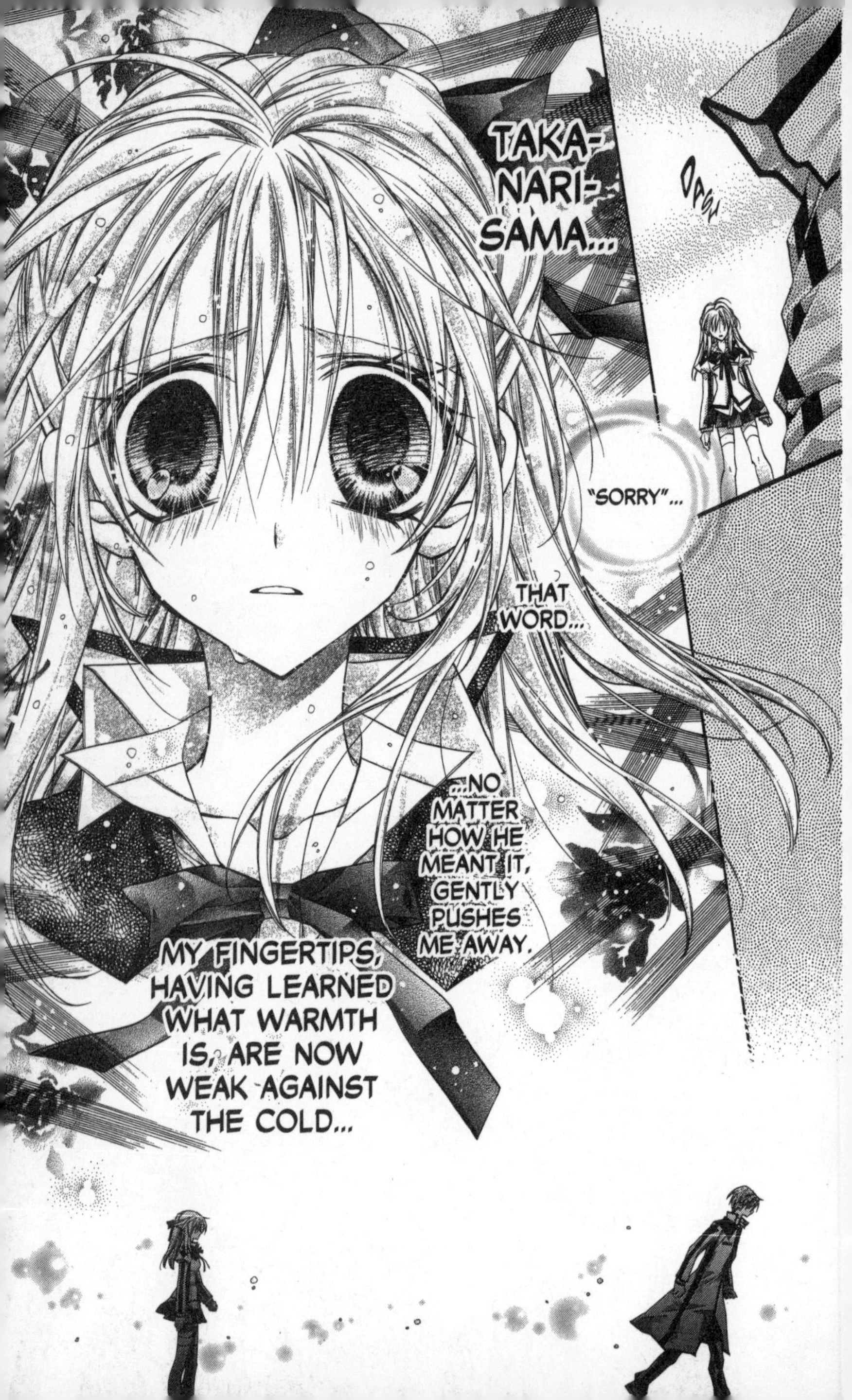
TAKA-NARI-SAMA...
"SORRY"...
THAT WORD...
...NO MATTER HOW HE MEANT IT, GENTLY PUSHES ME AWAY.
MY FINGERTIPS, HAVING LEARNED WHAT WARMTH IS, ARE NOW WEAK AGAINST THE COLD...

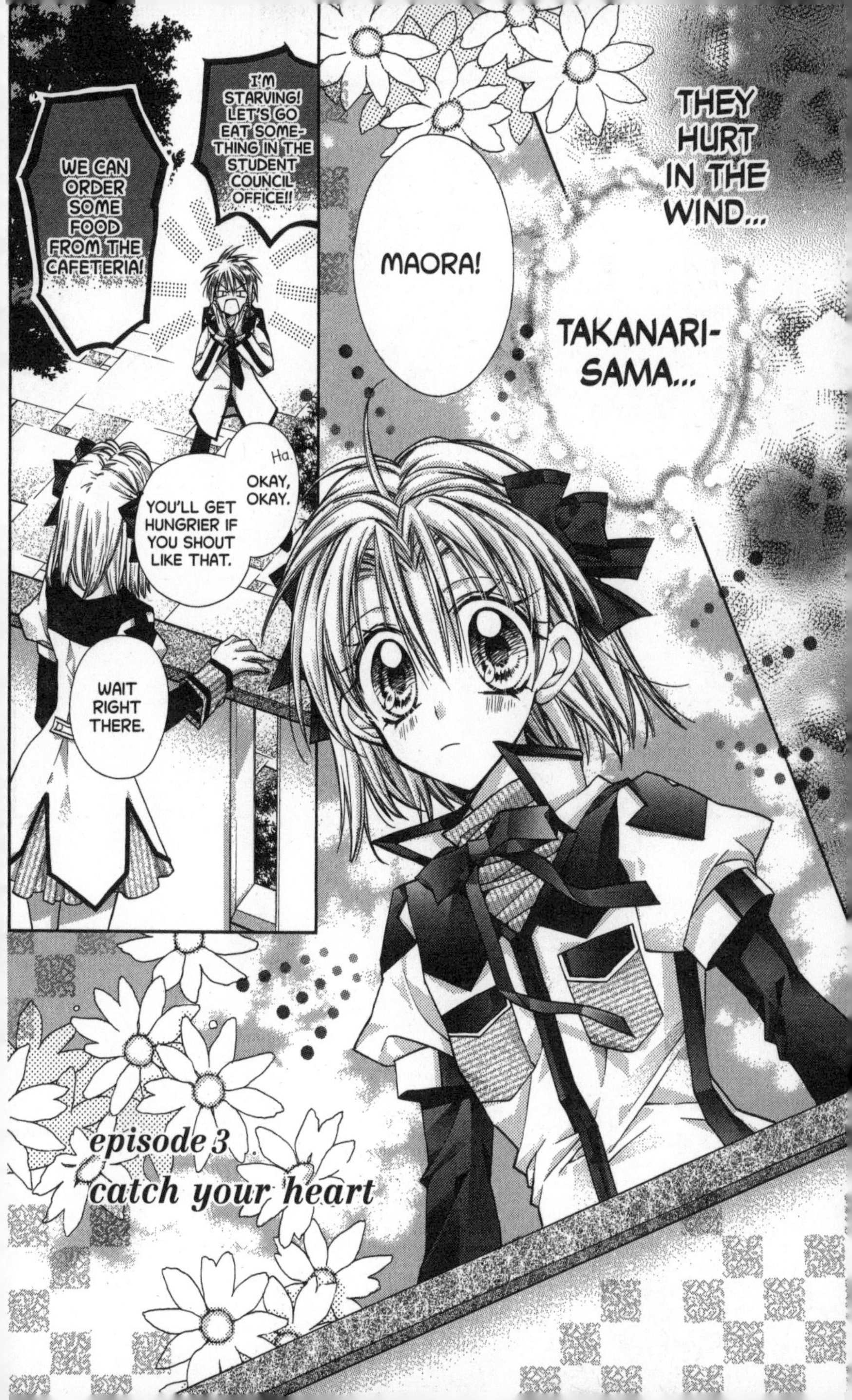
THEY HURT IN THE WIND...
TAKANARI-SAMA...
MAORA!
I'M STARVING! LET'S GO EAT SOME-THING IN THE STUDENT COUNCIL OFFICE!!
WE CAN ORDER SOME FOOD FROM THE CAFETERIA!
Ha.
OKAY, OKAY.
YOU'LL GET HUNGRIER IF YOU SHOUT LIKE THAT.
WAIT RIGHT THERE.
episode 3
catch your heart

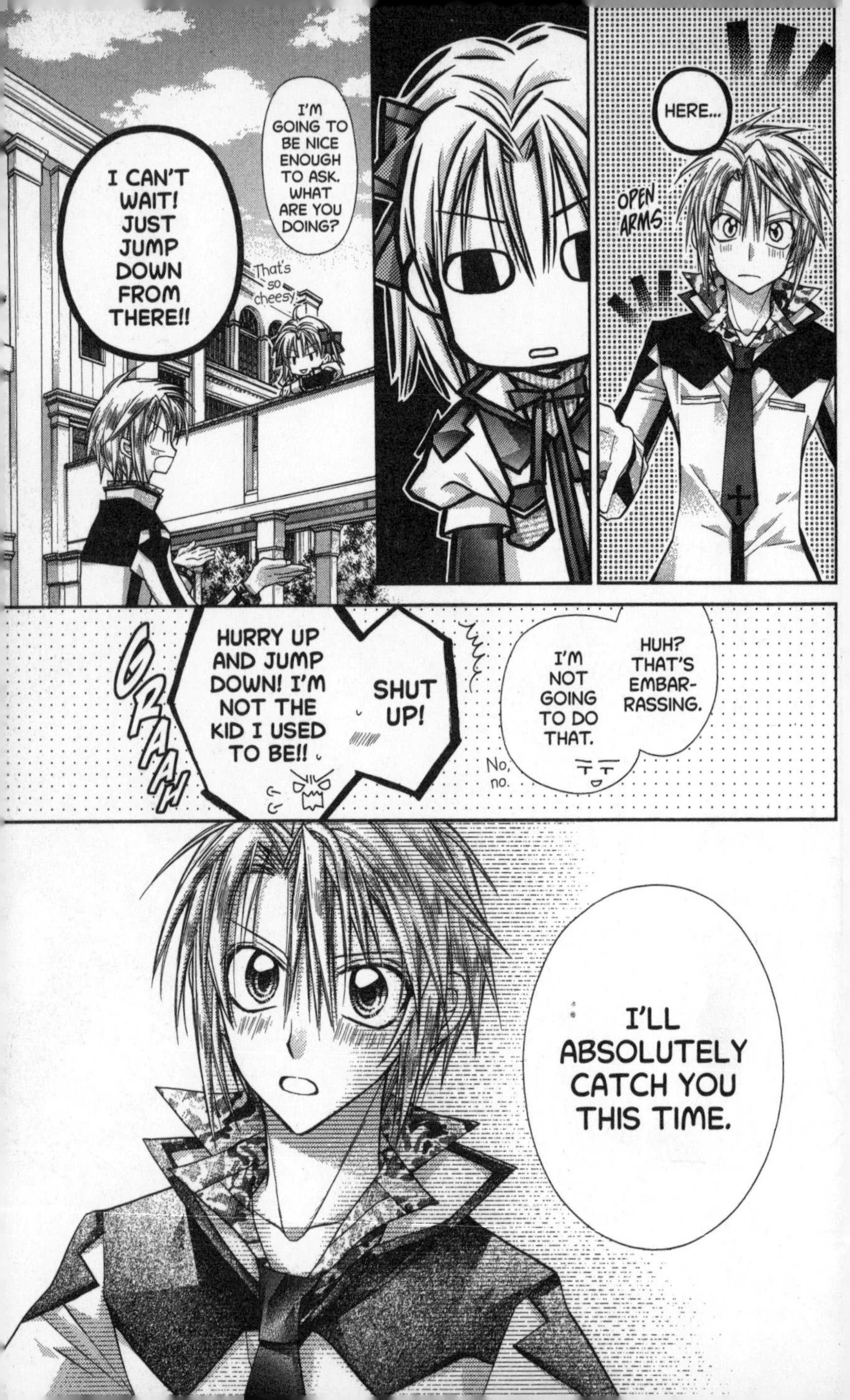

HERE...
OPEN ARMS
I'M GOING TO BE NICE ENOUGH TO ASK. WHAT ARE YOU DOING?
I CAN'T WAIT! JUST JUMP DOWN FROM THERE!!
That's so cheesy!
HUH? THAT'S EMBARRASSING.
I'M NOT GOING TO DO THAT.
No, no.
SHUT UP!
HURRY UP AND JUMP DOWN! I'M NOT THE KID I USED TO BE!!
GRAAH
I'LL ABSOLUTELY CATCH YOU THIS TIME.

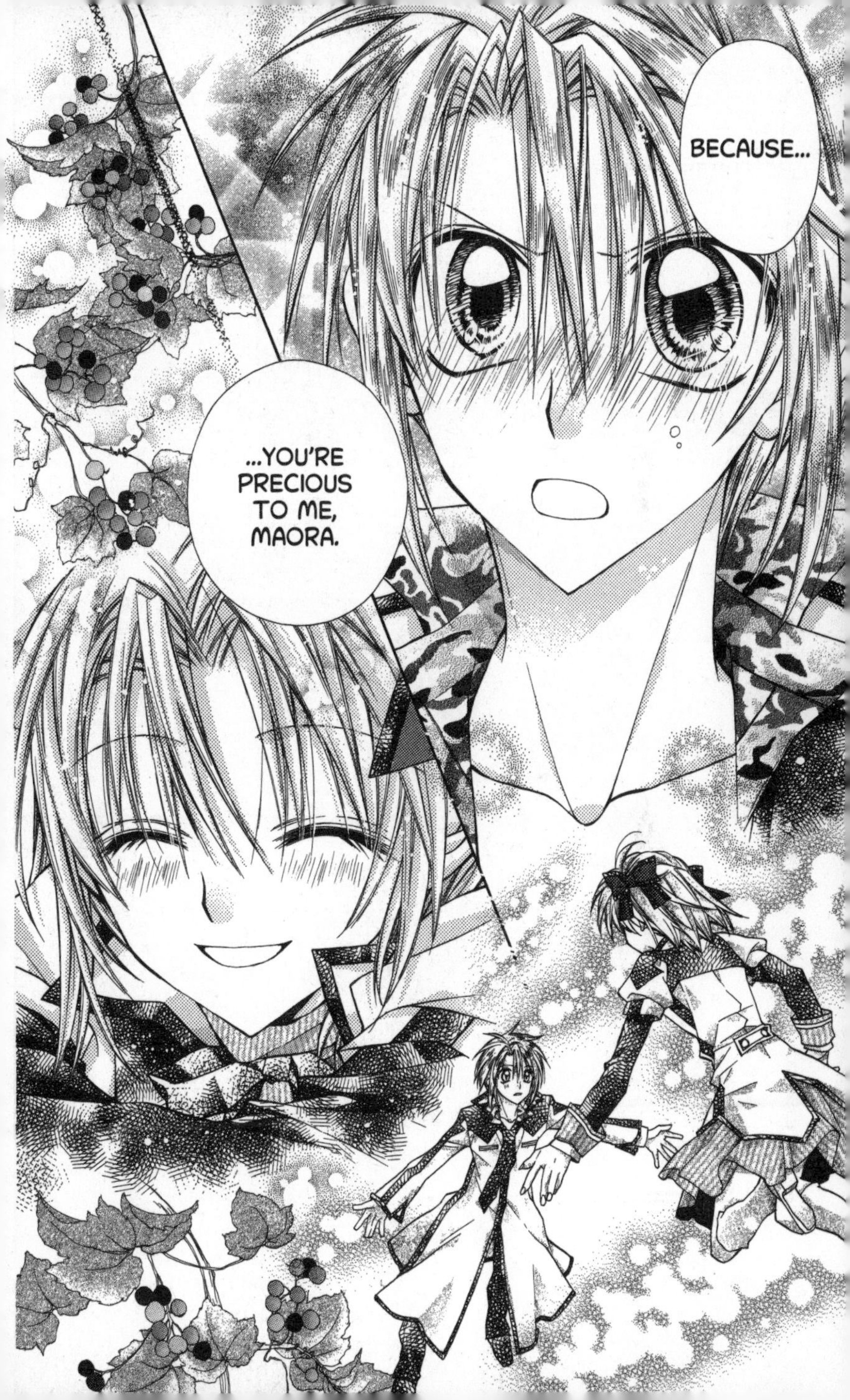
BECAUSE...
...YOU'RE PRECIOUS TO ME, MAORA.

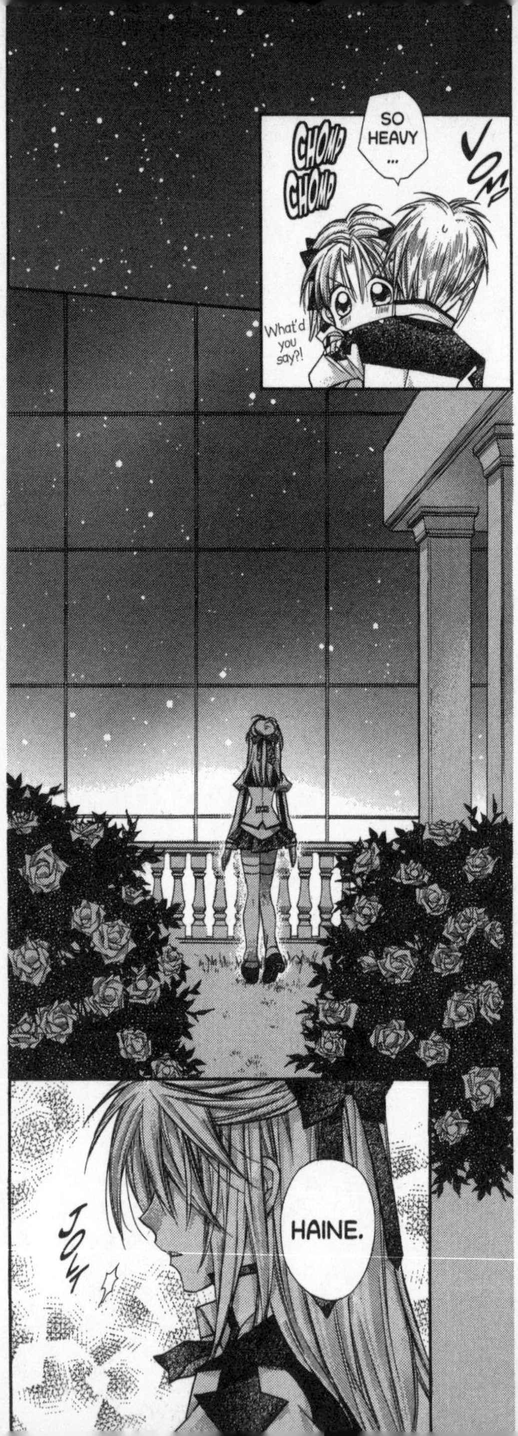
VONP
SO HEAVY ...
CHOMP CHOMP
What'd you say?!
HAINE.
JOLT

Final Greetings

Oh? It's already over.
I could only do three sidebars.
I'm sorry.

But to tell you the truth, I really don't have much to talk about... I've already written most of the things I wanted to talk about in the series.

2009

My next series will start in the January edition of *Ribon*. It will be a Heian-period fantasy story(?). I'm not too sure how it'll turn out though... But I'd like to put all my effort into it.

Special Thanks

Nakame Saori

Chihiron

Iyo-chan Mi-chan
Yuki-chan Shoko-chan
Sa-chan Hina-chan
Saki-chan Tomo-chan

Shueisha
Everybody at the
Ribon Editorial Department
Supervisors S-sama, K-sama

Ammonite Ltd.

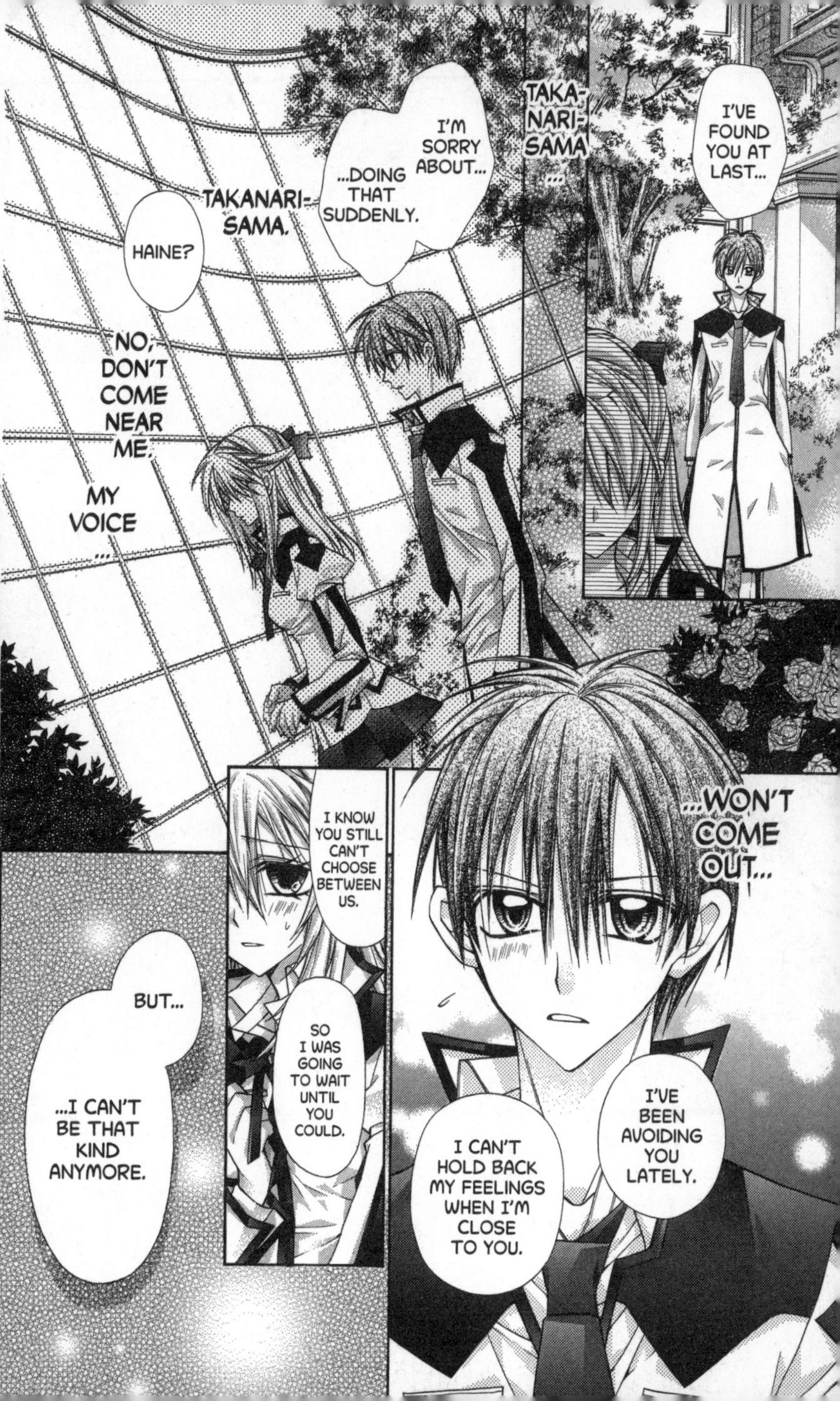
I'VE FOUND YOU AT LAST...
TAKANARI-SAMA...
I'M SORRY ABOUT...
...DOING THAT SUDDENLY.
TAKANARI-SAMA.
HAINE?
NO, DON'T COME NEAR ME.
MY VOICE...
...WON'T COME OUT...
I'VE BEEN AVOIDING YOU LATELY.
I CAN'T HOLD BACK MY FEELINGS WHEN I'M CLOSE TO YOU.
I KNOW YOU STILL CAN'T CHOOSE BETWEEN US.
SO I WAS GOING TO WAIT UNTIL YOU COULD.
BUT...
...I CAN'T BE THAT KIND ANYMORE.

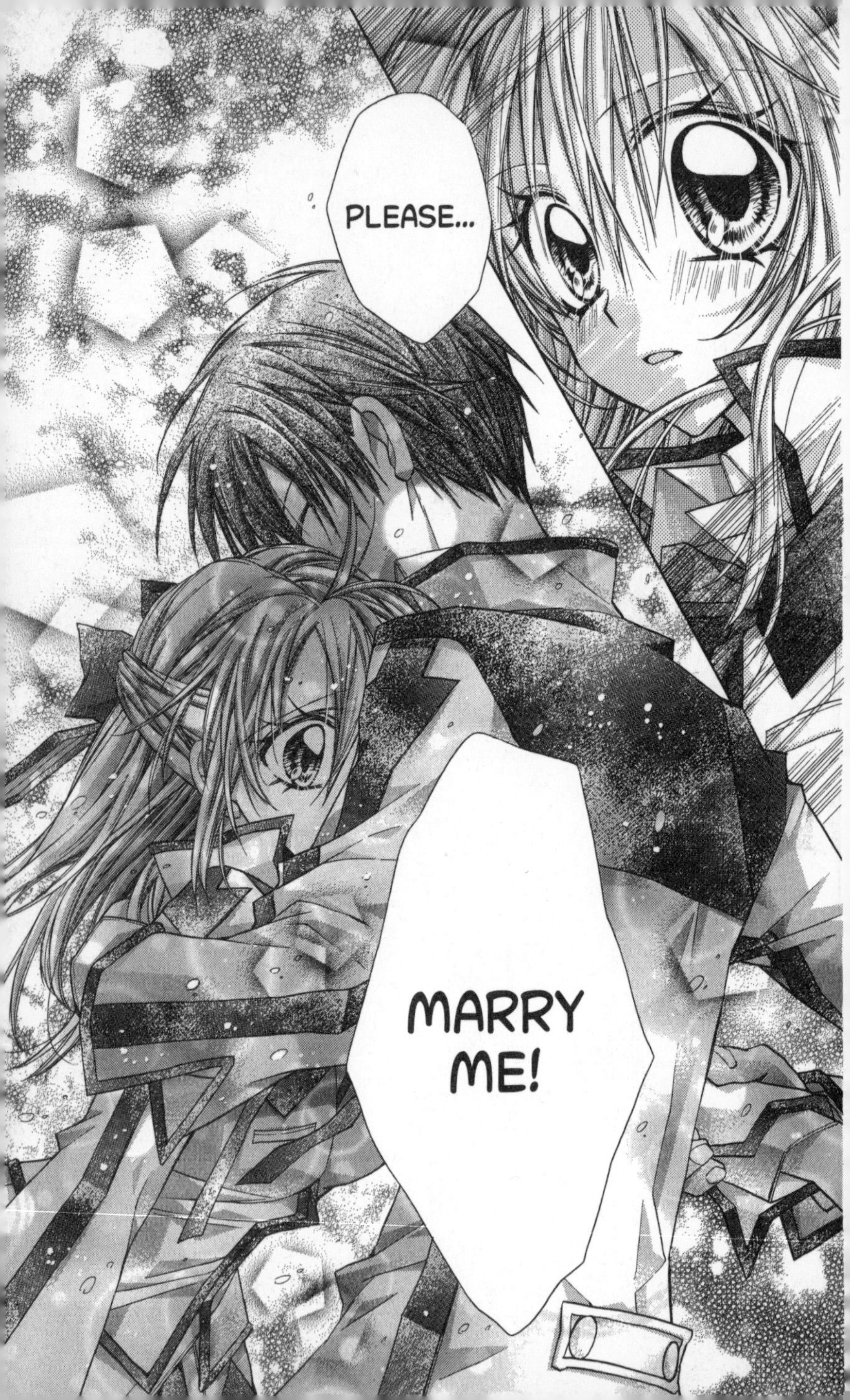
PLEASE...
MARRY ME!

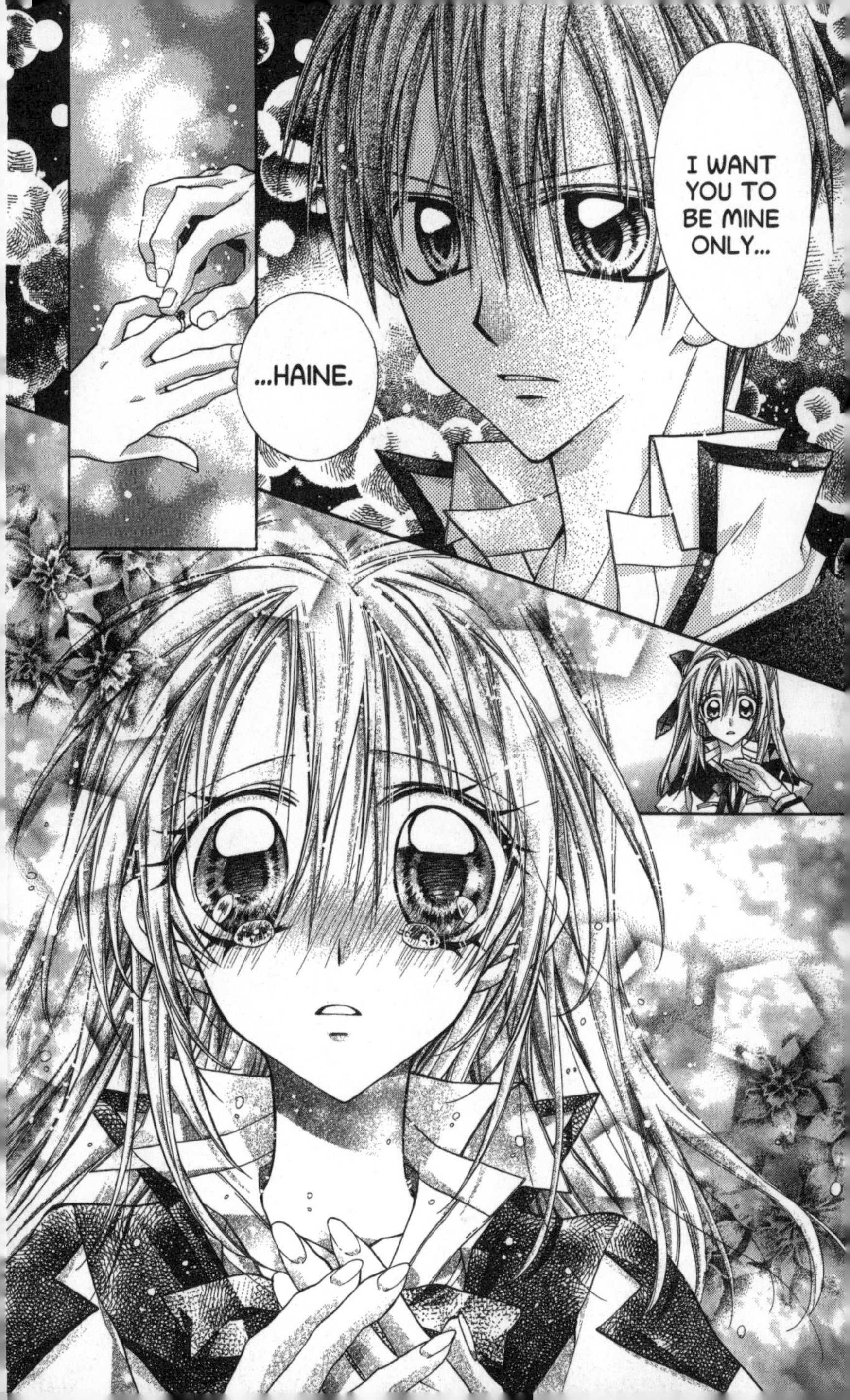
I WANT YOU TO BE MINE ONLY...
...HAINE.

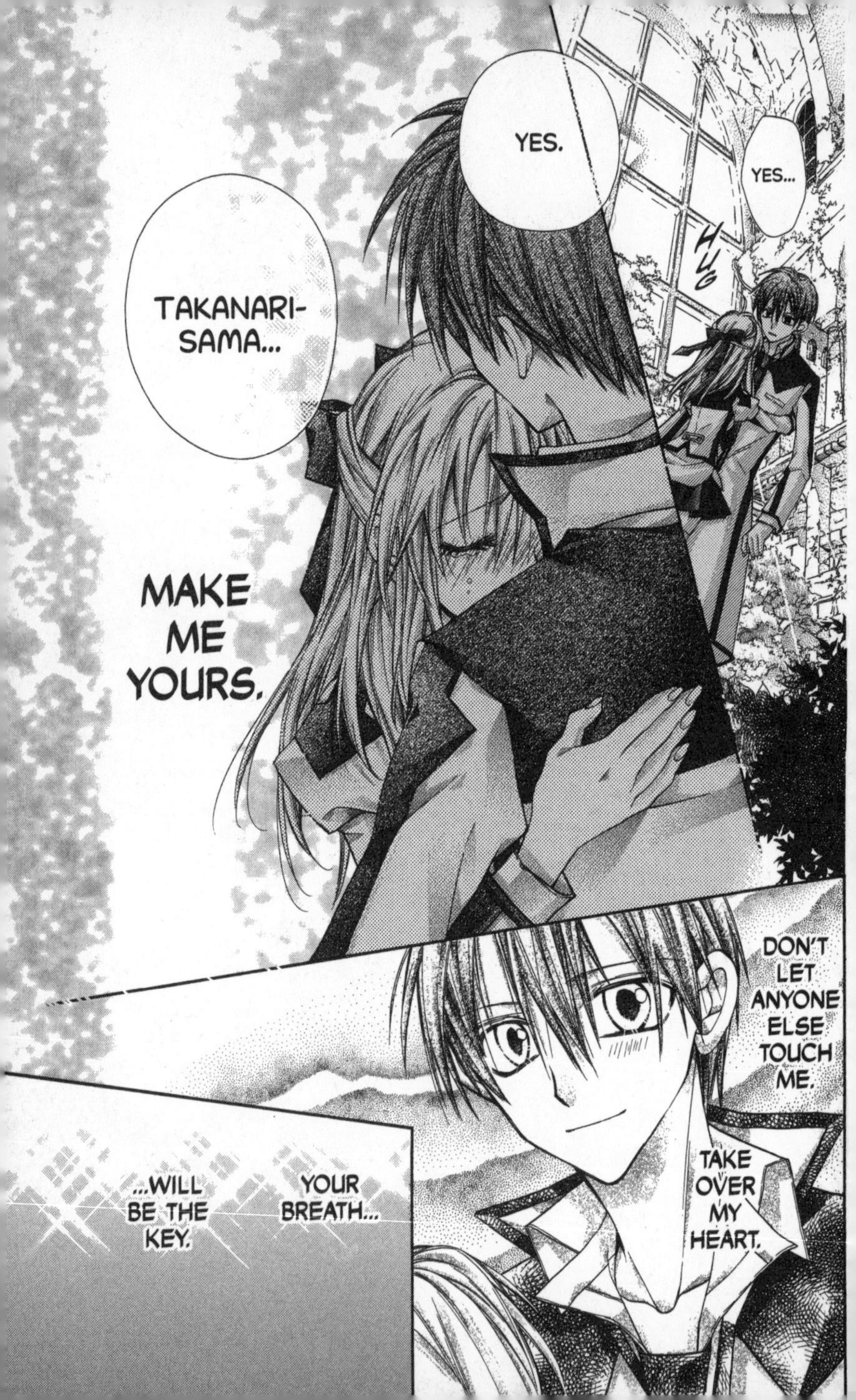
YES...
HUG
YES.
TAKANARI-SAMA...
MAKE ME YOURS.
DON'T LET ANYONE ELSE TOUCH ME.
TAKE OVER MY HEART.
YOUR BREATH...
...WILL BE THE KEY.

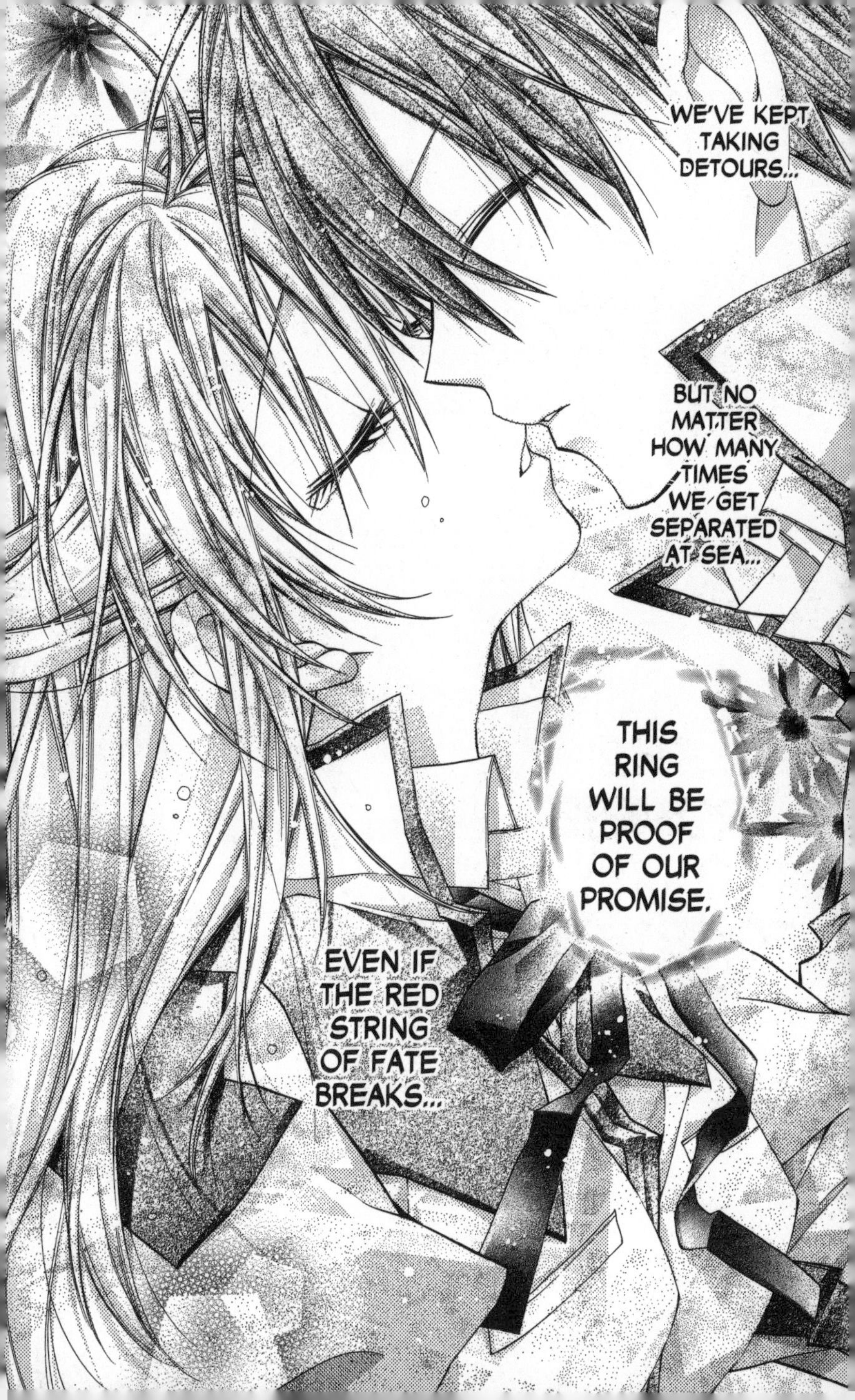
WE'VE KEPT TAKING DETOURS...
BUT NO MATTER HOW MANY TIMES WE GET SEPARATED AT SEA...
EVEN IF THE RED STRING OF FATE BREAKS...
THIS RING WILL BE PROOF OF OUR PROMISE.

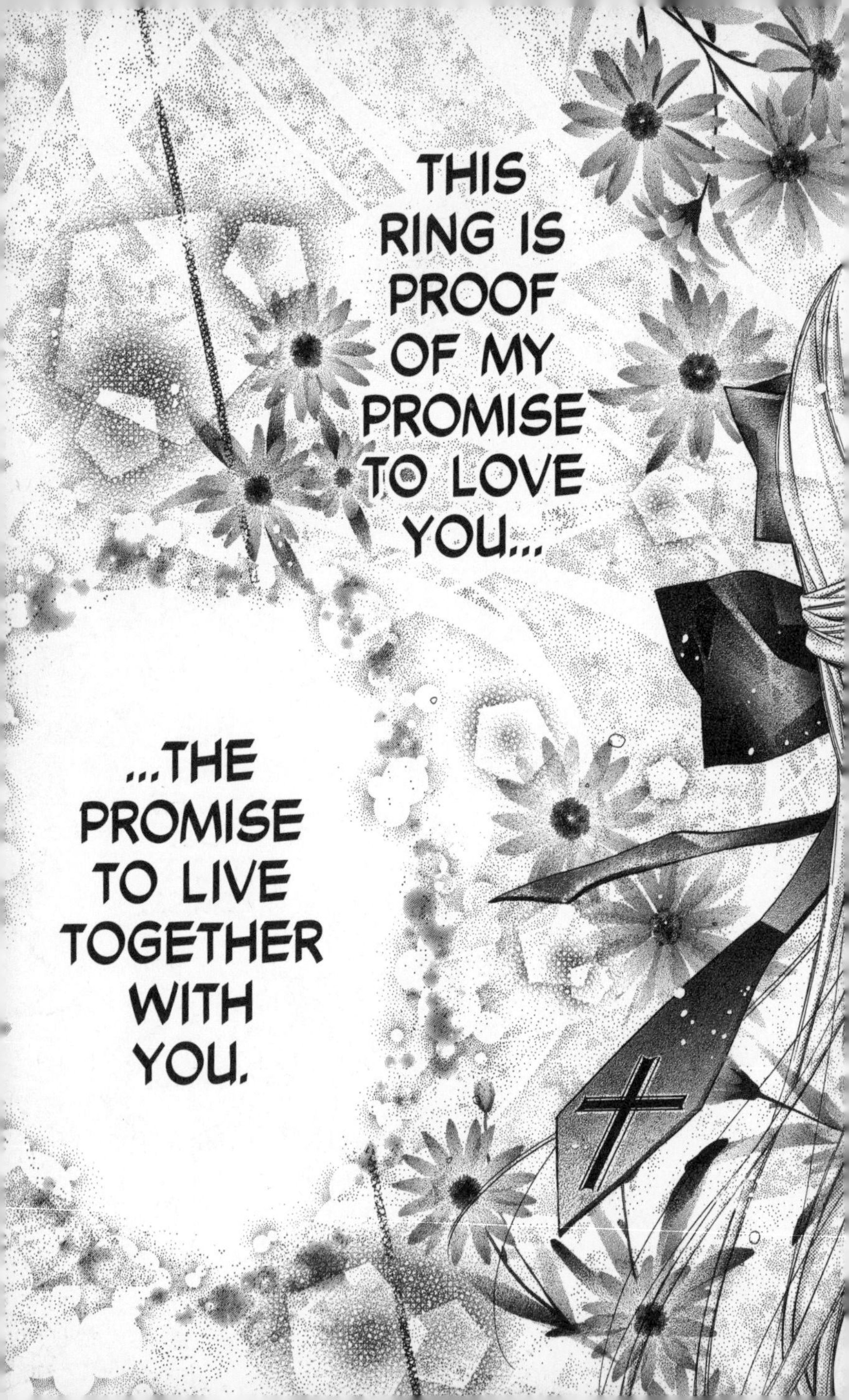
THIS RING IS PROOF OF MY PROMISE TO LOVE YOU...
...THE PROMISE TO LIVE TOGETHER WITH YOU.

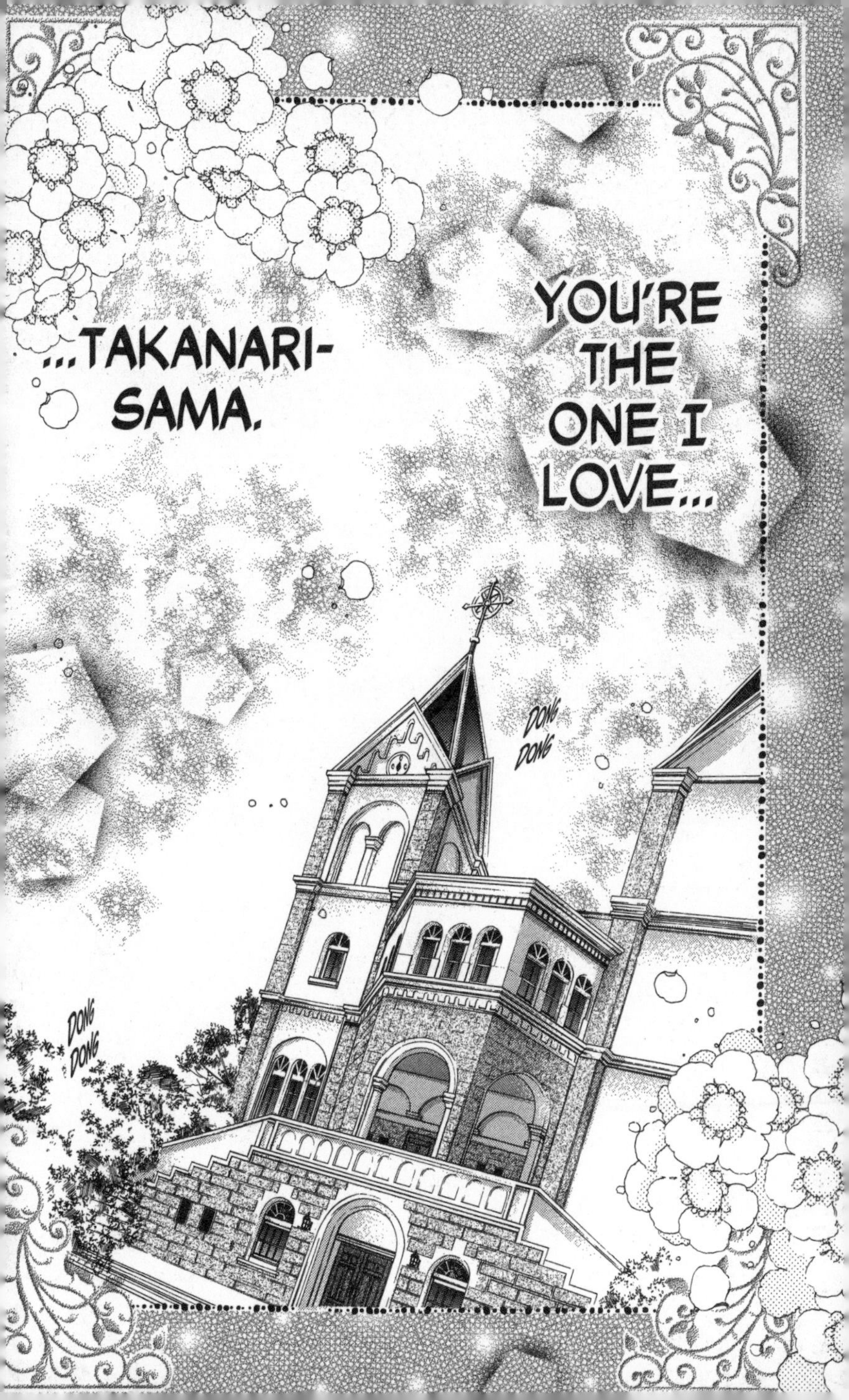
YOU'RE THE ONE I LOVE...
...TAKANARI-SAMA.
DONG DONG
DONG DONG

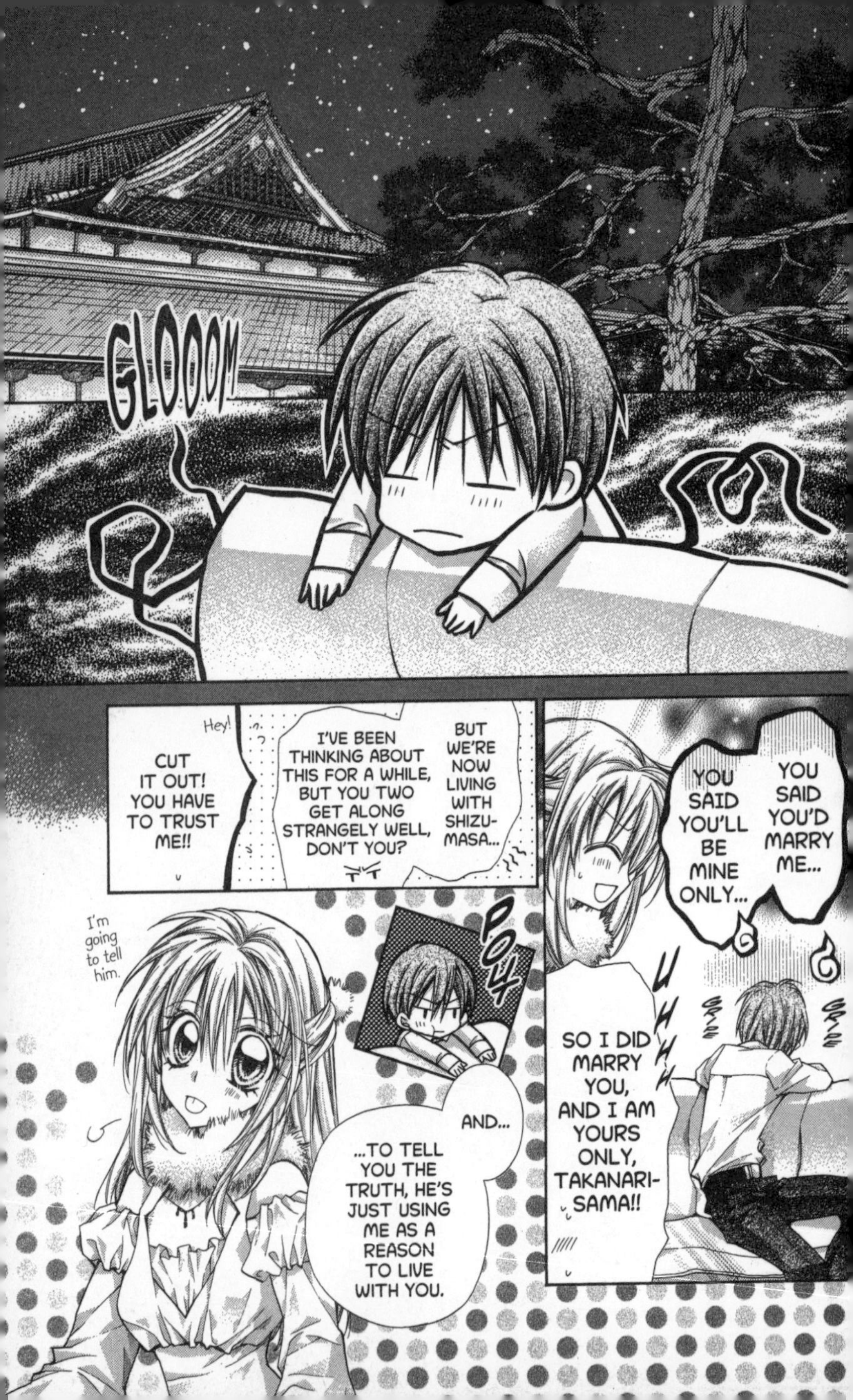
GLOOOM
YOU SAID YOU'D MARRY ME...
YOU SAID YOU'LL BE MINE ONLY...
UHHHH
GRIPE
GRIPE
SO I DID MARRY YOU, AND I AM YOURS ONLY, TAKANARI-SAMA!!
BUT WE'RE NOW LIVING WITH SHIZU-MASA...
I'VE BEEN THINKING ABOUT THIS FOR A WHILE, BUT YOU TWO GET ALONG STRANGELY WELL, DON'T YOU?
CUT IT OUT! YOU HAVE TO TRUST ME!!
Hey!
POUT
AND...
...TO TELL YOU THE TRUTH, HE'S JUST USING ME AS A REASON TO LIVE WITH YOU.
I'm going to tell him.

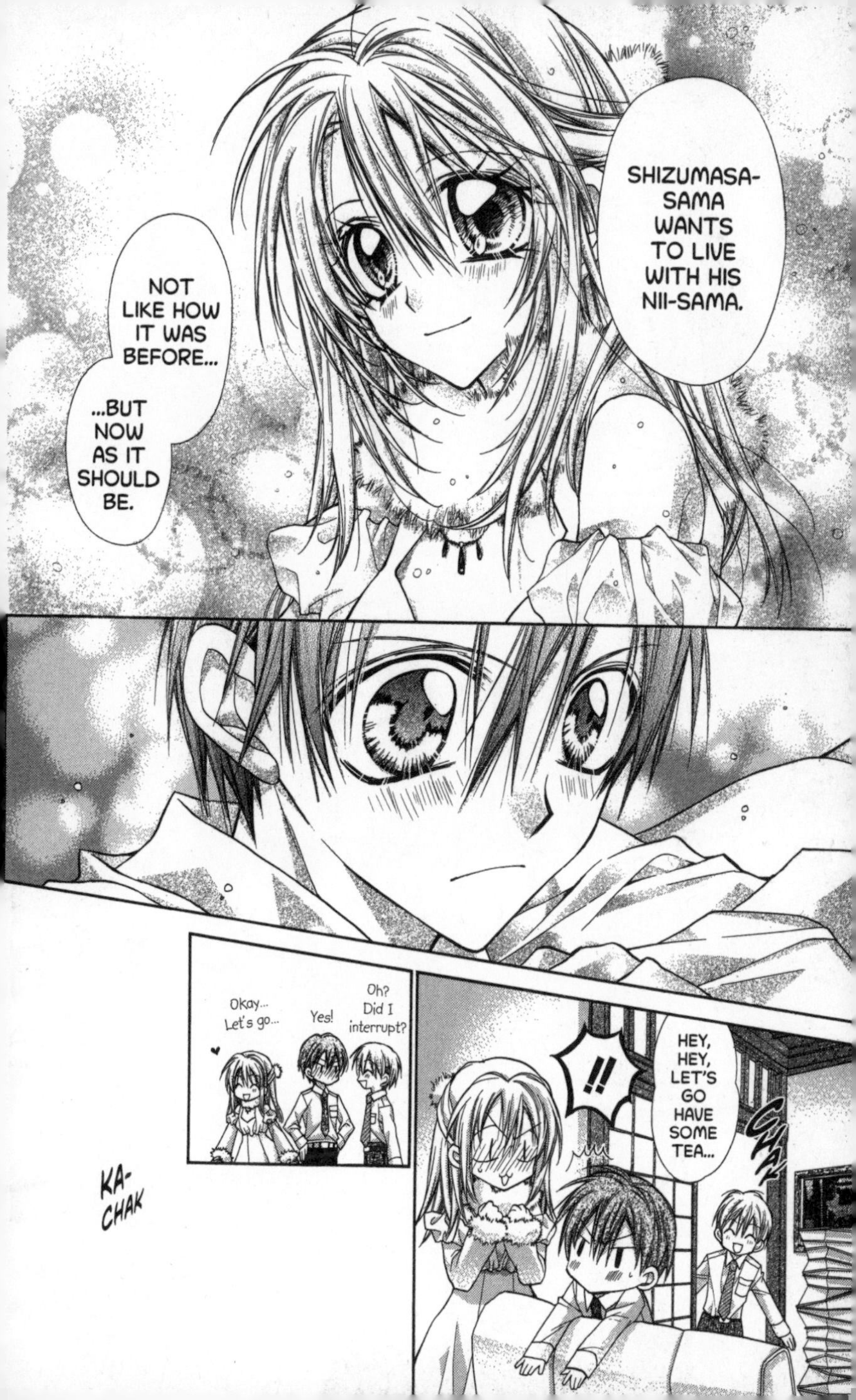
SHIZUMASA-SAMA WANTS TO LIVE WITH HIS NII-SAMA.
NOT LIKE HOW IT WAS BEFORE...
...BUT NOW AS IT SHOULD BE.
HEY, HEY, LET'S GO HAVE SOME TEA...
!!
Oh? Did I interrupt?
Yes!
Okay... Let's go...
KA-CHAK

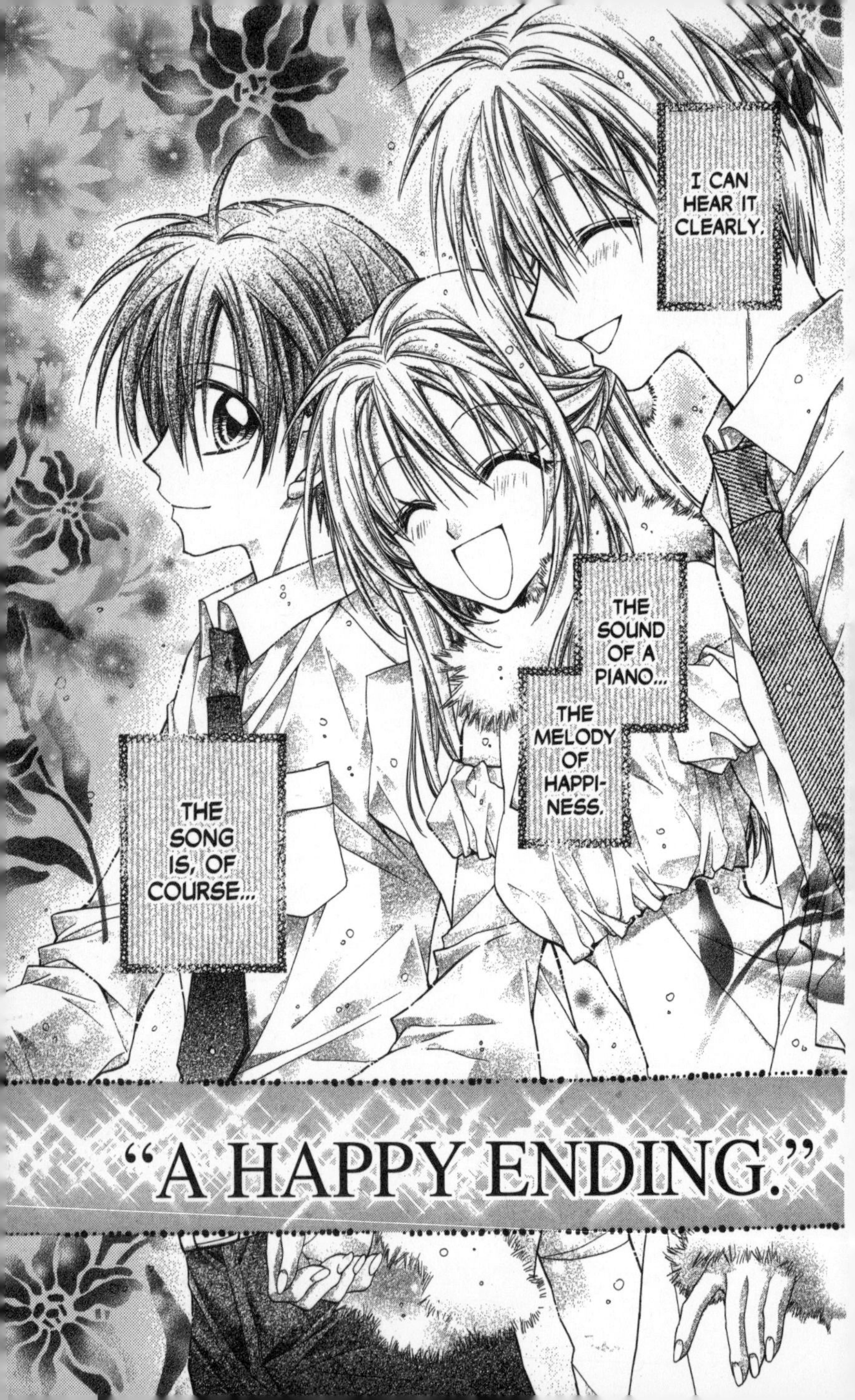
I CAN HEAR IT CLEARLY.
THE SOUND OF A PIANO...
THE MELODY OF HAPPI- NESS.
THE SONG IS, OF COURSE...
"A HAPPY ENDING."

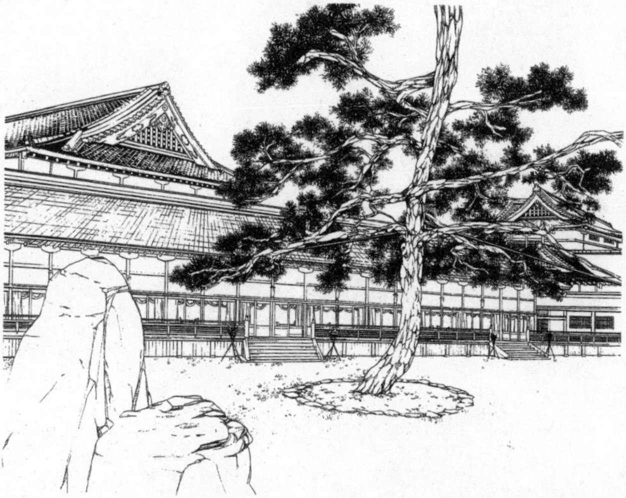

↑ Togu Family House

I looked at a *book* to draw this. I went through *books* on the Imperial Palace and arranged it myself.

Gentlemen's Alliance Gallery

You can see the window of the room where Takanari had been locked up. ↓

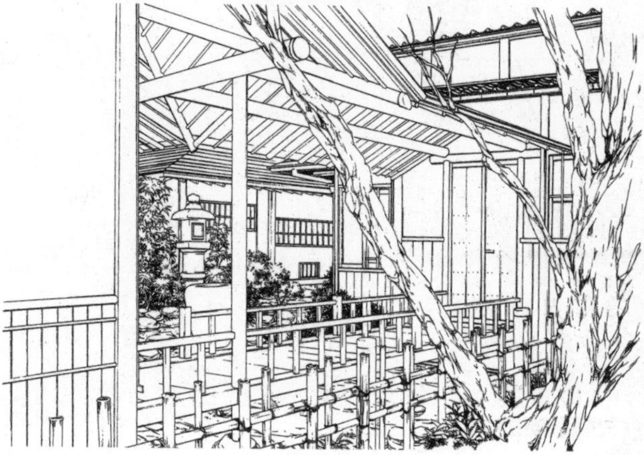

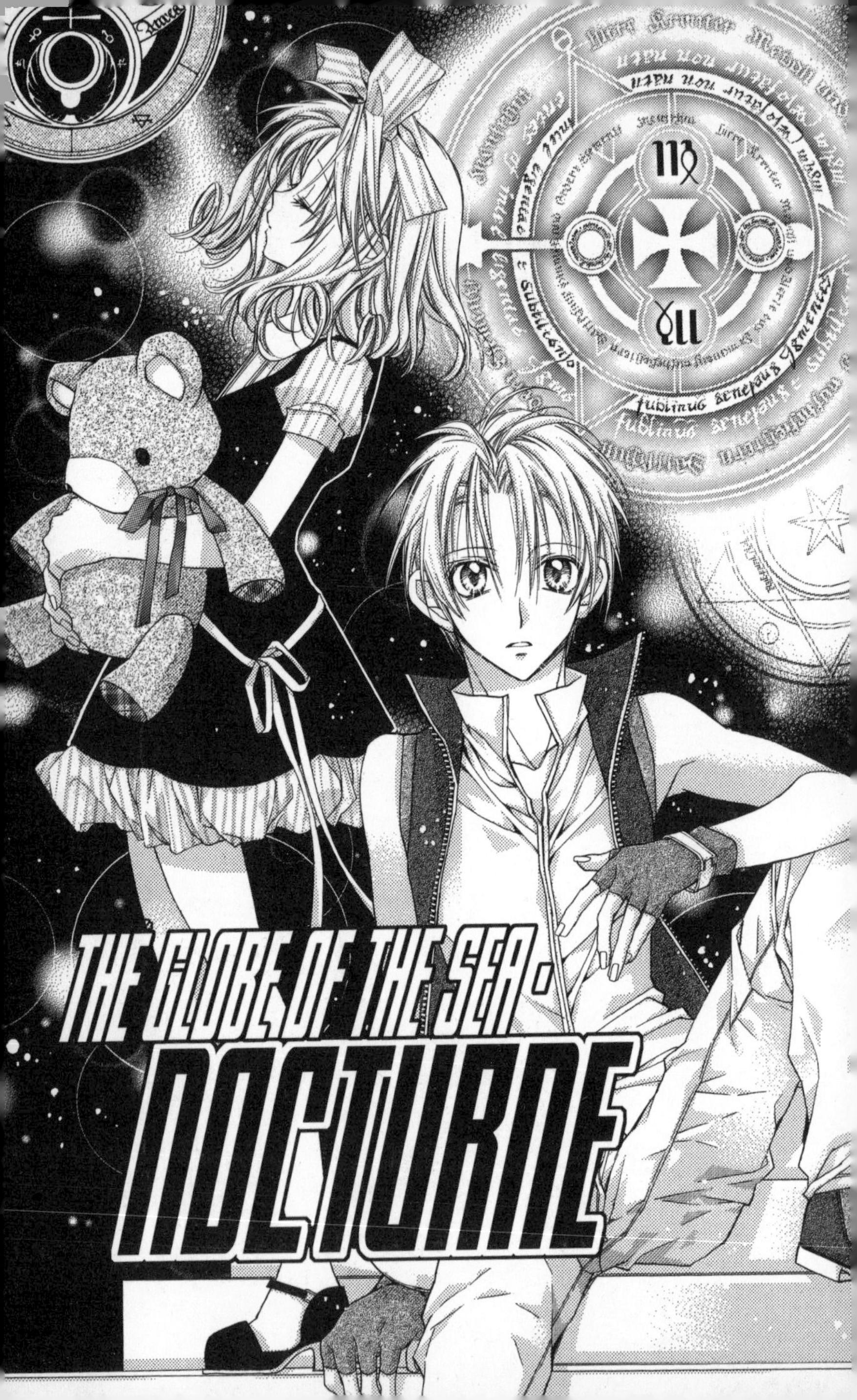
THE GLOBE OF THE SEA·
NOCTURNE

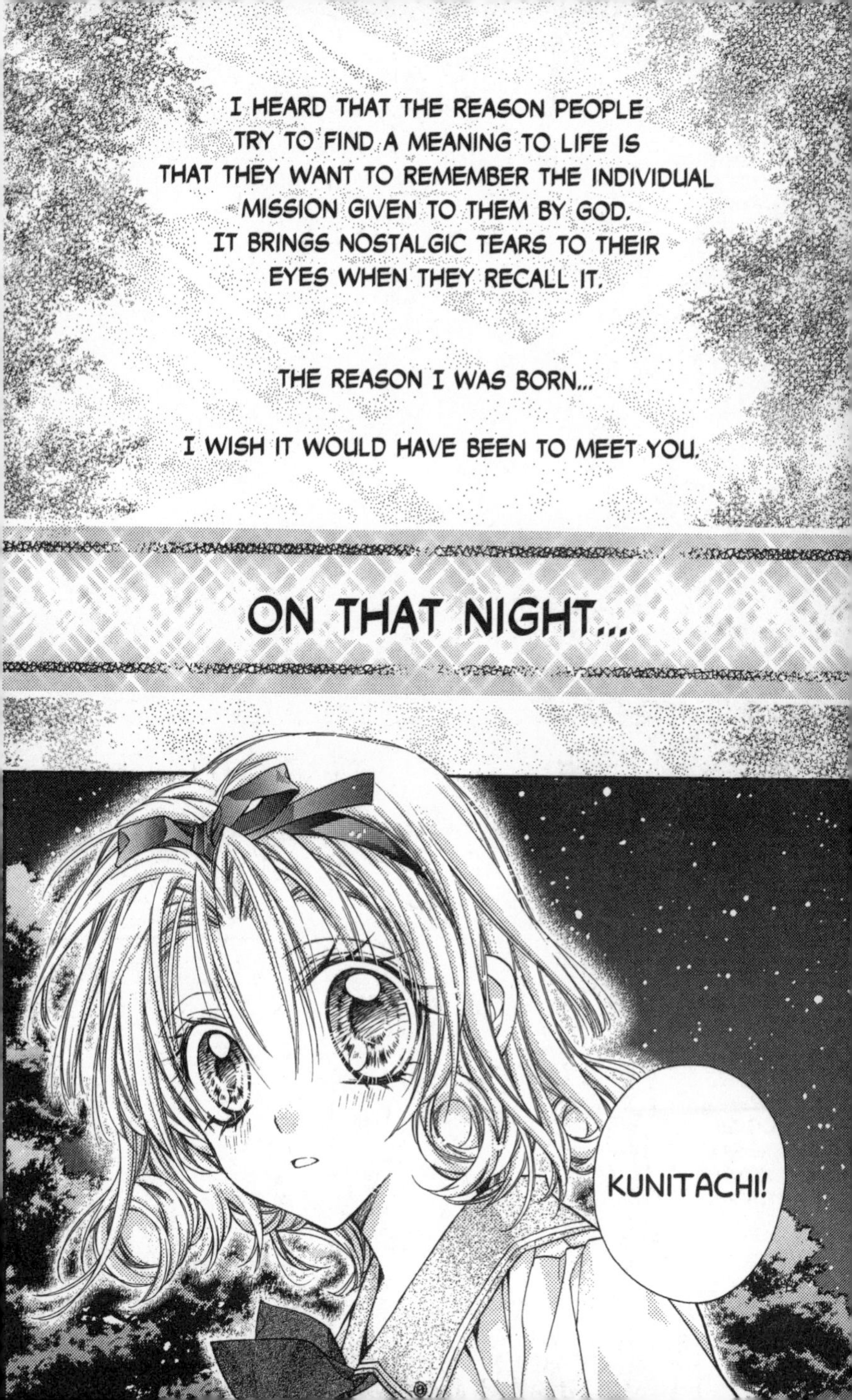
I HEARD THAT THE REASON PEOPLE TRY TO FIND A MEANING TO LIFE IS THAT THEY WANT TO REMEMBER THE INDIVIDUAL MISSION GIVEN TO THEM BY GOD. IT BRINGS NOSTALGIC TEARS TO THEIR EYES WHEN THEY RECALL IT.
THE REASON I WAS BORN...
I WISH IT WOULD HAVE BEEN TO MEET YOU.
ON THAT NIGHT...
KUNITACHI!

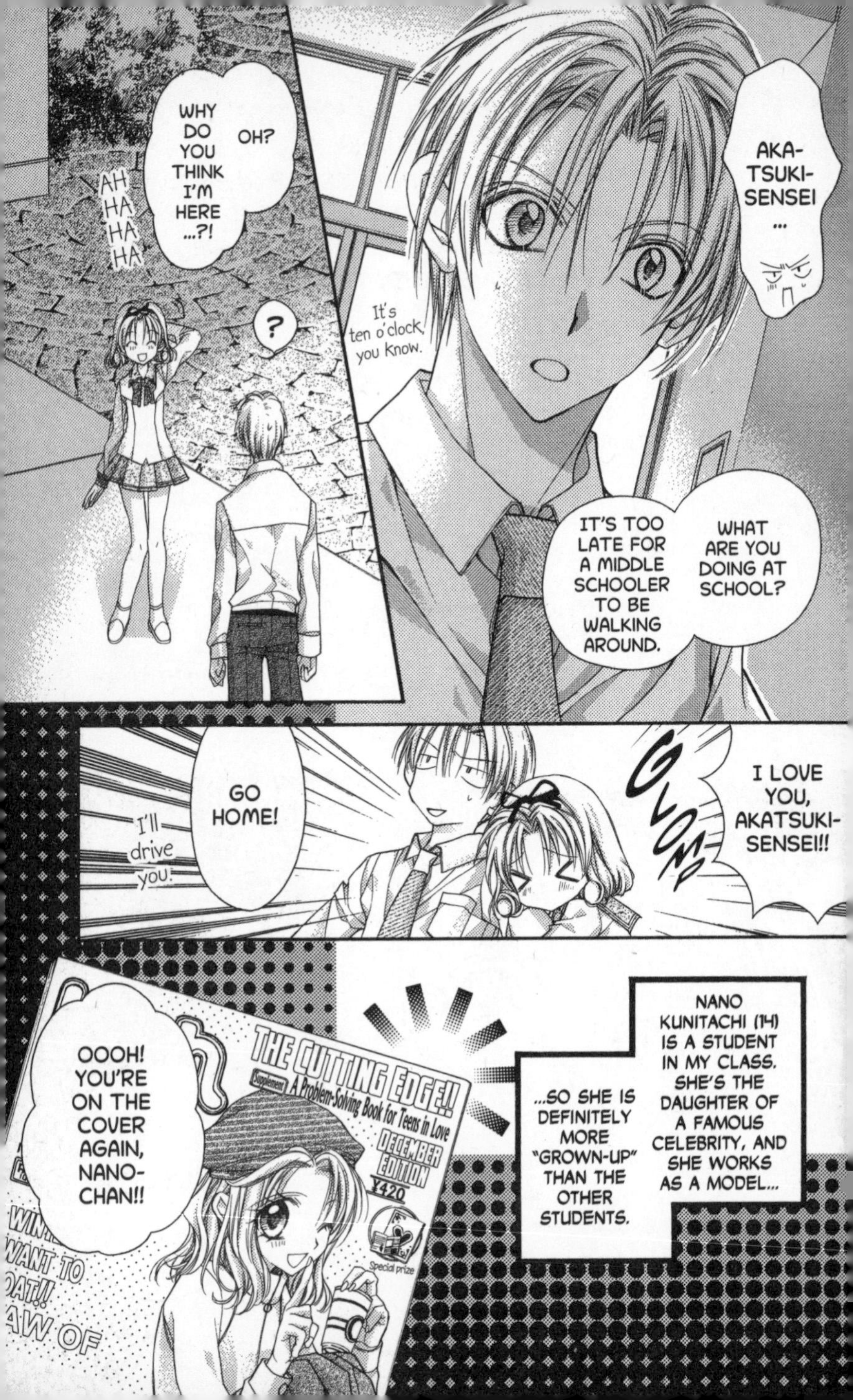
AKA-TSUKI-SENSEI ...
It's ten o'clock, you know.
WHAT ARE YOU DOING AT SCHOOL?
IT'S TOO LATE FOR A MIDDLE SCHOOLER TO BE WALKING AROUND.
OH?
WHY DO YOU THINK I'M HERE ...?!
AH HA HA HA
?
I LOVE YOU, AKATSUKI-SENSEI!!
GLOMP
GO HOME!
I'll drive you.
NANO KUNITACHI (14) IS A STUDENT IN MY CLASS. SHE'S THE DAUGHTER OF A FAMOUS CELEBRITY, AND SHE WORKS AS A MODEL...
...SO SHE IS DEFINITELY MORE "GROWN-UP" THAN THE OTHER STUDENTS.
THE CUTTING EDGE!!
Supplement A Problem-Solving Book for Teens in Love
DECEMBER EDITION
¥420
Special prize
OOOH! YOU'RE ON THE COVER AGAIN, NANO-CHAN!!

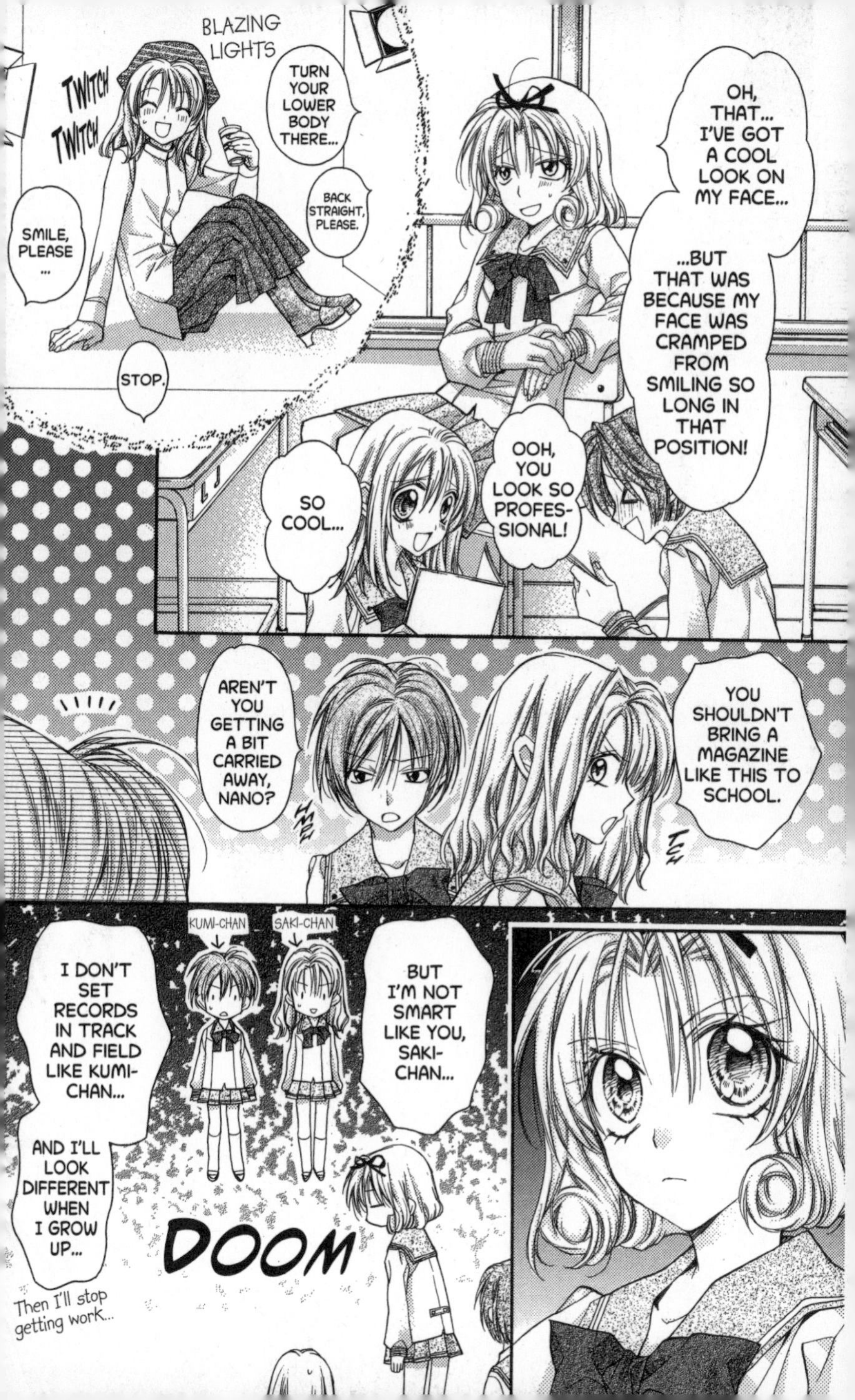
OH, THAT... I'VE GOT A COOL LOOK ON MY FACE...
...BUT THAT WAS BECAUSE MY FACE WAS CRAMPED FROM SMILING SO LONG IN THAT POSITION!
BLAZING LIGHTS
TURN YOUR LOWER BODY THERE...
BACK STRAIGHT, PLEASE.
TWITCH TWITCH
SMILE, PLEASE ...
STOP.
OOH, YOU LOOK SO PROFES- SIONAL!
SO COOL...
YOU SHOULDN'T BRING A MAGAZINE LIKE THIS TO SCHOOL.
AREN'T YOU GETTING A BIT CARRIED AWAY, NANO?
BUT I'M NOT SMART LIKE YOU, SAKI- CHAN...
SAKI-CHAN
KUMI-CHAN
I DON'T SET RECORDS IN TRACK AND FIELD LIKE KUMI- CHAN...
AND I'LL LOOK DIFFERENT WHEN I GROW UP...
DOOM
Then I'll stop getting work...

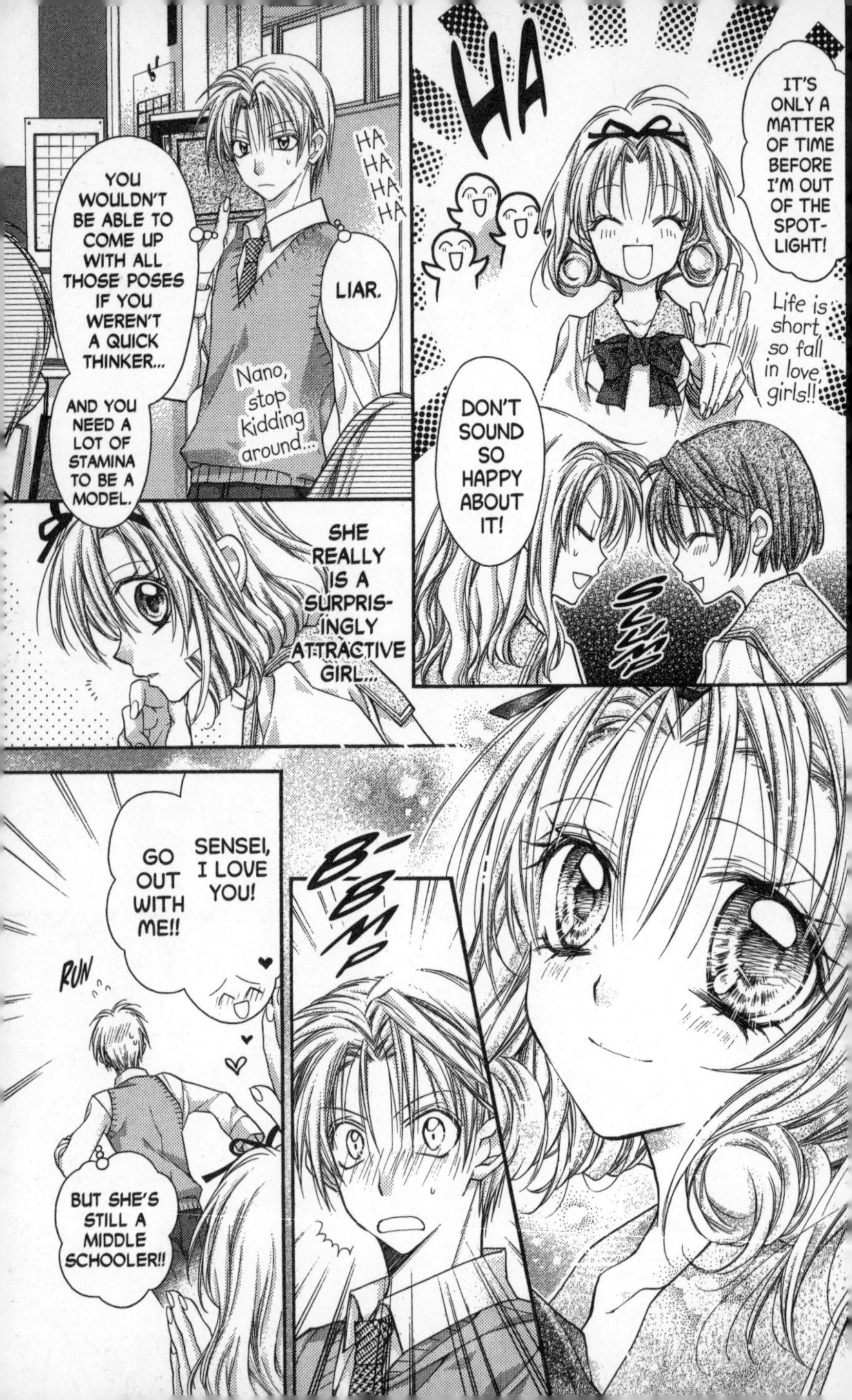
HA
IT'S ONLY A MATTER OF TIME BEFORE I'M OUT OF THE SPOT-LIGHT!
Life is short, so fall in love, girls!!
DON'T SOUND SO HAPPY ABOUT IT!
SLUMP
HA HA HA HA
LIAR.
Nano, stop kidding around...
YOU WOULDN'T BE ABLE TO COME UP WITH ALL THOSE POSES IF YOU WEREN'T A QUICK THINKER...
AND YOU NEED A LOT OF STAMINA TO BE A MODEL.
SHE REALLY IS A SURPRIS-INGLY ATTRACTIVE GIRL...
B-BUMP
SENSEI, I LOVE YOU!
GO OUT WITH ME!!
RUN
BUT SHE'S STILL A MIDDLE SCHOOLER!!

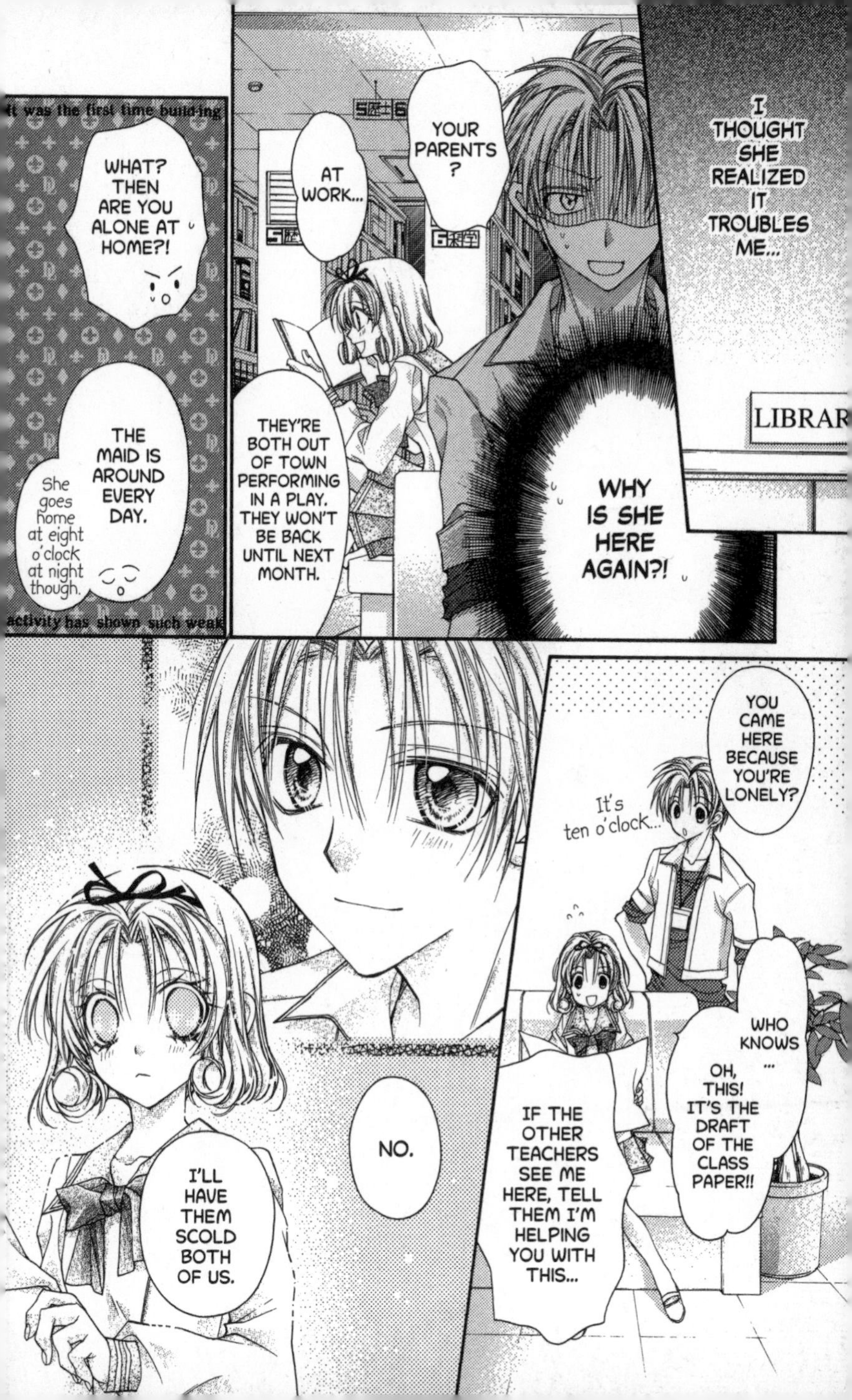

I THOUGHT SHE REALIZED IT TROUBLES ME...
LIBRAR
WHY IS SHE HERE AGAIN?!
YOUR PARENTS?
AT WORK...
THEY'RE BOTH OUT OF TOWN PERFORMING IN A PLAY. THEY WON'T BE BACK UNTIL NEXT MONTH.
It was the first time building
WHAT? THEN ARE YOU ALONE AT HOME?!
THE MAID IS AROUND EVERY DAY.
She goes home at eight o'clock at night though.
activity has shown such weak
YOU CAME HERE BECAUSE YOU'RE LONELY?
It's ten o'clock...
WHO KNOWS...
OH, THIS! IT'S THE DRAFT OF THE CLASS PAPER!!
IF THE OTHER TEACHERS SEE ME HERE, TELL THEM I'M HELPING YOU WITH THIS...
NO.
I'LL HAVE THEM SCOLD BOTH OF US.

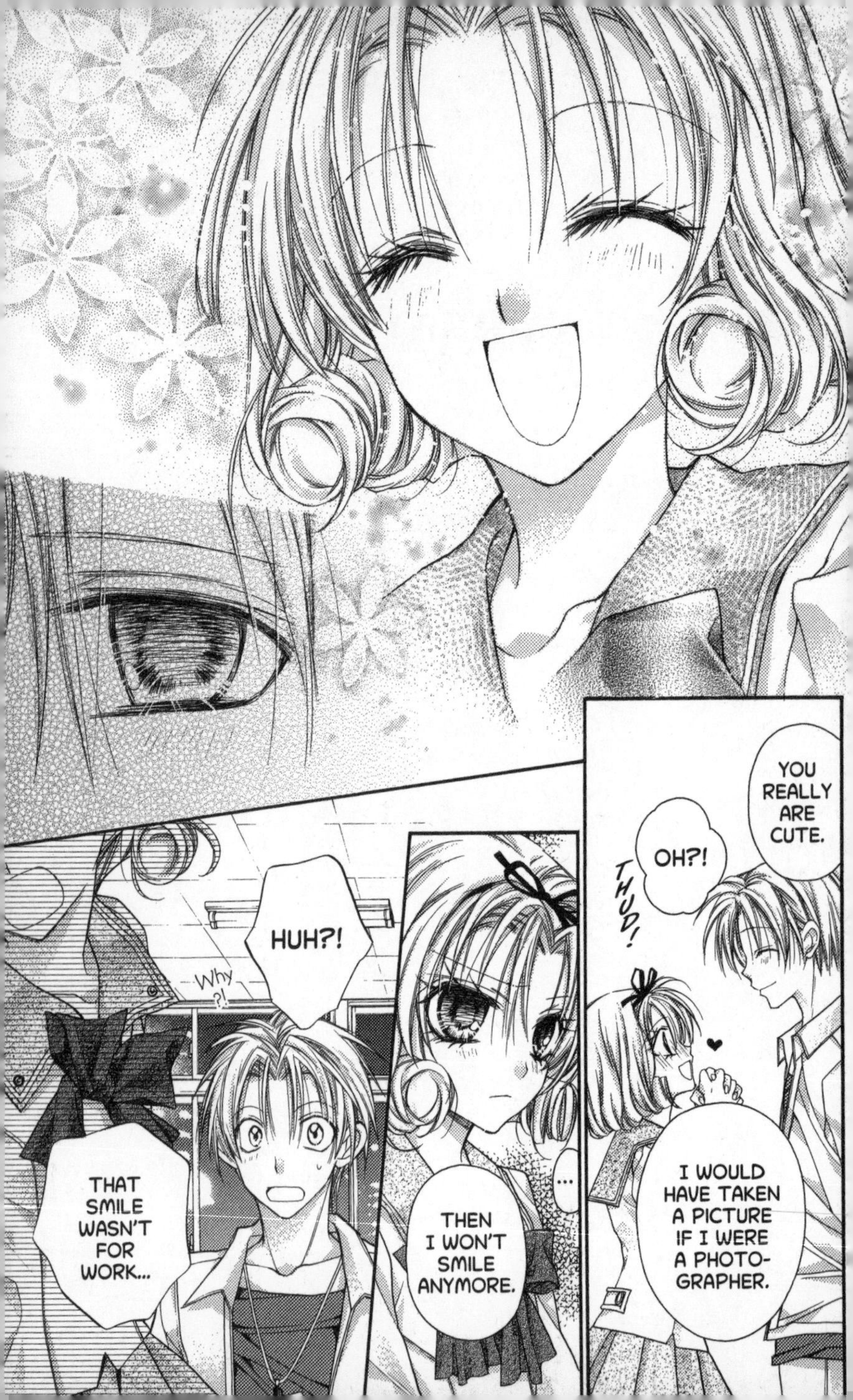
YOU REALLY ARE CUTE.
OH?!
THUD!
I WOULD HAVE TAKEN A PICTURE IF I WERE A PHOTO-GRAPHER.
...
THEN I WON'T SMILE ANYMORE.
HUH?!
Why ?!
THAT SMILE WASN'T FOR WORK...

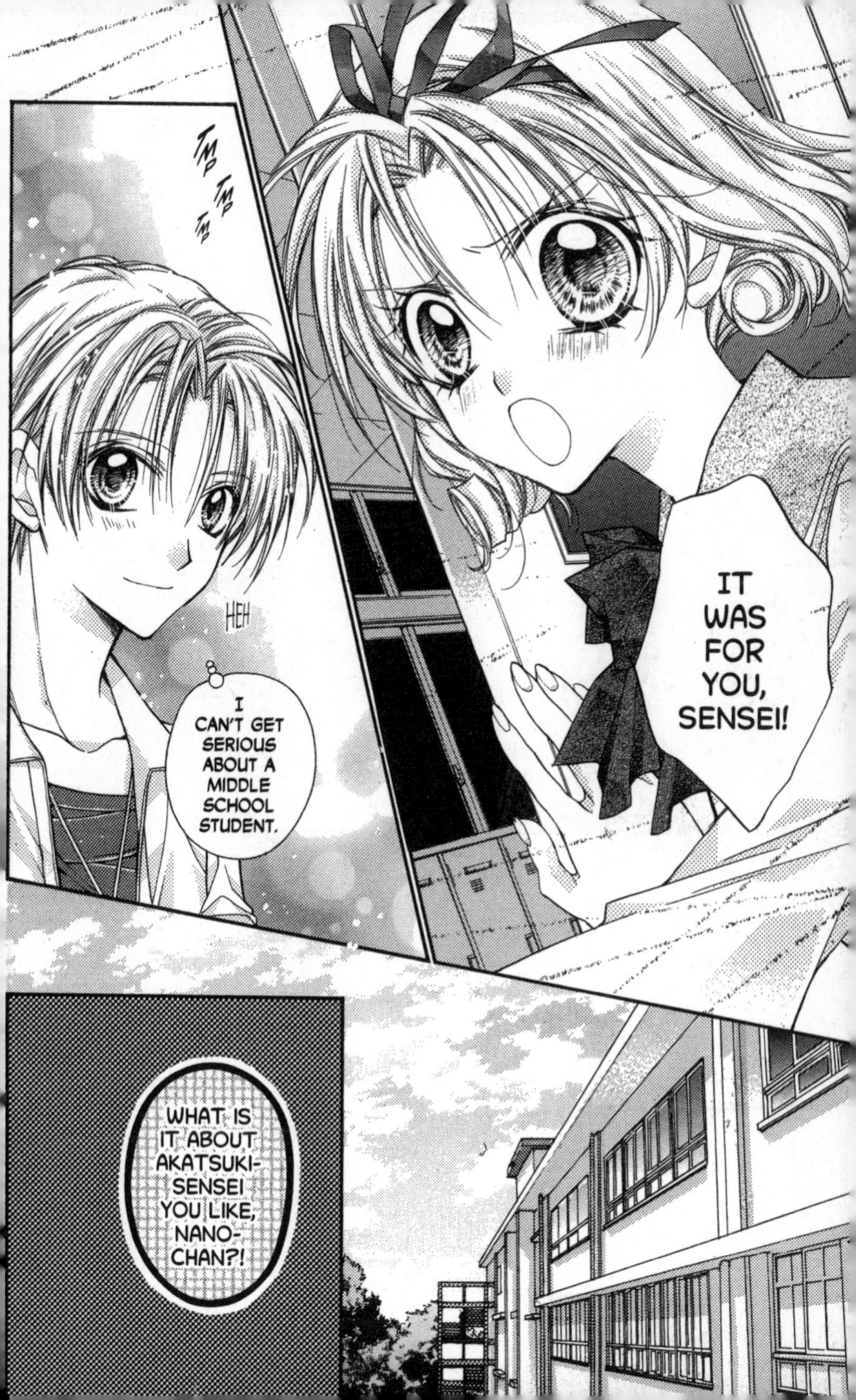
IT WAS FOR YOU, SENSEI!
TMP TMP TMP
HEH
I CAN'T GET SERIOUS ABOUT A MIDDLE SCHOOL STUDENT.
WHAT IS IT ABOUT AKATSUKI-SENSEI YOU LIKE, NANO-CHAN?!

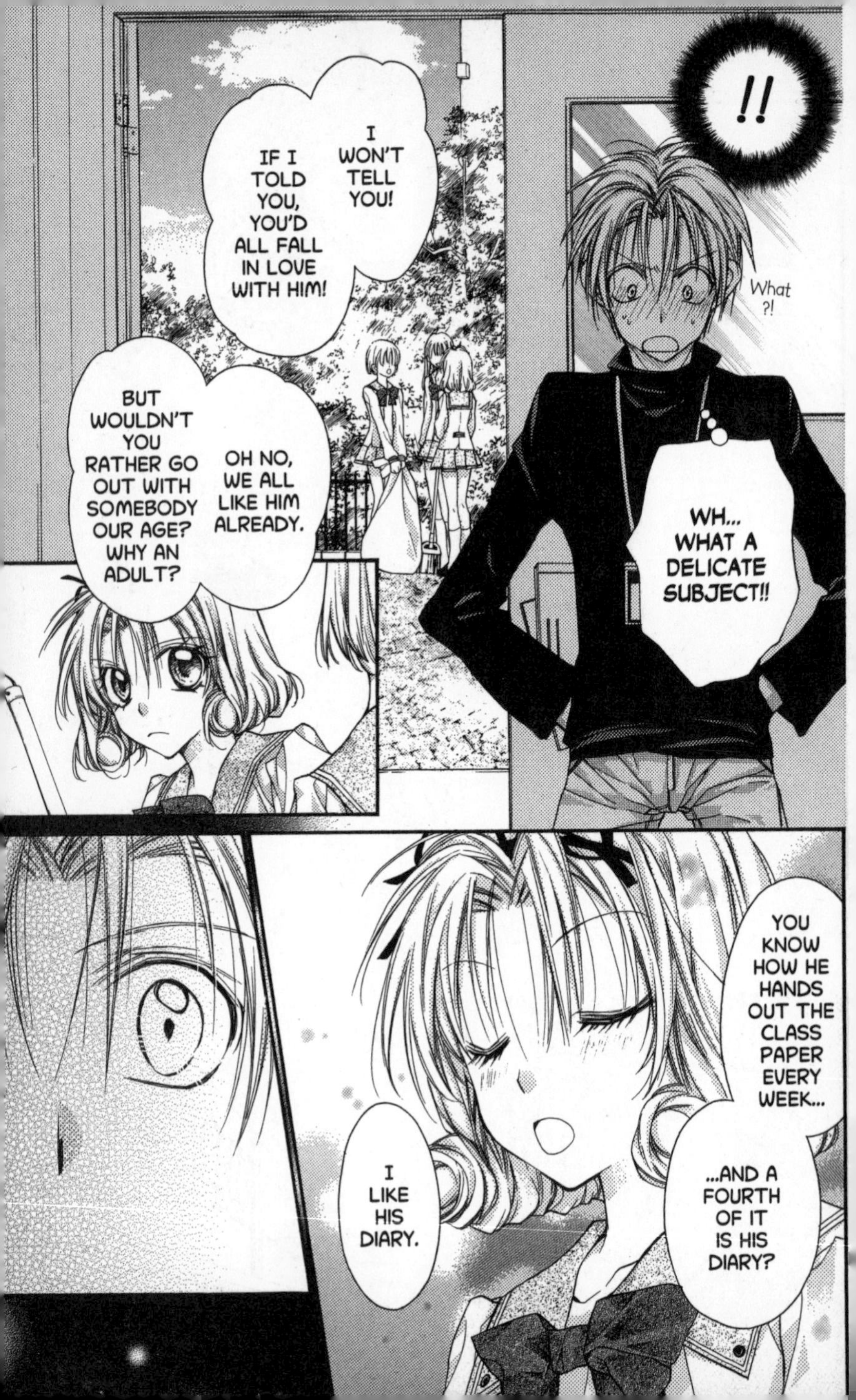
!!
What ?!
WH... WHAT A DELICATE SUBJECT!!
I WON'T TELL YOU!
IF I TOLD YOU, YOU'D ALL FALL IN LOVE WITH HIM!
OH NO, WE ALL LIKE HIM ALREADY.
BUT WOULDN'T YOU RATHER GO OUT WITH SOMEBODY OUR AGE? WHY AN ADULT?
YOU KNOW HOW HE HANDS OUT THE CLASS PAPER EVERY WEEK...
...AND A FOURTH OF IT IS HIS DIARY?
I LIKE HIS DIARY.

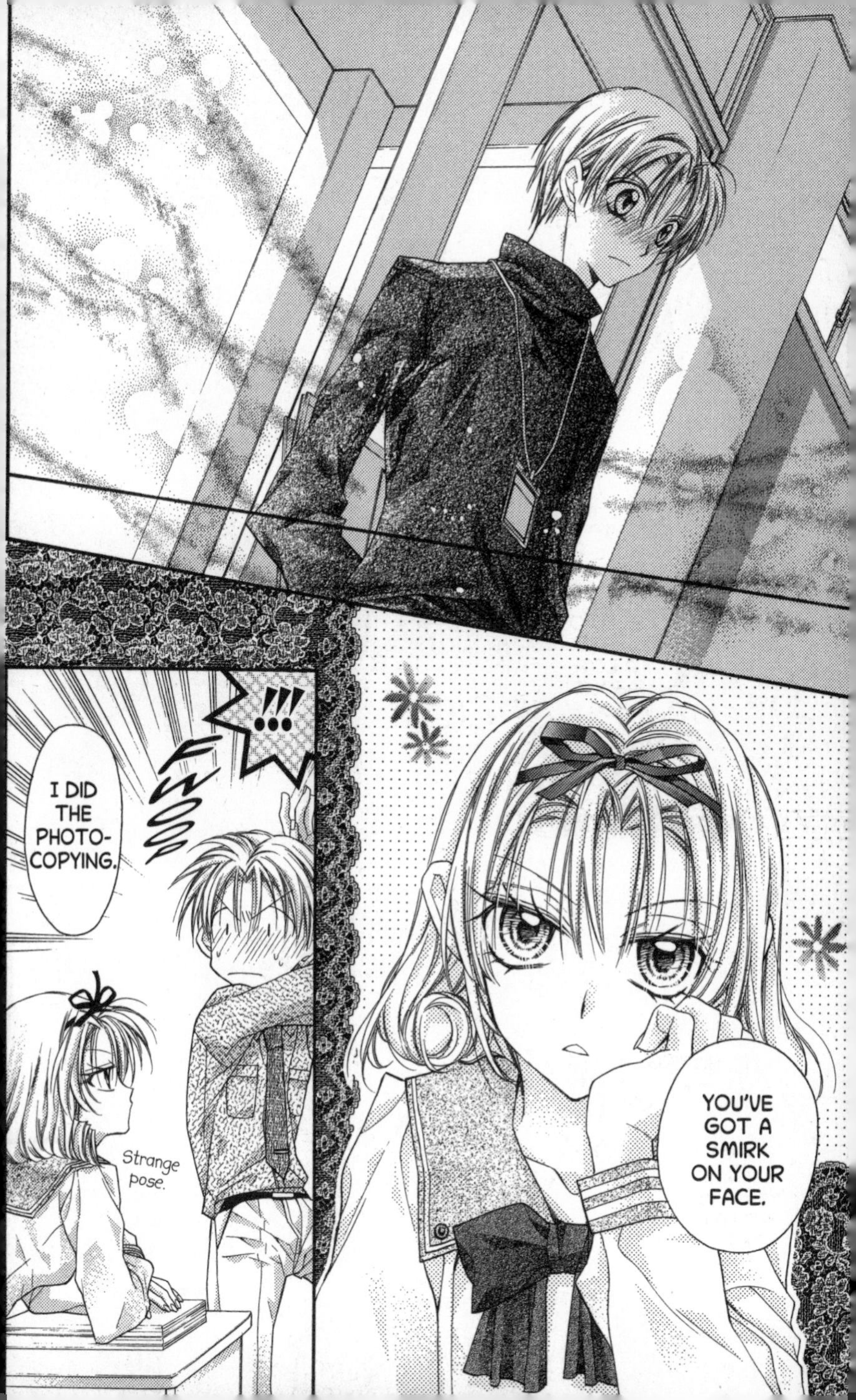
YOU'VE GOT A SMIRK ON YOUR FACE.
!!!
FWOOP
I DID THE PHOTO-COPYING.
Strange pose.

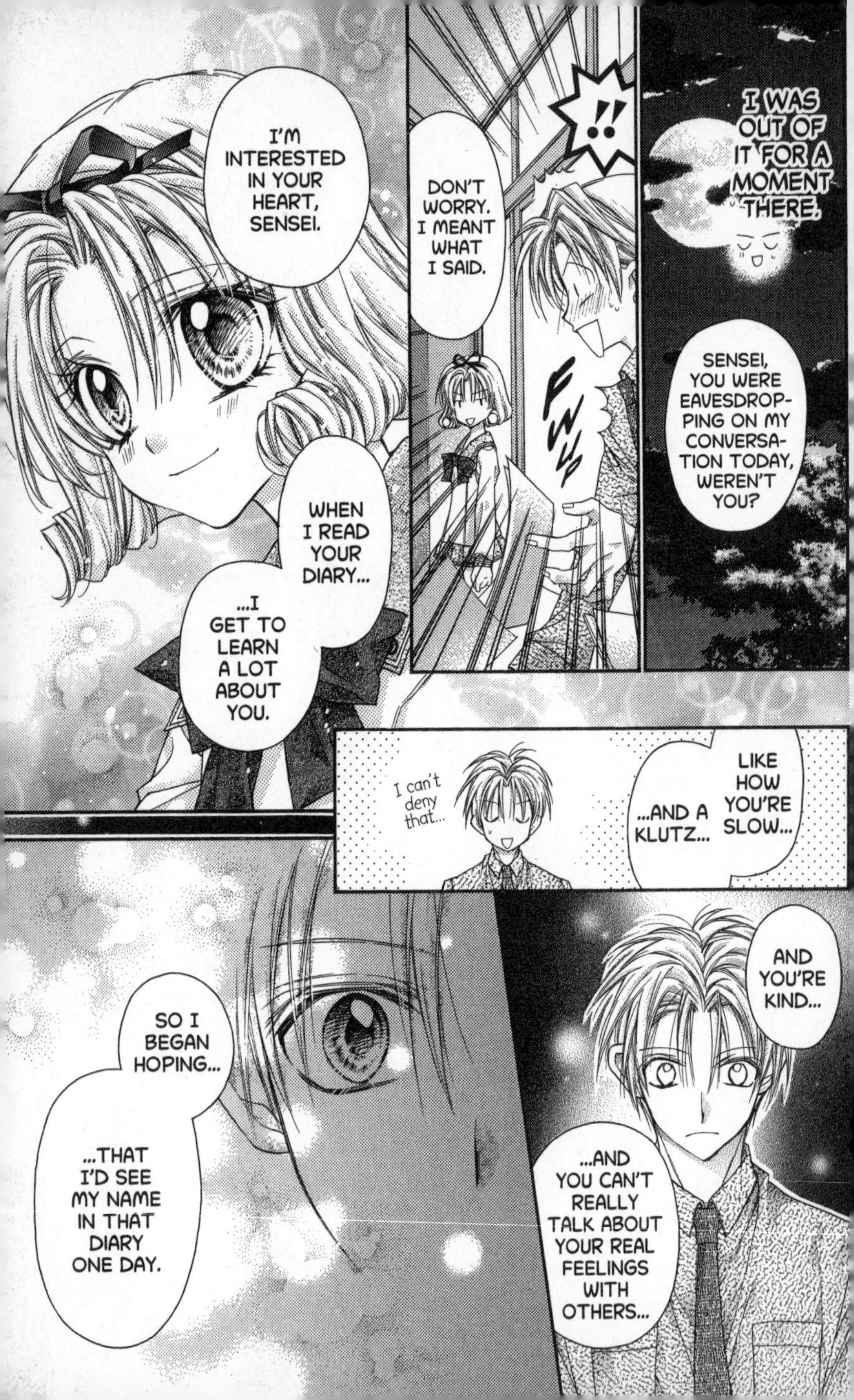
I WAS OUT OF IT FOR A MOMENT THERE.
SENSEI, YOU WERE EAVESDROPPING ON MY CONVERSATION TODAY, WEREN'T YOU?
!!
FWUP
DON'T WORRY. I MEANT WHAT I SAID.
I'M INTERESTED IN YOUR HEART, SENSEI.
WHEN I READ YOUR DIARY...
...I GET TO LEARN A LOT ABOUT YOU.
LIKE HOW YOU'RE SLOW...
...AND A KLUTZ...
I can't deny that...
AND YOU'RE KIND...
...AND YOU CAN'T REALLY TALK ABOUT YOUR REAL FEELINGS WITH OTHERS...
SO I BEGAN HOPING...
...THAT I'D SEE MY NAME IN THAT DIARY ONE DAY.

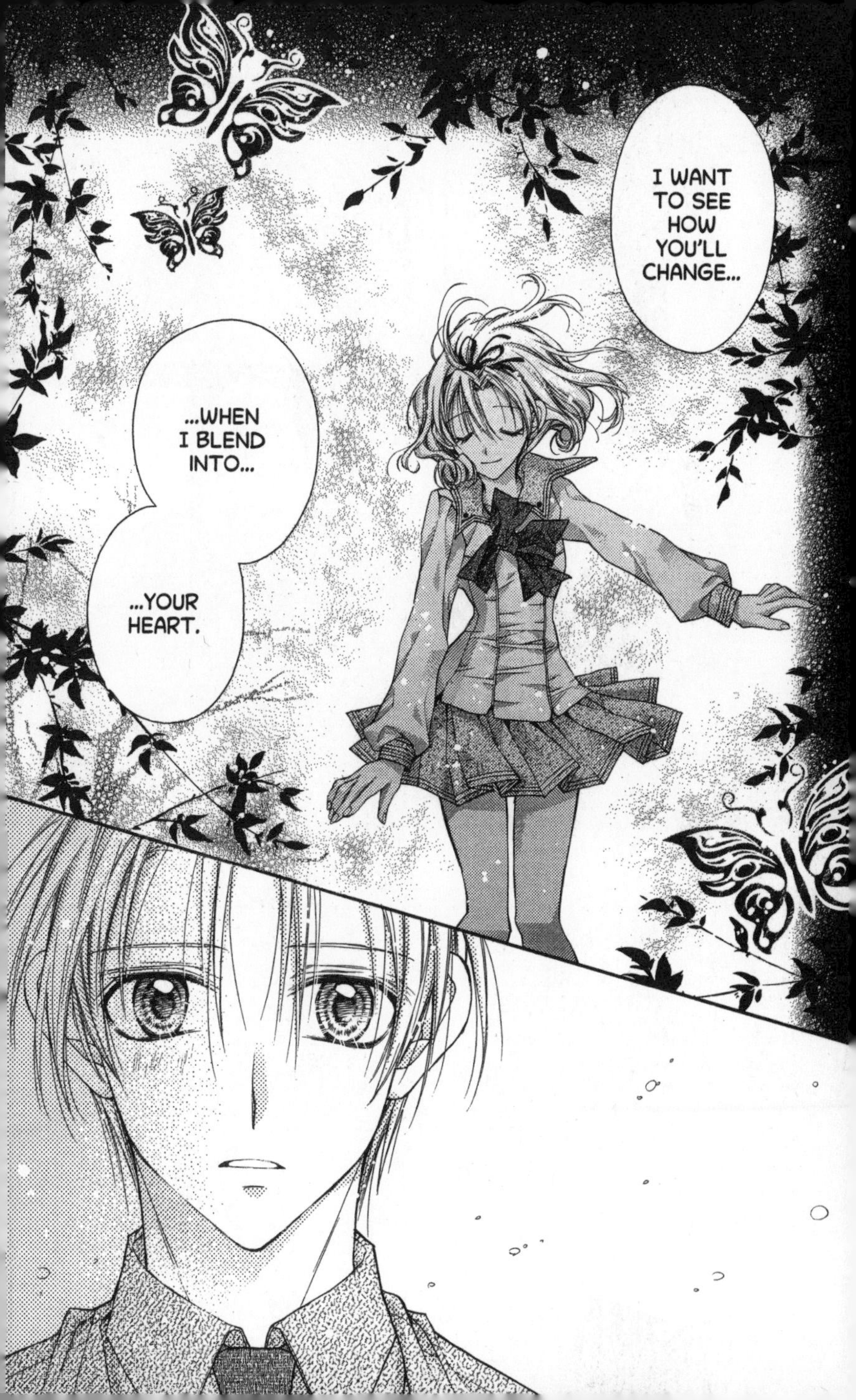
I WANT TO SEE HOW YOU'LL CHANGE...
...WHEN I BLEND INTO...
...YOUR HEART.

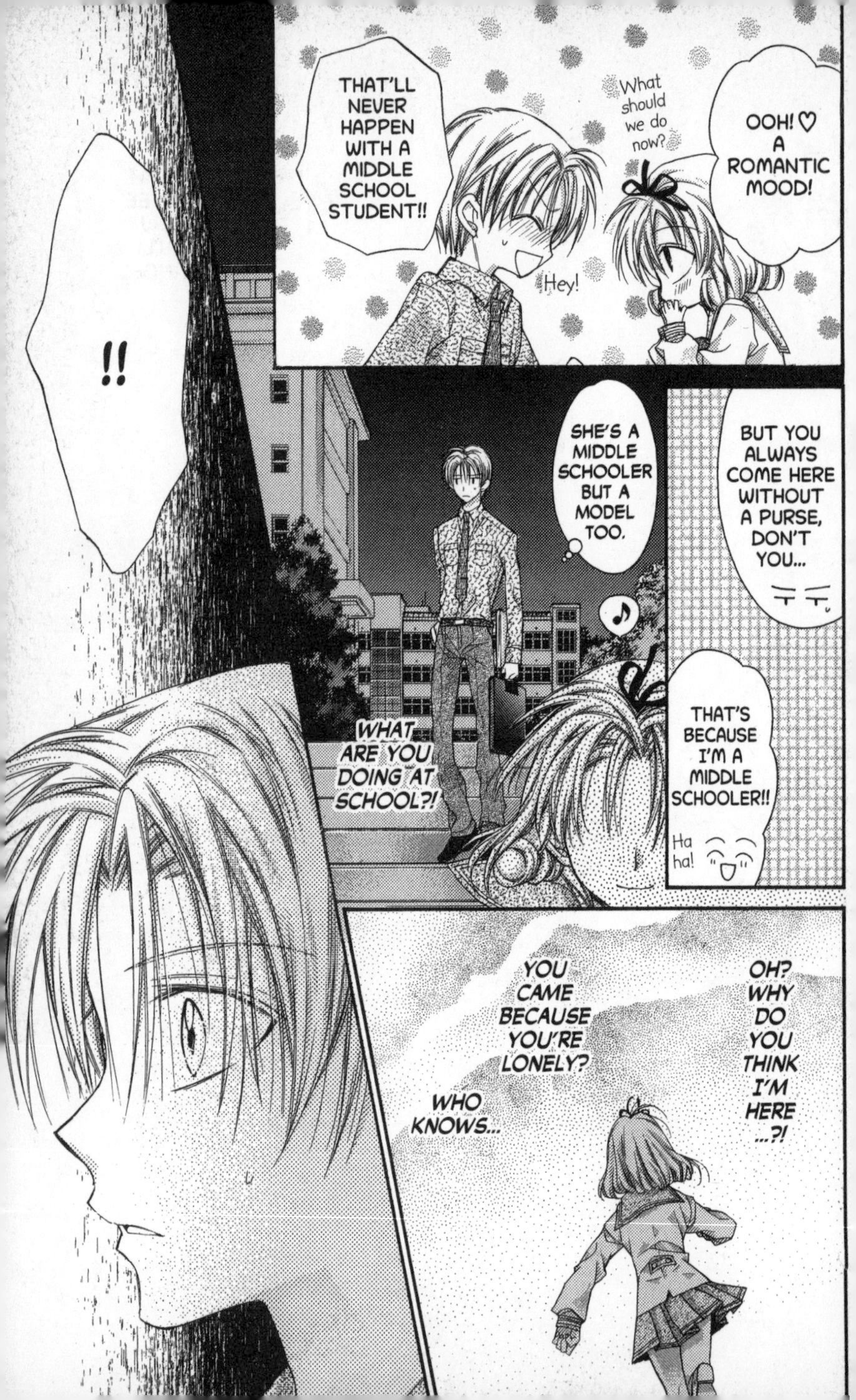

OOH! ♡ A ROMANTIC MOOD!
What should we do now?
THAT'LL NEVER HAPPEN WITH A MIDDLE SCHOOL STUDENT!!
Hey!
BUT YOU ALWAYS COME HERE WITHOUT A PURSE, DON'T YOU...
THAT'S BECAUSE I'M A MIDDLE SCHOOLER!!
Ha ha!
SHE'S A MIDDLE SCHOOLER BUT A MODEL TOO.
WHAT ARE YOU DOING AT SCHOOL?!
OH? WHY DO YOU THINK I'M HERE ...?!
YOU CAME BECAUSE YOU'RE LONELY?
WHO KNOWS...
!!

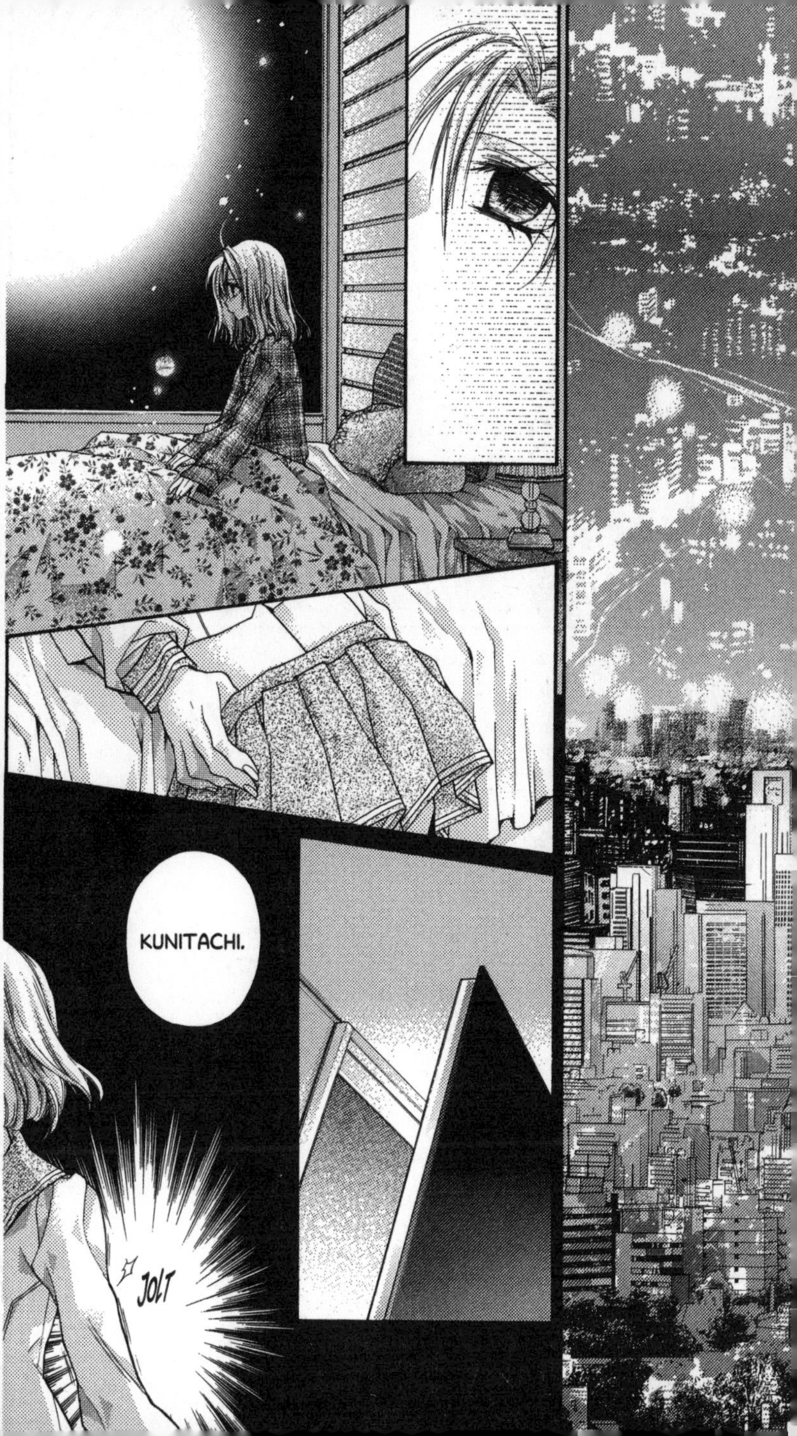
KUNITACHI.
JOLT

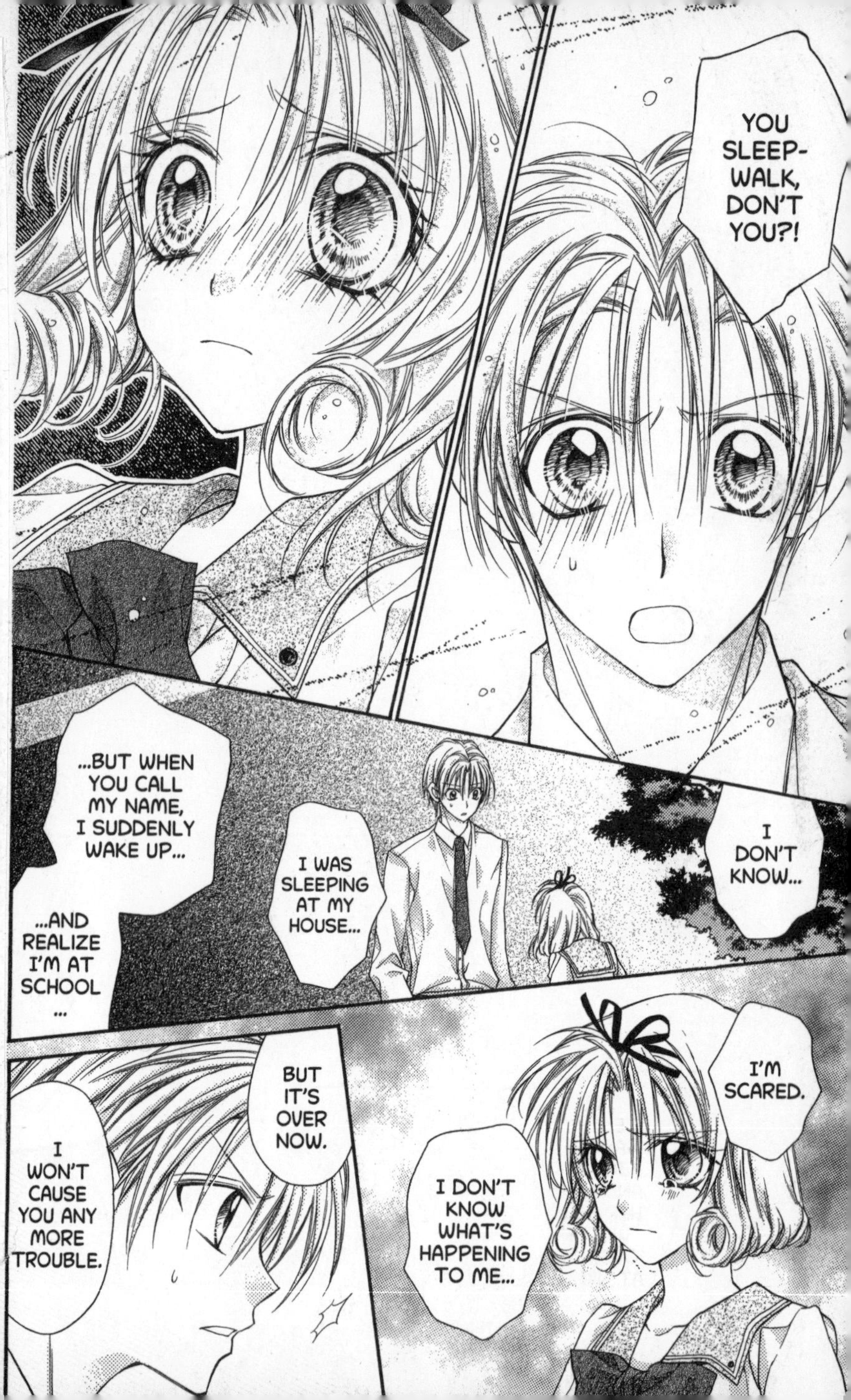
YOU SLEEP-WALK, DON'T YOU?!
I DON'T KNOW...
I WAS SLEEPING AT MY HOUSE...
...BUT WHEN YOU CALL MY NAME, I SUDDENLY WAKE UP...
...AND REALIZE I'M AT SCHOOL ...
I'M SCARED.
I DON'T KNOW WHAT'S HAPPENING TO ME...
BUT IT'S OVER NOW.
I WON'T CAUSE YOU ANY MORE TROUBLE.

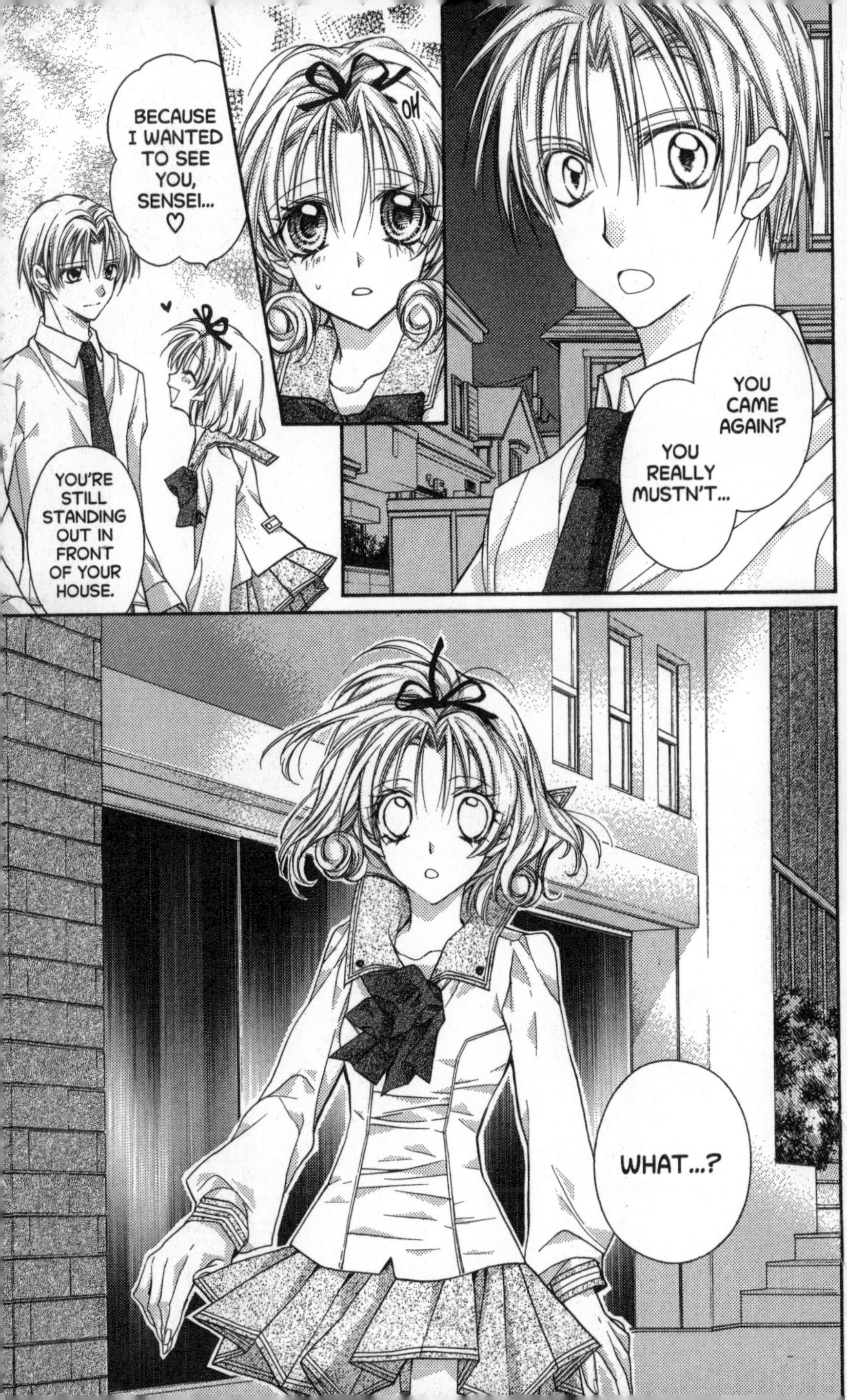
YOU CAME AGAIN?
YOU REALLY MUSTN'T...
OH
BECAUSE I WANTED TO SEE YOU, SENSEI... ♡
YOU'RE STILL STANDING OUT IN FRONT OF YOUR HOUSE.
WHAT...?

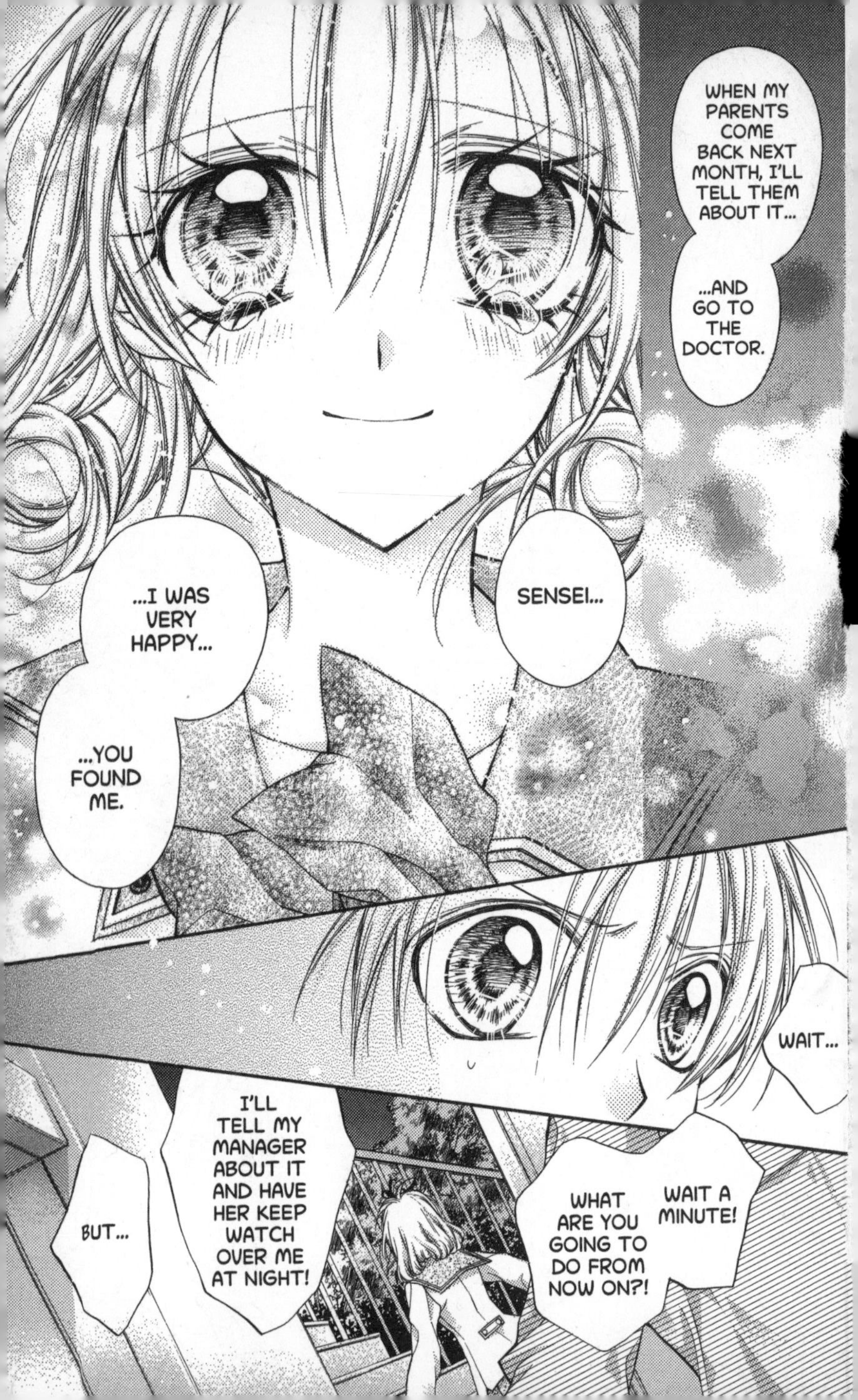
WHEN MY PARENTS COME BACK NEXT MONTH, I'LL TELL THEM ABOUT IT...
...AND GO TO THE DOCTOR.
SENSEI...
...I WAS VERY HAPPY...
...YOU FOUND ME.
WAIT...
WAIT A MINUTE!
WHAT ARE YOU GOING TO DO FROM NOW ON?!
I'LL TELL MY MANAGER ABOUT IT AND HAVE HER KEEP WATCH OVER ME AT NIGHT!
BUT...

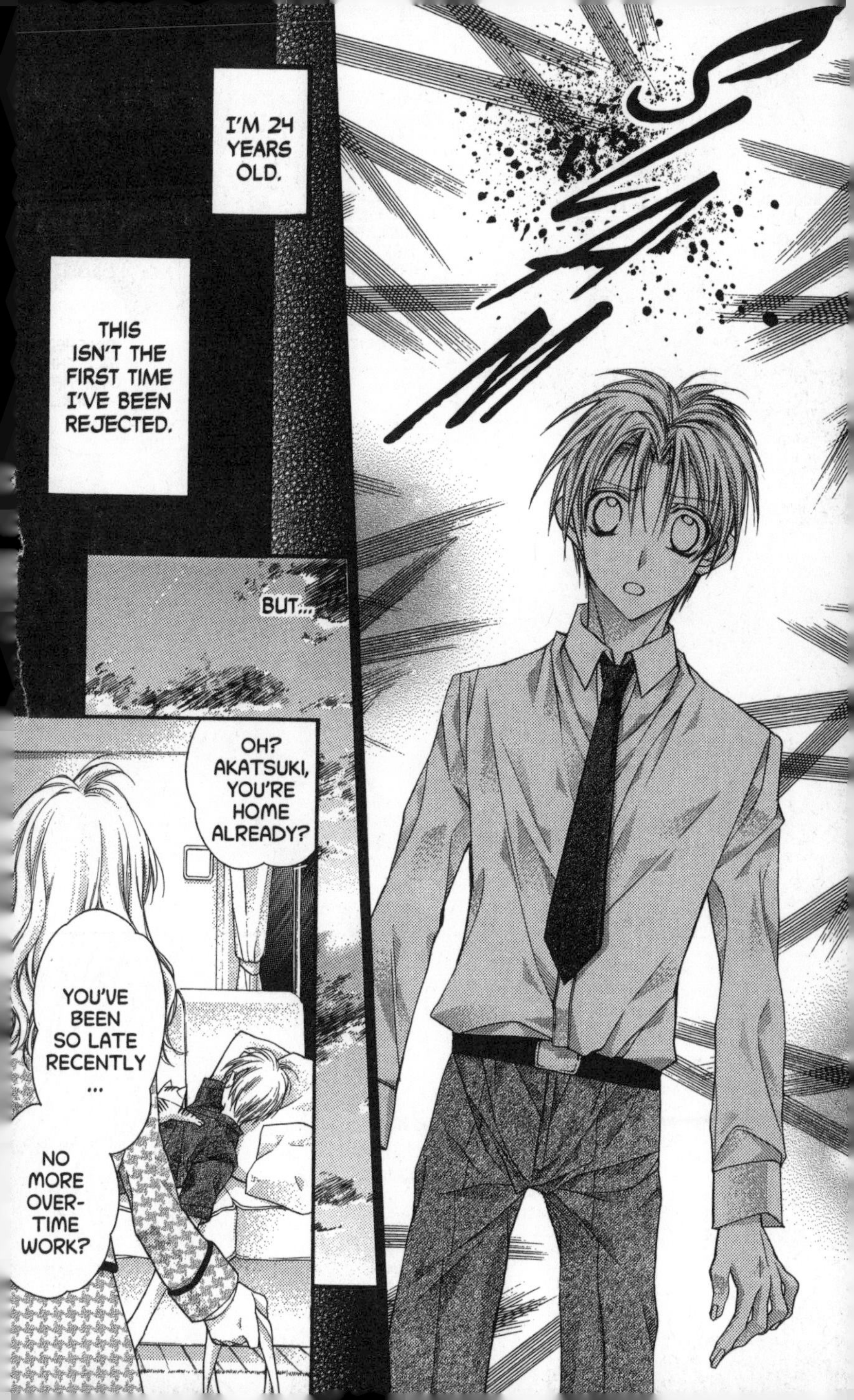
SLAM
I'M 24 YEARS OLD.
THIS ISN'T THE FIRST TIME I'VE BEEN REJECTED.
BUT...
OH? AKATSUKI, YOU'RE HOME ALREADY?
YOU'VE BEEN SO LATE RECENTLY ...
NO MORE OVER-TIME WORK?

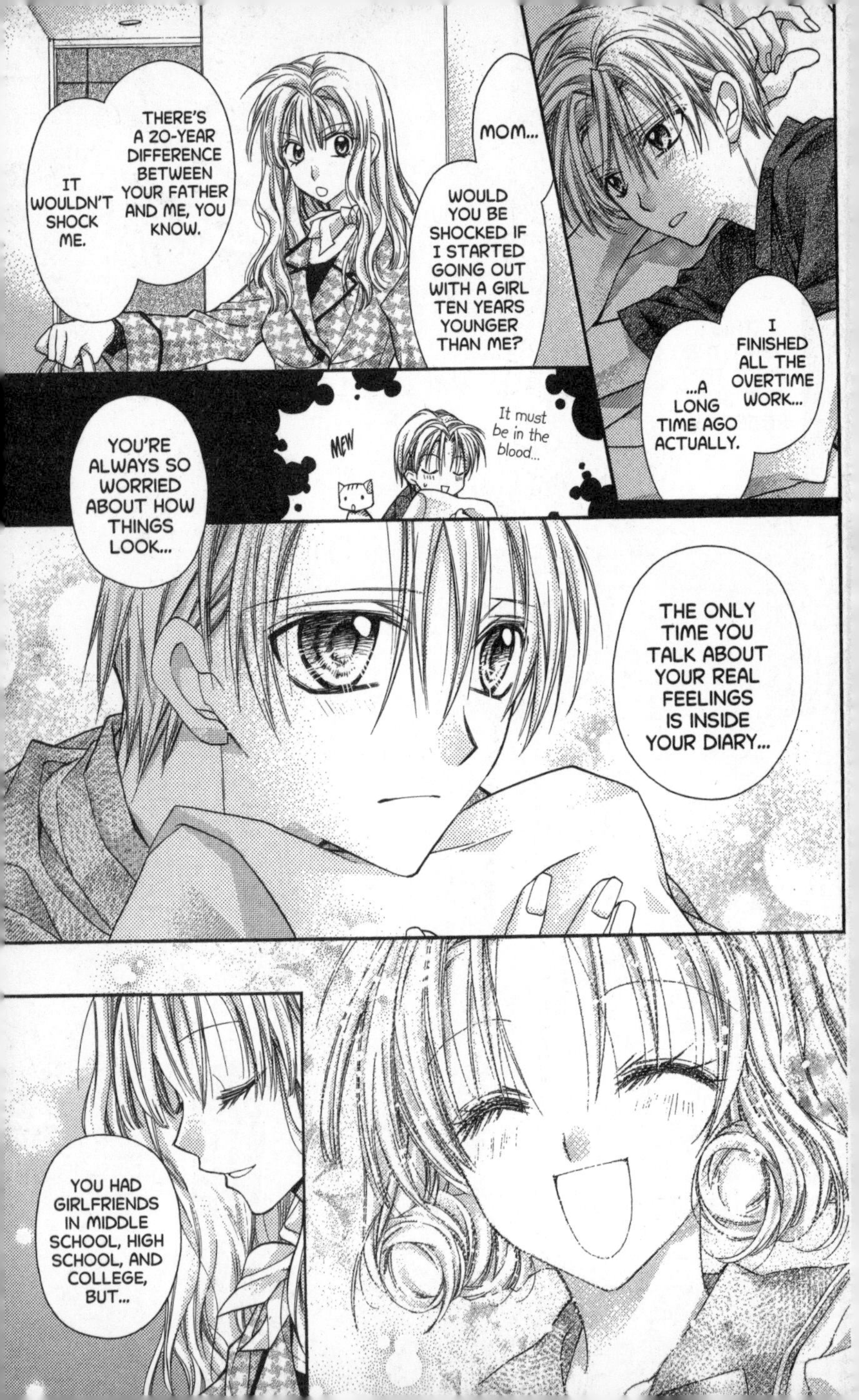
I FINISHED ALL THE OVERTIME WORK...
...A LONG TIME AGO ACTUALLY.
MOM...
WOULD YOU BE SHOCKED IF I STARTED GOING OUT WITH A GIRL TEN YEARS YOUNGER THAN ME?
THERE'S A 20-YEAR DIFFERENCE BETWEEN YOUR FATHER AND ME, YOU KNOW.
IT WOULDN'T SHOCK ME.
It must be in the blood...
MEW
YOU'RE ALWAYS SO WORRIED ABOUT HOW THINGS LOOK...
THE ONLY TIME YOU TALK ABOUT YOUR REAL FEELINGS IS INSIDE YOUR DIARY...
YOU HAD GIRLFRIENDS IN MIDDLE SCHOOL, HIGH SCHOOL, AND COLLEGE, BUT...

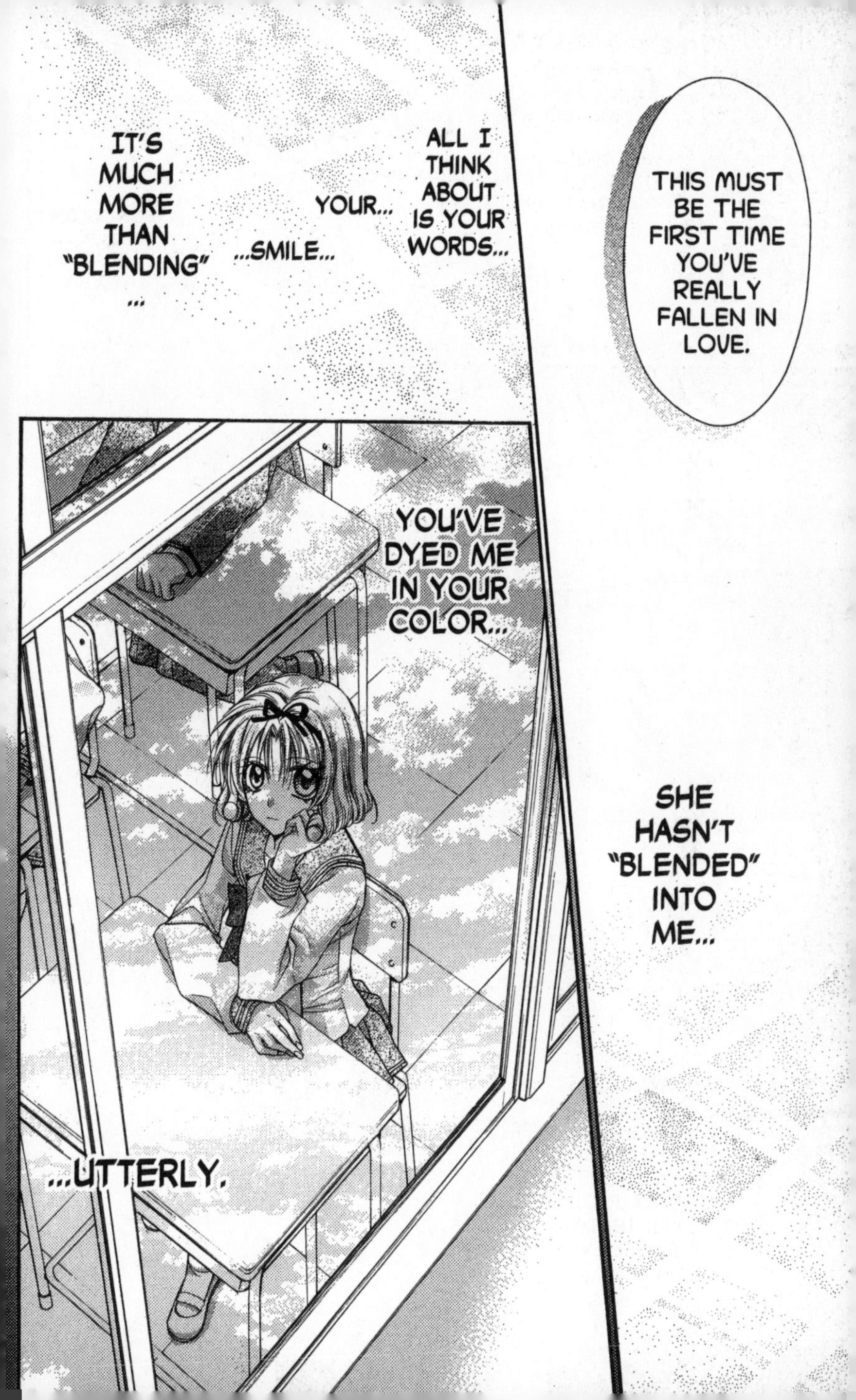
THIS MUST BE THE FIRST TIME YOU'VE REALLY FALLEN IN LOVE.
ALL I THINK ABOUT IS YOUR WORDS...
YOUR...
...SMILE...
IT'S MUCH MORE THAN "BLENDING"...
SHE HASN'T "BLENDED" INTO ME...
YOU'VE DYED ME IN YOUR COLOR...
...UTTERLY.

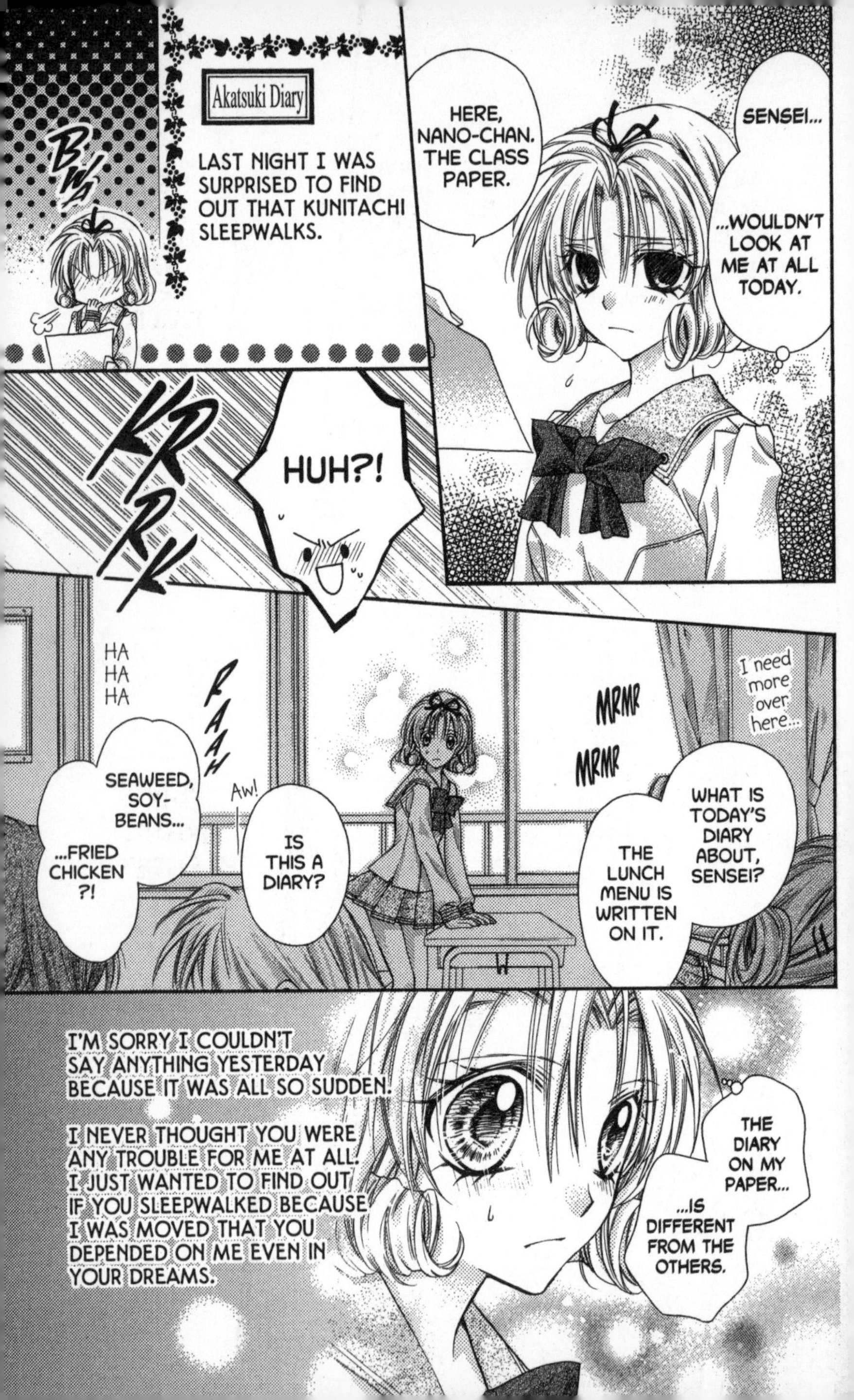
SENSEI...
...WOULDN'T LOOK AT ME AT ALL TODAY.
HERE, NANO-CHAN. THE CLASS PAPER.
Akatsuki Diary
LAST NIGHT I WAS SURPRISED TO FIND OUT THAT KUNITACHI SLEEPWALKS.
BWA!
HUH?!
KRRK
I need more over here...
MRMR
MRMR
WHAT IS TODAY'S DIARY ABOUT, SENSEI?
THE LUNCH MENU IS WRITTEN ON IT.
IS THIS A DIARY?
AW!
RAAAH
HA HA HA
SEAWEED, SOY-BEANS...
...FRIED CHICKEN ?!
THE DIARY ON MY PAPER...
...IS DIFFERENT FROM THE OTHERS.
I'M SORRY I COULDN'T SAY ANYTHING YESTERDAY BECAUSE IT WAS ALL SO SUDDEN.
I NEVER THOUGHT YOU WERE ANY TROUBLE FOR ME AT ALL. I JUST WANTED TO FIND OUT IF YOU SLEEPWALKED BECAUSE I WAS MOVED THAT YOU DEPENDED ON ME EVEN IN YOUR DREAMS.

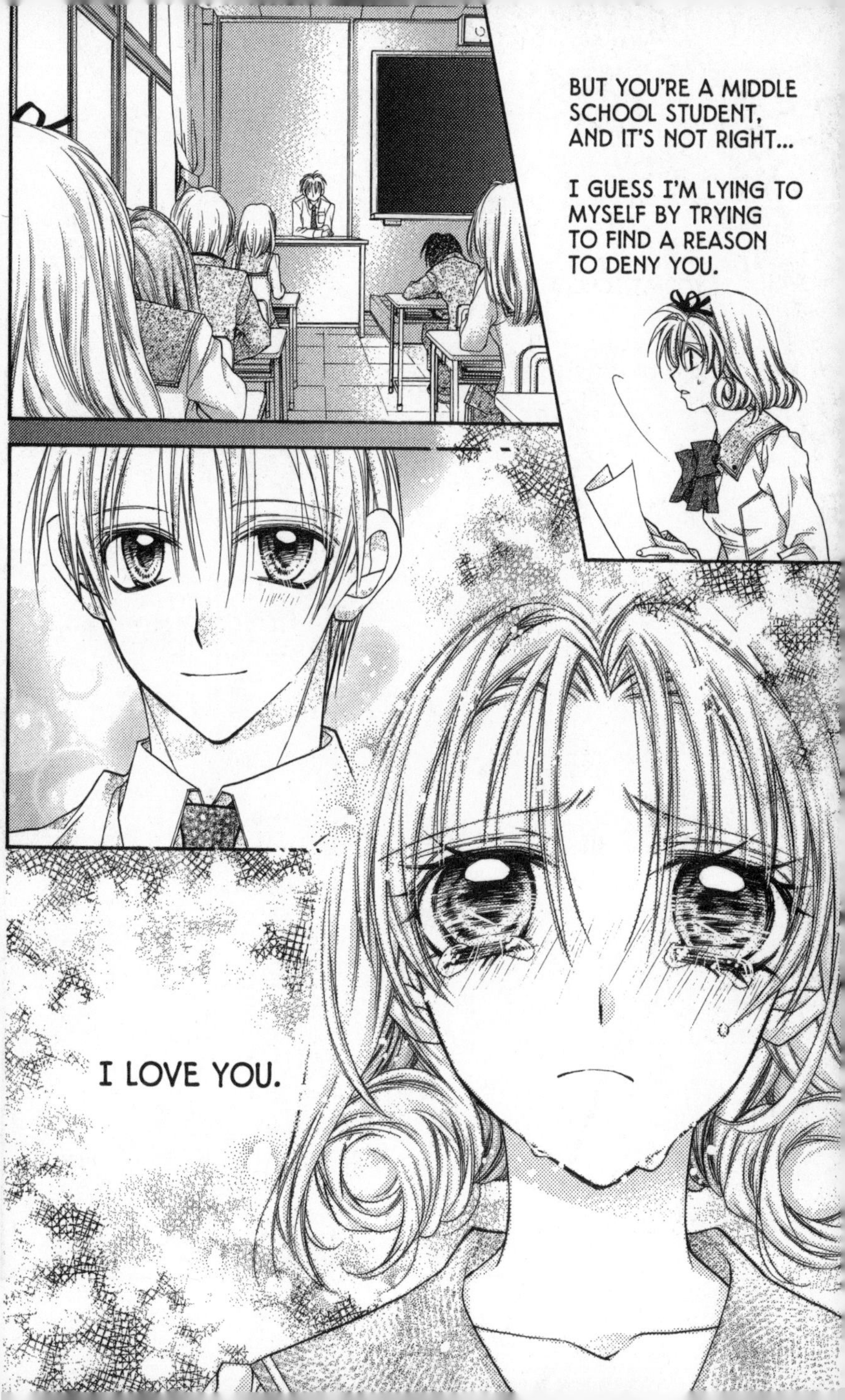
BUT YOU'RE A MIDDLE SCHOOL STUDENT, AND IT'S NOT RIGHT...
I GUESS I'M LYING TO MYSELF BY TRYING TO FIND A REASON TO DENY YOU.
I LOVE YOU.

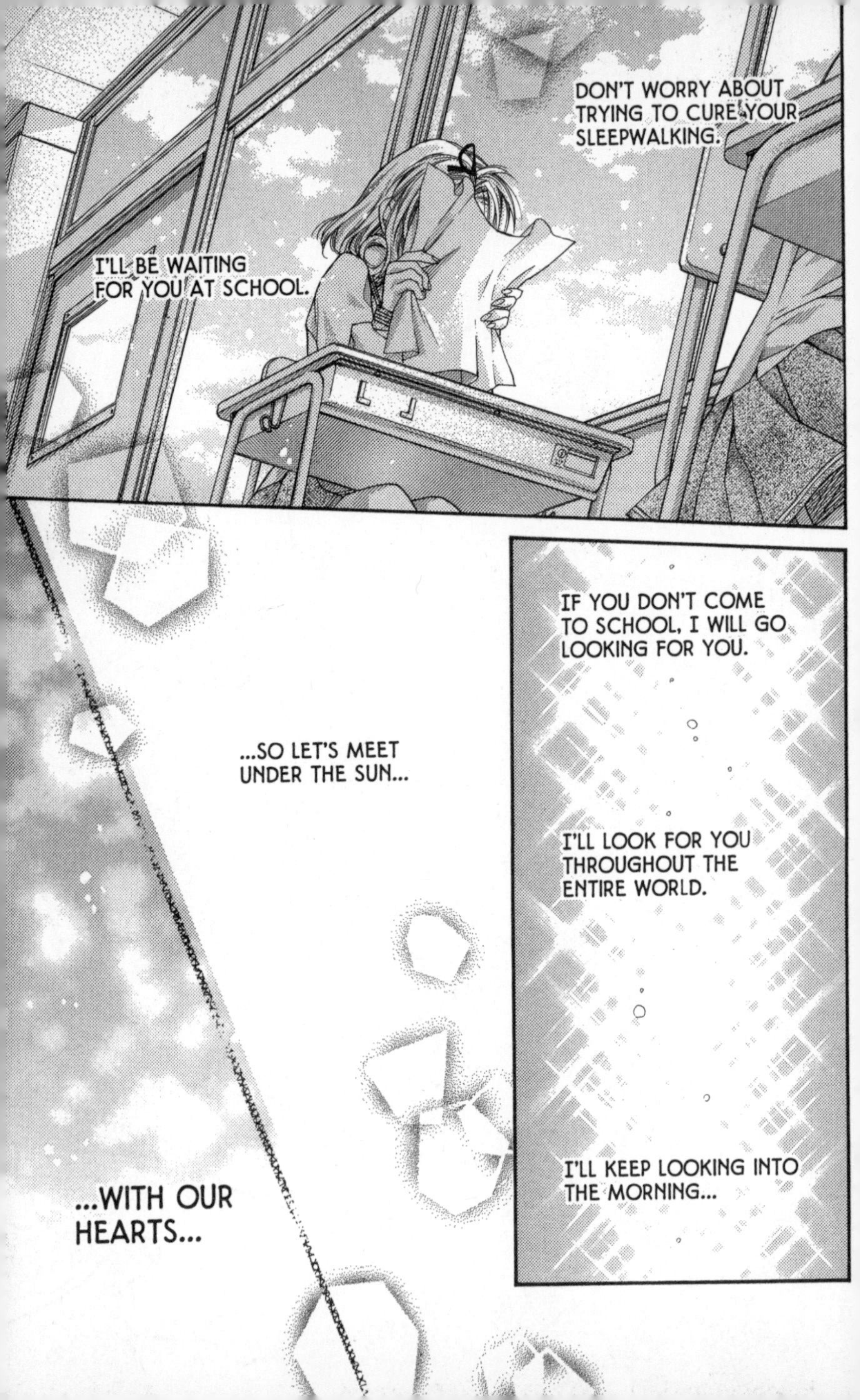
DON'T WORRY ABOUT TRYING TO CURE YOUR SLEEPWALKING.
I'LL BE WAITING FOR YOU AT SCHOOL.
IF YOU DON'T COME TO SCHOOL, I WILL GO LOOKING FOR YOU.
I'LL LOOK FOR YOU THROUGHOUT THE ENTIRE WORLD.
I'LL KEEP LOOKING INTO THE MORNING...
...SO LET'S MEET UNDER THE SUN...
...WITH OUR HEARTS...

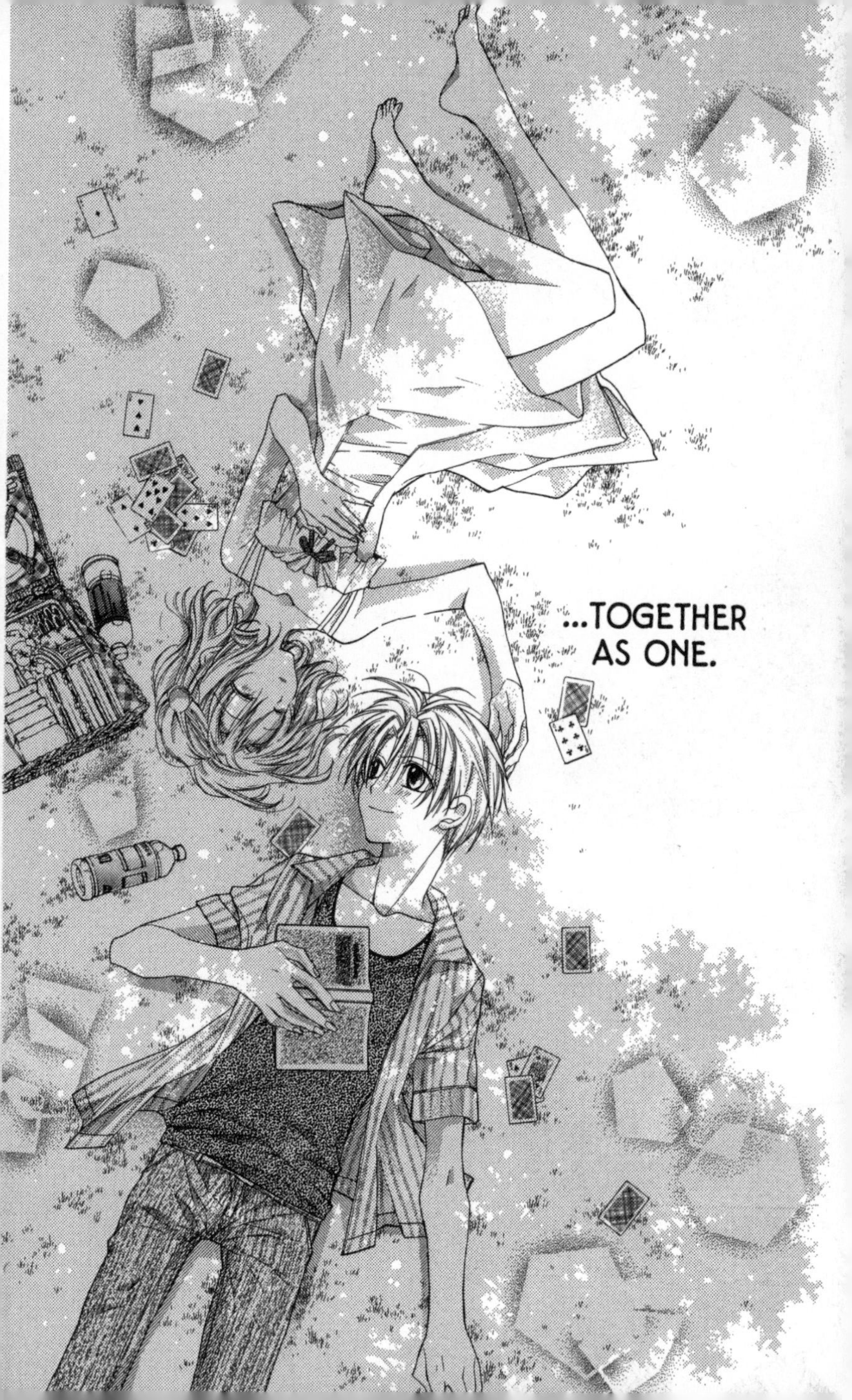
...TOGETHER AS ONE.

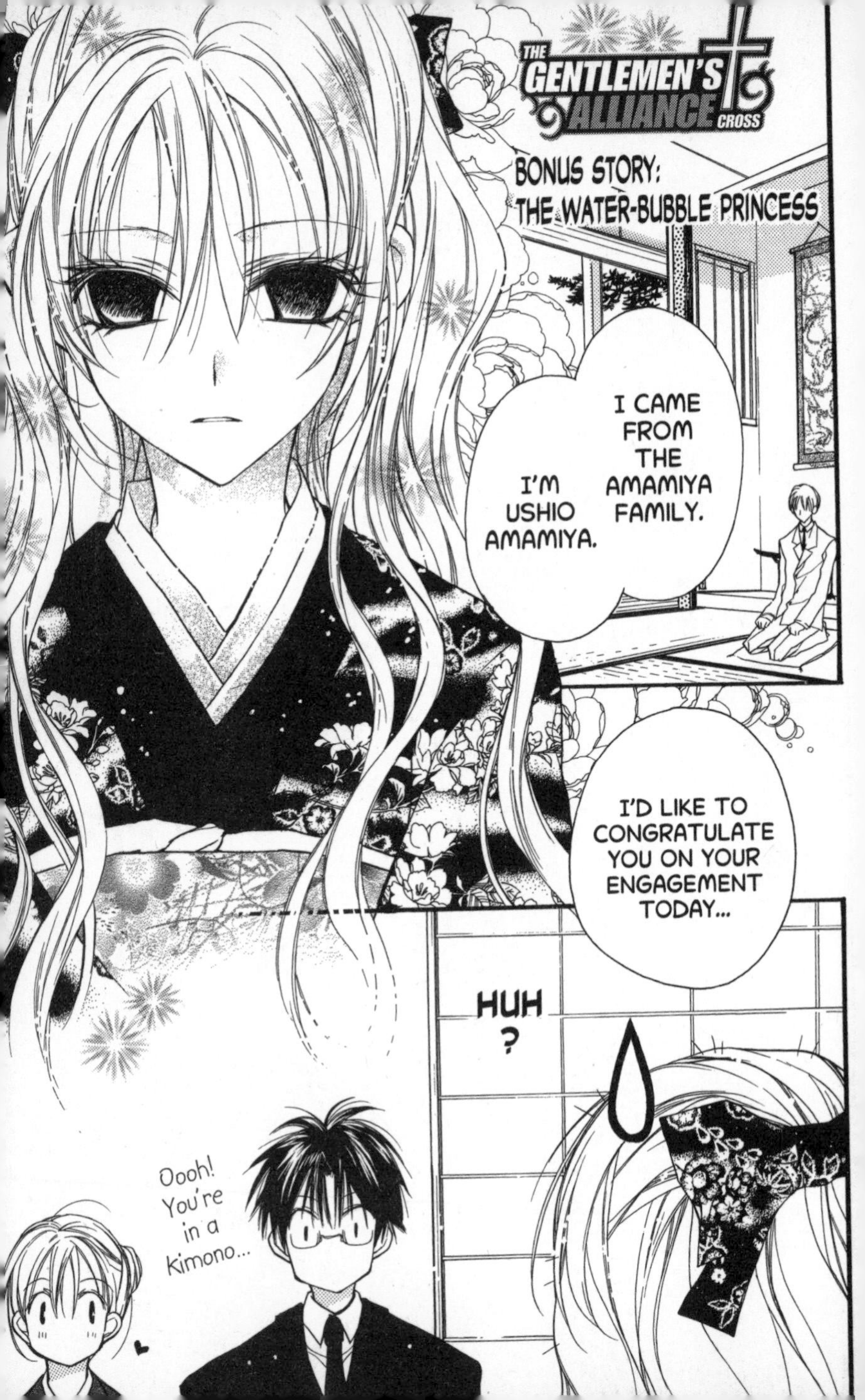
THE GENTLEMEN'S ALLIANCE CROSS
BONUS STORY: THE WATER-BUBBLE PRINCESS
I CAME FROM THE AMAMIYA FAMILY.
I'M USHIO AMAMIYA.
I'D LIKE TO CONGRATULATE YOU ON YOUR ENGAGEMENT TODAY...
HUH?
Oooh! You're in a kimono...

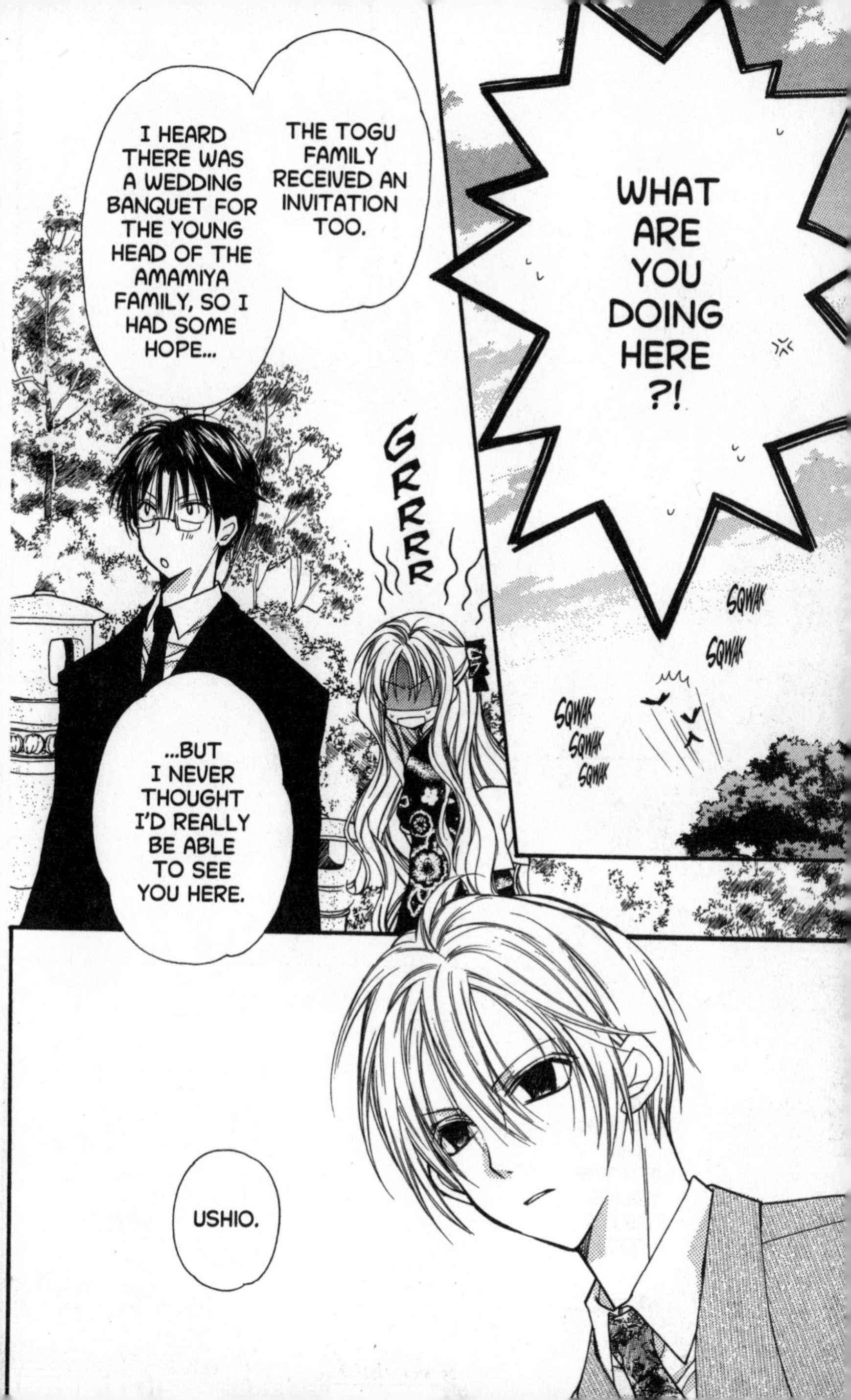
WHAT ARE YOU DOING HERE?!
SQWAK
SQWAK
SQWAK SQWAK SQWAK
THE TOGU FAMILY RECEIVED AN INVITATION TOO.
I HEARD THERE WAS A WEDDING BANQUET FOR THE YOUNG HEAD OF THE AMAMIYA FAMILY, SO I HAD SOME HOPE...
GRRRR
...BUT I NEVER THOUGHT I'D REALLY BE ABLE TO SEE YOU HERE.
USHIO.

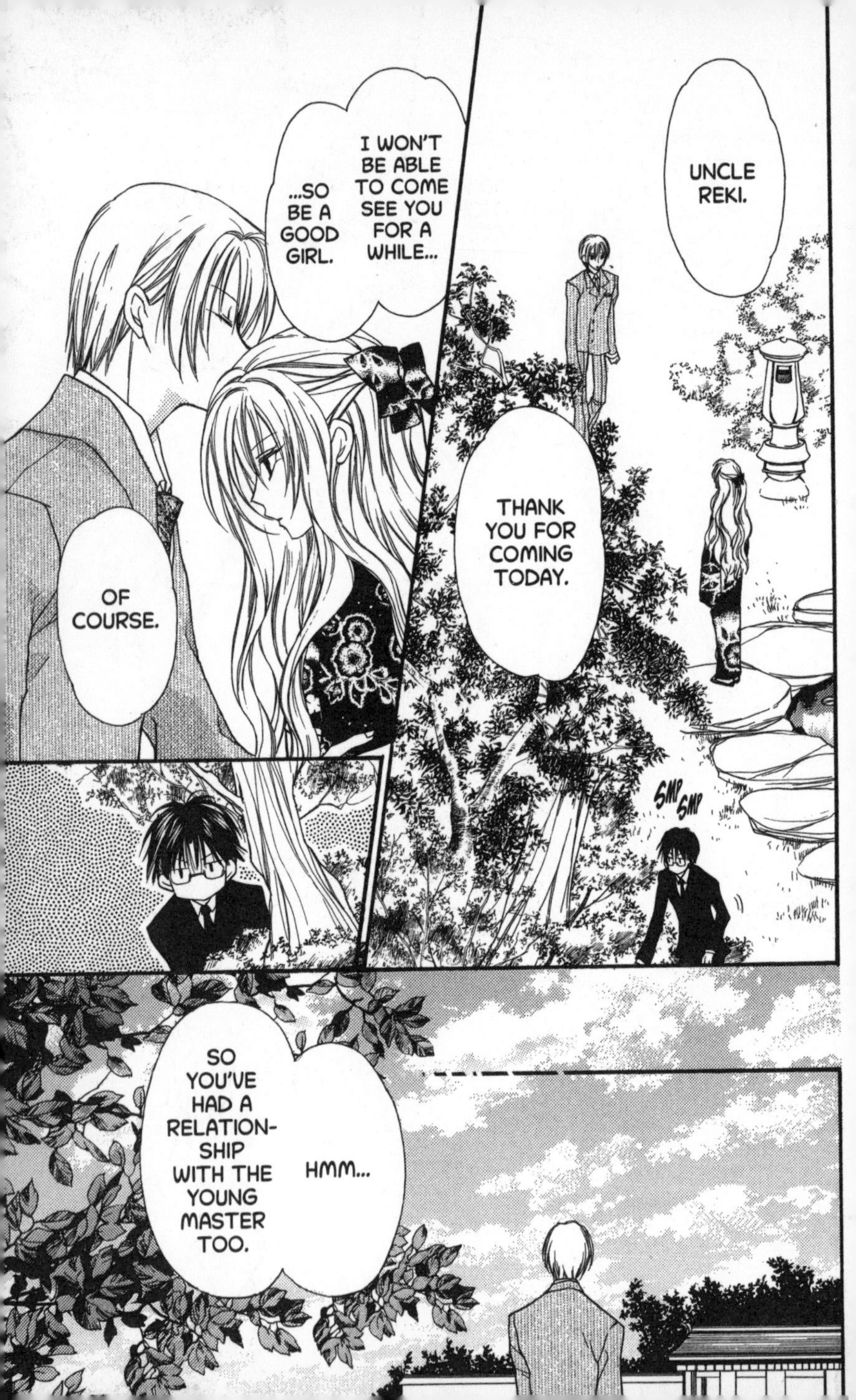
UNCLE REKI.
THANK YOU FOR COMING TODAY.
SMP SMP
I WON'T BE ABLE TO COME SEE YOU FOR A WHILE...
...SO BE A GOOD GIRL.
OF COURSE.
HMM...
SO YOU'VE HAD A RELATION-SHIP WITH THE YOUNG MASTER TOO.

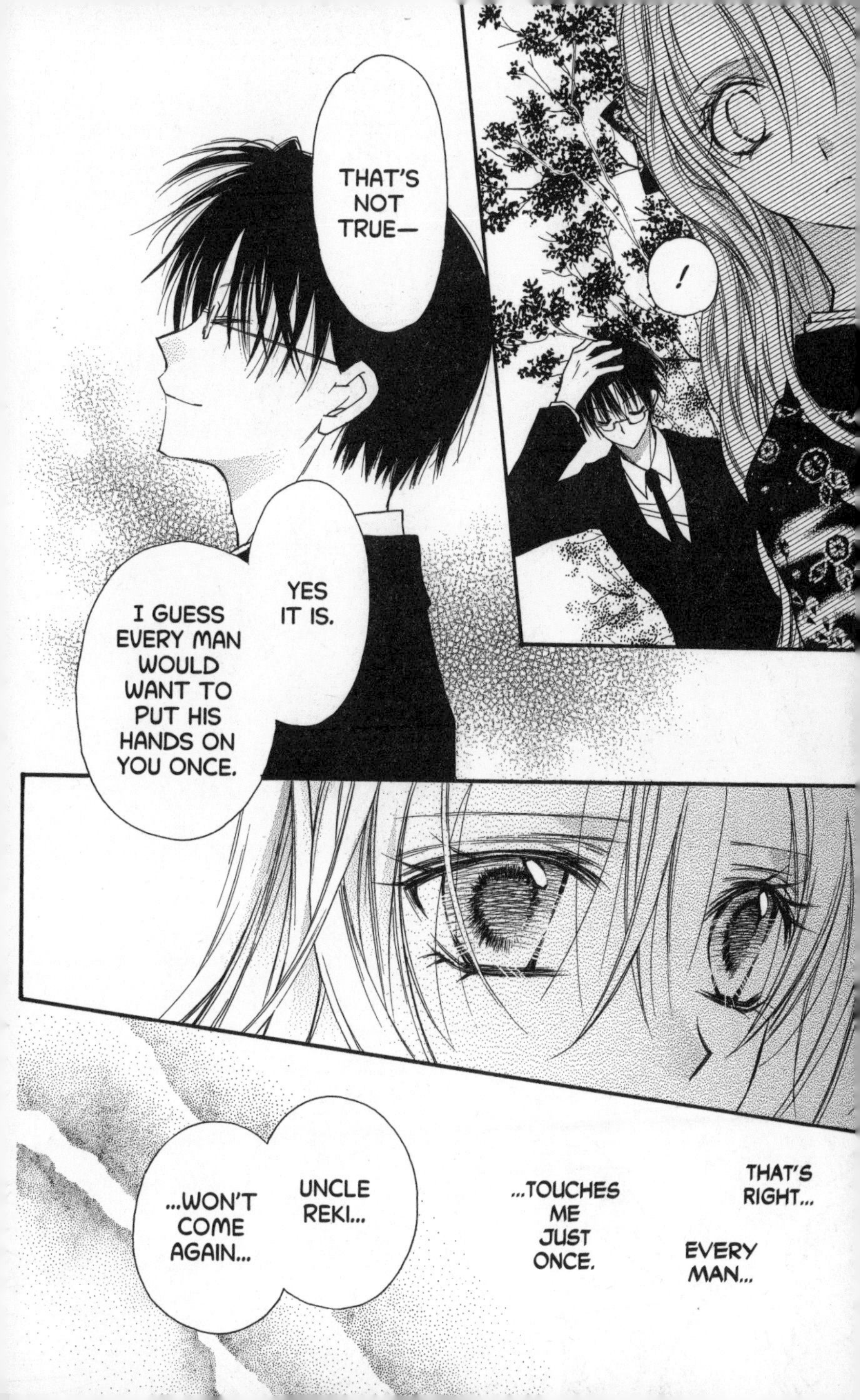
!
THAT'S NOT TRUE—
YES IT IS.
I GUESS EVERY MAN WOULD WANT TO PUT HIS HANDS ON YOU ONCE.
THAT'S RIGHT...
EVERY MAN...
...TOUCHES ME JUST ONCE.
UNCLE REKI...
...WON'T COME AGAIN...

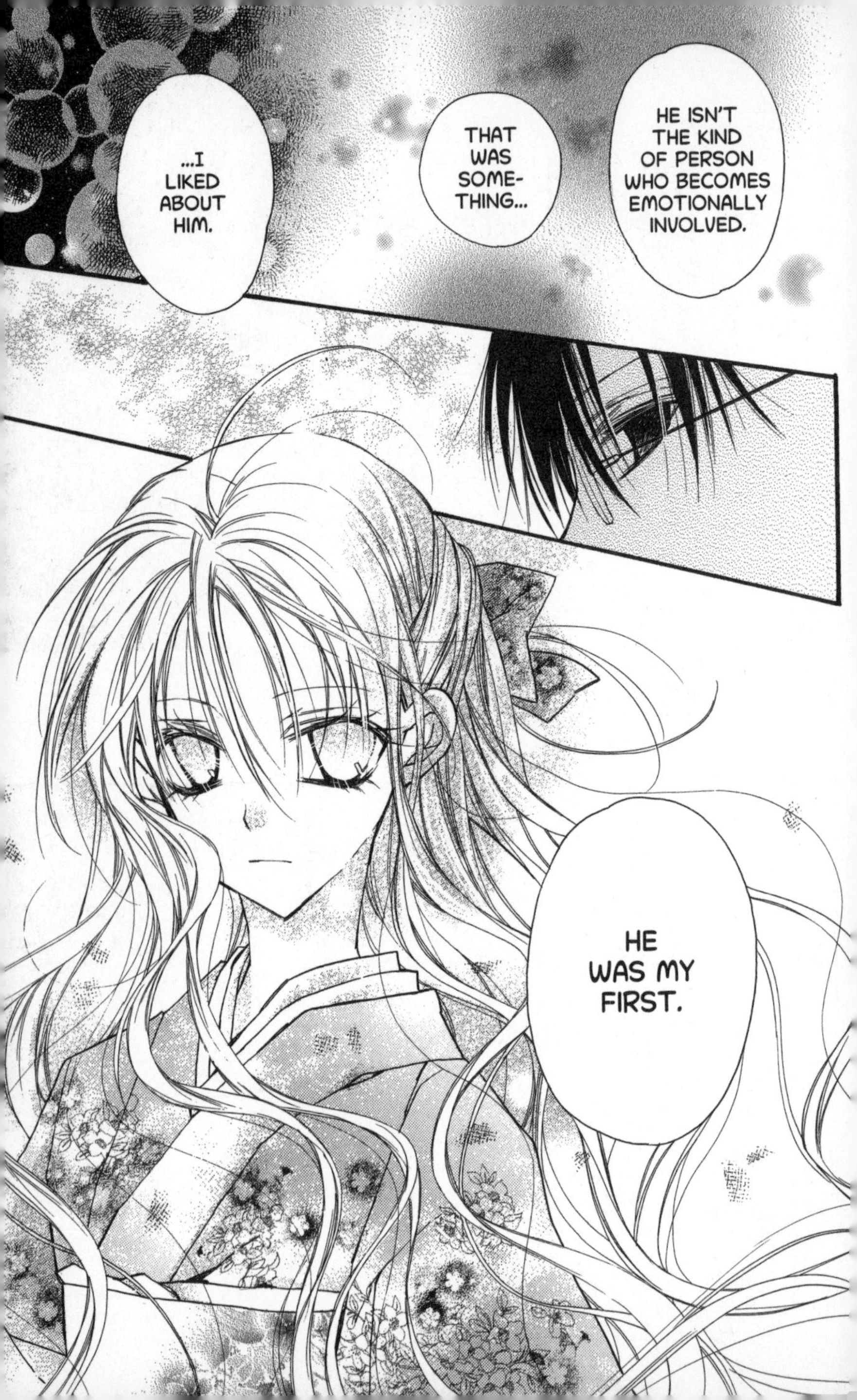
HE ISN'T THE KIND OF PERSON WHO BECOMES EMOTIONALLY INVOLVED.
THAT WAS SOME-THING...
...I LIKED ABOUT HIM.
HE WAS MY FIRST.

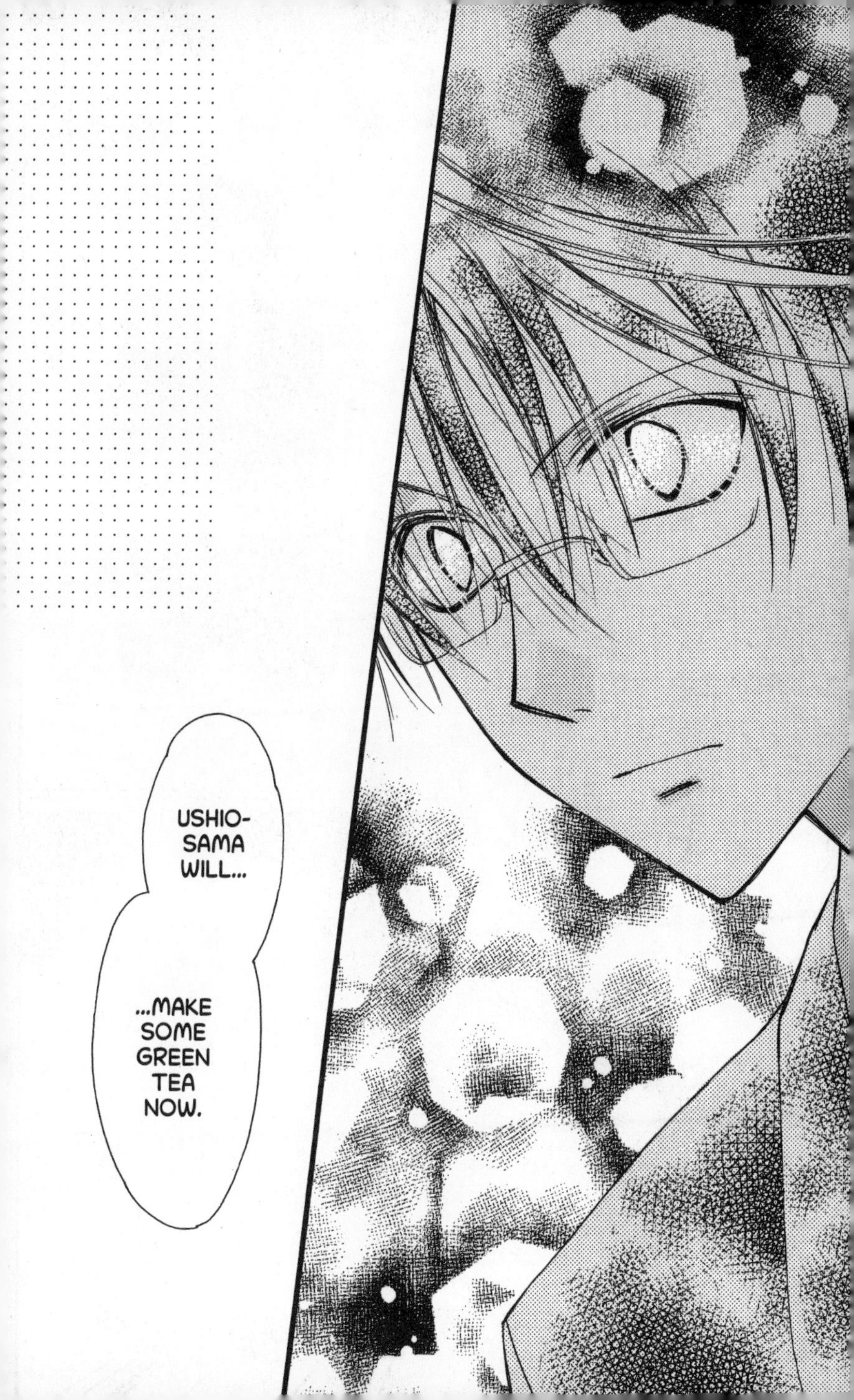
USHIO-SAMA WILL...
...MAKE SOME GREEN TEA NOW.

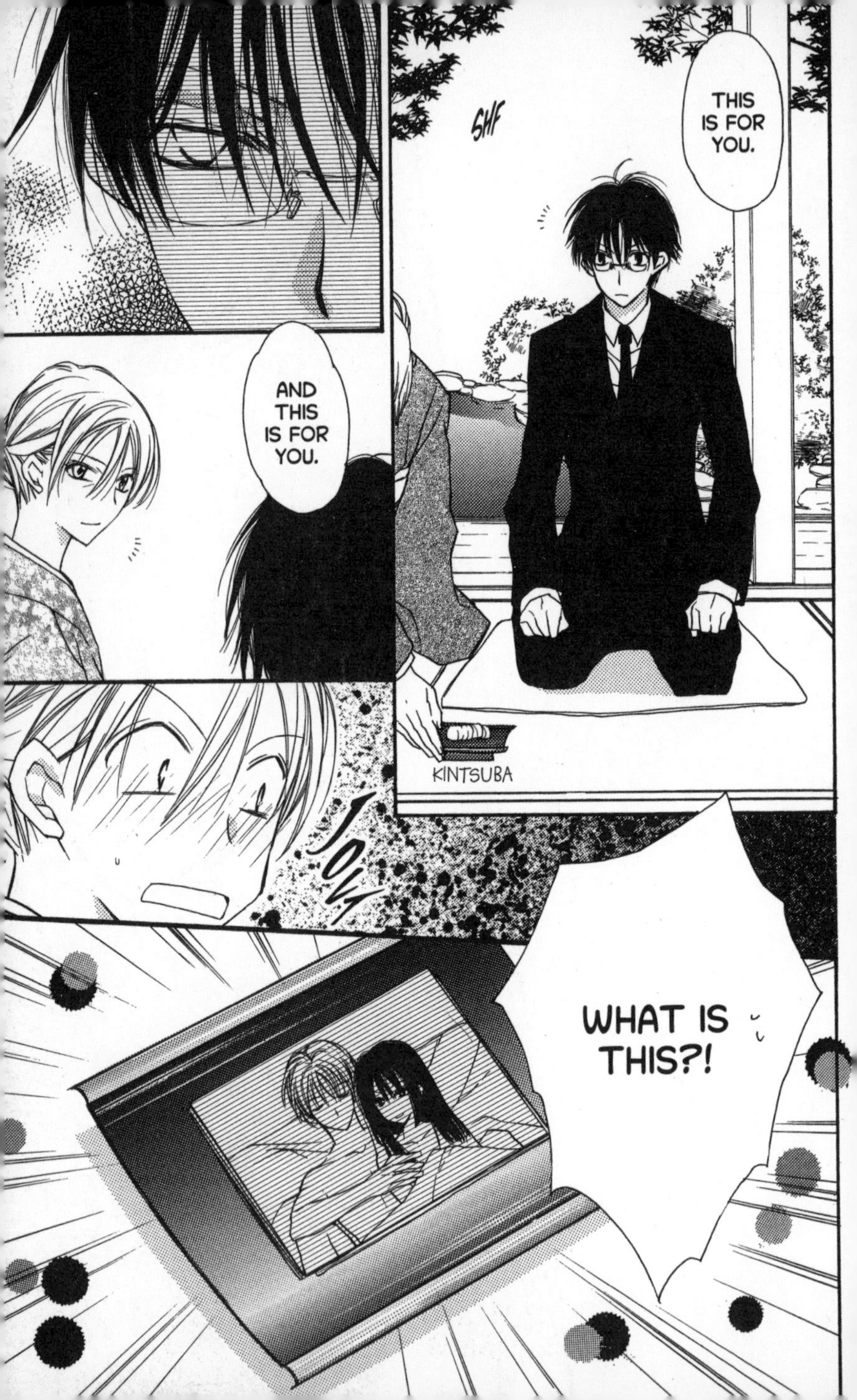
SHF
THIS IS FOR YOU.
KINTSUBA
AND THIS IS FOR YOU.
WHAT IS THIS?!

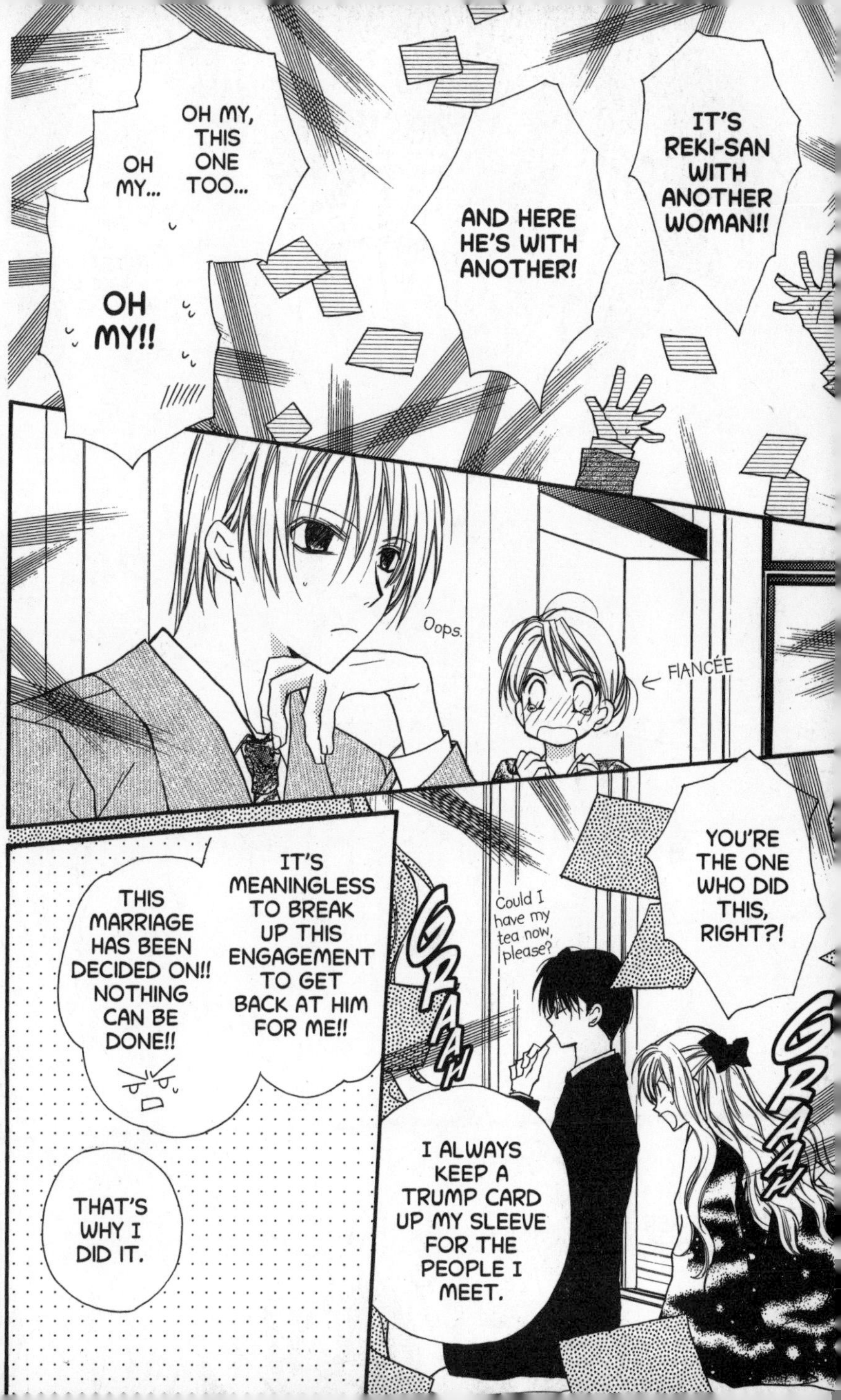
IT'S REKI-SAN WITH ANOTHER WOMAN!!
AND HERE HE'S WITH ANOTHER!
OH MY, THIS ONE TOO...
OH MY...
OH MY!!
Oops.
← FIANCÉE
YOU'RE THE ONE WHO DID THIS, RIGHT?!
GRAAAH
GRAAAH
Could I have my tea now, please?
I ALWAYS KEEP A TRUMP CARD UP MY SLEEVE FOR THE PEOPLE I MEET.
IT'S MEANINGLESS TO BREAK UP THIS ENGAGEMENT TO GET BACK AT HIM FOR ME!!
THIS MARRIAGE HAS BEEN DECIDED ON!! NOTHING CAN BE DONE!!
THAT'S WHY I DID IT.

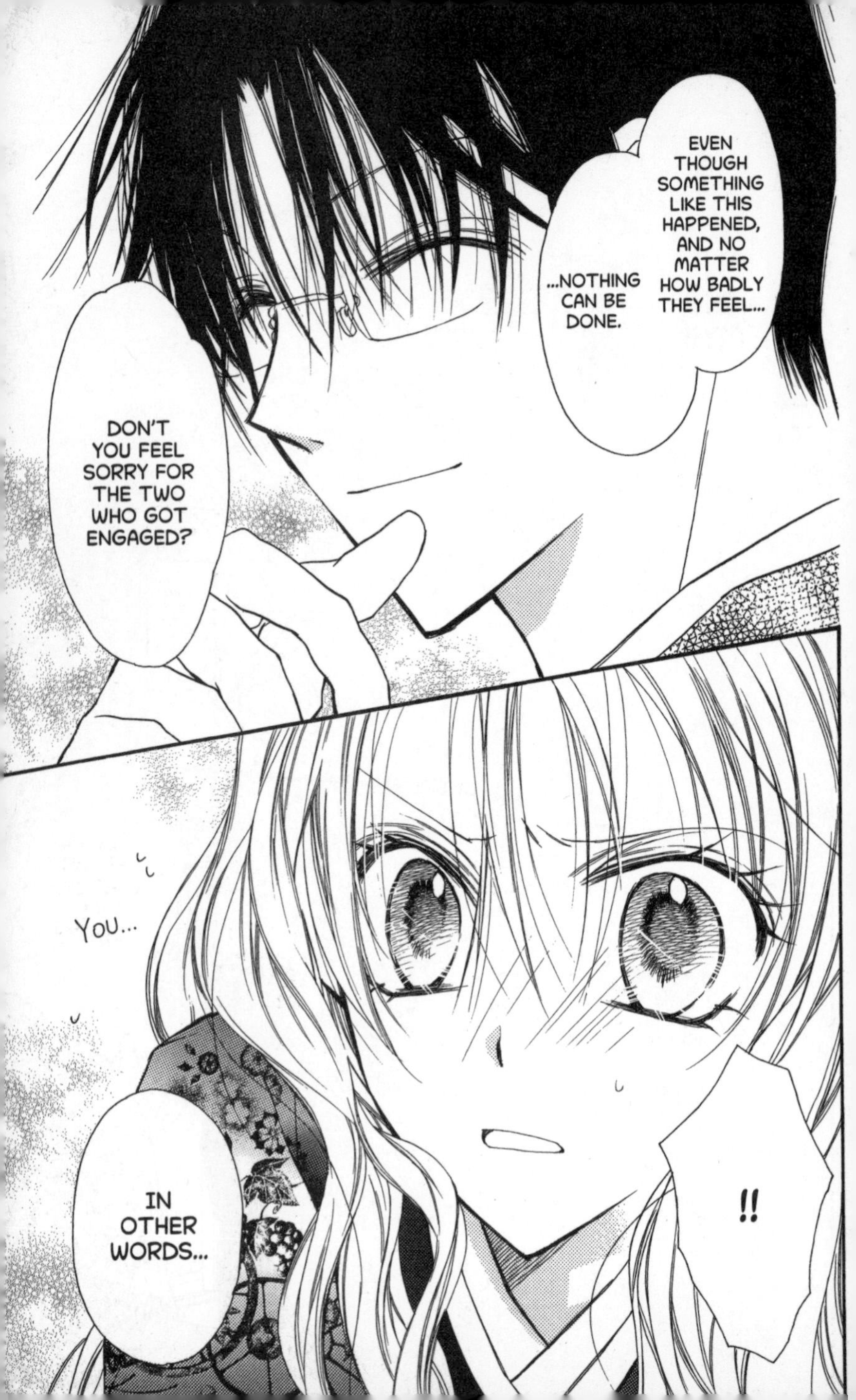
EVEN THOUGH SOMETHING LIKE THIS HAPPENED, AND NO MATTER HOW BADLY THEY FEEL...
...NOTHING CAN BE DONE.
DON'T YOU FEEL SORRY FOR THE TWO WHO GOT ENGAGED?
!!
YOU...
IN OTHER WORDS...

...YOU CAN'T BLAME ME...
...FOR BEING A LITTLE PISSED OFF, CAN YOU?

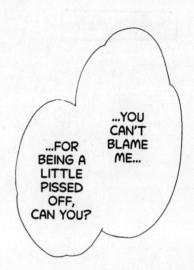

Character Collection

※ I drew these before the series started, so there may be things that are different. I hope you enjoy it.

The Gentlemen's Alliance †

Character File ① Main Character

Sold to the current family for 20 million yen. She became a yanki because of that. She met Shizumasa, fell in love with him, and turned over a new leaf in high school to become a cute girl.

Haine Otomiya

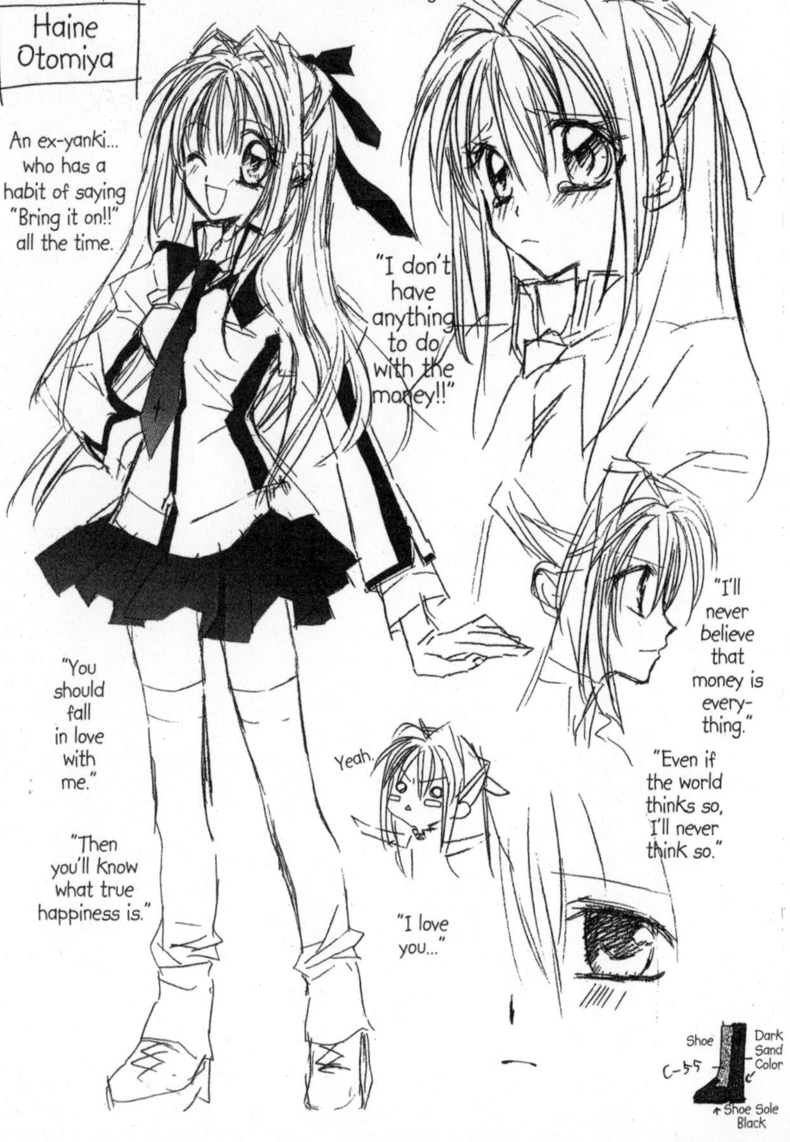
An ex-yanki... who has a habit of saying "Bring it on!!" all the time.
"I don't have anything to do with the money!!"
"I'll never believe that money is every-thing."
"Even if the world thinks so, I'll never think so."
Yeah.
"You should fall in love with me."
"Then you'll know what true happiness is."
"I love you..."
Shoe
Dark Sand Color
C-55
Shoe Sole Black

The Gentlemen's Alliance
Character File ②

The student council president of Imperial Academy who has the highest Gold rank. He rules over the school as a model student but also pays money to the Heretics to control them. He likes to be alone and disappears every now and then. He also comes up with a fake story to go missing.

He's popular with the girls, but he doesn't like it, and he spreads the rumor that he's gay.

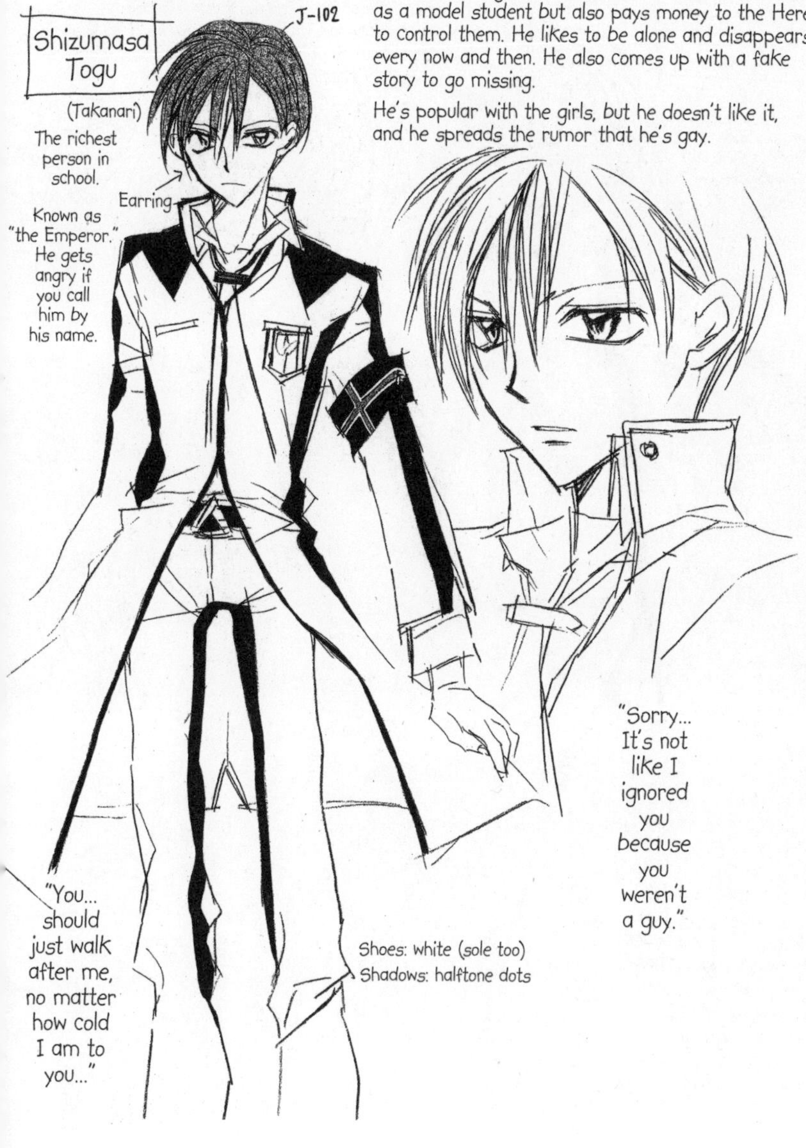

Shizumasa Togu
(Takanari)
The richest person in school.
Known as "the Emperor." He gets angry if you call him by his name.
J-102
Earring
"Sorry... It's not like I ignored you because you weren't a guy."
"You... should just walk after me, no matter how cold I am to you..."
Shoes: white (sole too)
Shadows: halftone dots

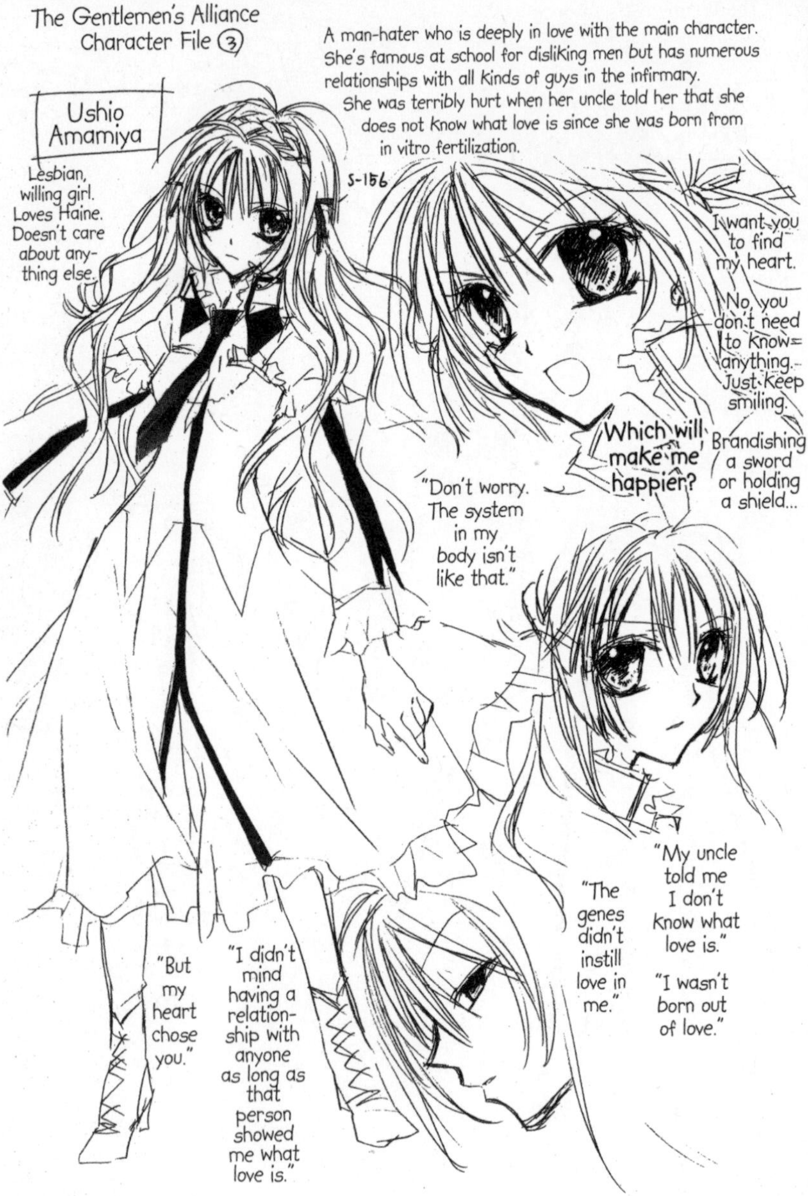
The Gentlemen's Alliance Character File ③
A man-hater who is deeply in love with the main character. She's famous at school for disliking men but has numerous relationships with all kinds of guys in the infirmary. She was terribly hurt when her uncle told her that she does not know what love is since she was born from in vitro fertilization.
Ushio Amamiya
Lesbian, willing girl. Loves Haine. Doesn't care about anything else.
S-156
I want you to find my heart.
No, you don't need to know anything. Just keep smiling.
Which will make me happier?
Brandishing a sword or holding a shield...
"Don't worry. The system in my body isn't like that."
"My uncle told me I don't know what love is."
"I wasn't born out of love."
"The genes didn't instill love in me."
"I didn't mind having a relationship with anyone as long as that person showed me what love is."
"But my heart chose you."

## The Gentlemen's Alliance Character File ④

Maguri-Kun's childhood friend (was in love in him). He started to cross-dress because Maguri didn't want to go out with a guy, but Maguri turned out to be gay, so the two got into a huge fight. Since then, they haven't been on good terms. He falls in love with Haine when she is still a yanki. ✓ Jumps for joy after being reunited with her at the student council. He thinks it's safer to remain as her friend and have a crush on her.

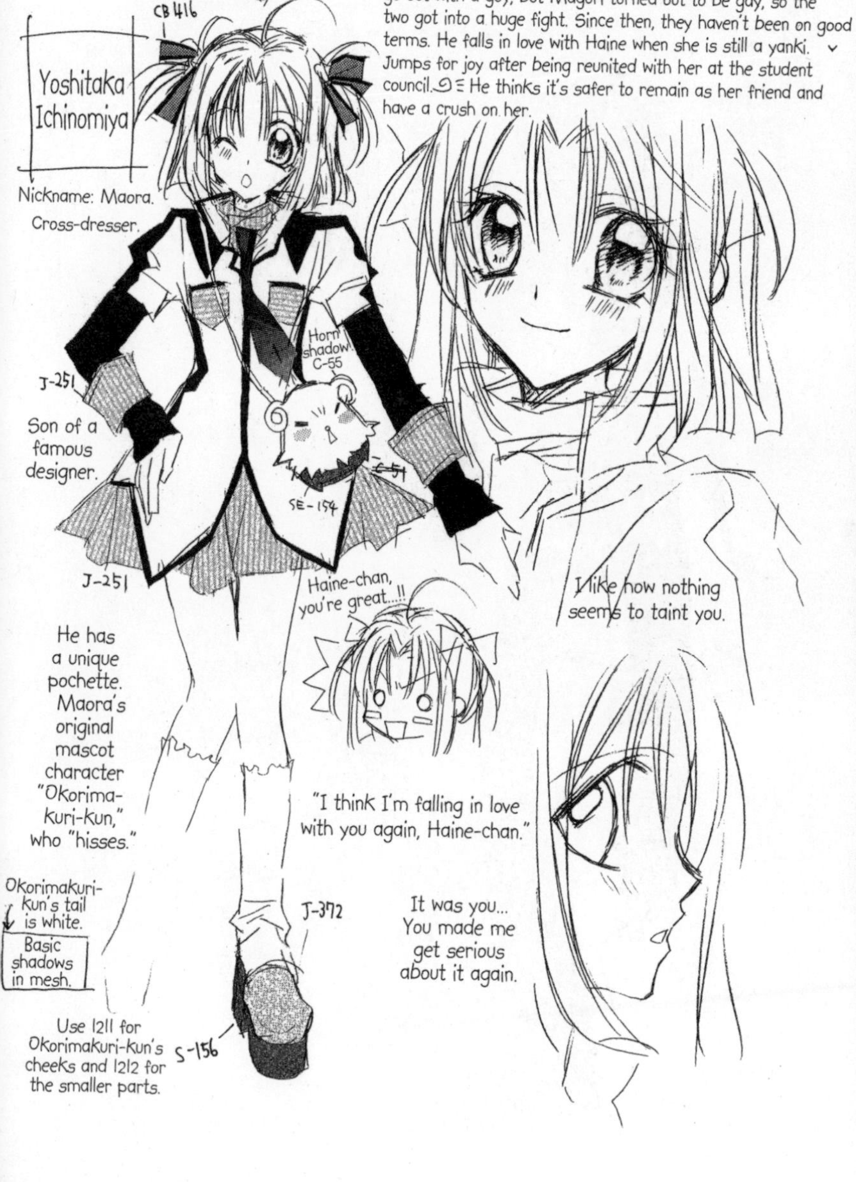
CB 416
Yoshitaka Ichinomiya
Nickname: Maora.
Cross-dresser.
Horn shadow: C-55
J-251
Son of a famous designer.
C-51
SE-154
J-251
Haine-chan, you're great...!!
I like how nothing seems to taint you.
He has a unique pochette. Maora's original mascot character "Okorimakuri-Kun," who "hisses."
"I think I'm falling in love with you again, Haine-chan."
Okorimakuri-kun's tail is white.
Basic shadows in mesh.
J-372
It was you... You made me get serious about it again.
Use 1211 for Okorimakuri-Kun's cheeks and 1212 for the smaller parts.
S-156

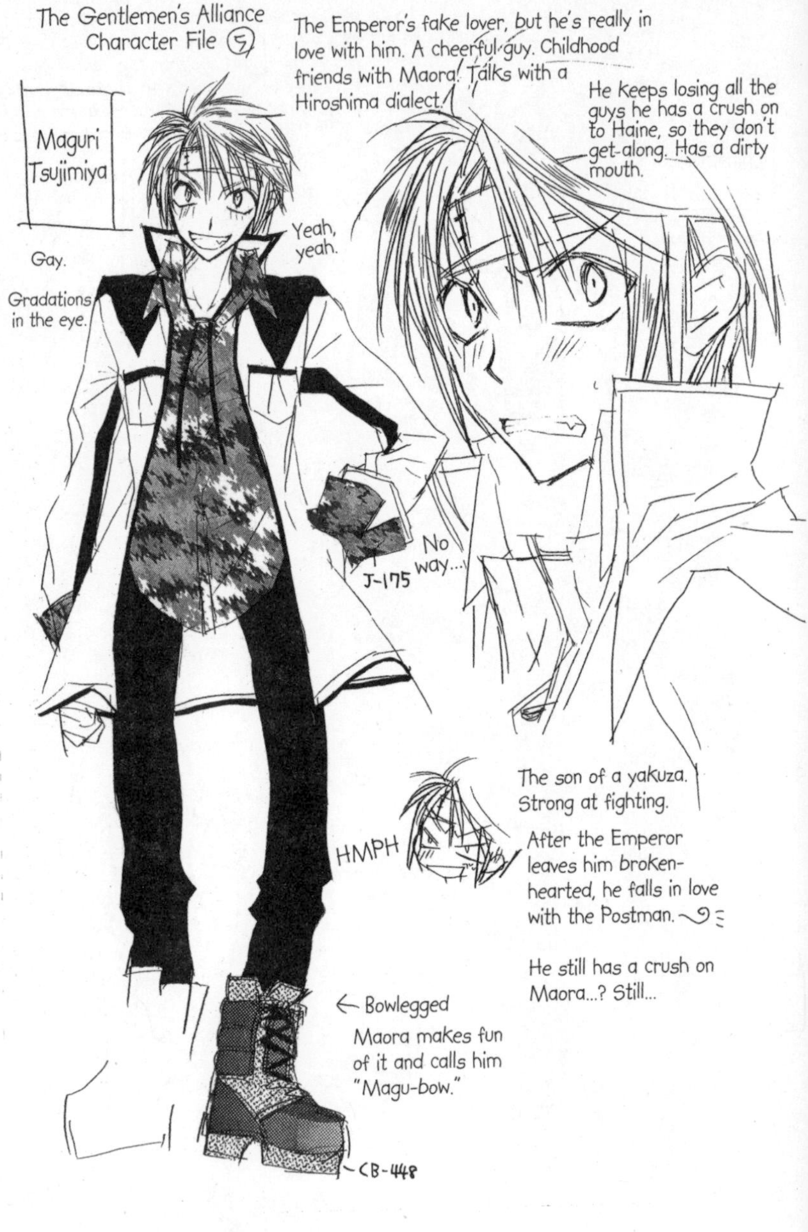
The Gentlemen's Alliance Character File 5
Maguri Tsujimiya
Gay.
Gradations in the eye.
Yeah, yeah.
The Emperor's fake lover, but he's really in love with him. A cheerful guy. Childhood friends with Maora! Talks with a Hiroshima dialect!
He keeps losing all the guys he has a crush on to Haine, so they don't get along. Has a dirty mouth.
No way...
J-175
The son of a yakuza. Strong at fighting.
HMPH
After the Emperor leaves him broken-hearted, he falls in love with the Postman.
He still has a crush on Maora...? Still...
← Bowlegged
Maora makes fun of it and calls him "Magu-bow."
CB-448

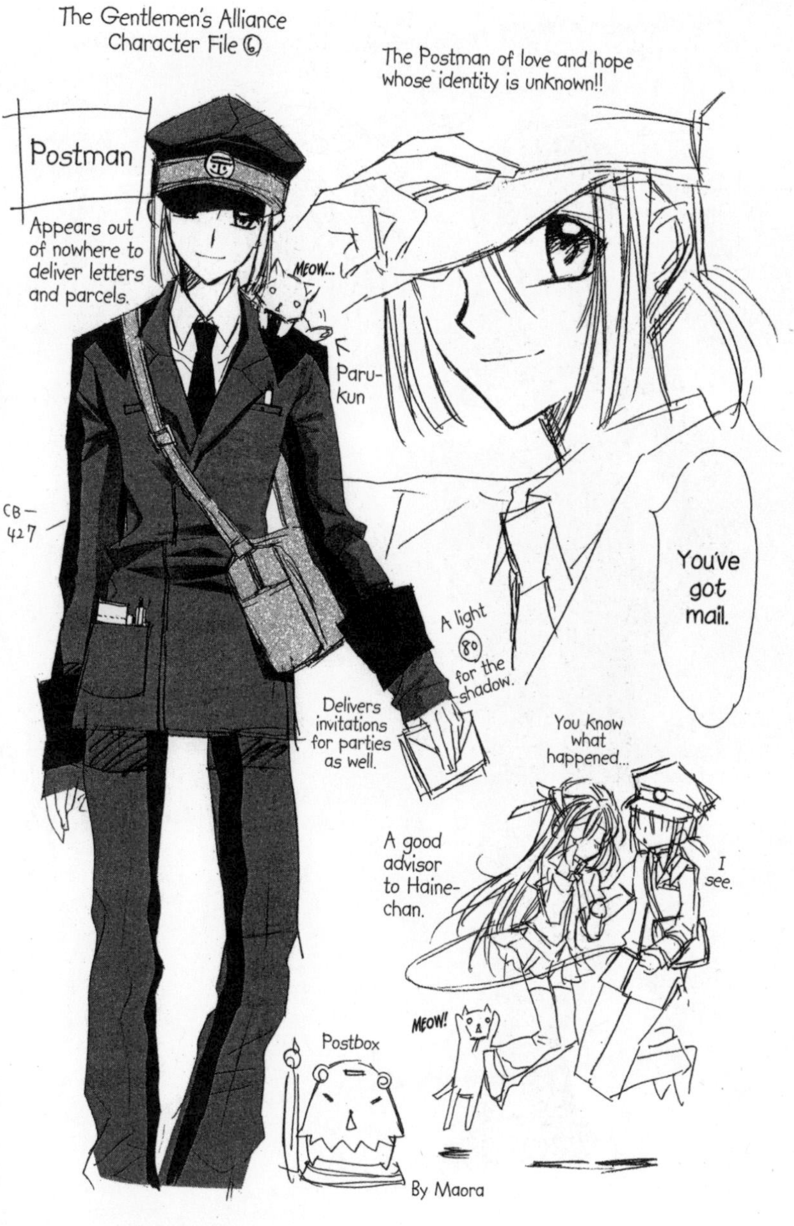
The Gentlemen's Alliance
Character File 6
The Postman of love and hope whose identity is unknown!!
Postman
Appears out of nowhere to deliver letters and parcels.
MEOW...
Paru-kun
CB-427
You've got mail.
A light 80 for the shadow.
Delivers invitations for parties as well.
You know what happened...
I see.
A good advisor to Haine-chan.
MEOW!
Postbox
By Maora

The Gentlemen's Alliance Character File ⑰

In love with Haine. Earnest and hardheaded. Working part-time so he can marry Haine. Likes to save money.

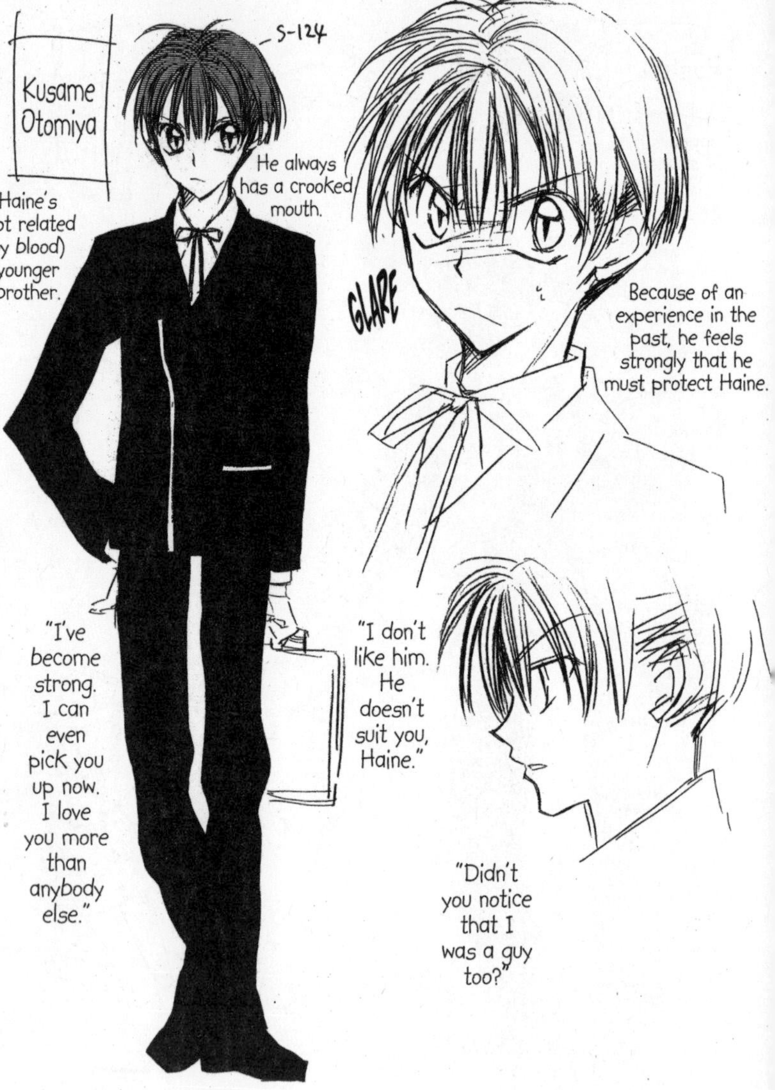
Kusame Otomiya
S-124
He always has a crooked mouth.
Haine's (not related by blood) younger brother.
GLARE
Because of an experience in the past, he feels strongly that he must protect Haine.
"I've become strong. I can even pick you up now. I love you more than anybody else."
"I don't like him. He doesn't suit you, Haine."
"Didn't you notice that I was a guy too?"

# The Gentlemen's Alliance Character File ⑧

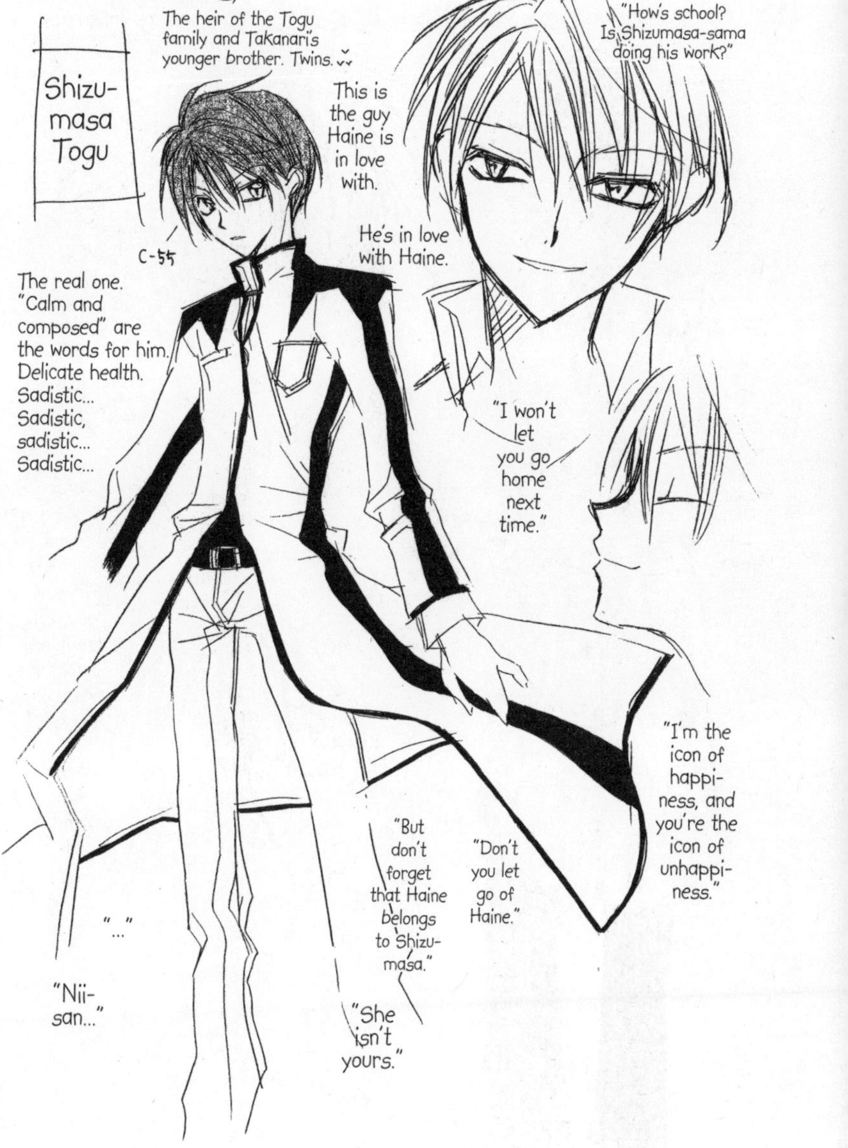

Shizu-masa Togu
The heir of the Togu family and Takanari's younger brother. Twins.
"How's school? Is Shizumasa-sama doing his work?"
This is the guy Haine is in love with.
He's in love with Haine.
C-55
The real one. "Calm and composed" are the words for him. Delicate health. Sadistic... Sadistic, sadistic... Sadistic...
"I won't let you go home next time."
"I'm the icon of happiness, and you're the icon of unhappiness."
"Don't you let go of Haine."
"But don't forget that Haine belongs to Shizumasa."
"..."
"Nii-san..."
"She isn't yours."

The Gentlemen's Alliance Character File ⑨

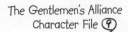

A bad teacher who doesn't do anything even when Ushio is doing all sorts of things in the infirmary.

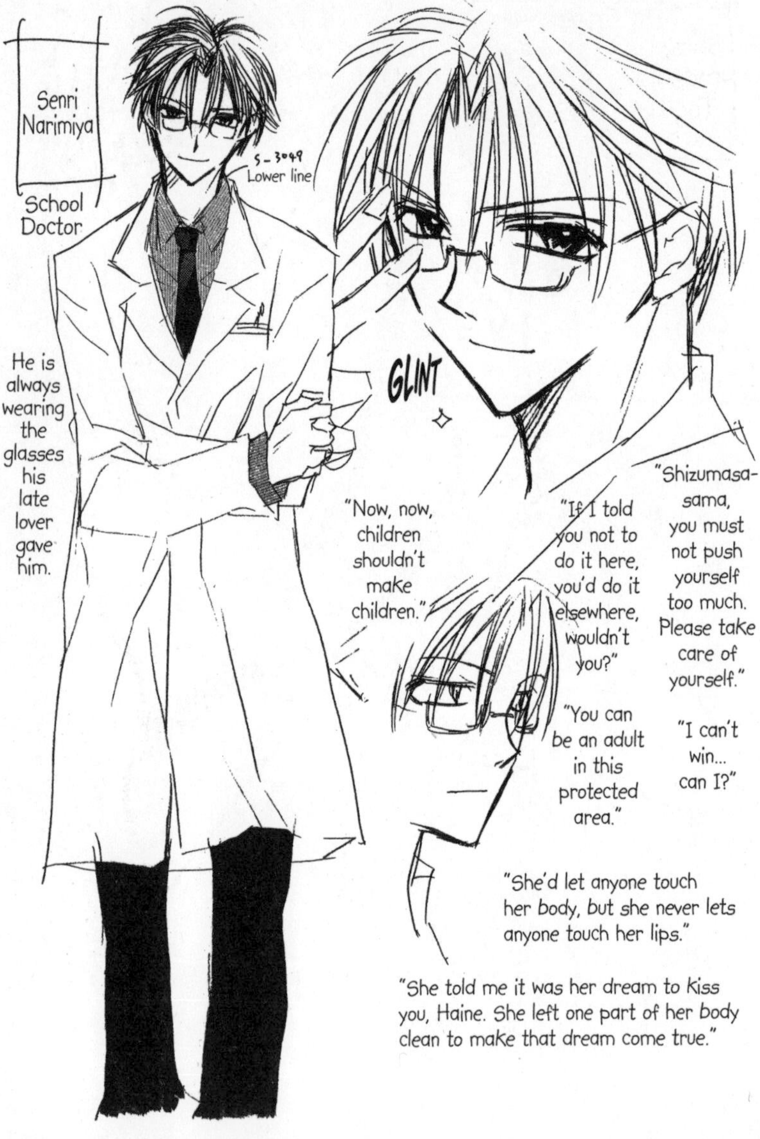
Senri Narimiya
School Doctor
S-3049
Lower line
He is always wearing the glasses his late lover gave him.
GLINT
"Now, now, children shouldn't make children."
"If I told you not to do it here, you'd do it elsewhere, wouldn't you?"
"Shizumasa-sama, you must not push yourself too much. Please take care of yourself."
"You can be an adult in this protected area."
"I can't win... can I?"
"She'd let anyone touch her body, but she never lets anyone touch her lips."
"She told me it was her dream to kiss you, Haine. She left one part of her body clean to make that dream come true."

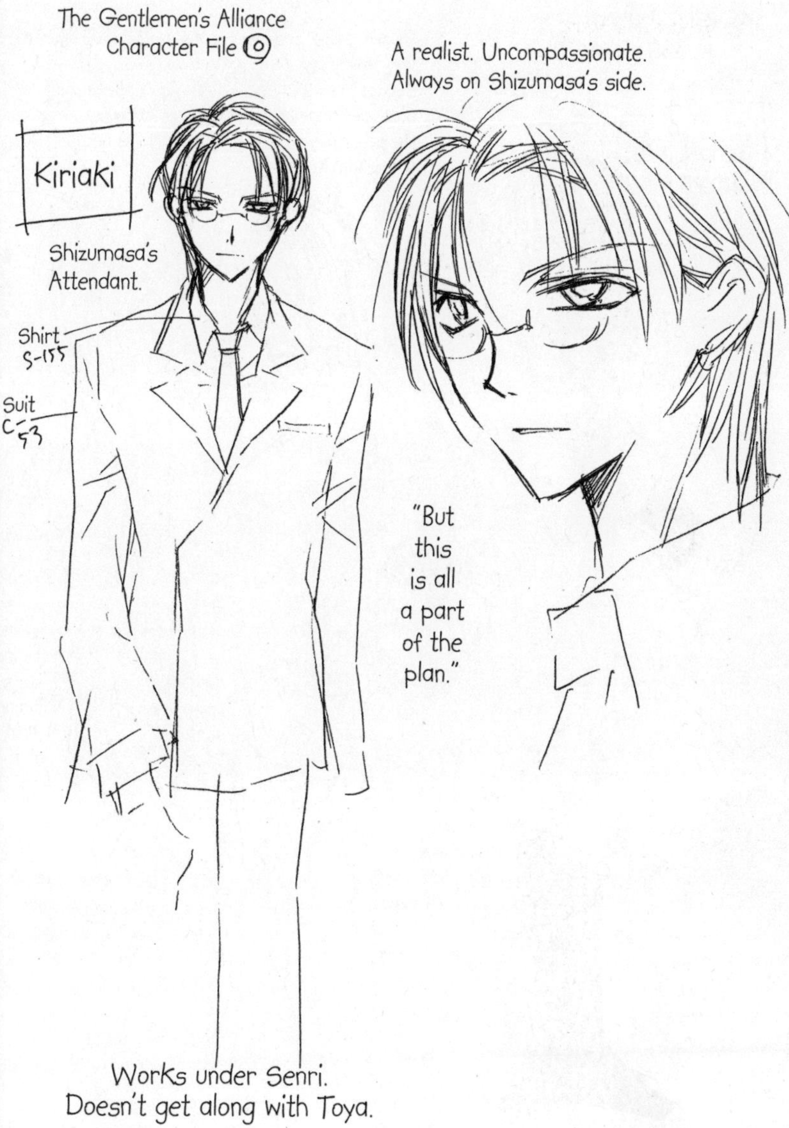
The Gentlemen's Alliance
Character File ⑩
A realist. Uncompassionate.
Always on Shizumasa's side.
Kiriaki
Shizumasa's
Attendant.
Shirt
S-155
Suit
C-53
"But
this
is all
a part
of the
plan."
Works under Senri.
Doesn't get along with Toya.

The Gentlemen's Alliance
Character File ⑪

Komaki
Kamiya

Student council president of the middle school division.
Very self-reliant. Does not get along with Kusame,
the vice president. She likes Haine, but since she
wants her to be happy in her present house,
she acts coldly so that Haine will not like her.
In love with Kusame.

Hmph!

Haine's
real sister.

Sand
color
CB-362

Sigh

Arm band.
Marble color.

"Could
you stop
saying
'Haine
this,
Haine
that'
all the
time?!"

"Can
I call
you...
Onee-
chan...?"

"What?
No one can
tell how
Onee-chan
feels, can
they?! Why
can't you just
leave her
alone?"

"I hope
they
don't
say...

"...we
should
have
sent you
away..."

Shoes C-52
(Sand)

# NOTES ON THE TEXT

**PAGE 89:**

**So I decided to use the character "宮" for all of their surnames!**
The kanji "宮" can be read as "miya," "gu," or "kyu."

**PAGE 92:**

**Collect seven of those and your wish comes true!!**
This is a reference to the *Dragon Ball* manga. If a character can collect seven dragon balls, his wish comes true.

**PAGE 132:**

**Even if the red string of fate breaks...**
The "red string of fate" refers to the belief that lovers who are destined to be together are connected by an invisible red string.

**PAGE 143:**

**Life is short, so fall in love, girls!!**
This is a line from a famous old Japanese song called "Gondora no Uta" (The Gondola Song).

**PAGE 169:**

**Kintsuba**
*Kintsuba* is a traditional Japanese sweet made of red beans.

So it's finally the last volume. I always feel this after finishing a series, but I feel like I've just lived through a full lifetime. I was able to finish this thanks to all your support. Thank you very much for showing your love for this series!

—*Arina Tanemura*

Arina Tanemura was born in Aichi, Japan. She got her start in 1996, publishing *Nibanme no Koi no Katachi* (The Style of the Second Love) in *Ribon Original* magazine. Her early work includes a collection of short stories called *Kanshaku Dama no Yuutsu* (Short-Tempered Melancholic). Two of her titles, *Kamikaze Kaito Jeanne* and *Full Moon*, were made into popular TV series. Tanemura enjoys karaoke and is a huge *Lord of the Rings* fan.

# THE GENTLEMEN'S ALLIANCE † vol. 11
## Shojo Beat Edition

### STORY & ART BY
## ARINA TANEMURA

English Translation & Adaptation/Tetsuichiro Miyaki
Touch-up Art & Lettering/Gia Cam Luc
Design/Amy Martin
Editor/Nancy Thistlethwaite

VP, Production/Alvin Lu
VP, Sales & Product Marketing/Gonzalo Ferreyra
VP, Creative/Linda Espinosa
Publisher/Hyoe Narita

Printed in Canada

Published by VIZ Media, LLC
P.O. Box 77010
San Francisco, CA 94107

10 9 8 7 6 5 4 3 2 1
First printing, April 2010

www.viz.com

www.shojobeat.com

# Arina Tanemura Series

### The Gentlemen's Alliance †

Haine Otomiya joins Imperial Academy in pursuit of the boy she's loved since she was a child, unaware that he has many secrets of his own.

### I•O•N

Chanting the letters of her first name has always brought Ion Tsuburagi good luck—but her good-luck charm is really the result of psychic powers!

### Full Moon

Mitsuki Koyama dreams of becoming a pop star, but she is dying of throat cancer. Can she live out a lifetime of dreams in just one year?

### Short-Tempered Melancholic

A collection of short stories including Arina Tanemura's debut manga, "In the Style of the Second Love"!

### Time Stranger Kyoko

Kyoko Suomi must find 12 holy stones and 12 telepaths to awaken her sister who has been trapped in time since birth.

**Art book featuring 216 pages of beautiful color images personally selected by Tanemura**

**Read where Mitsuki's pop dreams began in the manga—all 7 volumes now available**

**Complete your collection with the anime, now on DVD**

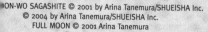

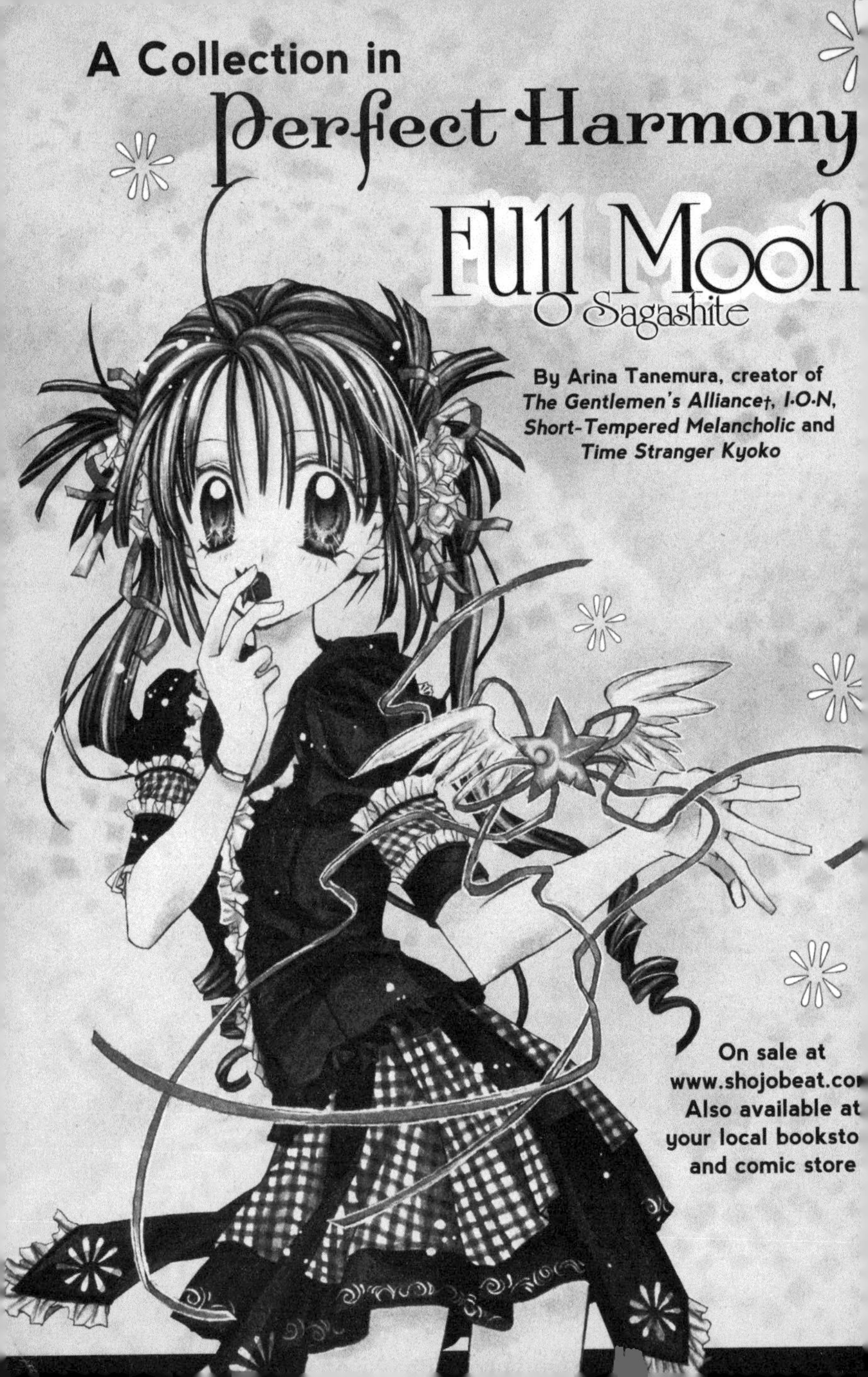
A Collection in
Perfect Harmony
Full Moon
O Sagashite
By Arina Tanemura, creator of
The Gentlemen's Alliance†, I·O·N,
Short-Tempered Melancholic and
Time Stranger Kyoko
On sale at
www.shojobeat.co
Also available at
your local booksto
and comic store

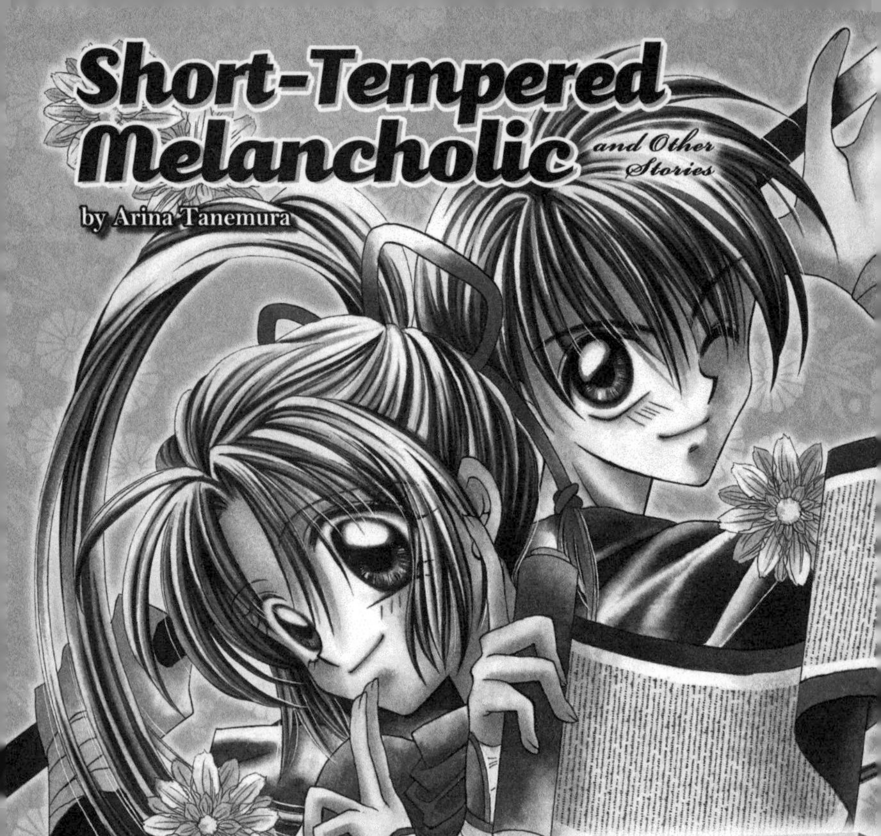
Short-Tempered Melancholic and Other Stories
by Arina Tanemura



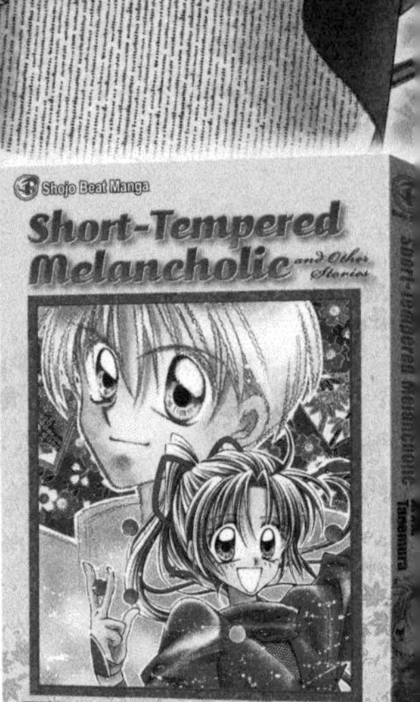
Shojo Beat Manga
Short-Tempered Melancholic and Other Stories
Story & Art by
Arina Tanemura

MANGA from the HEART

## OTOMEN
STORY AND ART BY
AYA KANNO

## VAMPIRE KNIGHT
STORY AND ART BY
MATSURI HINO

## Natsume's BOOK of FRIENDS
STORY AND ART BY
YUKI MIDORIKAWA

Want to see more of what you're looking for?

Let your voice be heard!

# hojobeat.com/mangasurvey

Help us give you more manga from the heart!